AN

OUTLINE HISTORY

AN

OUTLINE HISTORY

OF

Tioga and Bradford Counties in Pennsylvania, Chemung, Steuben, Tioga, Tompkins and Schuyler in New York,

BY

JOHN L. SEXTON

TOWNSHIPS, VILLAGES, BORO'S AND CITIES

KALPAZ

ISBN: 978-93-5128-865-7(HB)

First Published in 1885
Indian Reprint in 2017

Published by

Kalpaz Publications
C-30, Satyawati Nagar,
Delhi – 110052
E-mail: kalpaz@hotmail.com
Website: kalpazpublications.com
Ph.: +91-9212142040

Cataloging in Publication Data—DK
Courtesy: D.K. Agencies (P) Ltd. <docinfo@dkagencies.com>

Sexton, John L., author.
An outline history of Tioga and Bradford counties in Pennsylvania, Chemung, Steuben, Tioga, Tompkins, and Schuyler in New York by townships, villages, boro's and cities / written expressly for the Gazette Company, Elmira, N.Y. ; by John L. Sexton.
pages cm
Reprint. Originally published: Elmira, N.Y. : The Gazette company, 1885.
ISBN 9789351288657

1. New York (State)—History, Local. 2. Pennsylvania—History, Local. I. Gazette Company (Elmira, N.Y.) II. Title.

F157.T5S5 2017 DDC 974.7 23

AN OUTLINE HISTORY

—OF—

TIOGA COUNTY, PENNSYLVANIA.

By an act of the Legislature of the State of Pennsylvania, approved March 26th, 1804, Tioga County was formed. It contains an area of seven hundred and nineteen thousand, three hundred and sixty (719,360) acres, or one thousand one hundred and twenty-four (1,124) square miles. It is bounded on the north by the state line between New York and Pennsylvania and the counties of Steuben and Chemung in New York; on the east by the county of Bradford; on the south by the county of Lycoming and on the west by the county of Potter. Its population is about 50,000. The capital or shire town is Wellsboro, situated on Charleston Creek, near the geographical center of the county, a rich and flourishing borough, containing about three thousand inhabitants.

STREAMS.—The principal streams in Tioga County are Pine Creek, Canoe Camp Creek, Crooked Creek, Corry Creek, Marsh Creek, Babbs Creek, Long Run, Mill Creek, Lamb's Creek, Cedar Run, Troops Creek, Elkhorn, Fall Brook and the Tioga and Cowanesque Rivers. Pine Creek, one of the largest streams in the county, rises in Potter County and flows east and southward and empties into the West Branch of the Susquehanna River, near Jersey Shore, Lycoming County. The Tioga River rises in the highlands of Ward township, Tioga County and Armenia in Bradford County and at first flows southward, thence westward and thence northward, and uniting with the Cowanesque at the state line near Lawrenceville, Pa. The Cowanesque rises in Potter County and flows eastward through the valley of the Cowanesque, keeping near the northern boundary of the county and unites with the Tioga near Lawrenceville. Marsh Creek, Babbs Creek, Cedar Run and Long Run are tributaries of Pine Creek. Canoe Camp Creek, Cory Creek, Fall Brook, Lamb's Creek, Mill Creek, Elkhorn and Crooked Creeks are tributaries of the Tioga River. Troops Creek and Mill Creek are tributaries of the Cowanesque. There are many lesser creeks and rivulets running at every conceivable angle, which added to the numerous springs make Tioga County one of the best watered counties in Northern Pennsylvania.

SOIL.—The soil of the county is well adapted to the growing of wheat, corn, oats, barley, the orchard fruits and garden vegetables, together with some very fine alluvial soils, well suited to the cultivation of tobacco, which is raised in the valley of the Tioga as far south as Covington, and in the Cowanesque valley as far west as Westfield and the county line near Harrison Valley and upon the waters of Pine Creek in the townships of Gaines, Shippen and Morris—and upon the waters of Marsh, Charleston and Crooked Creeks large and profitable crops of tobacco are grown. Other portions of the county of which we shall speak more particularly in the history of townships, are well adapted to the pasturing of sheep, the raising of cattle and horses and the making of the golden rolls of butter and the manufacturing of cheese.

MINERALS.—Semi-bituminous coal is found in large quantities in Tioga County and mines are in operation at Blossburg, Morris Run, Fall Brook, Arnot, Antrim, Gurnee and Mitchell's. There are annually mined in the county about thirty million bushels, or over one million tons of coal which is marketed, by the Fall Brook Coal Company, the Morris Run Coal Mining Company, the Blossburg Coal Company, the Gaines Coal and Coke Company, the Coal Run Company, Jacob Jones, Alexander Hutchinson and Joseph Mitchell. The four latter named being miners for home consumption. The Blossburg Coal Company at Arnot and the Fall Brook Coal Company at Tioga are largely engaged in the manufacture of coke from semi-bituminous coal. Iron ore is found in paying quantities at Blossburg and in the township of Richmond near the borough of Mansfield. Fire brick clay and glass sand rock is found in large quantities in the southern portion of the county in the coal region.

TIMBER.—The county was originally covered with an immense growth of timber. Along the principal streams in the valleys the white pine predominated. On the rolling land hemlock attended with swails of beach, maple, birch, cherry, chestnut, oak and hickory was found. It it estimated that from the organization of the county in 1804 up to the year 1865, that one thousand million feet of white pine lumber was cut and marketed at an average price of about seven dollars and fifty cents per thousand, the citizens of Tioga County thus receiving about seven million five hundred thousand dollars for their white pine lumber, up to twenty years ago. What pine was then left was mostly owned by large and strong companies, who have received at the rate of about eighteen or twenty dollars per thousand for the pine they have sold. The market which the early lumbermen of Tioga County sought was the southern, and was reached by the waters of Pine Creek, Cowanesque, Tioga, Chemung and Susquehanna rivers, thus making the rafting and floating of lumber upon the bosom of these waters a great and exciting industry. About twenty years ago the hemlock lumber, or rather the hemlock became an object of considerable attention, on account of the value of its bark for tanning purposes. At first the hemlock was felled and the bark peeled from it and taken to the tanneries, the trunk suffered to remain in many instances in the woods to decay where it laid. By and by architects tested its strength and found that it was a valuable timber for building purposes, and a market for it soon sprung up. But the demand for the bark now exceeds the demand for hemlock lumber. Of this we shall write more fully under the head of tanning. The oak, hickory and chestnut are substantially gone, while here and there remain tracts of beech, maple, yellow birch and black birch, with cherry interspersed. But these lands are chiefly owned by Mining and Tannery Companies, and are not to any great extent in the hands of individuals. The Mining Companies of the county are owners of about seventy-five thousand acres of timbered and coal land; the Tanning Companies about forty thousand acres of timbered land, other companies about twenty-five thousand, making a grand total of about one hundred and forty thousand acres in the hands of a very few. The remainder of the timber land consists of small tracts, which are principally owned by those who desire them for their own use, or perhaps to carry on the business of lumbering upon a small scale.

Pioneers.—The pioneers in the settlement of Tioga County were generally men of intelligence. They came from all sections of the country, from Southern Pennsylvania, from Maryland, Virginia, Delaware, New Jersey, New York, Vermont, Massachusetts, Rhode Island and Connecticut, determined to make themselves a home in a land, which for centuries before 1784 had been in possession of the six nations of Indians. Their hardships and privations were many, yet inspired by the salubrity of the climate, the grandure of the forest scenery and the productiveness of the soil, the beautiful springs, rivulets, creeks and rivers, the abundance of game, they pursued their labors with untiring zeal and energy, and many of them lived to a ripe old age, and saw ere they slept with their fathers, where once the forest was unbroken, fields of waving grain and pastures green, the cabin torn down, and the comfortable farm house erected in its place, the rough corduroy wagon road, supplanted by the railroad with its iron horse and tireless energy, the post boy on horse back, yielding to the postal car, or telegraph. The names of the pioneers will appear in their respective villages, townships or borough histories.

SELECTION OF COUNTY SEAT, ETC.—In the year 1806, Wellsboro was selected as the county seat of Tioga County, and in the year 1813 the first court was held, Hon. J. Bannister Gibson, Circuit Judge, presiding. The court was held in a log house facing the public square. Pursuant to an act of the Legislature of March 14th, 1814, Hopestill Beecher, Timothy Ives and Ambrose Millard on the 6th of October 1814, apportioned the County into six districts for Justices of the Peace. The first district was composed of the township of Delmar, and contained eighty-seven taxables. Daniel Kelley was the Justice of the Peace. The second district was composed of Deerfield, and contained sixty-three taxables. The third district was composed of the township of Elkand, with seventy-nine taxables, with Dorman Bloss, Justice of the Peace. The fourth and fifth district was composed of the township of Tioga (then embracing what is now divided into a dozen or more townships) and William Rose, Justice of the Peace with one hundred and thirty-nine taxables. The sixth district was composed of the township of Covington, from which also a dozen townships have been formed, then containing ninty-five taxables, Daniel Lamb and Elijah Putnam being the Justices. The total number of taxables at that time in the county were four hundred and sixty-three.

OFFICERS.

COUNTY OFFICERS—*Representatives.*—John Ryon, 1822; James Ford, 1824; Curtis Parkhurst, 1827; John Beecher, 1829; Samuel W. Morris, 1831. (Tioga and Bradford Counties at that time composed one representative District, and in 1835 Doct Bullock and Israel Meyers, both of Bradford County were elected for the district). William Garretson, 1836. In 1838 Tioga and Potter Counties were a representative district, Lewis B. Cole, of the latter named county was chosen. John Wakeley, 1840; Daniel L. Sherwood, 1841; George Knox, 1843; John C. Knox, 1845; N. A. Elliott, 1847; James Black, 1849–51; J. J. Monroe, 1850; James Lowrey, 1852; Thomas

L. Baldwin, 1854; L. T. Williston, 1856; B. B. Strang, 1860; S. B. Elliott, 1861; C. O. Bowman. 1862; John W. Guernsey, 1863; William T. Humphrey, 1865; Jerome B. Niles, 1868; John I. Mitchell, 1871; C. V. Elliott, 1876; Hugh Young, 1876, served one year and resigned, and Benjamin Dorrance elected to fill vacancy; Charles Tubbs, 1880; Jerome B. Niles, 1880.

STATE SENATORS.—John Ryon, 1824; Daniel L. Sherwood, 1846, elected speaker; John W. Guernsey, 1852–3; Stephen F. Wilson, 1862–3; B. B. Strang, 1871–76; Charles H. Seymour. 1877–78.

MEMBERS OF CONGRESS.—James Ford, 1828–30; Samuel W. Morris, 1836; Stephen F. Wilson, 1864; Henry Sherwood, 1870; John I. Mitchell, 1876; Congressman at large, Mortimer F. Elliott, 1883.

UNITED STATES SENATOR.—John I. Mitchell, 1881.

UNITED STATES BANK EXAMINER.—Hon. Hugh Young, 1876, present occupant.

UNITED STATES REVENUE COLLECTOR.—Hon. S. B. Elliott, 1863; Massena Bullard, 1865 to 1883; Lucius Truman, 1883, present occupant.

HIGH SHERIFFS.—Alpheus Cheeney, 1812; Simeon Power, 1815; John Knox, 1818; Elijah Stiles, 1821; John Beecher, 1824; Robert Tubbs, 1827; Seth Daggett, 1830; Frances Weatherby, 1831; Benjamin Gitchell, 1836; John Wakely, 1837; Curtis Parkhurst, 1840; J. W. Guernsey, 1843; Henry M. Potter, 1846; John Mather, 1849 and in 1855; Henry A Guernsey, 1852; Simeon I. Power, 1858; Hezekiah Stowell, Jr., 1861; Leroy Taber, 1864; Jerome B. Potter, 1867; E. A. Fish, 1870; Stephen Bowen, 1873; Delos H. Walker, 1876; H. J. Landrus, 1879; Harry Baxter, 1882.

COUNTY SURVEYORS.—John Norris, from 1814 to 1827; Samuel McDougal from 1827 to 1836; E. P. Deane from 1836 to 1839; Samuel McDougal from 1839 to 1850; David Heise from 1850 to 1856; Henry Archer from 1856 to 1859; E. P. Deane from 1859 to 1863; D. L. Deane from 1863 to 1865; David Heise from 1865 to 1885.

PROTHONOTARIES.—John Norris, 1813; Uri Spencer, 1818; John Patton, 1821: Uri Spencer, 1824; J. Brewster, 1831; John F. Donaldson, 1836-7; A. S. Brewster, 1838; John F. Donaldson from 1839 to 1872; General Robert Cox from 1872 to 1885, present incumbent.

COUNTY TREASURERS.—Samuel W. Morris, 1811; Alpheus Cheeney, 1814; B. Thompson, 1815; Benjamin W. Morris from 1817 to 1819; Daniel Lamb, 1822; John Beecher, 1823-4; Thomas Putnam, 1825-6; William Willard, 1827-8; Lewis Vail, 1829-30; Elihu Hill, 1831-33; Thomas Dyer, 1834-5; John Barnes, 1836-7; Elihu Hill, 1838-41; Archibald Knox, 1842; R. G. White, 1844; John L. Robinson, 1846; A. H. Bacon, 1848; George Levergood, 1850; S. L. Hibbard, 1852; George Knox, 1854; Henry Rathbone, 1856; O. H. Blanchard, 1858; O. F. Taylor, 1860; J. S. Watrous, 1862; H. B. Card, 1864; A. M. Spencer, 1866; C. F. Miller, 1868; H. C. Bailey, 1870; R. C. Cox, 1873; H. Roland, 1875; Thomas Allen, 1878; Thomas Bryden, 1878, died during term of office; Charles F. Veile, appointed; John R. Bowen, 1881. Horton, 1883, present incumbent.

REGISTER AND RECORDER.—William Bache, 1821; Uri Spencer, 1824; B. B. Smith, 1831; Luman Wilson, 1836; James P. Madill, 1845: John N. Bache, 1848; James P. Madill, 1851; William D. Bailey, 1854; Henry S.

Archer, 1860; D. L. Dean, 1866; George C. Bowen, 1875, present incumbent.

COUNTY COMMISSIONERS.—Eddie Howland, 1809; Caleb Boyer, Uri Spencer, George Hart, Nathan Niles, 1810; Timothy Ives, 1812; Hopestill Beecher, 1814; Justus Dartt, 1815; Robert B. Elliott, 1816; John Knox, 1817; Asa Mann, 1818; Elijah Depue, 1819; John Ryon Jr., 1820; Oliver Willard 1821; Seth Daggett, 1822; Hiram Beebe, 1823; William Knox, 1824; Elijah Welch, 1825; Elijah Stiles, 1826; James Goodrich, 1827: L. Jackson, 1828; John Cochran, 1829; E. P. Gerould, 1830; Job Geer, 1831; A. Hammond, 1832; C. Olivert, 1833; Geo. Knox, 1834; Samuel Miller, 1835; C. N. Sykes, 1836; P. Doud, 1837; George Levergood, 1838; Buel Baldwin, 1839; Levi Elliott, 1840; C. O. Spencer, 1841; M. W. Stull, 1842; H. M. Potter, 1843; E. Howland, 1844: William Rose Jr., 1845; John Fox, 1846; Israel Merrick, 1847; David Ellis, 1848; Leander Culver, 1849; David Caldwell, 1850; Ansel Purple, 1851; Benjamin VanDuzen, 1852; Austin Lathrop, 1853; O. B. Wells, 1854; G. G. Stevens, 1855; C. V. Culver, 1856; John James, 1857; L. B. Seeley, 1858; Amos Bixby, 1859; A. Barker, 1860; Job Rexford, 1861; C. F. Miller in 1862, appointed to fill vacancy, elected in 1863; Myron Rockwell, 1863; E. S. Seeley, 1864; E. Hart, 1865; R. Van Ness, 1866; A. Barker, 1867; M. W. Wetherby, 1868; R. VanNess, 1869; A. Barker, 1870; T. O. Hollis, 1871; E. Hart. 1872; L. B. Sheives, 1873; E. Klock, 1874; L. B. Smith, E. J. Purple, 1875; N. A. Elliott, A. O. Smith, 1878; N. A. Elliott, A. O. Smith, 1881; James E. Peters, 1878-81, C. M. Rumsey and John J. Reese, 1881; William Kimble, W. H. Baxter and John Karr, 1884.

COUNTY SUPERINTENDENTS OF SCHOOLS.—The supervision of the common schools by County Superintendents, commenced in the year 1854. Superintendents are chosen by a convention of school directors of the various townships and boroughs of the county. The term of office is three years. They have been Rev. N. L. Reynolds, Rev. J. F. Calkins, H. C. Johns, S. B. Price, Elias Horton, Jr., Miss Sarah I. Lewis and M. F. Cass. An election takes place in the month of May 1885.

JUDGES OF THE COURT OF COMMON PLEAS, who have resided in Tioga County.—Hon. Robert G. White, two terms from 1851 to 1871; Henry W. Williams, additional Law Judge from 1865 to 1871, President Judge from 1871 to 1881, re-elected in 1881, term expires in 1891; Judge Stephen F. Wilson, appointed additional Law Judge in 1871 to fill the vacancy occasioned by the promotion or election of Judge Williams to the office of President Judge —elected additional Law Judge in 1872 and served until the year 1882.

MEMBERS OF THE CONSTITUTIONAL CONVENTIONS.—Robert G. White, 1837; Mortimer F. Elliott and Jerome B. Niles, 1873.

COURT AND BAR OF TIOGA COUNTY.—*President Judge*—Hon. Henry W. Williams. *Associate Judges*—Hon. Harvey Lamkin, Hon. George H. Baxter. *Prothonotary or Clerk of the Court*—Gen. Robert C. Cox. *Clerk of Orphan's Court*—George C. Bowen. *District Attorney*—J. H. Matson.

ASSOCIATE JUDGES.—Since the organization of the courts of the county the Associate Judges have been: Samuel Morris and Ira Kilbourn from 1813 to 1830; since that time John Ryon, Curtis Parkhurst, Jonah Brewster, Simeon Power, Levi J. Nichols, Edwin Dyer, J. C. Whittaker, Abel Humphrey, Victor Case, Royal Wheeler, Charles F. Veile, E. T. Bentley, L. B. Smith, D. McNaughton, John F. Donaldson, M. K. Retan, Peter VanNess. George H. Baxter and Harvey Lamkin. Present incumbents, George H. Baxter and Harvey Lamkin.

BAR OF TIOGA COUNTY.—Some of the most distinguished men in the state have been members of the Tioga County bar, and have filled places of distinction and honor, such as Judges of the Supreme Court, Attorney-Generals, Members of Congress and United States Senators, and Auditor Generals. The present members are.

Wellsboro.—Hon. Henry Sherwood, Walter Sherwood, Mortimer F. Elliott, F. Watrous, Jerome B. Niles, Henry M. Foote, George W. Merrick, S. F. Channell, Alfred J. Shattuck, John I. Mitchell, David Cameron, Jeff. Harrison, John N. Bache, D. L. Deane, Robert C. Simpson, Thomas Allen, A. L. Ensworth, John W. Mather, J. H. Matson, A. S. Brewster, Hugh Young, Ezra B. Young, L. P. Williston, Horace B. Packer, Stephen F. Wilson, Herbert Huntington, Burt M. Potter, Clark W. Beach.

Mansfield.—Henry Allen, Frank W. Clark, John W. Adams.

Tioga.—A. Redfield, F. E. Smith, H. L. Baldwin, Norman H. Ryon.

Lawrenceville.—Wallace P. Ryon, Horace M. Darling.

Blossburg.—John C. Horton, G. P. Smith.

Millerton.—Samuel Kirkendall.

Elkland.—John S. Ryon, Robert T. Wood.

Knoxville.—John T. Geer.

Westfield.—D. W. Baldwin, M. L. Foster.

ROADS.—In 1792, General Williamson, under the immediate supervision of Robert and Benjamin Patterson, caused a road to be constructed from Northumberland via Williamsport, Trout Run, Block House and Blossburg down the Tioga valley to Painted Post, thence up the Conhocton River to Bath.

. In 1806, the Legislature of the state passed an act, authorizing the building of a road from the Moosic Mountains in Luzern to Towanda, thence via of Troy, Covington, Wellsboro to Coudersport. By a supplement to this act, the road was authorized to be continued westward to Smethport and Warren thence to Erie. The road through Tioga County was completed in the year 1809.

A road was constructed very early in the history of the county from Newberry in Lycoming County near Williamsport via Englishtown, Babbs Creek to Wellsboro.

After the county was completely organized, roads were constructed in various sections, as necessity required, and they were succeded by the laying out of the township roads.

RAILROADS.—At the session of the Pennslyvania Legislature held in 1826, a "General Improvement Act" was passed. About this time action was taken by enterprising citizens of Tioga County for the formation of a navigation Company. Prominent among these citizens was Hon. Samuel W. Morris of Wellsboro. A charter was obtained and by successive supplements the navigation company obtained the right to construct a railroad from Blossburg to the state line at Lawrenceville. Another company was formed in the state of New York, with power to construct a railroad from where the flourishing village of Corning now is to Lawrenceville, and intersect or connect with the railroad to be constructed by the citizens of Pennsylvania. These railroads were constructed and completed in the year 1840, and were first known as "The Corning and Blossburg Railroad." The road bed was graded, and flat rails of iron spiked upon timbers. The road was in operation about thirteen years, when new companies were formed, and the strap or flat rail taken up, and a T rail put in its place. The Hon. John Magee and his co-adjutors operated and owned that portion of the railroad situated in the state of New York, and a company whose principal stockholders were residents of Philadelphia, Pa., operated and controlled that portion situated in Pennsylvania. The length of the road was, in New York fifteen miles, in Pennsylvania twenty-five miles, total, forty miles. In 1854 four miles of railroad were constructed from Blossburg to Morris Run, where mines of semi-bituminous coal was opened. Col. Pharon Jarret, of Lock Haven, was the engineer of the latter road, and Col. W. E. Fox, of Towanda, engineer of the road constructed in 1840. In 1866, a railroad four miles in length, reaching from Blossburg to the present village of Arnot was constructed. In 1876, about twenty miles of railroad was constructed from Elmira, N. Y., intersecting the old Blossburg road in the township of Lawrence. All the roads, excepting the one from Lawrenceville to Corning, is now known as "The Tioga and Elmira State Line Railroad," and is operated by the New York, Lake Erie and Western Railroad Company, of New York. In the year 1859, a railroad was constructed by the Fall Brook Coal Company, Hon. John Magee, president, from Blossburg to the present borough of Fall Brook, a distance of about seven miles. In 1872, a railroad was constructed by the Fall Brook Coal Company, from Lawrenceville via Tioga, Hollidays, Middlebury, Niles Valley, Stokesdale, Wellsboro; Round Top, to where the present mining town of Antrim is located. In the year 1872–3, a railroad was also constructed from Lawrenceville, via of Nelson up the Cowanesque river to Elkland, a distance of about twelve miles. This road, about ten years afterwards, was extended westward up the Cowanesque valley via Academy Corners, Osceola, Knoxville, Cowanesque; Westfield to Harrison Valley in Potter County.

In the years 1882-3 a railroad was constructed from Stokesdale down Marsh Creek to Ansonia on Pine Creek, thence down Pine Creek to Jersey Shore, thence down the west branch of the Susquehanna to Williamsport, connecting with the Philadelphia and Reading lines. This road is under the management of the Fall Brook Coal Company, and is known as the Jersey Shore and Pine Creek railroad. Hon. Henry Sherwood of Wellsboro is the President of this road.

In the year 1882 a railroad was built from Arnot to Hoytville, a distance of fourteen miles, known as the Arnot and Pine Creek railroad. It connects at Arnot with the Tioga and Elmira State Line R. R., and is under the same management as that railroad.

Also during the year 1882 a narrow guage railroad was constructed from Addison, Steuben County, New York, into the Cowanesque Valley, Tioga County, Pa., touching Nelson, Elkland, Academy Corners, Osceola, Knoxville, Westfield, thence south up Mill Creek to Sabinsville, and down Long

Run to Gaines on Pine Creek, with a branch ascending the mountains to Gurnee, a mining town owned by the Gaines Coal and Coke Company. This line during the year 1884 was extended up Pine Creek to Pike Mills or Galeston, a distance of five miles. The length of the entire line now is about forty-six miles.

CORNING, COWANESQUE AND ANTRIM RAILROAD, OFFICERS.—George J. Magee, President; Daniel Beach, Vice President, Secretary and Treasurer; Anton Hardt, Chief Engineer; Alonzo H. Gorton, General Superintendent. Directors, George J. Magee, Daniel Beach, Alfred L. Edwards and Henry Sherwood.

PINE CREEK RAILWAY, OFFICERS.—Henry Sherwood, President; George J. Magee, Vice President; William Howell, Secretary; Cornelius Vanderbilt, Treasurer; Anton Hardt, Chief Engineer. Directors, George J. Magee, William H. Vanderbilt, Cornelius Vanderbilt, Chauncey M. Depew, William Howell, E. G. Schiefflein, Walter Sherwood, Jefferson Harrison, Jerome B. Niles, Anton Hardt, John W. Bailey and Henry Sherwood.

TIOGA AND ELMIRA STATE LINE RAILROAD, OFFICERS.—John King, President; R. B. Cable, Superintendent; C. C. Drake, Secretary and General Agent; D. S. Drake, Treasurer.

ARNOT AND PINE CREEK RAILROAD, OFFICERS.—Levi H. Shattuck, President; David S. Drake, Secretary and Treasurer.

ADDISON AND NORTHERN PENNSYLVANIA RAILROAD, OFFICERS.—Hon. Thomas C. Platt, President; William Brookfield, Vice-President; William C. Shelden, Treasurer; James E. Jones, Secretary; Frank M. Baker, General Superintendent; H. C. Hitchcock, Auditor; James P. Wright, Road-Master.

MINING OF SEMI-BITUMINOUS COAL.—As early as 1792, when Robert and Benjamin Patterson were conducting General Williamson's party of five hundred German and English emigrants or settlers to the Pultney estate in New York, they discovered coal in the mountains, within the present borough limits of Blossburg. In the year 1806, Aaron Bloss removed from Covington to "Peter's Camp," a camp made by the Williamson party in 1792, erecting an inn where he entertainned travelers who were journeying upon the Williamson road between Painted Post, Williamsport and Northumberland. This inn was situated in the southern portion of the present borough of Blossburg. Mr. Bloss opened up in a rude manner the vein of coal near his dwelling or inn and at about the same time Clemmons, who resided about two and a half miles north of Mr. Bloss opened up a vein of coal situated in the northeastern portion of the present borough of Blossburg. From these small and temporary openings has the immense coal trade of the Blossburg semi-bituminous coal been brought about. We have not the space to enter into all the details in relation to the development of the trade, but must content ourselves with a concise and brief statement of the leading facts.

The finding of the coal in such quantities, was the main-spring which set in motion the construction of the Blossburg and Corning Railroad in 1837 which was completed in 1840. Its existence also had much to do in influencing the Legislature of New York to pass an act for the digging of the Chemung Canal and Feeder, which was completed in 1833. After the completion of the Blossburg and Corning Railroad in 1840, the Arbon Coal Company opened up the mines upon the Clemmons property at Blossburg, and commenced the shipment of coal. They shipped from 1840 to 1843, 49,633 tons. The mines then passed into the hands of William M. Mallory & Co., who from 1844 to 1856 shipped 405,116 tons; D. S. Magee then became the operator and shipped 78,996 tons, making a total of 533,745 tons taken from the Blossburg mines for shipment by rail.

In 1852 mines were opened at Morris Run, an account of which will appear in the history of that place. Mines were opened at Fall Brook in 1859, and shipment commenced. Mines were also opened at Arnot in 1866, and at Antrim in 1869-70 and shipment commenced in 1872. Mines of semi-bituminous coal were opened at Gurnee, in the township of Gaines in the year 1882, and shipment per rail commenced in the year 1883.

The total amount of coal mined and shipped to market since the year 1840 from Tioga County up to January 1st, 1885, is about in round numbers sixteen million five hundred thousand tons.

Glass Manufacturing.—There are two well conducted window glass manufactories, one located in Blossburg and one in Covington. They are now both operated by Hirsch, Ely & Co., upon the co-operative plan. The Blossburg glass manufactory was erected in the year 1847, by William Dezang of Geneva, and the one at Covington several years later. The sand rock suitable for the manufacture of glass exists in inexhaustible quantities in the southern portion of the county. The history of the manufacture of glass in Tioga County will more fully appear in the histories of Blossburg and Covington.

Tanneries.—The tanning of sole leather in the County of Tioga has assumed grand proportions within the past few years. To give the reader an idea of the magnitude of its business, we would state, that it takes the hemlock bark from one hundred and eighty million feet of hemlock timber to supply the annual demand of the tanneries of the county. The value of the products of the tanneries is counted by the million.

Agricultural Societies.—There are two flourishing agricultural societies in existence in the county—one holding its annual exhibition and fair at Wellsboro and one at Mansfield. These will be more fully described in the history of those boroughs.

Institutions of Learning.—From the early settlement of Tioga County to the present, great interest has been manifested by the citizens of the county in the establishment and maintainance of suitable institutions of learning, whether it was at a time when a few neighbors joined and erected a log school house, or whether it was in the establishment of an academy, graded or normal school, with facilities for imparting knowledge commensurate with the wants of the public.

As early as 1817 an academy was established at Wellsboro and some of the most prominent and intelligent men in the county selected as trustees. Pursuant to an act of incorporation of March 25th, 1817, Ambrose Millard, Daniel Lamb, William Bache, John Norris, Nathan Niles, Jr., Asa Mann, Alpheus Cheeney, John Knox, Joseph McCormick, Isaac Baker, Samuel W. Morris, Eddy Howland, Robert Tubbs, Uri Spencer, William D. Bacon,

Nathan Rowley, Jr., James Gray and Justus Dartt were appointed trustees and received from the state an endowment of two thousand dollars. The academy erected then remained in use until a few years ago, when it was superseded by the elegant graded school.

Tioga County was among the first counties in the state to accept the provisions of the common school act of 1834.

SOLDIERS' ORPHANS' SCHOOL.—The Soldiers' Orphans' School was established at Mansfield, October 1st, 1867, under the direction of the State Superintendent of Soldiers' Orphans' School, and Prof. F. A. Allen, the late eminent scholar and teacher, appointed principal. The school opened at first with only twenty-five students, but increased in usefulness and numbers until there were about two hundred pupils, sons and daughters of deceased soldiers, and children of indigent soldiers who were not able to give their children suitable educational advantages elsewhere. Prof. Allen was untiring in his efforts for nearly thirteen years in looking after their educational and moral training. The writer of this sketch has frequently visited the institution, while it was under the direction of Prof. Allen, and was pleased beyond expression, witnessing the paternal care exercised by the late Professor over these wards of the old Keystone state. The Professor was very fortunate in his selections of assistants, and was ably seconded by Mrs. Allen and his corps of teachers. After the death of Professor Allen, which occurred February 11th, 1880, his widow became the head of the institution, which position she still occupies. Prof. Vine R. Pratt, for nearly fifteen years was one of the principal teachers and managers in the institution. In the year 1872, a farm consisting of about one hundred and fifty acres, located upon the west side of the Tioga river, about half a mile from the school, was purchased, and where the boys are given lessons in practical farming. Prof. Allen was practical in his teaching, and aimed to give these orphans an education, which would enable them to gain a livelihood after they should pass from under his care. Hundreds will point to him as their best friend.

STATE NORMAL SCHOOL.—On the 11th of December, 1862, the State Normal School for the fifth district of Pennsylvania was established. The building for several years previous had been used as a seminary of learning under the auspices of the M. E. Church. Its history as a seminary is eventful and marked by a heroic struggle of its founders. When the aid of the state was called in, its friends disappointed in some degree, nevertheless joined heartily in making it a success as a State Normal School. It was financially embarrassed and the sheriff was at its door. By an united effort on the part of its friends, appropriations were secured, which placed it temporarily out of danger and finally after years of financial difficulties it was placed upon a solid foundation; new and additional buildings were erected commensurate with its requirements. To enumerate all its friends would be to write the names of every citizen in the borough of Mansfield, township of Richmond and surrounding country. There are however names which deserve especial mention and which it would be rank injustice not to write out. We therefore name, J. S. Hoard, Dr. J. P. Morris, P. M. Clark, W. C. Ripley, A. Bixby, R. B. Buttler, John Voorhes, B. M. Bailey, A. J. Ross, Phillip Williams, Hon. Simon B. Elliott, Rev. W. Cochran, C.

W. Bailey, Prof. F. A. Allen, Mart King, John Murdaugh, Daniel Pitts, Capt. A. M. Pitts, Alvin Gaylord, William Hollands, R. Videan, Jr., Hon. John Magee, the latter not only lending it money, but presenting it with $3,332.50, Col. N. A. Elliott, A. M. Spencer, Dr. C. V. Elliott, E. Burley, R. C. Shaw, J. P. Bennett, T. J. Berry, J. C. Howe, J. A. Fellows, L. Beach, Jr., Rev. N. L. Reynolds, Prof. J. C. Doane, Lemuel Ammerman, Jr., Rev. J. N. Fradenburg, Prof. Charles M. Verrill, John H. French, who devoted their time, money and influence to the building up the walls of the institution and giving it a reputation.

Prof. F. A. Allen was chosen principal in May, 1864, and remained at the head of the institution for five years, or until 1869, when Prof. J. T. Streit was chosen. His health did not permit him in assuming the active duties of the position. He died soon after being selected as principal, and Prof. Charles H. Verrill assumed the prosition, which he occupied with honor for four years, and was succeeded by Prof. J. N. Fradenburg, who retained the position for two years, when Prof Verrill again was chosen principal and served in that capacity for two years, when Prof. F. A. Allen, whom the people regarded as the father of the school, again resumed the principalship and was acting in that capacity when his last illness and death occurred, Feb. 11th, 1880. Since the death of Prof. Allen, Prof. D. C. Thomas has been at the head of the school. The first graduating class was in 1866. The total number of graduates up to this date (1885) is about five hundred.

It is one of the most prosperous schools of the kind in the state. It is the only State Normal School in Northern Pennsylvania. The grounds, buildings, furniture, library and cabinet, have cost about one hundred and twenty-five thousand dollars.

Patriotism.—During the late rebellion, no county in the Commonwealth according to the population, did more nobly than Tioga. It sent forth to battle over two thousand soldiers and the various townships and boroughs raised four hundred thousand dollars for bounties and the county about six hundred thousand dollars, making in round numbers one million dollars ($1,000,000.00.) No portion of this vast amount remains unpaid.

Townships and Boroughs.—There are twenty-eight townships and twelve boroughs in the county of Tioga. The following will show when they were organized and from what territory taken:

Tioga from Lycoming, in 1808; Delmar from Lycoming, in 1808; Deerfield from Delmar, in 1814; Elkland (this township no longer exists), 1814; Covington from Tioga, in February, 1815; Jackson from Tioga, in September, 1815; Sullivan from Covington, in February, 1816; Lawrence from Tioga and Elkland, in December, 1816; Charleston from Delmar, in December, 1820; Westfield from Deerfield, in December, 1821; Middlebury from Delmar and Elkland, in September, 1822; Liberty from Delmar and Covington, in February, 1823; Shippen from Delmar, in February, 1823; Richmond from Covington, in February, 1824; Morris from Delmar, in September, 1824; Rutland from Jackson and Sullivan, in February, 1828; Chatham from Deerfield, in February, 1828; Farmington from Elkland, in Februray, 1830; Union from Sullivan, in February, 1830; Gaines from Shippen, in March, 1838; Bloss from Covington, in June, 1841; Clymer from Westfield and

Gaines, in December, 1850; Ward from Sullivan and Union, in February, 1852; Elk from Delmar and Morris, in February, 1856; Osceola from Elkland, in December, 1854; Nelson from Elkland, in December, 1857; Hamilton from Bloss, in December, 1872; Duncan from Delmar, Charleston and Morris, in December, 1873; Wellsboro from Delmar, in May, 1830; Lawrenceville from Lawrence, in May, 1831; Covington from Covington, in May, 1831; Elkland from Elkland, in May 1850; Knoxville from Deerfield, in May, 1851; Mansfield from Richmond, in Februray, 1857; Mainesburg from Sullivan, in February, 1859; Tioga from Tioga, in February, 1860; Fall Brook from Ward, in August, 1864; Westfield from Westfield, in January, 1867; Blossburg from Bloss, in August, 1871; Roseville from Rutland, in February, 1876.

Post Offices, and towns in which they are located in Tioga County, Pa. Ansonia, Shippen; Antrim, Duncan; Arnot, Bloss; Barfelden, Liberty; Blossburg, Blossburg; Brookfield, Brookfield; Canoe Camp, Richmond; Charleston, Charleston; Chatham Valley, Chatham; Cherry Flats, Charleston; Covington, Covington; Cowanesque Valley, Westfield; Crooked Creek, Middlebury; Daggetts Mills, Jackson; Delmar, Delmar; East Charleston, Charleston; East Chatham, Chatham; East Point, Liberty; Elkland, Elkland; Elk Run, Covington; Fall Brook, Fall Brook; Farmington Center, Farmington; Farmington Hill, Farmington; Gaines, Gaines; Hammond, Middlebury; Keeneyville, Middlebury; Knoxville, Knoxville; Lamb's Creek, Richmond; Lawrenceville, Lawrenceville; Liberty, Liberty; Little Marsh Chatham; Lloyd, Morris; Landrus; Morris; Mainesburg, Mainesburg; Mansfield, Mansfield; Maple Ridge, Charleston; Marshfield, Gaines; Middlebury Center, Middlebury; Millerton, Jackson; Mitchell's Creek, Tioga; Mixtown, Clymer; Morris, Morris; Morris Run, Hamilton; Nauvoo, Liberty; Nelson, Nelson; Niles Valley, Middlebury; Ogdensburg, Union; Osceola, Osceola; Potter Brook, Westfield; Round Top, Charleston; Rutland, Rutland; Sabinsville, Clymer; Somer's Lane, Lawrence; Stony Fork, Delmar; Sullivan, Sullivan; Tioga, Tioga; Wellsboro, Wellsboro; West Covington, Covington; Westfield, Westfield.

Brookfield Township.

Brookfield Township was organized Feb., 1827, taken from the northern portion of Westfield township. It is situated in the extreme northwestern portion of Tioga County, Pa., and bounded on the north by Steuben County, New York; on the east by the township of Deerfield, Pa.; on the south by Westfield, and on the west by Potter County, Pa. Its mean elevation above tide is about 1,550. Its largest stream is Troop's Creek, which flows eastward and southward, emptying into the Cowanesque river at Knoxville, Pa. It is well watered by springs, rivulets and brooks, and is fast gaining a position as an agricultural township. Its early settlers were Bedford George, Titus Ives, Elihu Hill, and Curtis Cady, who located with their families within the present limits of the township, about the year 1809. They were followed by John Joseph, Ira Baker, Amos Baker, John Brown, Godfrey Bowman, Luman Seeley, Simeon Lewis, Benjamin Seeley, Asahel Nobles, William George, J. B. Seeley, William Simmons, Azel Nobles,

Samuel Baker. These settlers came principally from the state of New York. They endured many privations and hardships in clearing up their farms and making themselves homes in the wilds of northern Pennsylvania. Several times when the water was low in the Cowanesque and Tioga rivers, they were obliged to go to Painted Post to get their milling done—a distance of about fifty miles. The forests were full of wild animals, and much trouble and annoyance were experience by the settlers, from them. The deer however, were plenty, and in season, they were certain of an abundance of meat, which they preserved by drying and smoking. It was suitable medical attendance, sugar, tea, coffee and calico, and the thousand and one articles which go to make life agreeable that they were deprived of. But they persevered, and others took courage from their example; the forest was cut down, comfortable and elegant dwellings were erected, and the fields of waving grain, soft meadows, and green pastures, where herds of cattle and sheep are grazing, are the fruits of their perseverance and their triumph over the rugged hand of nature.

—Titus Ives erected the first framed house in Brookfield.

—William Simmons was the first merchant in Brookfield.

—The first orchard in Brookfield township was set out by Elihu Hill.

—The first road in the township of Brookfield was the "North Road."

—The first church edifice erected in the township was in the year 1858.

—The first justices of the peace were Titus Ives and Godfrey Bowman.

—Men worked for a yard of calico per day in the early settlement of Brookfield.

—The first tavern or public house erected in the township was by William Corwin, in 1853.

—Rev Thomas Magee held the first religious services in the township. He was a Methodist.

—Rev. Nathan Fellows held a series of revival meetings in the year 1836, making many conversions.

—The Free Will Baptists effected a church organization in 1840, and 1861 a church edifice was erected,

—The first school in the township was taught by Asa Bushnell, in the year 1817, at the house of Curtis Cady.

—Close Communion Baptists organized a church May, 25th, 1848, and erected a church edifice in 1859; first meeting June, 1860.

—The first marriage in the township was that of William Simmons and Mary A. Brown. Simmons was about sixteen years of age,

—The first church, (M. E. Church) was organized in 1818. Ira Baker, Amos Baker, Samuel Baker, John Joseph, Azel Nobles and their wives, were among the first members. Hannah Joseph, Deborah Joseph, Curtis Cady, were also members.

—The Rev. Samuel Conant taught the first school in the first school house erected in the township. The school house was a log one, with desks and seats made from split boards of basswood. Anna VanCamp and Luman Seeley were his successors.

—William and John Simmons were for many years justices of the peace in the western portion of the township; John G. Holmes many years in the eastern portion.

—A cheese factory was erected by Wood & McBride in 1866.

—The first mowing machines used in the township were owned by William Simmons and D. W. Nobles.

Bloss Township.

The original limits of the township of Bloss have been so materially lessened by the formation of the borough of Blossburg in the year 1871, and the township of Hamilton in December, 1872, that substantially the inhabitants of Bloss township are to be found in the village of Arnot. The township of Bloss was formed in the year 1841, and taken from the southern portion of the township of Covington. Of the portion which now remains of the township we shall proceed to write, giving the early history of the township in connection with the borough of Blossburg.

The Blossburg Coal Company obtained its charter by an act of the Legislature of Pennsylvania, approved April 11th, 1866. The company consisted of Constant Cook, John Arnot, Charles Cook, Henry Sherwood, Franklin N. Drake, Ferral C. Dininny, Henry H. Cook and Lorenzo Webber. Hon. Constant Cook, John Arnot, Charles Cook, Henry Sherwood and Lorenzo Webber are dead, and of the original corporators, only three survive, viz: Franklin N. Drake, Ferral C. Dininny and Henry H Cook.

The Blossburg Coal Company immediately after obtaining their charter commenced the construction of a railroad from Blossburg southwest up Johnson Creek to their coal lands, a distance of about four miles. This railroad was completed during the year 1866. While the road was being constructed the opening up of the mines was carried on with activity. A saw mill was erected and the construction of dwellings, shops schutes, stores, offices, etc. were hurriedly built. For a time this new coal town was known as Drakeville, in honor of Franklin N. Drake, the executive manager of the company; but it was finally christened "Arnot" in honor of Hon. John Arnot, Sr., of Elmira.

In 1867 Mr. Franklin N. Drake removed from Steuben County, New York to Blossburg, in order to be near the work. He was for many years the President of the Company and Ferral C. Dininny, Superintendent. Under his management (F. N. Drake's), churches and schools were erected He demonstrated the feasibility of making coke from semi-bituminous coal, causing two hundred coke ovens to be constructed under the immediate direction of S. B. Elliott, civil and mining engineer.

The first inhabitants were principally from Blossburg, Morris Run and Fall Brook, men who had been engaged in mining or lumbering at those places. The Dunsmores, Sullivans, Landrus, Camerons, Herons, Jones, Davis's, Çoles, Allens, Harrisses, Logans, Dugans, had formerly been employed by either the Morris Run Coal Company or the Fall Brook Coal Company.

—There are four schools in Arnot.

—Arnot contains about 3,000 inhabitants.

—For many years the citizens of Arnot maintained a reading room.

—Fred Wingrave has been employed many years by the company.

—Arnot contains five church edifices and seven church organizations.

—The company own a steam fire engine which is housed near a reservoir of water.

—November 28th, 1880, coal washer destroyed by fire at Arnot. Loss about $20,000.

—Col. W. F. Fox was for many years cashier at Arnot, handling large sums of money.

—William Harris made the first coke in open pits at Arnot before coke ovens were constructed.

—Mr. Jason Higgins has served the company in the capacity of store agent for many years successively.

—In May, 1884, destructive fire in the woods surrounding Arnot. Seventeen buildings were destroyed in Arnot.

—Among the teachers were R. E. Howland and wife, S. A. Gaskill, Frederic L. Gray, Mrs. David McIntyre.

—The Blossburg Coal Company are engaged largely in lumbering, having three mills whose total capacity is 30,000,000 feet.

—When F. N. Drake was president of the company he gave the miners and their families a free ride to Elmira and return.

—The site of Arnot was covered with a dense growth of timber, when the Blossburg Coal Company commenced operations in 1866.

—Since the mines were opened up to date there has been mined and shipped over four million tons of coal and about three hundred thousand tons of coke.

—The population of Arnot is composed of a very great number of different nationalities, among whom are native Americans, English, Irish, Scotch, Welsh, Swede, Poles and Germans. They live very peacefully together.

—Henry J. Landrus has been the active manager at the mines at Arnot for the past three years. He served several years before in the same capacity and resigned, S. B. Elliott, taking his place. Mr. Elliott after several years resigned and Mr. Landrus again accepted the position.

—The Blossburg Coal Company purchased the Tioga railroad, extending from Blossburg to Lawrenceville and from Blossburg to Morris Run, which added to their own road made them the owners of thirty-four miles of first-class railroad. This was accomplished in the year 1867.

—Arnot contains "A Friendly Society," Ivorites, Catholic Temperance Association, Good Templars, Patrons of Temperance, Catholic Knights of America, Knights of Pythias. There are quite a number of Odd Fellows and Free Masons, but they are members of Blossburg lodges.

—Andrew Bowers, Dr. D. C. Waters, James Cameron, John Cameron, William Dunsmore, John Dunsmore, John J. Davis, Alexander Logan, Samuel Heron, James Smith, John McKay, James Cleary, John Hill, Thomas M. McCay, Jason Higgins, Richard Smith, Fred Wingrave, George Lee, John Burke, Nicholas Shultz, Michael Clark, Campbell Cole, James Patterson, Theodore Williams, George Tylee, Charles Logan, William Bowers, Frank Howland, William Reynolds, W. R. Logan, Robert Pendleton, Thomas Llewellyn, H. G. Boardman, R. F. Cummings and E. K Mandeville have held prominent positions under the company.

Chatham Township.

The early settlers of southern Deerfield township were great admirers of Lord Chatham, (William Pitt) and in February, 1828, they petitioned the court of Common Pleas of Tioga County, for the formation of a township to be taken from the southern portion of Deerfield township, to be known as "Chatham." The court answered their prayer, and the township of Chatham was duly organized; such organization to take effect in the year 1829. In the year 1829, Allen Fraser, Jr., assessor, returned to the county commissioners the first assessment for the new township. The names of the taxables were Cyrus Ames, Aaron Alba, James Allen, Francis Burrell, Alexander Burrell, Beersheba Bates, Asa Bates, Silas Billings, Daniel Baker, Martin Boardman, John Bates, Nathan Baker, Stephen Colvin Joel Crandall, Samuel Carpenter, Allen Fraser, Jr., Eddie Howland, Jr., Joseph Howland, John Knox, William Knox, David Lesure, John Macumber, Joseph Matson, David Seamens, Lovell Short, Samuel Strawn, John P. Tracey, Elijah Thompson, Samuel Taylor, Widow A. W. Tracey, William Wass, Joseph Yarnall.

Several of the above named was non-residents. The northern portion of the township facing the Cowanseque valley was peopled by settlers who came in from New York by that route, and the southern and eastern portion by those who came up the Tioga and Crooked Creek valleys. The early settlers along the valley of Crooked Creek, were W. L. Merrick, William Spalding, Doctor Harvey Leach, John Short, Rensalaer Toles, Robert Hill, Asa Short, Nehemiah Beach, H. B. Leonard, David Lesure, George Hawley, Lovell Short, Daniel Hill. In the locality now known as the "Close District," were Caleb Close, Reuben Close, Charles Avery, Armand Close, Abel Close, Amasa Clark, Samuel Miller, John McCumber, William Wass, Russell Temple, Sylvester Treat, Benjamin VanDusen. Upon the south and central, were Benoni Hill, Z. Burdick, Frank Spencer, Aurora Spencer, Calvin Davis, Moses Wilhem, Joseph Wheeler, Whit Wheeler and Calvin Wheeler, Azariah Slocum, Samuel Main, Jesse Moffett, Artemus Crippin. At Shortsville, in Chatham township, the early settlers were Lovell Short, John Short, Jr., Miletus Brown, Peter Hoteling, Lemuel Jackson, James Gee, C. A. Carpenter. Other early settlers were Burdick Hill, Daniel Shoves, Asher Manning, Harlow Boyce, Ezra Allen, Phillip Erway, Samuel King, Winchester Cooper, Abram Wormer, Alexander Lattimer, John Winters, William Brong, James Doane, Daniel Doane, Jerry Garner. The township, like all the territory in Tioga County, was covered with a heavy growth of timber. Some of the finest pine in Tioga County, grew along Crooked creek and its tributaries in Chatham township, and in the early history of the township, lumbering was carried on extensively. Mr. John L. Sexton, Jr., in his history of Chatham, written for W. W. Munsell & Co., says: "Few of the present day appreciate the hardships and the privation of the pioneers, who forty or fifty years ago came into the wilderness and began clearing up new farms. These privations and hardships we have often alluded to in our general and township histories. In Chatham there was the same experience as elsewhere; conflicts with the panther, bear and wolf, and sport with the deer, elk and fish; the log house, the sheep or cattle fold, the clearing of fallows, the logging bees, the raisings, the social gatherings, the cutting out of roads, the erection of mills, school houses and churches, the humble fare, the rigid economy, sickness, deaths, marriages and births, and were we to relate them, it would form a section almost identical with those on other localities. The words 'pioneer,' and 'early settler,' convey to the mind of the readers all these experiences and lead them back to the times when this our land was new."

—The mean altitude of Chatham is about 1,500 feet above tide.

—The first saw mill was erected by Nehemiah Beach on "Nate Mead's" brook.

—Crooked creek is a tributary of the Tioga river, uniting with that stream at Tioga.

—Wheat, oats, corn, buckwheat, potatoes and the orchard fruits are grown with profit.

—The villages in Chatham township are Little Marsh, Shortsville and Keeneyville.

—Tobacco has been raised quite extensively in the valley of Crooked creek, in the township of Chatham.

—In point of agricultural wealth, Chatham stands twelfth out of a list of twenty-eight townships in Tioga County.

—There are fourteen schools in the township, where about five hundred pupils were instructed for seven months in the year.

—The principal stream in the township, is Crooked creek. Its principal tributaries are Norris brook and Nate Mead's brook.

Covington Township.

Covington township was formed from the township of Tioga, and originally contained the territory now chiefly composed of the township of Bloss and Blossburg Borough, Sullivan and Mainesburg Borough, Ward and the borough of Fall Brook, Union, Liberty and Morris. The earliest settler in the township was Aaron Bloss, who located in the township in the year 1801, and subsequently removed and founded Blossburg, five miles further up the Tioga river in the year 1806. The next early settlers were David Clemmons Hovey, Washburne, Mallory, Sackett, Levi Prentiss, John Patten, Tilley Marvin, J. Coonrod Youngman, Asahel Graves, Absalom Kingsbury, Isaac Walker, Peter Keltz, Sumner Wilson, Robert Searles, Samuel Negley, Christopher Huntington and Nathaniel Elliott.

The first assessment made by Ichabod Rowley to the county commissioners John Knox, Asa Mann and Elijah Depuy, when Covington contained the territory now embraced in some nine townships and five boroughs, showed the following list of taxable inhabitants, David Austin, Samuel Aldrich, Ebenezer Burley, David Burley, Alpheus Button, Joseph Bunn, Rufus Butler, Aaron Bloss, Gideon Briggs, Abner Cockran, Henry Campbell, John Cochran, Elijah Clark, Seth Clark, David Clemmons, Stillman Cannon Samuel Campbell, Levi Elliott, Eli Gitchell, Aaron Gillett, Charles Gillett, Asahel Graves, Josiah Graves, Levi Gifford, Noah Gifford, Samuel Higley, George Higley, Timothy Higley, Christopher Huntington, S. Huntington, John Keltz, Peter Keltz, Henry Knowlton, Absalom Kingsbury, Daniel

Lamb, Henry Lamb, Gad Lamb, Minnard Lawrence, John Levergood, Silas Lamphear, Erastus Lillibridge, Jacob Miller, Richard Miller, George Mateer John Marvin, Asa Mann, Samuel Negley, Thomas Overton, Elias Pratt, Rufus Pratt, William Patten, Levi Prentiss, Thomas Putman, Elijah Putman, Nathan Rowley, Nehemiah H. Ripley, Ichabod Rowley, Cephas Stratton, Thomas Sampson, Joshua Shaw, Amos Spencer, L. H. Spencer, Ichabod Smith, John Shaffer, Jonathan Sebring, Nathan Whitman, Isaac Walker, Archelius Wilkins, Daniel Wilkins, Tilley Marvin, David Harkness, David Harkness Jr., Royal Walker, Lorrian Lamb, Seneca Stratton, William Merritt. Sullivan township was taken from Covington township in the year 1816, and returned to the county commissioners its assessment to them, by their assessor, James Gray, Jr., at the same time as Ichabod Rowley did that of Covington and that is the reason why the names of the taxables of the whole township of Covington as embraced in the above list does not appear. By referring to the list made by the Sullivan assessor, the reader will obtain a complete list of the taxables then (1817) in the territory now composed of Sullivan township, Rutland township, Mainsburg borough, Roseville borough, Fall Brook borough, Bloss township and borough, Hamilton, Ward, Union and Liberty townships.

—The Tioga and Elmira State Line Railroad runs across the township about centrally.

—Dr. Henry Kilbourne was one of the early and prominent physicians in Covington borough and township.

—Covington township has many acres of highly cultivated lands with elegant farm houses and good barns

—Victor Gray, one of the first engineers on the Corning and Blossburg Railroad resides in the township of Covington.

—David Clemmens, a native of Hampshire County, Massachusetts, settled on the west side of the Tioga River in Covington township, in 1806.

—The early settlers on the Elk Run road were Alonzo Reddington, Jonathan Jennings, Isaac Bliss, father of the evangelist and Asahel Graves.

—Covington township is bounded on the north by Richmond township, on the east by Sullivan and Ward, on the south by Hamilton and Bloss and Blossburg borough and on the west by Charleston.

—Asahel Graves settled in 1817; Tilley Marvin in 1817; Sumner Wilson in 1818: Ephraim B. Gerould in 1822; Richard Videau in 1831; David Caldwell in 1836; John Copp, a native of Rhode Island was the first settler in "Copp Hollow."

—Settlers on the state road west of Covington borough were Norman Rockwell, Avery Gillett, Levi Elliott and Nathaniel Elliott. Matthew Skelley about forty-five years ago settled on the west side of the Tioga River; in the eastern portion of Covington the early settlers were Lyman Frost, James T. Frost, Samuel and Lewis Walker, Joseph Jacques, Peter Whittaker, Silas Lamphere, John Cleveland. Sumner Wilson and James Negley settled on the Williamson road about a mile and a half north of Covington borouhg.

Clymer Township.

From the year 1845 to 1869, William B. Clymer grandson of Hon. George Clymer a signer of the Declaration of Independance, was agent for the sale of the Bingham lands situated in Tioga, Potter, McKean and other northern counties of Pennslyvania, with his office or head quarters at Wellsboro.

Through his liberal offers many citizens of the state of New York, were induced to settle upon the Bingham lands in Tioga county. A large number of these New Yorkers located upon lands in the southern portion of the township of Westfield, Tioga county, along the valley of Mill Creek, a tributary of the Cowanesque, and upon the plateaus and hard wood ridges on the east and west sides of Mill Creek Valley and the head waters of Long Run and Potter Brook. These settlers in the years 1850 petitioned the court to form a township to be taken from the townships of Westfield and Gaines, to be named Clymer.

The court granted the request in the year 1850. The first annual assessment was made in the year 1852. The taxables were John Ackley, Roswell Ackley, George Ackley, J. F. Allen, W. R. Burdick, Edmond Bristol, George O. Bristol, George Briggs, Francis Briggs, Levi Blue, Enos Babcock, John Brown, William Bradley, Willis Babcock, Washington Blue, Rockwell Bentley, Charles Burlingame, Hamilton Boardman, John Baty, Isaac Burnside, Seth Boothe, Benoi Boardman, Samuel Briggs, Hiram Burdick, J. B. Benn, William Benn, J. M. Bush, Squire Briggs, Isaac Beach, E. M. Brown, Thomas Barber, J. B. Beach, Henry Brigham, Sylvenus Coe, Eli Chapman, F. W. Calkins, George Cass, Samuel Carlin, C. D. Cameron, Sylvester Davy, George Davy, Jared Davis, John Davis, Alvah Dickens, Robert Dickens, Charles P. Douglass, B. Dutcher, William Douglass, Horace Dimond, Thomas Eldridge Jr., Horace Eldridge, Thomas Eldridge, Chester Ellsworth, Andrew Frasier, Ransom Freemond, Squire Guile, Philo Griffin, Silas Griffin, Daniel Gower, Charles Gum, Benjamin Grew, W. G. Grew, Peter Griffin, G. W. Heiler, George Heiler, Lott Hackett, Elmer Hackett, Burton Howe, George Hawley, Benjamin Howe, Elijah Hancock, J. W. Hancock, Lyman Hancock, E. G. Hill, Charles Hoag, Erastus Hill, H. K. Hill, Henry Hill, Z. Hemminger, William Head, Job Head, Doctor J. W. Hamer, James Hill, George Harvey, George Hurlburt, James Johnson, Alonzo King, Hiram King, H. King, A. King, Harvey King, John King, Alfred King, Charles King, David Kilbourn, Henry Larrison, W. Larrison, William Lebar, George Lebars Thompson Lebar, A. Lebar, Charles Lebar, Chauncy Lebar, James Lovell, Peter Lovell, John Lovell, Nelson Lindsey, W. Larrison, G. Larrison, George Larrison, William McNeil, Benjamin Madison, Henry McFall, Mose, Newton, M. W. Newton, Samuel Niver, Norman Orris, Andrew Ormes, Cyrus Paddock, D. A. Paddock, Lyman Pritchard, James Richards, Charles Richards, Ira Potter, Willard Potter, Orson Pemblaton, Cheeney Pendleton, John Rushmore, William Rogers, Rosel Rogers, Dennis Roberts, William Runnells, Willard Rowland, Silas Rushmore, Peter Rushmore, Jonas Rushmore, Jonas Schoonover, Thomas Schoonover, Christopher Schoonover, Hiram Schoonover, John Sykes, Charles Sykes, Charles

Southard, Dixson Southard, Chauncey Southard, C. B. Skelley, David Short, E. G. Smith, E. W. Smith, James Smith, Abram Smith, Peter Smith Marvin Swimelar, Thomas Straight, Orrin Stebbins, E. H. Stebbins, Stephen Straight, A. G. Sabin, Henry Steele, E. F. Skinner, Nathaniel Skinner, C. R. Skinner, W. B Skinner, James Scott, Luke Scott, Levi Scott, Rufus Scott, Charles Scott, Samuel Swimelar, Samuel Scoville, Merritt Thompson, J. O. Thompson, Caleb Trowbridge, H. E. Tanner, J. C. Tanner, Watson Trowbridge, Noah Weeks, Freeman Wilcox, Willian Wright, Aaron Yale. Much attention is directed to agricultural pursuits in the township, the raising of neat cattle and sheep, and the making of butter and cheese.

—Sabinsville contains about 300 inhabitants.

—Sabinsville is a station on the A. & N. R. R. R.

—Simon Rexford settled at Mixtown in the year 1820.

—George O. Bristol settled in Mixtown in the year 1820.

—Equitable Aid Union No. 253, organized March 5, 1881.

—The first black-smith in the township was Cyrus Paddock.

—The first hotel in Sabinsville was kept by C. P. Douglass.

—The first mail through Sabinsville was carried by Samuel Losey.

—The mean elevation of Clymer township is about 1,575 feet above tide.

—The first store in Sabinsville was built by the late Honorable Butler B. Strang.

—The early settlers made large quantities of maple sugar for the market.

—The first regular school house was erected at Mixtown in the year 1826.

—The first regular physician in Clymer township was Doctor John M. Haner.

—The first election held in the township was at the house of C. P. Douglass.

—James Mix was the first settler at Mixtown, in Clymer township, in the year 1818.

—The first grist mill was erected by Orrin Stebbins and Elijah Hancock in Sabinsville.

—Sabinsville was named in honor of Alonzo G. Sabin. a prominent citizen of the place.

—There are three post offices in the township, viz: Sabinsville, Mixtown and Long Run.

—The post office was established at Sabinsville in the year 1849. C. P. Douglass post master.

—Sabinsville lodge No. 2,300 Knights of Honor instituted by W. H. Fuller, D. D. G. D., October 2, 1880.

—The Addison and Northern Pennsylvania Railroad, passes through the central portion of the township from north to south.

C. P. Douglass settled in Sabinsville in the year 1837. Orrin Stebbins and Elijah Hancock made settlements at about the same time.

—There are two church edifices in the township, Methodist church erected in the Ackley district in the year 1858. A Baptist church was erected in Sabinsville in 1879.

Charleston Township.

In the year 1820 the township of Charleston was formed. It was taken from the eastern side of the township of Delmar, and occupies a central position in the county of Tioga. It was originally covered with a heavy growth of timber embracing many varieties—hemlock, white pine, beach, maple, ash, cherry, white, yellow and black birch, chestnut and oak. It occupies elevated land between the Tioga, Charleston creek and Crooked creek valleys. Its pioneer settlers were principally from New York and the New England states. Its second pioneers on the south were from Wales. It is well watered, although occupying a mean elevation of fifteen hundred feet above ocean level. It is one of the most productive townships in the county, and is substantially "cleared up." The prevailing pursuit of its inhabitants is agriculture. Its first assessment was made in the year 1821, by Nathan Niles, Jr., Oliver Willard, Hiram Beebe and Seth Daggett, commissioners; David Lindsay, commissioners' clerk.

The names of the taxable inhabitants were A. Atherton, Caleb Austin, Rosel Bailey, Jesse Catlin, Nelson Catlin, William Catlin, Timothy Culver, Joseph Culver, Cyrus Catlin, Gideon Dewey, Justus Dartt, Justus Dartt, Jr., James G. Dartt, Daniel Dennison, John Dailey, Calvin Eli, Israel Greenleaf, Benjamin Gitchell, Frederic Hilbot, David Henry, James Henry, Nathan Niles, Jr., James Porter, Jr., Thomas Prentiss, Daniel Packer, Leonard Porter, John Porter, Elijah Starkweather, Peter Shumway, Heman Shumway, Vine Sager, John Starkweather. Adam Seeley, Thomas Sampson, Isaiah Wilson, Daniel Wilson, Moses Wheeler, Lyman Wetmore, Andrew Wetmore, Oliver Willard, Joseph Wilson, Orlando Willard, William Fanton, Cyrus Dartt, John Domine, John Lovell, James Pettis, William Hill. There were then less than fifty taxables. There is now over six hundred, with a population of about twenty-five hundred. The territory of Charleston sixty-five years ago, included not only its present boundaries but that of the present township of Duncan. The villages or hamlets in the township of Charleston, are Cherry Flats, Whitneyville, Dartt Settlement, Catlin Hollow, Hill's Creek, Round Top and Welsh Settlement. The first settler of Cherry Flats was Timothy Culver. Timothy and Joseph Culver were early settlers in the "Welsh Settlement." Thomas Evans, Lewis Lewis, Miles Harris, David G. Edwards, David Morris, were also pioneers in that locality. At Whitneyville the first settlers were Lemuel Churchill, Asa Churchill, T. and Solomon Rice. Whitneyville was named in honor of Nelson Whitney, an enterprising farmer, merchant and lumberman, who located there in 1848. During the late rebellion he raised a company and did distinguished service. Dartt Settlement obtained its name from the first settler, Colonel Justus Dartt, a soldier of the revolutionary war, who settled there in the year 1811. When he settled in Dartt settlement there were only eight other settlers in the township, viz: Moses Wheeler, Levi Elliot, Oliver Willard, —— Shumway, Caleb Austin, Nathan Niles, Rosel Bailey and Timothy Culver.

—In 1837, Robert Pratt settled at Whitneyville.

—Norman Rockwell was the first post master at Cherry Flats.

—The first school in Charleston was opened at Dartt Settlement.

—In 1840, a Welsh Chapel was erected in the "Welsh Settlement."

—Tobacco is raised quite extensively on Col. Justus Dartt's old farm.

—The state road built in the year 1808 runs through Cherry Flats village.

—Aaron Gillett settled at Cherry Flats, Charleston township, in the year 1812.

—A lodge of Knights of Honor was established at Whitneyville, January 24th, 1881.

—Robert Adams, a native of Ireland, about the year 1840, settled on Hill's Creek.

—The first church edifice erected in Charleston township, was in Catlin Hollow, and the second in Dartt Settlement.

—About the year 1820, Lemuel Churchill erected a small tannary near Hill's Creek, in the northern portion of Charleston township.

—Col. Justus Dartt died July 5th, 1838, aged 81 years. His wife Hannah January 14th, 1844, aged 86 years. They are buried in the Dartt Settlement graveyard.

—The first election for the township of Charleston, was held at the house of Justus Dartt, March 19th, 1824. The first officers were, supervisors, Thomas Sampson and Royal Porter. David Henry and Oliver Willard were elected constables. Justus Dartt, and Daniel Wilson acted as judges of the election.

—The pioneer on Hill's Creek was Jacob Schlefflein, who purchased several thousand acres in Lycoming and Tioga Counties and located on Hill's Creek in the year 1828. He was a physician but never practiced. Was acquainted with Aaron Burr, Santa Anna, Robert Fulton, Dewitt Clinton. He died at Tioga, December 27th, 1880, aged 87 years.

Dearfield Township.

Some of the very earliest settlements in Tioga County were made within the present limits of the township of Deerfield, upon the Cowanesque river near the mouth of Troops Creek. Patents were obtained for several warrants, located in this township from the state of Pennsylvania as early as 1785. It contains an area of nearly twenty one thousand acres. Its mean elevation is about 1500 feet above the ocean's level. It contains some of the richest alluvial soil in the state. It is bounded on the north by Steuben county New York, on the east by Osceola and Farmington in Pennsylvania, on the south by Chatham, on the west by the township of Brookfield. The Cowanesque river and Troops Creek are its principal streams. The Cowanesque river enters the township near its south western boundary and flows in a north easterly direction, and passing out of the township near the center of its north and south lines. It was formed from Delmar in the year 1814, and originally contained within its limits, territory which has since been organized into several townships and boroughs. At the organization of Deerfield township, there were only sixty three taxable innhabitants in the township containing an area of about 106,000 acres or a fraction over one seventh of the entire county of Tioga.

—Union Academy established in 1847.

—September 15th, 1848, great freshet in the Cowanesque river.

—Levi Cook had a blacksmith shop in 1809.
—Rev. David Short became a settler in 1806.
—In 1804 Eddy Howland erected a saw mill.
—In 1801, Bethlehem Thompson became a settler.
—Joshua Colvin erected a distillery in the year 1815.
—John Knox built a hewed log hotel in the year 1819.
—Eddy Howland established a store in the year 1814.
—Eddy Howland erected a cider mill in the year 1817.
—Butler or Chatham Baptist Church, organized in 1852.
—First Baptist Church organized, (regular Baptist) in 1843.
—Bethlehem Thompson erected a log grist mill in the year 1811.
—Free Will Baptist Church of Deerfield organized in March, 1829.
—Doctor Simeon settled in Deerfield in 1803, and remained about five years.
—In 1803 Eddy Howland and John Howland, his father, made a settlement.
—In 1842 William J. Knox built a store at Academy Corners, in Deerfield township.

—Martin Bowen erected a tannery in the year 1820. Peter Rushmore built a tannery the same year.

—The first settlers in Deerfield on the Cowanesque, were William Knox and Ebenezer Seelye in the year 1797.

—The first chidren born in Deerfield, were Sally Seelye, daughter of Ebenezer Seelye, and James Knox, son of William Knox.

—John Colton Knox was born in Deerfield, February, 1817; studied law and became one of the Judges of the Supreme Court of Pennsylvania.

—In the year 1785 and 1786, James Strawbridge and Col. Thomas Proctor obtained patents from the Land Department of Pennsylvania, for lands in the Cowanesque Valley.

—In the year 1807 at sheriff s sale held at Williamsport, Pa., a nephew of James Strawbridge, George Strawbridge became the owner of the Strawbridge lands in Deerfield.

—In the year 1807, Emmer Bowen, Newberry Cloos, James Falkner, John Falkner, William Falkner, became settlers—also about the same time Jonn Short, Reuben Short, Jonathan Rogers, Curtis Cady, James Yarnall, the latter from near Philadelphia, Zadoc Bowen and Joshua Colvin, became settlers.

—The first school taught in Deerfield township, was by Betsey Bodwell, in the year 1802. This school was in a log house. Among the scholars who attended the school were Reuben Cook, Ashael Rexford, Harvey Seelye, John Knox, David Rexford, Alanson Seelye, Archibald Knox, Abel Cloos, Anna Seelye, William Knox, Matilda Cloos, Mehetitable Seelye, Betsey Knox, Julius Seelye, Lucinda Seelye, Betsey Seelye.

Duncan Township and Village of Antrim.

Duncan township was formed from the townships of Delmar, Charleston and Morris, by a decree of the Court of Common Pleas held in and for Tioga County, at the December Term, in the year 1873, and Thomas Gaffney and E. H. Tremain were authorized to hold the first township election, February 17, 1874. At an election held pursuant to the above decree, Thomas Gaffney and E. H. Tremain were chosen supervisors; Isaac S. Marshall and J. Shumway justices of the peace; W. W. Lownsberry constable; William E. Butts asssessor; and for school directors, David Cooper was elected for six years; A. Lake, six years; Dr. E. George, four years; W. P. Thomas, two years; Joseph Murray, two years; John Hinman was elected treasurer, and Thomas Farrer, auditor for one year; George W. Rice, for two years and Chas. G. Hinman for three years; Wm. W. Forrest, town clerk; Jerry Austin, judge of election, and Chas. Prothero, D. D. Holleday, inspectors of election; thus was the official machinery of the township put in motion. A greater portion of the lands in the township are owned by the Fall Brook Coal Company and the largest portion of its population is centered in the mining town of Antrim. The mean elevation of the township is about 1700 feet above sea level. It is situated in the southern central portion of Tioga county, about seven miles north of the Tioga and Lycoming county lines. Antrim the center of population of the township is a mining village containing about two thousand inhabitants, and the southern terminus of the Corning, Cowanesque and Antrim railroad. The streets are many of them graded and the village laid out in a systematic manner. Nearly all the dwellings are painted, and everything kept as clean and neat as it is possible in a mining town, in fact it is the model mining town of Pennsylvania.

—Antrim Hall, erected in 1879.

—James Pollock is the mining engineer.

—Antrim Lyceum organized December, 1879.

—David Cooper was the first master carpenter.

—John Hinman was the first store agent and cashier.

—The Antrim graded school dedicated in July, 1880.

—Methodist Episcopal class organized in April, 1874.

—William Howell, Jr., is now manager at the mines.

—Samuel Heron is the chief book keeper and paymaster.

—The managers and paymasters office was erected in 1873.

—The Antrim Fall Brook Coal Company store erected in 1874.

—Workingmen's Benevolent Association, organized June, 1876.

—A Baptist Church was organized at Antrim, February 20th, 1873.

—The capacity of the Antrim coal mines is about 1,800 tons per day.

—Charles Hoff was the first weighmaster. John Forrest was a weighmaster for many years.

—Thomas Gaffney was the first mining boss at Antrim, and held the position at his death in 1884.

—Thomas Farrer held the position of manager of the mines from their opening in 1867, to 1883.

—James Ketchum was the first overseer of lumbering and outside work. He still retains the position.

—L. J. Stothoff the first station agent at Antrim, was killed by the cars at Antrim, February 15, 1877.

—Ella Cooper, Mary Hinman, Theodore P. Whiting, Frances Whiting in the order named were the first teachers at Antrim.

—In December, 1867, Titus Drainsfield moved his family into a shanty at Antrim which had formerly been used as a camp by the explorers.

—October 28th, 1872, first locomotive over the Corning, Cowenesque and Antrim Railroad entered Antrim. Joseph Boyle, engineer. John Wilson, conductor.

—Welsh Congregational Church, organized in 1876. Church completed in 1878, cost $1,104.46 of which the Fall Brook Coal Company donated half the amount.

—Explorations for coal were made by Thomas Farrer and John Smith employees of the Fall Brook Coal Company, in the year 1866 ,at Antrim. It was then a wilderness.

—Duncan Lodge, I. O. O. F., organized December 29th, 1879, Thomas Gaffney, Noble Grand ; Isaac Cook, Vice Grand ; George Makin, Recording Secretary ; David Nichol, Assistant Secretary ; William Young, Treasurer.

—In 1868 Duncan S. Magee christened the place Antrim. Hon. Daniel E. Howell, of Bath, Gen. George J. Magee, John Lang and Charles Crawford of Watkins, N. Y., Hon. Charles C. B. Walker and A. H. Gorton of Corning, John Magee, Jr., of Watkins, N. Y., S. S. Ellsworth, of Penn Yan, N. Y., Anton Hardt, John Smith, Thomas Farrer, R. F. Cummings, James Hoffman, of Fall Brook were present.

—Trinity Church organized by Dr. Charles Breck, of Wellsboro, at Antrim July 24th, 1872. Through the munificent bequest of John Magee, Jr., the Trinity Church edifice was erected and completed in the year 1881. It is built of cut stone and cost about $13,000. He provided in his will for the erection of five Episcopal Churches, whose total cost should not exceed $50,000. He died very suddenly of pneumonia, at Watkins, N. Y., April 26th, 1873, aged about 29 years.

—Thomas McMahon, A. J. Pollock, John Curran, David J. Davis, James Maloy, Andrew K. Fletcher, W. W. Forrest, Samuel Heron, William Howell, Jr., Simon Keating, Thomas Burton, James Gaffney, Charles Prothero, James Ketcham, James Pollock, Joseph Lodge, Charles Burgess, William B. James, D. M. Edwards, Thomas Gaffney, William Buckley, John Forrest, James Ketcham, Titus Drainsfield, Michael Keating, Sr.. James Gardiner and Samuel Strong are old employees, some of them having been employed continuously by the Fall Brook Coal Company, for the past twenty years or more.

Delmar Township.

The act of the Legislature authorizing the formation of Tioga County from Lycoming County in the year 1804, was not fully complied with until the year 1813, when the first court was held at Wellsboro. The formation of the township of Delmar in the year 1808, was by the authority of the court of common pleas of Lycoming County and the assessment was not made and returned to the county of Lycoming until the year 1815. Tioga township was organized also by the same authority in 1808 and these two town ships were the original townships from which the twenty-six other townships have been formed.

Delmar township is situated nearly in the geographical center of the county and its mean altitude is about 1,550 feet above tide. Its surface is diversified by valleys, hills and plateaus. It is supplied with living springs of water and numerous creeks. Pine Creek a stream navigable for rafts of lumber or timber during a freshet, washes its southwestern boundary. The early settlers in Delmar (before the borough of Wellsboro was formed) were from Delaware, Maryland, Virginia and Philadelphia. The first settlers in the township were Benjamin Wistar Morris, John Norris, David Lindsey, Alpheus Cheeney, David Kelsey, William Wells, Gideon Wells, James Iddings, James Dixson, Richard Jackson and Rev. Caleb Boyer. This was in the years 1801 and 1802. In christening the township, out of compliment to the states from which they had emigrated they called it Virdelmar, the abbreviations of Virginia, Delaware and Maryland. When it was incorporated as a township the abbreviation *Vir.* was omitted and it went upon record as Delmar. Notwithstanding the edict of the court several of the settlers who had acquired the custom of calling it Virdelmar persisted in thus naming it. Benjamin W. Morris was a Philadelphian and was the leading spirit in the settlement. He had met with reverses in Philadelphia, and came into the wilderness of Northern Pennsylvania to hide his chagrin or recover his former financial standing. William Wells was from Maryland and located about two and one half miles southwest of the spot where Mr. Morris had located. He brought several slaves with him which in a few yeaars he manumitted, giving them his Delmar poperty, house, lands and personal effects.

The assessment in the year 1815, the first that was returned to the commissioners of Tioga County and which then was embraced in the township of Delmar, covering the territory now composed of Delmar, Charleston, Middlebury, Shippen, Clymer, Gaines, Elk, Morris, Duncan, a portion of Liberty with the borough of Wellsboro. The names of these taxables appear: John Allington, Roswell B. Alford, Caleb Austin, Asahel Anderson, Rosel Bailey, William Babb, William Bache, Gideon Briggs, David Brant, Alpheus Cheeney, Jediah Carpenter, Timothy Culver, Jas. Dickinson, J. G. Dartt, Justus Dartt, Jr., Asaph Ellis, Consider Ellis, Richard Ellis, Chas. Daniels, Justus Dartt Sr., Peter Fulkrson, Aaron Furman, Jos. Irish, Sam'l W. Fisher, David Greenleaf, Isaac Greenleaf, Richard Gooden, Jacob Hines, Reuben Harrington, David Henry, Samuel Hampson, William Hill, William Hoadley, J. R. Harrison, George Haven, Hezekiah Haven, James Henry, Roswell Ives, Ezekiel Jones, Lorentus Jackson, Ebenezer Jackson, Luther Johnson, Sarah Kelsey, Daniel Kelsey, Thomas Kinney, Uriah Lute, Samuel W. Morris, Miss Mathews, B. W. Morris, James Madison, Eben Murray, Samuel Miller, Morderica Moore, Israel Merrick, Asa Mann, Israel Merrick, Jr., William Mitchell, John Norris, Aaron Niles, Nathan Niles, Jr., Richard Phillips, John Phenix, Daniel Phillips, Thomas Printer, James Porter, James Porter, Jr., Elias Spencer, Orange Hotchkiss, Robert Hale, Peter Shumway, Elijah Starkweather, Henry Sligh, Jonathan Thorndyke, Munson Thompson, T. A. Whitman, Daniel Willson, J. W. Whitman, Samuel Whitman, Daniel Warner, Elijah White, Oliver Willard, Josiah Wilson, O. Wheeler, Andrew Whitmore, J. N. Kilbourn, David Kilbourn, Francis Conkright, William Conkright, William Dickson, Morderica Jackson, John Smith, D. H. Baker, Joseph Brown, Henry Hulburt, Joseph Trimbler, Daniel Salmon, Thompson Alden, Gordon Benjamin, Samuel Dill and James Tremain.

Alvin Willard, assessor; Hopestill Beecher, Justus Dartt and John Knox, county commissioners; David Lindsay, clerk; Nathan Niles and Caleb Austin, collectors. Rate of tax one per cent

—The first teacher in Delmar was Beadle Skull.

—There are twenty-five school houses in Delmar.

—Israel Stone was one of the pioneers in Delmar.

—John McEwen was one of the pioneers of Delmar.

—The family of Bacons were pioneers in Delmar township.

—Delmar is one of the best cultivated agricultural townships in Tioga County.

—Robert Campbell, one of the most successful farmers in Tioga County, settled in Delmar, in the year 1837.

—Robert Karr, a native of Wilmington, Delaware, settled in Delmar near Stony Forks in the year 1836. He died July, 1875, aged 75 years.

—David Heise, a native of Germany, a celebrated land surveyor, settled in Delmar in the year 1820. He used the compass over sixty years.

—Erastus P. Deane, a teacher, surveyor and farmer, settled in Delmar in 1834. He was one of the most accurate and well known land surveyors in Pennsylvania.

—William Eberenz, a native of Germany, settled in Delmar in the year 1817. He became one of the prominent citizens of the township and left a fine estate. He died June 7th, 1880, aged 79 years.

Elk Township.

Elk township was formed from the townships of Delmar and Morris in the year 1856. It is mountainous and sparsely settled, lying west of Pine Creek, and in the southwestern portion of Tioga County, bounded on the west by Potter County and on the south by Lycoming, on the east by Morris and Delmar townships. Pine Creek touches its northeastern boun dary. Cedar Run and the Billings branch of Kettle Creek are its principle streams Silas Billings, the elder, erected a steam saw mill upon the head-waters of Cedar Run in the year 1847, and constructed a plank road down the Run, nine miles to its junction with Pine Creek in Brown township, Lycoming County, Pa. Mr. Billings erected a dwelling which for many years was known as the "White House" together with several other dwellings for his men. The township abounded with white pine and hemlock timber. The pine timber has been pretty generally cut down and marketed. In 1856 Silas X. Billings and his brother-in-law, P. S. McNiel, erected a steam mill about two miles farther down Cedar Run and engaged extensively in lumbering. They also erected several dwellings. It was known as "Billings Camp" and a post office by that name established.

It was at this time (1856) that the township was organized. Its first taxables were Jehiel Beach, George Bendle, William Bendle, J. F. Bristol, John Cramer, S. S. Dingman, James Farley, Benjamin Frever, Edward Fridley, Charles Fisher, Henry Fisher, Daniel K. Fitch, G. W. Howd, George Maynard, Sarah Maynard, John Maynard, Peter S. McNiel, Daniel Minsker, A. P. Roberts, C. F. Roberts, D. W. Ruggles, Homer Ruggles, Jason Smith, John E. Smith, Lyman Thompson, Joseph Thompson, Columbus Wells,

J. F. Westcott, Lauren Wetmore, John Wetherell. A large portion of the above named persons were employees of Billings & McNiel. In the northern portion of Elk township the actual settlers were John Maynard, George Maynard, Loren Wetmore, John E. Smith, Jehial Beach, Homer Ruggles, D. W. Ruggles, Benjamin Freyer, James F. Westcott, Jason Smith, G. W. Howd. Of these John Maynard was the pioneer; he made a permanent settlement in the northwestern portion of the township, purchased sixteen hundred acres of wild land, cleared one hundred and fifty acres, set out four orchards containing about one thousand trees, erected dwellings, barns, etc. He died December 9th, 1878, aged 67 years.

In the year 1879, a company styling itself the "Cedar Run Tanning Co.," erected a large tannery at Billing's Camp, having the year previous, (1878,) secured the hemlock bark from Silas X. Billings, growing upon about 20,000 acres, surrounding the tannery. To accommodate their workman they erected fifty or more dwellings, a school house; opened a store and changed the name of the place from "Billings Camp" to Leetonia in honor of Mr. William Lee, one of the principal owners of the tannery. Mr. William Lee, Jr., erected a fine residence in the year 1880

—There are now four school houses in the township.

—James F. Palen was the first Postmaster at Leetonia.

—Dr. E. P. Luce was the first resident physician of Leetonia.

—Miss Mary Harrington was the first school teacher at Leetonia.

—The first post office in the township was called "Malone" and Loren Wetmore postmaster.

—A convenient school house was erected in 1879, which is used for school and church purposes.

—In 1879 Lee & Co. experienced much difficulty in getting their heavy machinery to Leetonia.

—Augustus B. Snyder was the first superintendent with James Gilbert assistant, at Leetonia.

—A portion of Elk township, a few years since was annexed to Gaines township on the north.

—James Thompson was the first superintendent at the tannery; and James F. Palen the first store agent.

—The first school in the township was taught by Miss Marion Watrous. Among the early teachers were Martha Dennison, Albina Vermilye, Mary Kelley, Selana Hart, Carrie Wilcox, Phebe Wetmore.

—The first public road in the township was constructed under contract by John Maynard and others in 1856, and led from Gaines in Tioga County to Germania in Potter County, a distance of twelve miles.

—Silas Billings the elder, was engaged for forty days with a large complement of men in cutting a road from Gaines on Pine Creek to where he located his mill, in 1847. His road was over one of the highest mountains in Tioga County.

Farmington Township.

Farmington Township was formed from the township of Elkland, in the year 1830. It contains an area of about 24,000 acres lying south of the Cowanesque river opposite the township of Nelson and the borough of Elkland.

Its mean elevation is about 1,500 feet above sea level. Its inhabitants are now almost exclusively devoted to the pursuit of farming. It was originally covered with a heavy forest, but the untiring industry of two generations and their accumulations, the third or present generation have succeeded in making it productive. Elegant farm houses, good barns, smooth fields, good fences, improved agricultural implements greet the traveler at every point.

Its first settler was David Bryant in the year 1820, and he was soon followed by a race of hardy, industriuus and frugal citizens. The Chamberlains, the Pierces, Halls, Cadys, VanDusens, Casbeers, Redfields, Gees, Herricks, Hoyts, Babcocks, Butts, Buckbees, Crippins, Bottoms, Blanchards, Baxters, McCallums, Prestons, Fosters, and others have made Farmington one of the best townships in the county.

Gaines Township.

The township of Gaines was formed in the year 1838, taken from the western portion of the township of Shippen. It is the third township south of the New York State line, and second on the north from the Lycoming County line, and is bounded on the north by the township of Clymer, on the east by the township of Shippen, and south by the township of Elk. The streams in the township are Pine Creek, Painter's Run, Rexford Run, Long Run, Lick Run, Elk Run, Phenix Run and Mill Run. All these Runs are tributaries to Pine Creek, a stream navigable for the floating of logs. lumber and shingles during the freshets. The lands along the valleys of Pine Creek are very productive, as well as those in the valley of Elk Run and Long Run. The mountains north and south of Pine Creek reach an elevation at some points of over 2,000 feet above the level of the sea. Pine Creek passes nearly through the center of the township from west to east. In the mountains above referred to are deposits of coal and iron. The coal in the mountains north of Pine Creek has been developed and mining of the same carried on quite extensively by the Gaines Coal and Coke Company, to which we shall hereafter refer. Josiah Furman was the first settler within the present boundaries of Gaines, having located upon two hundred and sixty-five acres of land two and one-half miles east of the present village of Gaines in the year 1804. Between the years 1804 and 1818, he purchased at Northumberland two hundred and twenty apple trees, put them in dug-outs or canoes and poled them up the West Branch of the Susquehanna to the mouth of Pine Creek, thence up Pine Creek to Gaines, a distance from Northumberland of over one hundred miles, and set out two orchards. Many of the trees are yet standing and bearing fruit. Josiah Furman was a native of Shamokin, Northumberland County, Pa.

—Great freshet on Pine Creek in 1832.

—Stephen Babcock was the first merchant.

—John Persing settled in Gaines in the year 1824.

—Benjamin Barse erected a hotel in 1848.

—John L. Phenix built a saw mill in 1836.

—Gaines was a great resort for fishing and hunting.

—John L. Phenix built a saw mill on Elk Run in 1845.

—John Benn erected a saw mill in 1835 for Silas Billings.

—First school house in the township, erected in the year 1813.

—August, 1882, commenced the construction of the A. & N. P. R. R.

—In 1828 Silas Billings purchased land in Gaines (then Shippen) township.

—Horace C. Vermilyea came to Gaines in 1855, and rented the Barse hotel.

—Tyadaghton Lodge No. 981, I. O. O. F., instituted November 18, 1881.

—The first saw mill on Long Run was built by Wheaton Hewett in 1845.

—August 26, 1882, "Barrens" purchased by the Gaines Coal and Coke Co.

—Silas X. Billings came to Gaines in 1855. D. A. Paddock came to Gaines in 1855.

—H. C. Vermilyea died, June, 1878, aged 63 years. He was post master twenty-two successive years.

—James Carsaw was the first assessor in Gaines township and John L. Phenix the first collector.

—In the year 1812 the Indians left Pine Creek, as it was supposed, to join the British in the Canadian frontier.

—February, 1882, John L. Sexton, Jr., of Blossburg, makes a preliminary exploration for coal upon the "Barrens."

—In 1860 Silas X. Billings erected the "Izaak Walton House" and Horace C. Vermilyea purchased it and kept it for eight years.

—David Rexford, Esq. son-in-law of Josiah Furman, owns and occupies the pioneer farm upon which Josiah Furman settled in 1804.

—First train of cars over the Addison and Northern Pennsylvania Railroad, arrived at Gaines, January 1st, 1883. Henry Maxson, engineer, Frank Wedge, fireman.

—Marshfield, named in honor of D. K. Marsh, is situated at the junction of Maynard and Wetmore branches of Elk Run. It contains two churches, a store and post office, a saw mill and several dwellings.

—March, 1882, John L. Sexton, Jr., employed by Col. James E. Jones, Col. Henry Baldwin, H. C. McKay and John Hinman, to make further investigation in relation to coal upon the "Barrens." Makes a favorable report, and the 10th of June, 1882, again makes further investigations, assisted by a number of workmen.

—Gurnee is a coal mining village in the township of Gaines, situated upon the "Barrens" about four and one-half miles northeast of the village of Gaines. There are about 350 inhabitants. The mines are operated by the Gaines Coal and Coke Co. The coal is shipped by the Addison and N. P. Railroad. Its elevation is about 2,300 feet above the ocean.

—Gaines is a village situated on Pine Creek, near the mouth of Elk Run, contains one church, (erected by Silas X. Billings,) a school house, several stores, one hotel, drug store, depot of Addison and Northern Pennsylvania Railroad, several industrial establishments, and contains about five hundred inhabitants. It is named in honor of Gen. Gaines, the hero of the Creek Indian removal.

—The taxable inhabitants of Gaines township when it was organized were Harry Allen, Roland Blackmar, Horace Broughton, Oliver Babcock, Riley Burdick, Stephen Babcock, Stephen B. Barnes, Simeon Babcock, Conrad Benaur, William Babcock, Silas Billings, Isaac Beech, John Blue, Jr., John B. Benn, William J. Benn, David Crandall, W. Champney, James Carsaw, Sylvester Davie, Henry Erway, Jacob Erway, Benjamin Furman, D. H. Furman, Aaron K. Furman, William Furman, David Furman, Levi Furman, William B. Furman, Aaron Furman, Josiah Furman. William Griffin, George Harvey, Zackariah Herringer, Dudley DeWitt, George Huyler, Wheaton Hewett, Joshua T. Jackson, William Larrison, William I. McNiel, Asa McIntyre, Calvin Newton, Nathaniel Owen, John L. Phenix, N. Prouty, Moses Pierce, John Robbins, Scoville & Babcock, William Steele, Henry Steele, John Schoonover, William W. Tate, S. N. Shelley, Aaron Stiles, Henry Scleick.

Hamilton Township.

The township of Hamilton was formed in the year 1871, from the townships of Ward and Bloss. The inhabitants of the township, with the exception of two or three families are located in the village of Morris Run. This village is located in a direct line about two miles east of Blossburg and situated upon Morris Run, a tributary of the Tioga River. The inhabitants are chiefly engaged in the mining of semi-bituminous coal upon the Bloss veins, and in lumbering. They are employed by the Morris Run Coal Mining Company. Morris Run contains one store, tinshop, drug store, hotel, meat market and grocery combined, a graded school, Odd Fellows Hall, a public hall, several churches and about 2,500 inhabitants. Its mean elevation is about 1,500 feet above tide.

—C. T. A., organized November 22, 1874.

—Morris Run contains about 360 dwellings.

—Welsh Congregational Church organized 1864.

—In 1852 first dwelling erected of logs at Morris Run.

—John James, Jr., first postmaster at Morris Run, 1865.

—Stephen Bowen of Morris Run, elected sheriff in 1873.

—Delos H. Walker of Morris Run, elected sheriff in 1876.

—Catholic Church erected in Morris Run in the year 1883.

—Iron coal diggers first used in Morris Run, December, 1879.

—P. F. O'Donnell has been paymaster at Morris Run since 1866.

—Welsh Baptist Church organized in 1864. Church erected in 1873.

—Morris Run I. O. O. F., No. 678, instituted January 22, 1870.

—First hotel erected at Morris Run, 1864, F. Caldwell, proprietor.

—Louisa Lodge, No. 105, Daughters of Rebeckah, organized May 14, 1875.

—Tioga Lodge, No. 304, Knights of Pythias, organized June 22, 1871.

—Explorations made for coal at Morris Run in 1852, with good results.

—Grand excursion of Knights of Pythias to Watkins, N. Y., Aug. 1879.

—Primitive Methodist Church organized 1869. Church edifice cost about $2,200.

—In 1862, the Salt Company of Syracuse leased the mines and enlarged the works.

—J. Norman Anderson has been employed in the paymaster's office for the past ten years.

—Thomas V. Keefe has been employed in the office of the company for the past ten years.

—In 1853 John Young opened an office and a supply store in a hewed log building at Morris Run.

—The first weigh-masters at Morris Run were James Brown, Peter Cameron, Jr., and H. J. Landrus.

—The Tioga Improvement Company mined and marketed, from 1853 to 1862 about 323,174 tons of coal.

—W. L. Richards, appointed State Inspector of bituminous mines by Gov. John F. Hartranft, May, 1877.

—*Caradog Ap Bran*, No. 11, *Adran F.*, Ivorites, a Welsh social and benevolent association, organized May 14th, 1872.

—U. S. Z., a social organization, established November, 1869. Mart G. Lewis, Pres.; J. L. Lewis, Sec.; W. W. Halsey, Treas.

—In 1864, the Morris Run Coal Company assumed control by lease of the mines. W. S. Nearing, chief engineer and superintendent.

—The inhabitants of Morris Run are native born Americans, English, Irish, Scotch, Welsh, Swede, Polanders, Germans and French.

—1853 railroad surveyed by Col. Phaon Jarrett, H. Brewer and J. Livingston, from Blossburg to Morris Run. Railroad completed that year.

—Alfred Jones, of Philadelphia, was the first sole agent of coal and paymaster for the Tioga Improvement Co. His office was in Corning, N. Y.

—In 1863, Major T. B. Anderson was employed as store agent, which position he has continued to hold under the various changes which have since taken place.

—In 1877, Morris Run Coal Company ceased to exist and the Morris Run Coal and Mining Company organized in its stead. The Fall Brook Coal Company becoming a large stockholder.

—The appliances for successful mining at Morris Run are not excelled in the United States. This was accomplished under the personal direction of W. S. Nearing, chief engineer and manager.

—Morris Run mines were then owned (1853) by the Tioga Improvement Company, in which Joseph W. Ryers, Coffin Calket and the heirs of the late Judge Samuel W. Morris, were chief stock-holders.

—At the completion of the railroad in 1853 there were at the mines sixteen log houses, occupied by Joseph Mitchell, Henry Mitchell, James R. Cameron, Joseph Hughes, Frank Smith, Samuel Vickers, John Nailon, William Kelley, Andrew Baird, William R. Gilmour, William Bland, Dennis Mooney, John Kelley, James Brown, with John Young superintendent.

Jackson Township.

The township of Jackson was organized in the year 1815, and stands sixth in the order of organized townships in Tioga County. Much of its original territory has been taken from it, to form other townships, yet it now contains an area of nearly 29,000 acres. It is situated upon highland in the extreme north-eastern portion of Tioga County, and is bounded on the north by the State line between New York and Pennsylvania, on the east by Bradford County, Pa., on the south by Rutland township, on the west by Tioga and Lawrence townships. Jackson Summit, Millerton, Daggett's Mills and Job's Corners are villages in the township, the largest of which is Millerton. The Tioga and Elmira State Line Railroad passes through the township in a north-easterly and south-westerly course.

Millerton is a new and sprightly village, situated on the line of the Tioga and Elmira State Line Railroad, and contains about four hundred inhabitants. The elections for the township of Jackson are held here. The *Millerton Advocate*, a weekly newspaper, edited and published by Harry T. Graves, is published at Millerton.

Daggett's Mills is the oldest village in the township. It contains a population of about one hundred and seventy-five.

Jackson Summit is a new village which has sprung up since the completion of the Tioga and Elmira State Line Railroad. It contains about one hundred inhabitants.

—M. E. Church erected at Millerton, 1853.

—Baptist Church erected at Alder Run in 1879.

—M. E. Church erected at Jackson Center, 1872.

—Joshua Spencer erected the first hotel in the township.

—Dr. Nathaniel Smith settled in Jackson, in the year 1844.

—Methodist Episcopal Church erected at Daggett's Mills, 1855.

—The first school in the township was erected at Daggett's Mills.

—Millerton Lodge, No. 935, I. O. O. F., instituted July 19th, 1876.

—*Millerton Advocate* established April 26th, 1877, by A. C. Lumbard.

—Seth Daggett erected the first saw mill in Jackson township, at Daggett's Mills.

—Garret Miller settled within the present limits of Jackson township in the year 1800.

—Seeley Creek Lodge, I. O. O. F., No. 641, at Daggett's Mills, instituted October 9th, 1868.

—The sons of Garret Miller were Garret, Joshua, Samuel, James, Nathan, George. They became prominent citizens.

—Reuben Daggett, Jr., and Seth Daggett, erected a grist mill in the year 1836. The millwright work was done by Allen S. Gibson and Lyman Gibson, from Chenango County, N. Y., and subsequently citizens of Elmira,

—In the year 1860, Samuel E. Kirkendall settled in Millerton, and for thirteen successive years taught school. In 1873 he commenced the practice of the law, having been admitted to the Tioga County bar in the year 1859.

—Reuben Daggett settled in the township in the year 1807. He was father of Major Seth Daggett who was elected Sherriff of Tioga County in the year 1830, who died in the borough of Tioga January 2, 1874, aged 84 years.

Lawrenceville Township and Borough.

The township of Lawrence was organized from Tioga and Elkland townships in December, 1816. The borough of Lawrenceville was organized May, 1831, taken from the township of Lawrence. The history of the township and borough are so intimately connected that they will be treated under one head.

It was upon the banks of the Tioga River that the first white man made a settlement within the limits of Tioga County. Samuel Baker, afterwards Judge Baker of Steuben County, N. Y., settled upon the west bank of the Tioga River, in the year 1787 and resided there until the year 1794, when General Williamson induced him to purchase lands of the Pultney estate, which he did and located in Pleasant Valley, Steuben County, N. Y., until his death in the year 1840, at the advanced age of 80 years.

Lawrence township is bounded on the north by the state line between New York and Pennsylvania, on the east by Jackson township, on the south by Tioga township and Farmington and on the west by Farmington and Nelson. The northern boundary of the borough of Lawrenceville is the state line, the other boundaries are the township of Lawrence. This borough is situated ninety miles west of the Delaware river, on a parallel of 42 degrees. The Tioga and Cowanesque rivers unite a few rods north of its northern boundary in the township of Lindley, N. Y.

—Daniel Walker came to Lawrenceville in 1810.

—St. John's Episcopal Church organized in 1860.

—Curtis Parkhurst located at Lawrenceville in 1816.

—J. F. Rusling, Esq., settled in Lawrenceville in 1860.

—Iron foundry established in Lawrenceville in the year 1812.

—Lawrenceville Lodge, No. 913, I. O. O. F., instituted July 14, 1875.

—Dr. Lewis Darling, Sr., graduated at Dartmouth College in the year 1829.

—The Lawrenceville Academy was formed in 1849, by Rev. Sidney Mills.

—From 1845 to 1860, Lawrenceville was the centre of a great lumber trade.

—Lawrenceville Equitable Aid Union, No. 198, established Dec. 18, 1880.

—Lawrenceville Encampment of Patriarchs, No. 227, instituted April 22, 1878.

—Dr. L. Granger, settled in Lawrenceville in 1845 and practiced medicine about forty years.

—*Lawrenceville Herald*, a weekly newspaper, established by A. Redfield & Son, in the year 1880.

—In the year 1831, the C. L. Ford dwelling was erected. It was the second brick building in the county.

—In 1816 Hon. James Ford erected a dwelling, which for many years was known as the "Ford Mansion."

—In 1806 Eleazer Baldwin settled at Lawrenceville. Dr. Simeon Power also made a settlement the same year.

—Hon. James Ford served two terms in the state Legislature and two terms in Congress of the United States.

—Lathrop and Dunning are stations in Lawrence township, on the Corning, Cowanesque and Antrim Railroad.

—Somer's Lane and Tioga Junction are stations in Lawrence township on the Tioga and Elmira State Line Railroad.

—Lawrenceville Fire Department organized March 5th, 1859. Kasson Parkhurst foreman of the engine company and Austin Lathrop, Jr., of the hose company.

—The *Valley Enterprise*, a weekly newspaper, founded by Henry C. Mills in 1871; in 1872 office removed to Mansfield.

—Dr. Lewis Darling, Sr., located at Lawrenceville, in the year 1831, and practiced medicine over fifty years in that place.

—The Corning Cowanesque and Antrim Railroad, and the Tioga and Elmira State Line Railroad each have a depot at Lawrenceville.

—Hon. John Ryon, of Lawrenceville, elected member of the state legislature in 1822, representing Tioga and Bradford counties.

—Samuel Baker was the first settler within the borough limits of Lawrenceville and the first in the county. William Holden settled soon thereafter.

—Hiram Beebe, a prominent business man, settled at Lawrenceville in 1815. He was the first treasurer of the Tioga Navigation Company, afterwards the Corning and Blossburg Railroad Company.

—The first Methodist Church was erected in 1836. The structure was of brick. The church organization becoming involved, the church edifice was purchased by Peter Reep, Esq., and torn down. New church built in 1849.

—In 1816 the settlers at Lawrenceville consisted of Hon. James Ford, Judge Ira Kilburn, Jacob Geer, Curtis Parkhurst, Micazah Seeley, Daniel Walker, Hiram Beebe, Dr. Simeon Power, John Ryon, Eleazer Baldwin, and William Holden.

—Lawrence and Lawrenceville were named in honor of Captain James Lawrence of the navy, who was killed during the war of 1812, while he was commanding the United States ship Chesepeake in its encounter with the British ship Shannon. Hon. James Ford gave it the name.

—The First Presbyterian Church, organized in Lawrenceville, by Rev. Daniel Higgins, of Bath, N. Y., and Rev. Henry Ford, of Elmira, in the year 1824. Rev. E. D. Wells became the stated pastor in the year 1831. The first ruling elders were Johnson Butts, John Peters, Loren Butts, Erastus Butts. The first trustees were Hon. James Ford, Hon. Curtis Parkhurst and Micazah Seeley.

—In 1834 the businesss men of Lawrenceville were Hon. James Ford, merchant and lumberman; Judge Ira Kilburn, lumberman; Job Greer, contractor and builder; Curtis Parkhurst, physician, lumberman and real estate dealer; Micazah Seeley, lumberman and merchant; Daniel Walker, farmer; Hiram Beebe, merchant and lumberman; Lewis Darling, physician; John Barnes, contractor and hotel keeper; Pardon Damon, lawyer; Joel Adams, tanner, currier and shoemaker; Samuel Chapman and Samuel Bogert, blacksmiths; Job Herrick, groceryman; Simeon Power, physician; Clark Slawson, inn keeper; E. D. Wells, Presbyterian minister; Henry Potter, hotel keeper and farmer, Johnson and Loren Butts, carpenters and joiners; Erastus Butts, stone mason: Alanson Beebe, glove maker; Asa Lincoln, merchant; Norman Purple, lawyer; Ralph Kimball, doctor; ——— Higgins, lawyer; Pleny Powers, doctor; Lemuel Maynard, minister, father of Hon. John W. Maynard, Rev. Mr. Platt, a Baptist minister; Calvin Cowley, lumberman; Clarendon Rathbone, lawyer and real estate dealer; William Seeley, farmer; Daniel Seeley, gentleman; Moses Baldwin and Buel Baldwin, farmers.

Liberty Township.

Liberty township is one of the southern tier townships of Tioga County, bounded on the south by Jackson township in Lycoming County, on the west by Morris township, on the north by Bloss and east by Union townships. It was formed from Covington and Delmar in the year 1823. Liberty and Nauvoo are its principal villages, with Barfelden, Veeltown and East Point, hamlets.

Liberty is a thriving village, situated upon Block House Creek, adjoining the Lycoming County line. Nauvoo is situated on Zimmerman Creek in the southwestern portion of the township.

Its mean elevation above tide is about 1,600 feet.

The inhabitants are chiefly engaged in farming. It stands fifth in point of valuation of the several townships of the county. The Williamson road which was made in 1792, passes north and south through the township.

—Joseph Reed settled in Liberty in 1821.

—Felix Costerison was the first merchant.

—John F. Hart settled in Liberty in 1824.

—Frederic Harrer settled in Liberty in 1830.

—Great fire in Liberty village December 5th, 1879.

—Horace Fellows settled in Liberty in the year 1840.

—Jonathan Sebring died in February, 1879, aged 96 years.

—Isaac Foulkrod taught the first school in Liberty in 1821.

—C. A. Miller & Co., erected their brick block in the year 1880.

—William Dieffenbacher erected the first woolen mill in Liberty.

—John Sebring was a soldier of the war of 1812. He came to Liberty in 1820.

—John Neal came to Liberty in 1822; he was a soldier of the war of 1812.

—There are now twelve school buildings in Liberty township where thirteen teachers are employed.

—Mrs. Lydia Jane Pierson, a poetess, settled in the western portion of Liberty township in the year 1821.

—A post route was established between Painted Post, N. Y., and Williamsport, Pa., via Liberty, in the year 1816.

—Leonard Miller came to Liberty in the year 1825; was a soldier under Napoleon, and received a medal for his bravery.

—Isaac Foulkrod settled in Liberty in the year 1821. He was a man of letters. His father, Jacob Foulkrod, was a revolutionary soldier.

—Isaac Werline settled in Liberty in 1829. He erected the first tannery in the township, was killed by the falling of a tree in the year 1846, aged 53 years.

—John Sheffer, Jr., of Liberty, in the years 1816-17-18, when only thirteen years of age, carried the U. S. Mail from Williamsport to Painted Post, a distance of eighty miles.

—April 20, 1861, the news of the firing upon Fort Sumpter was received; it was on Sunday morning. Major, afterwards General R. Cox, started that day for Wellsboro to organize companies. A band of martial music paraded the streets of Liberty village; the ministers dismissed their congregations.

—Block House Lodge, No. 398, I. O. O. F. was instituted February 25th, 1850. December 5th, 1879, a fire destroyed the lodge, books and regalia; new ones were immediately purchased.

—A colony of settlers came into Liberty and vicinity, about the year 1813, among whom were George Miller, Jonathan Sebring, —— Keagle, Peter Secrist, Jacob Beck, Frederic Bower, Peter Moyer.

—"Block House" erected in 1792, in the present village of Liberty, by Robert and Benjamin Patterson, who were conducting General Williamson's party of five hundred German and English emigrants or settlers to Bath, N. Y.

—A man by the name of Anthony kept a hotel in the "Block House" about the year 1800, and was succeeded by his sons. It was a disreputable place. In 1813 Jonathan Sebring came into possession and was a very respectable and honored citizens.

—The early settlers of Liberty were Joseph Opdegraff, Isaiah Thompson, Leonard Harrer, Peter Sheik, Samuel Keagle, Frederic Harrer, John Harrer; Fred Schambacher, Isaac Foulkrod, James Merrell, Jonathan Sebring, Daniel Hartsock, Michael Linck, John Sheffer, Felix Costrison, Charles A. Hénsler, Brown Miller, Jacob Benner, John Sebring, John Keller, Robert C. Sebring, George Bastian, George Wheeland, Leonard Miller, John Lovegood, Daniel Spangler, Casper Moyer, Harvey Root, John Marquot, Solomon Roup, Christian Carson, Jacob Shraner, Isaac Werline, John Neal, James McEvoy, John C. Beiser, George Hebe, John F. Hart, Thomas Black, Samuel Hartman, Jeremiah Black, —— Zimmerman, Caleb Comstock, John Ridge, Horace Fellows, Charles J. Minnich, Jacob Mannaval, John Cochran, John Lenhart, John Herman, Abram Kohler, William Cox, Robert C. Cox, George R. Sheffer.

Morris Township.

Morris township, named in honor of Hon. Samuel W. Morris, a distinguished citizen of Wellsboro, was formed in September 1824, taken from the township of Delmar. It is one of the southern tier townships of Tioga county bordering upon Lycoming county line. Its principal waters are Pine Creek, Babbs Creek, Sand Run, Zimmermans Creek and Stony Fork; the largest being Pine Creek and Babbs Creek, these latter named creeks are skirted on either side by mountains from eight hundred to one thousand feet above their bed. The lowest point in the township is about 825 feet above tide, and its highest point 2000 feet. In the eastern portion of the township along Babbs Creek, and on the highlands east of the valley are some good farming lands. Along Pine and Babbs Creeks were the Indian paths of the six nations. At the confluence of these creeks was the site of an Indian village, some of the trees surrounding the village bearing marks which were made by an ax or metal tomahawk in the year 1732.

—Samson Babb died in October, 1815.

—Job Doane was an early settler and erected a saw mill.

—Rev. George Higgins, a Baptist minister, held services in 1835.

—Samson Babb built the first saw mill in the township in the year 1806.

—The Arnot and Pine Creek railroad completed from Arnot to Hoytville in the year 1882.

—The Jersey Shore and Pine Creek railroad has a station at Blackwell's.

—Robert Campbell, a revolutionary soldier, settled in Morris at an early day.

—Mr. John Link, of eastern Mórris, is one of the wealthiest men in the county.

—Wm. Wells was a member of the English Land Company. He settled at Wellsboro in 1802.

—Samson Babb was commissioned a Justice of the Peace by Gov. Simon Snyder in the year 1813.

—Enoch Blackwell, grandson of Enoch Blackwell, the pioneer, has resided 60 years in Morris township.

—The Pine Creek Land Company owned large tracts in Morris and the adjoining territory of Lycoming as early as 1799.

—In the year 1881, Hoyt Brothers, of New York, erected a tannery upon Babbs Creek for the tanning of sole leather. It is the largest tannery in the world.

—The first white settler in Morris township was Samson Babb, a native of Wilmington, Delaware, who settled and gave the name to Babbs Creek in the year 1800.

—Hoytville was founded in the year 1881; it contains about 500 inhabitants and is one of the most active business centers in the southern portion of the county. Lumbering and tanning are carried on very extensively.

—Enoch Blackwell, senior, a member of the English Land Company, who owned twelve thousand acres in Morris township, Tioga co., and Lycoming county settled in Morris township in the year 1810. He had previously settled in Pine township in the year 1805. He was a native of England.

Nelson Township.

Nelson township was formed from the township of Elkland, in the year 1857. It is located upon the north and south sides of the Cowanesque River and bounded on the north by the Pennsylvania and New York state line, east by Lawrence township, south by Farmington and west by Elkland. The Corning, Cowanesque and Antrim Railroad runs through the centre of the township, having a station at Nelson village. The Addison and Northern Pennsylvania Railroad touches its northwestern boundary. The principal village in the township is Nelson, for many years known as Beecher's Island. Its inhabitants are chiefly engaged in agriculture, occupying some of the finest farms in Tioga County. Tobacco is extensively raised in the township.

The earliest settlers within its present limits were John and Hopestill Beecher, who made a settlement at Beecher's Island, (now Nelson) in the year 1802. Hopestill Beecher became one of the prominent men of the county, was one of the first county commissioners in the year 1811. His wife Abigail, died in Charleston, October 14, 1879, in her one hundredth year.

The township was originally covered with an immense growth of timber and for many years the business of lumbering was carried on extensively. The pine lumber was generally rafted into the Cowanesque River and floated

After the year 1865 the white pine lumber being generally exhausted, the inhabitants devoted themselves to farming and the result is the present highly cultivated and richly productive farms.

—Daniel Strait settled in the township in the year 1806.
—Dr. Albert M. Loop settled in Nelson in the year 1840.
—Artemus Losey settled in the township in the year 1830.
—In the year 1849, Judge George H. Baxter settled in Nelson.
—Hiram Beebe, of Lawrenceville, erected a store in Nelson in 1830.
—W. H. Baxter, of Nelson, elected County Commissioner, Nov. 1884.
—Harry Baxter, of Nelson, elected Sheriff of Tioga county, Nov. 1882.
—Enoch Blackwell came to Nelson in the year 1814, still remains in the township.
—M. F. Cass, of Nelson, elected County Superintendent of Schools in May, 1882.

down to the southern portion of Pennsylvania and Maryland, where a market was found for it.

Osceola Township.

Osceola township, named in honor of the great Seminole Chieftain by that name. was organized December 1851, taken from the western portion of the township of Elkland.

It is located in the beautiful and fertile valley of the Cowanesque, the Cowanesque river passing nearly through its center from west to east. Along the valley the soil is alluvial, and upon the hill and mountain sides which skirt the valley the soil is clay, shale and loam. Its inhabitants are chiefly engaged in agriculture, producing most excellent crops of wheat, corn, oats, barley, patatoes, broom corn, sorgum, tobacco and orchard fruits

Two railroads pass through the valley with stations at Osceola the principal village of the township. The railroads are the Corning, Cowanesque and Antrim, and the Addison and Northern Pennsylvania, both constructed through the valley and township in the summer of 1882.

—Osceola brass band organized in 1855.
—In 1865 a well was sunk for oil—dry hole.
—Henry Mott erected a blacksmith shop in 1810.
—The Cowanesque Railroad incorporated in 1869.
—In 1882 Charles L. Hoyt erected a sorghum mill.
—Nathen Seelye opened the first hotel in the year 1812.
—Tannery erected in 1852 by Messrs Tubbs and Crandall.
—Knights of Honor No. 843 established January 8, 1877.
—Osceola Plank Road Company incorporated March 25 1852.
—Equitable Aid Union No. 219 established January 18, 1881.
—Alfred J Sofield Post G. A. R., established January 18, 1876.
—Israel Bulkley built a carding and fulling mill in the year 1814.
—In 1870 Morgan Seeley opened a bank in the village of Osceola.
—Free and Accepted Masonic Lodge No. 421, organized July 22, 1868.
—In 1836 Benson Tubbs opened the first store in the village of Osceola.
—Sash and blind factory erected in 1854 by Enoch Steen and Eleazer Clark.
—Paul Gleason was the first shoemaker in the township; he settled in 1809.

—In 1804 Cooper Cady made a settlement.
—M. E. camp meeting held September 1828.
—Mail route established through Osceola in 1822.
—Presbyterian church organized December 26, 1844.
—Israel Bulkley erected a grist mill in the year 1814.
—Nathan Seelye settled in the township in the year 1812.
—George H. Gee, of Osceola, was a soldier in the Mexican war.
—Ebenezer Taylor built a saw mill upon Holden brook in 1810.
—Methodist Episcopal church was the pioneer church in Osceola.
—First physician in Osceola was Adolphus Allen in the year 1813.
—First graveyard in the township was on the banks of Holden Brook.
—The Addison and Northern Pennsylvania railroad incorporated July 1882
—Israel Bulkley established an apple nursery in the year 1800 in the township.

—In 1813 Andrew Bozzard, the first carpenter and jointer, settled in the township.

—Josiah Holcomb erected a shop for the manufacture of hollow wooden ware in 1827.

—Knights and Ladies of Honor, Vidette Lodge No. 115, established December 20, 1878.

—Nathaniel P. Moody and Reuben, two revolutionary soldiers are buried in the old graveyard.

—Robert Tubbs settled in the year 1811. His father Samuel Tubbs, Sr., was a revolutionary soldier.

—In 1807 Israel Bulkley sent Calvin Chamberlain to Onondaga with a herd of mules to pack home salt.

—The first permenent settler was Israel Bulkley in the year 1800. He brought a female negro slave.

—William Holden was the first settler in the township. Holden brook was named after him ; he settled in 1795.

—The first school house was erected in 1822. Osceola high school erected in 1860. Osceola music school opened in 1872.

—Asahel Nobles chopped an acre of pine timber for a barrel of salt in the year 1807. Nobles resided in Deerfield township.

—In the year 1876 new cemetery established, Abner Gleason was the first interred within the old graveyard in the year 1812.

—In 1857 Doctor William T. Humphreys located at Osceola. He afterwards became surgeon in the "Buck Tail Regiment."

—Dr. William T. Humphrey, of Osceola, was a representative in the Pennsylvania State Legislature 1865, 1866, 1874, 1875, 1876.

—In 1806 Pamelia Taylor and her three sons, Ebenezer, Phillip and Mitchell made a settlement. They were from near Wilkes-Barre, Pa.

—Robert Tubbs erected the first brick dwelling in Osceola township in the year 1829, it was the first brick edifice in Tioga county, it is occupied at present.

—Charles Tubbs, of Osceola, was Transcribing Clerk in the House of Representatives in the year 1869, and representative in the legislature 1881—served two years and was re-elected.

—The first teacher in Osceola was Miss Mary Ann Landon in the year 1812. The text books were the Testament and Webster's spelling book.

—Military organization in Cowanesque valley in the year 1812. A number of citizens went to the rescue of Buffalo in 1814. Samuel Tubbs, David Taylor, Reuben Cook and Andrew Bosard went from Osceola.

Richmond Township and Mansfield Borough.

Richmond township was organized from the northern portion of Covington township in February, 1824. It is bounded on the north by Tioga and Rutland townships, on the east by Rutland and Sullivan townships, on the south by the township of Covington, and on the west by the townships of Charlestown and Middlebury.

It is situated principally in the Tioga valley, about fifteen miles south of the state line at Lawrenceville, and contains a variety of soil, embracing the alluvial and sandy soils of the valley and the clay and red shale of the upland The Tioga River passes through it centrally from south to north, the principal streams of the township are the Tioga River, Corey Creek, Canoe Camp Creek and Lamb's Creek, the three latter tributaries of the Tioga river. The citizens of Richmond are chiefly engaged in agriculture. Iron ore is found in paying quanities, and has been quite extensively manufactured into "pig metal."

The Tioga and Elmira State Line Railroad passes through the township, following the valley of the Tioga, and has two stations in the township, exclusive of the one at Mansfield borough. The stations in the township are at the villages Canoe Camp and Lambs Creek.

Mansfield was incorpated as a borough, taken from the township of Richmond in the year 1857. It is one of the most flourishing boroughs in Tioga county, being the seat of the State Normal School, the Soldiers State Orphan School, the Mansfield Business College, and is deemed the educational center of the county.

—Great flood in Tioga river, May 1833.

—Doct Cannon settled in Mansfield in 1813.

—Elijah Clark settled in Richmond in 1806.

—Peter Keltz erected a frame house in 1810.

—E. W. Hazzard, first lawyer at Mansfield 1834.

—In 1810 Amos Spencer erected a grist mill at Canoe Camp.

—Elijah P. Clark was born at Lambs Creek in the year 1807.

—Candler Mann erected the first tannery in Mansfield in 1824.

—Graded school house erected in the year 1881, at cost of $13.000.

—Miss Susannah Allen taught school in Mansfield, in the year 1821.

—Mart King established a funiture manufactory in Mansfield in 1869.

—Chandler Mann organized a military company in 1836 in Mansfield.

—In 1841 Benjamin Gitchell erected the first brick dwelling in Mansfield.

—Mansfield business college organized by Professor Fred M. Allen in 1880.

—In 1804 Asa Mann founded Mansfield. He erected the first hotel and store.

—In 1872 Valley Enterprise, a newspaper office removed from Lawrenceville to Mansfield by H. C. Mills. It is now published under the name of "Mansfield Advertiser."

–In 1824 Almon Allen and Solon Richards erected a woolen mill in Mansfield.

—Jerusha Lamb organized the first Sunday School in Richmond township in the year 1826.

—Mansfield soldiers orphan school organized by Prof. F. A. Allen, October 1, 1867.

—Jacob Allen, a lieutenant in the continental army, died at Mansfield December 11 1836, aged 73 years.

—In the year 1803 Elihu Marvin built the first saw mill, and in 1805 the first grist mill in Richmond township.

—Andrew Sherwood, the geologist, was born in Richmond township, July 16, 1848. He resides now in Mansfield.

—Gad Lamb was the first permanent settler in Richmond township. He settled at Lambs Creek in the year 1797.

—Mansfield classical seminary organized February 15, 1855, completed and opened for school purposes in January 1857.

—In 1822 Amos Spencer was post master at Canoe Camp. It was the first post office within the limits of Richmond township.

—Arks loaded with Blossburg Coal at Canoe Camp, in the year 1836, by Christain Sykes and others, and floated down the river.

—In 1814 Miss Sally Elliott opened school at Canoe Camp. Martin Stratton, Esq., now of Blossburg Pa., was one of the pupils.

—Dr. J. P. Morris, James Lowrery, William Bache, Stephen F. Willson, John F. Donaldson contracted with Charles F. Swan for the erection of an iron furnace in 1854.

—Seminary re-organized and became a state normal school for the fifth district, being the third school of the kind organized in the state, December 11, 1862, with Rev. W. D. Taylor, principal.

—The Balance, a newspaper published in Mansfield in 1856, by I. M. Ruckman. The type and fixtures were afterwards removed to Kansas, and during ruffian agitation were thrown into the Missouri river.

—First officers of Mansfield borough in 1857, were Burgess, Henry Allen, Councilmen, P. Gaylord, L. H. Elliott, J. M. Cassels, H. Davis, M. Kelley. Justices, Lyman Beach, William Adams ; Constable, Alvin Gaylord.

—July 5, 1832, Presbyterian church organized at Mansfield. Baptist church at Mansfield organized April 10, 1840. Methodist church, February 10, 1845. St. James Episcopal church, in March 1865. Universalist church organized in 1882.

—Among the early settlers of the township of Richmond were, Isaac Lownsberry a soldier of the revolution, who was born December 21, 1757, and died at Canoe Camp April 4 1851, aged 94 years, Cephas Stratton, Mr. Negley, Ichabod Rowley, Mayor Ripley, John Cochran, Amos Spencer, Elijah Clark, Ebenezer Burley, Hezekiah Gaylord, Dyer J. Butts, Thomas Jerrald, Elihu Marvin, John Keltz, Peter Keltz, Jacob Keltz, Henry Daniels.

Rutland Township and Roseville Borough.

Rutland township was formed from the townships of Jackson and Sullivan, in the year 1828. It is bounded on the north by the township of Jackson, on the east by the county of Bradford, Pa., on the south by Sullivan and Richmond townships, on the west by Richmond and Tioga townships; its mean elevation above tide is about 1,500 feet. Mill Creek is its principal stream, which flows westward and discharging its waters into the Tioga river.

The lands in the township are under a good state of cultivation, with some of the finest farms in the county. The chief pursuit of the inhabitants is farming. Its first settlers were largely from the Green Mountain State, and hence they named their township Rutland, in honor of the county from which they came.

In the year 1829, when the first assessment of the township was made by William Howland, assisted by Ezra Wood and William Rose, the taxables were Stewart Austin, John Argetsinger, Isaac Benson, Ephraim Bryant, Bethuel Bently, Ebenezer Bacon, Daniel Bunker, Halsey Burton, Hiram Benson, Green Bentley, Jacob Benson, Caleb Burrell, Silas Burrell, Sylvester Benson, Hiram Beeles, Constant Bailey, Peter Burrell, John Benson, Joseph Beeman, Johnson Brewer, John Britton, Peter Backer, Abraham Brown, W. D. Bacon, Sylvenus Benson, William M. Corey, Jabez M. Corey, Asa Crippen, David Crippen, Sydney Clark, Cornelius Clark, Seeley Cook, Hiram Cooley, Edwin Currie, Joseph Clark, Samuel Clark, Lemuel Clark, Harris Corey, John Crippen, Enos Curtis, Samuel H. Coates, Isaac Clymer, John Drake, James Dann, James Dann, Jr., John B. Dann, Joseph Fletcher, Judah Gifford, Nathan Gifford, Nathan Goodwin, Gardiner Gould, Jonathan Gray, Eli Gray, Justus Garretson, —— Goff, Calvin Hathaway, Hosea Howland, William W. Howland, John R. Howland, James Husted, Nathaniel Howland, Henry Hull, Seth E. Howland, Baldwin Haywell, Isaac Hager, David Huntley, Calvin W. Handmer, Thomas Johnson, James Job, Daniel King, Benjamin Lawrence, Nathan Newberry, Sylvester Newberry, Lucinda Newberry, Elisha Nash, Levi Osgood, Richard Lamberton, David Prutsman, Erastus Rose, Virgil Rose, William Rose, Levi Rose, Samuel Reynolds, D. B. Reynolds, John Reynolds, Avery Smith, Jesse Smith, Betsey Sherman, Jacob C. Stout, Harvey Smith, I. S Smith, Isaac Smith, Cornelius Sharp, Andrew Sharp, Herman Soper, Jefferson Sherman, Robert Searles, John Selover, John Snyder, Silas Smith, E. Strong, John Slingerland, Tunis Slingerland, Albert Slingerland, William Turner, William Updike, John Updike, Henry Updike Abram Updike, Jonathan Wood, Solomon Wood, William Wolf, Ira Weldon, Daniel Wattles, Seth Ward, William M. Ward, Justus Wood, Lewis H. Weldon, Ezra Wood, Solomon Wood, 2nd, James Rosell.

Roseville Borough formed from Rutland was organized Feb. 3, 1876. Its first officers were Burgess, Sandford Johns; Council, G. W. Sherman, Myron Mills, L. C. Benson, C. L. Strait, John M. Barden, Daniel Watson; Justices of the Peace, Daniel Watson, John D. Longwell; Constable, Josephus Stout; Street Commissioner, D. W. Hibbard; Treasurer, Myron Mills; Assessor, Warren Rose; Assistant Assessors; D. W. Hibbard, Lyman C. Benson: Judge of Election, G. W. Soper; Inspectors, D. W. Stout, H. M. Reynolds; Auditors, C. L. Strait, Amos Mansfield, H. H. Soper.

—The assessed valuation of property in Rutland township and boro is about $250,000—the real value is about $750,000.

—The first school house in Rutland was on the Mill Creek road.
—The first settler at Roseville was William Rose, in the year 1806.
—There are now twelve school houses in the township and borough.
—Erastus Rose, son of William Rose, lived sixty nine years in Rutland.
—Harris Soper was one of the early school teachers in Rutland township.
—Capt. E. R. Backer, of Rutland, raised a company during the rebellion.
—There are five churches in the township of Rutland and Roseville boro.

Shippen Township.

The township of Shippen was organized in the year 1823, taken from Delmar. Pine Creek runs centrally through the township from west to east for about four miles, and then abruptly turns to the southward near the mouth of Marsh Creek, one of its tributaries. For many years the business of lumbering in the pineries of the township afforded the chief industry of the inhabitants.

The late Hezekiah Stowell, Phelps, Dodge & Co., were among the prominent lumberman, as well as Scovill & Babcock, Hon. Robert G. White and others. The land along the valley of Pine Creek and Marsh Creek and in the southeastern portion of the township are under a fair state of cultivation, but a large portion of the township is not well adapted to agricultural pursuits, on account of the high and rugged mountains, which are a thousand or more feet in height above the waters of Pine Creek. The Jersey Shore and Pine Creek railroad passes through the township, following the valley of Marsh and Pine Creeks. Ansonia is a station on the line of the railroad in the township.

The first assessment of the township was made in 1824, by Asaph Ellis, before the township of Gaines was formed. The taxpayers in what was then Shippen, and now composed of Shippen, Gaines and a portion of Elk, were: John Benn, Coonrod Bennauer, Elijah Dimmick, Paul Dimmick, Sylvester Davy, Richard Ellis, John Ellsworth, Asaph Ellis, David Ellis, Consider Ellis, Richard Ellis, John Ellis, Robert Francis, Benjamin Furman, Josiah Furman, Aaron Furman, William Furman, Reuben Harrington, George Huyler, Dudley Hewitt, Jr., John Smith, Wheaton Hewitt, Dudley Hewitt, Levi Murdock, Morris Miller, Richard Phillips, John L. Phenix, John Steele, Robert Steele, Jas. Steele, Ephraim Steele, Frederic Tanner.

—Josiah Furman was the first settler in the township. He came up in a boat from Jersey Shore and made a settlement near the mouth of Marsh Creek on Pine Creek in the year 1804. Many of his descendants, still reside in the township.

—David Ellis was the first collector of taxes in the year 1824.

—The Indians did not vacate Pine Creek in Shippen township until the war of 1812.

—Reuben Harrington, one of the early settlers died, April 17th, 1862.

—Presbyterian church erected by the employes of Phelps and Dodge in the year 1843. Rev. T. Forster of Harrisburg, then located at Wellsboro, officiating as minister.

—Graveyard near Presbyterian church established April 1844. Israel Merrick who came from the state of Delaware in 1809, died April 30th, 1844, aged 78 years, is buried there.

Sullivan Township and Mainsburg Borough.

Sullivan township was formed in the year 1816, taken from Covington township. It is situated upon high table lands facing the Tioga valley on the west and the Sugar Creek valley of Bradford county and the upper waters of the Tioga River on the east. Its mean elevation above tide is about 1,600 feet.

It embraces some of the best cultivated lands in the county. Its soil is particularly adapted to grazing and the growing of oats, corn, wheat, potatoes and the orchard products.

It was named in honor of General John Sullivan of revolutionary fame. Its territory at its formation embraced what is now several townships.

At its organization its taxables were: John Andrews, Isaac Baker, Annais Baker, Simeon Briggs, Simeon Briggs, Jr., Griffin Bailey, Constant Bailey, Thomas R. Corey, Paul Cudworth, James Cudworth, David Crippen, Jacob Collins, Peleg Doud, Josiah Dewey, Joseph Dewey, John Ellis, David Fellows, James Gray, John Gray, Silas Gray, Aaron Gitchell, David Jones, Timothy Knowlton, John King, Uri Loper, Allen Lane, Jr., Lemuel Lane, Allen Lane, John Luddington, William Luddington, Benjamin Lawrence, Henry Lawrence, Asa Mann, Reuben Merritt, Ira Mudge, Eli McNett, John Newell, Jesse Orvis, Joseph Orvis, Timothy Orvis, David Palmer, John Packard, Jonathan Patridge, Stephen Palmer, H. Pitts, Clement Paine, Samuel Reynolds, Enos Rose, Daniel Rose, Jeremiah Rumsey, Noah Rumsey, Smith Rumsey, Thomas Raxford, Elisha Rush, John Simpkins, Gardiner Seaman, Jesse Smith, Jonathan L. Spencer, Lyman Spencer, Benjamin Trout, Nathaniel Welch, Elijah Welch, Nathaniel Welch, Jr., Roswell Webster, Zebedee Woodward, Abiah Webster, Noah Wiest, John Watson, Ephraim S Marsh, Eli Gitchell, Joseph Ford, Lyman Rumsey, Abijah Hawley, Samuel Harding, Robert Potter, Apolis Cudworth, John Benson, Jr., Daniel James, Levi Fox, Isaac Benson, Thomson Bennett, Benjamin Harrison.

—County road cut out in 1808 and 1809.

—The first school house was made of logs.

—Peleg Doud settled in Sullivan in the year 1808.

—In 1832, John Fox opened a store at Mainesburg.

—Jeremiah Rumsey settled in Sullivan in the year 1806.

—John Gray built the first saw-mill in the township in 1811.

—In 1809, Noah Rumsey erected a flouring mill in Mainsburg.

—The first Post Office was established in the township in 1814.

—The first assessor of Sullivan township was James Gray, Jr.

—In 1816, John Gray erected and opened a store in Gray's Valley.

—John Maine erected a distillery in Mainesburg about the year 1820.

—Mainesburg Lodge No. 754, I. O. O. F. was organized March 15, 1871.

—State Road constructed through the township in the years 1807 and 1808.

—Ira Mudge and William Luddington were the first Supervisors of the township.

—In the year 1831 flouring mill erected at what is now Chandlersburg, Sullivan township.

—First religious services held in the township by Rev. Joseph Mitchell about the year 1808.

—Capt. James Gray, the first settler in Gray's Valley, Sullivan township, was a revoultionary soldier.

—William Luddington settled on the county road in 1808. He was one of the wealthiest men in the township. Genial and kind hearted.

—There are two churches in Mainesburg. An elegant brick structure owned and occupied by the Methodist Episcopal, and a neat wooden structure owned and occupied by the Christain or Disciples.

—Mainesburg contains about 200 inhabitants and is surrounded by a good agricultural country. It is situated upon Corey creek, about five miles east of Mansfield and about one and a half miles north of the old state road.

—Mainesburg was organized as a borough in March 1859. Taken from Sullivan township. It was named in honor of John Maine, Esq. Its first officers were, Burgess, John Fox; Councilmen, A. C. Witter, E. R. Maine. G. W. Carman, A. B. Austin, P D. Parkhurst; Treasurer, Alpheus Peters; Street Commissioners; D. S. Peters, G. W. Carman; Collector, James Packard; Clerk of Council, A. C. Witter.

Tioga Township and Borough.

Tioga township originally contained the entire area of the present county of Tioga. It was then a portion of Lycoming County, Pa. On the formation of Tioga County, in March, 1804, by an act of the Legislature it was created an election district on the 3rd of April 1804, and the house of Thomas Berry designated as the place of holding elections. It will be recollected that Tioga County, then (1804), was only in its incipient state and not fully organized until the year 1813.

The present township of Tioga is bounded on the north by the township of Lawrence, east by Jackson and Rutland townships, south by Richmond, west by Middlebury and Farmington townships. Its principal streams are the Tioga river and its tributaries, Crooked, Elkhorn, Mill and Mitchell's Creeks. It is situated in and on both sides of the Tioga valley, comprising some of the best alluvial and upland soils in the State.

Tioga borough was formed from the township of Tioga in February, 1860. It is beautifully situated in the valley of the Tioga on the Tioga River, near the mouth of Crooked and Elkhorn Creeks, and contains about one thousand inhabitants. The Tioga and Elmira State Line Railroad has a station on the eastern side of the borough and the Corning, Cowanesque and Antrim Railroad, a station on its western side.

—Catholic church erected in 1881.
—Episcopal church organized in 1860.
—Thomas Berry settled at Tioga in 1799.
—Ira McCallister settled in Tioga in 1805.
—Tioga village cemetery established in 1829.
—Baptist church organized in the year 1813.
—Park Hose Co. organized December, 1874.
—Destructive fire at Tioga, February 9th, 1871.
—John Gordon settled in Tioga in the year 1801.
—Lyman Adams settled in Tioga in the year 1809.
—Odd Fellows Lodge established October 8th, 1847.

—Dr. William Willard settled in Tioga in 1799.

—Tioga Grange, No. 241, organized May 6th, 1874.

—*Tioga County Express* established at Tioga in 1873.

—B. C. Wickam, merchant, settled in Tioga in 1833.

—Richard Mitchell settled at Mitchell's creek in 1795.

—Allen D. Caulkins settled in Tioga in the year 1813

—William Rathbone settled in Tioga in the year 1812.

—Nicholas Prutsman settled in Tioga in the year 1800.

—Timothy Ives settled in Tioga township in the year 1797.

—Levi and Joseph Guernsey settled in Tioga in the year 1825.

—Tioga Lodge, Free Masons, No. 373, established October 16, 1866.

—Willardsburg Lodge, Free Masons, established about the year 1820.

—Tioga River Lodge, I. O. O. F., No. 797. established July 10th, 1872.

—Knights of Honor, Phenix Lodge, No. 933, established March 7th, 1878.

—Elijah Depue settled at Tioga. 1809. He died March 17, 1853, aged 80 years.

—James Goodrich, an enterprising citizen, settled in Tioga in the year 1819.

—Richard Mitchell, son of the pioneer was born at Mitchell Creek, in 1801.

—Harry Hotchkiss, a revolutionary soldier, settled in Tioga in the year 1804.

—Presbyterian church organized by Rev. J. S. McCullough. Jan. 25, 1852.

—A. C. Bush establishes a Free Park on the east side of the Tioga River in 1873.

—Henry H. Goodrich, poet, writer and historian, born at Tioga, February 28th, 1825.

—In 1796 Benajah Ives settled in the township of Tioga, three miles north of the village.

—Tioga village was originally known as "Willardsburg," named in honor of Dr. Willard.

—Hon. William Garretson settled in Tioga in the year 1827. He was an editor and lawyer.

—Uriah Spencer settled at Tioga in 1798. He was the first post master at Willardsburg in the year 1805.

—In 1827 *The Tioga Pioneer*, a weekly newspaper removed from Wellsboro to Willardsburg, (now Tioga).

—Hon. John W. Gurnsey, elected first burgess of Tioga borough in 1860, held the office for four consecutive years.

—William Garretson elected Justice of the Peace in the borough of Tioga in 1863. Nathan Niles was the first justice in 1808.

—Ambrose Millard settled in Tioga in 1805. He was one of the county commisioners when the county was fully organized in 1813.

—A. C. Bush, merchant, lumberman and prominent business man settled in Tioga in the year 1831. He was the founder of Bush's Park.

—Coke Ovens, for the manufacture of coke from semi-bituminous coal, were constructed in the year 1882–3, by the Fall Brook Coal Company at Tioga. They number about 500.

—The First Methodist church organized at the house of James Goodrich, June 24th, 1826. First tru tees William Willard, Jr., Elisha Booth, and Jacob Prutsman; Chairman, Benjamin Bentley; Secretary, William Willard, Jr.

—Dr. William Willard died at Willardsburg, (now Tioga), October 28th, 1836, in the 75th year of his age. He was a native of the State of Vermont. His widow died February 1864, aged 94.

—Jesse Losey was the first settler in Tioga, in the year 1794. He was a revolutionary soldier and died March 12th, 1844, aged 85 years, 5 months and 7 days, and is buried in a grave-yard south of Hollidaytown, in Middlebury township, Tioga County.

Union Township.

The township of Union, in Tioga County, Pennsylvania, is situated in the southeastern corner of Tioga County, and is bounded on the north by the townships of Hamilton and Ward; on the east by the county of Bradford, on the south by the county of Lycoming, and on the west by townships of Liberty and Hamilton.

Its mean elevation above tide is about sixteen hundred feet. Its lowest point is about 940 feet and its highest point nearly twenty-four hundred feet above tide. It was formed from the township of Sullivan in February, 1830. The villages in the township are Roaring Branch, Ogdensburg and Gleason. The streams of the township flow in an easterly and southeasterly direction and empty into the Lycoming Creek or river, with the exception of one in the northeastern portion of the township, which discharges its waters into a tributory of the North Branch of the Susquehanna. The lands of the township generally face the east and south, and although they occupy an elevated position, they produce most excellent crops of oats, grass, potatoes and buckwheat with fine orchard fruits.

The early settlers were Uriah Loper, Eli McNett, Samuel McNett, John McNett, William Taylor, Wright Rutty, Nelson Rutty, Jewett Spencer, Sr., Jewett Spencer, Jr., Lyon Spencer, Charles O. Spencer, Martin Robinson, Labon Landon, Ezra Landon, Joseph Groover, John Newell, Charles M. Dibble, John Ogden, Luther Ogden, Joseph Wilber, George W. Terry, Alfred Jackson, Jay Whitehead, Nathan Palmer, Martin Middaugh, Martin I. Harrington, Peter Skelley, Patrick Skelley, Abram Rundell, William Barrows, Joshua Reynolds, Thomas Tebo, Ithiel B. Reynolds, Thomas Stull, William Rathbone, Thomas Nichols, Thomas Decoursey, G. G. Collins, Patrick McCormick, Peter B. Harrington, Hiram Gray, Charles Whitcomb.

—Baptist church organized in the year 1844.

—John Newell settled in Union township in the year 1814.

—Joseph Groover settled in Union township in the year 1827.

—Methodist church in the Newell District, erected in the year 1877.

—Uri Loper was the first settler in Union township in the year 1800.

—The first saw mill in the township was built by Labon X. Landon.

—Methodist church at Roaring Branch, erected in 1883. Cost about $2,800.

—Jay Whitehead, a prominent farmer, settled in Union, in the year 1849.

—John Ogden, the founder of Ogdensburg, in Union township, settled there in 1839.

—"The Yankee Path," so well known by lumbermen and rivermen forty years ago, was cut out by Alfred Jackson, Esq., of Union, in the year 1840 He is still living.

—The first school house in the township was built of logs. It stood near the residence of Charles M. Dibble, Esq.

—Swamp church (Baptist) erected in 1860. There is a small swamp near it, which is the reason that it is termed, "The Swamp Church."

—Patrick McCormick founded the "Irish settlement" in Western Union in 1841. Peter Skelley and Thomas Skelley were associated with him.

—The first township election was held at the house of Eli McNett, in the year 1831. Township and general elections are now held at Ogdensburg.

—The first hotel in the township was kept by Samuel McNett. It was situated in the eastern portion of the township on the highway leading from Elmira, Troy, Canton to Ralston and Williamsport.

—The Catholic church in the Irish settlement was completed and dedicated in March, 1880. Mrs. Mary Skelley Birmingham, widow of the late John Birmingham gave the ground upon which the church is erected.

Ward Township.

The township of Ward was formed from the townships of Sullivan and Union, in the year 1852. Within its boundaries are the highest points in Tioga County, or Northern Pennsylvania. It was named in honor of Hon. Christopher L. Ward, of Towanda, Pa., who at one time owned nearly the entire lands in the township. Within its boundaries as formed in 1852, were to be found the largest deposits of semi-bituminous coal in Northern Pennsylvania. The borough of Fall Brook was taken from its territory in 1864, where mining of coal has been carried on since 1860, and a portion of Hamilton was taken from Ward in 1872. Mining is carried on by the Morris Run Coal and Mining Company, and quite a large portion of the coal is taken from the township of Ward, although it is brought to the surface in the township of Hamilton. The heirs of the late Christopher L. Ward still own considerable coal lands in the township, though in an undeveloped state. The Tioga river flows from the north-east through the township, receiving its first tributaries in that township. There is a tradition that some of the very first settlements in Tioga County were made within the limits of Ward township, by those claiming title under the grants made by the state of Connecticut. There is a place known as the "Old Possessions," which had been made prior to 1808--but by whom, the oldest settler in Ward and the neighboring township of Sullivan cannot definitely determine. In 1808 these "Old Possessions" had the appearance of having been made and abandoned from fifteen to twenty years prior to that date. It is not known therefore, who the first settler was in the township of Ward. William McIntosh, Simon McIntosh and Matthias McIntosh settled in what is now known as "McIntosh Hollow," in the township of Ward, in the year 1837. Harry Coovert settled near them about the same time. James Lyon, Andrew Kniffin, Erastus Kiff, William R. Lyon, Daniel Hager, John Purvis, Waterman Gates and others, soon thereafter located in the township. A number of these were from Delaware county New York.

—The first election was held in 1852, at the house of William R. Lyon.

—The first school house in the township was made of logs. It was located in McIntosh Hollow, and was erected in the year 1838.

—Erastus Kiff built a saw mill in 1863.

—A Farmers' Grange was established in the year 1879.

--The first schools in the township were taught at private houses.

—Rev. John Spalding was the first clergyman who preached in the township.

—Among the first teachers in the township were Mary Welsh and Susannah Bascomb.

—Mr. Wood erected a saw mill in Ward, in the year 1844. William McIntosh erected one a few years later.

—There are several religious organizations in the township, but no church edifices. The school hous..s are used for religious services.

—Tracey O. Hollis, A. J. Teeter, John Kiff, A. P. Gray, Miles Furman, Stephen Segar, Hugh Crawford, H. R. Wilcox, are a few of the prominent business men and farmers of the township.

—It will be borne in mind that Fall Brook was not taken from Ward until August, 1864. During the rebellion, Fall Brook and Ward, with a total voting population of 148, furnished, either by commutation, substitute or drafted men, 366 persons for the Union armies.

Westfield Township and Borough.

The township of Westfield was formed from the township of Deerfield, in in the year 1821. It is bounded on the north by Brookfield township, on the east by Deerfield and Chatham townships, on the south by Clymer township and on the west by Potter county. The Cowanesque river runs through the township from west to east, near the northern boundary line between it and Brookfield. Its mean elevation above tide is about 1,600 feet. Its inhabitants are now chiefly engaged in farming. The original settlers were generally of New England origin, and had been former residents of the State of New York, Chenango, Cortland and Delaware counties being largely represented. Among the first settlers were Porter Lapham, Nathaniel Mann, Ayres Tuttle, Reuben Cook and John Thomas.

Westfield borough was formed from Westfield township in the year 1867. It is situated upon the banks of the Cowanesque river, at the mouth of Mill Creek, and is one of the most prosperous and growing boroughs in the valley of the Cowanesque. The Corning, Cowanesque and Antrim railroad and the Addison and Northern Pennsylvania railroad companies have each a station, express office and telegraph office in the borough. It contains several large industrial establishments, a graded school, several churches, a number of stores, saloons, groceries and shops, two hotels, a newspaper printing office, and is rapidly increasing in wealth and population.

—Samuel Phillips erected the first saw mill in the borough.

—David Close remodeled a house and kept a hotel in the year 1842.

—Butler B. Strang was the first burgess of the borough of Westfield.

—Wesleyan Methodist church organized under the ministration of Rev. Francis Strang in 1850.

—Rev. Francis Strang was the first merchant in Westfield borough. He opened a store in 1840.

—Richard Phillips erected the first grist mill in Westfield borough. There had been a small one in the township years before.

—Westfield tannery erected in the year 1876.

—Methodist Episcopals held service in the township in the year 1830.

—Corning, Cowanesque and Antrim R. R. completed to Westfield Nov. 1882.

—Addison and Northern Penna. R. R. completed to Westfield Nov. 1882.

—Hon. Butler B. Strong, died in May 1884, at his home in Westfield. He was one of the most able and distinguished citizens of Tioga County.

—The locomotive engineer who ran the first engine into Westfield over the A. & N. P. R. R., was Edward Bryant, (Spike); Daniel Conderman, fireman.

—Col. James E. Jones wore a straw hat into Westfield November 7, 1882, upon the completion of the A, & N. P. R. R., to fulfil his prophecy made in June previous, that the road would be completed to Westfield before he discarded his summer hat.

—The A. & N. P. R. R was located from Westfield to Knoxville by Wm. E. Worme'sdorff, chief engineer, Wm. O. Bristol, level, Charles Nelson, rodman, Samuel M. Sexton, transit, John McGee; head chainman, Richard Laney, rear chainman, Hawkins Simpson, James Metcalf, axemen, Charles Kimber, peg agent, Lyman Swan, flagman.

—Knights of Honor, No. 1206, organized Sept. 16, 1878. The first officers were, D., W. H. Fuller; V. D., Charles Krusen; A. D., B. F. Mulford; G., James H. Metcalf; R., J. B. Tubbs; T. R., E. H. Ashcroft; Treas., William A. Omans; Chaplain, A. S. Mindoyne; Guardian, Seth W. Harris; Sentinel, E. V. Eaton; Med. Ex, A. L. Bottom, M. D.

—Westfield Lodge No. 477, F. A. M., organized in Westfield borough Dec. 28, 1870; first stated meeting held January, 1871. The officers were: T. C. Sanders, W. M.; N. J. Krusen, S. W.; Edwin B. Bulkley, J. W.; A. D. Ashcroft, S. D.; Nelson Doty, J. D.; E. H. Stebbins, Sec.; Isaac Plank, Treas.; A. K. Sayles, Tiler. The charter members were T. C. Sanders, Edwin B. Bulkley, Sylvester D. Phillips, James Masten, Isaac Plank, E. H, Stebbins, John Davis, Philetas L. Corbin, E. P. Fish, Nelson Doty, Charles Bliss, Levi Skinner, N. J. Krusen, Norman Buck, A. D. Askcroft, A. K. Sayles.

Blossburgh Borough.

In 1792, when Benjamin and Robert Patterson were conducting the German and English settlers to the Pultney estate, where Bath, in Steuben county, is now located, they tarried for some days near where the present bridge across the Tioga river in the southern portion of the borough of Blossburg is now located.

They erected a hugh oven and cleared away the timber, and made a "camp" which was afterwards known as "Peter's Camp."

In the year 1806, Aaron Bloss located upon this camp, and erected a dwelling, which was for many years was used as an Inn. His nearest neighbor to the southward was ten miles away; his Inn was located however upon the Williamson road, which then was the only road between Williamsport on the west branch of the Susquehanna, and Painted Post at the mouth of the Conhocton river. The coal which had been pronounced good by the English who accompanied the Patterson brothers, soon began to attract attention. In the meantime, David Clemmons had located two and one half miles to the northward upon the banks of the Tioga river, and purchased several warrants of land. He also opened up the coal where years afterwards the Arbon Coal Company first commenced operations. Among the early settlers within the present limits of Blossburg Borough were Absalom Kingsbury, Isaac Walker, Ashael Walker, Royal Walker, Judge John H. Knapp, D. P. Freeman, Lewis Saynisch and Samuel Weeks, when the construction of a railroad from Blossburg to Corning, or soon thereafter Col. Joseph Yonkin, Alexander H. Gaylord, John L. Evans, James H. Gulick, Francis Welch, John James, Thomas Turner, a brother-in-law of Hon. Erastus Corning, William Butler, Clarendon Rathbone, Franklin R. Smith, John G. Boyd, P. P. Cleaver came on and located. Hon. Horatio Seymour in 1837 visited Blossburg, and in company with Hon. Amos P. Granger and Hon. Thomas P. Davis of New York and Curtis Parkhurst and Hon. James Ford of Lawrenceville, Pa, purchased lands and sold lots within the present borough limits. When the railroad was completed in 1840, from Blossburg, another large instalment of settlers came. The first store, saw mill and furnace were erected by Judge John H. Knapp, as early as 1826. It was claimed by Miller Fox, the chief engineer of the Corning and Blossburg R. R., that the time would come when one hundred thousand tons of coal would pass over the railroad, his statements then were ridiculed. A million tons annually now go over the railroad, and are marketed. There were some, however, who believed in his prophecies and govern themselves accordingly.

The consumption of bituminous coal at that time was very limited, and but compartively few were acquainted with its use, only as a substitute for charcoal to a limited extent in blacksmithing. The era of steam had not fully arrived.

The prosperity of Blossburg depended largely upon the coal trade, which was fickle and unstaple. The Arbon Coal Company was succeeded by William M. Mallory, and he by Duncan S. Magee. The transferring of the mining operations of the Magees' from Blossburg to Fall Brook in the year 1859-60-61, was a great blow to the prosperity of Blossburg. In 1862 there were from forty to fifty vacant dwellings in Blossburg, the town was nearly deserted. The establishment of the Tioga railroad shops at this point at that time revived business materially, and Blossburg again entered upon a new lease of prosperity.

In the year 1847, William Dezang, of Geneva New York, erected a window glass manufactory in the northern portion of Blossburg, built a store and ten or twelve dwellings. This manufactory was conducted by Mr. Dezang several years, and subsequently by James H. Gulick and O. F. Taylor, and in the year 1867 it was leased by Messrs. Hirsch, Ely & Co., and conducted up to the present by that firm under the co-operative plan. Blossburg was incorporated as a borough in August, 1871. It now contains an Episcopal, Methodist, Baptist, Welch Congregationalist, Irish Catholic and Polish Catholic Churches. A fine graded school, employing one principal and six assistant teachers, a bank, printing and news paper office (Blossburg Register) a window glass manufactory, two saw mills, a planing mill and feed mill, a very large tannery, a foundry and machine shop ; the shops of the Tioga R. R. three boot and shoe stores, with shops attached, one shoe making and repair shop, one harness shop, two blacksmith shops, one wagon shop, two paint shops, four licensed hotels, a city hall with rooms for the fire companies, the council and burgess, school board, high constable, election board and for a prison or lock-up, five eating saloons, two billiard rooms, three furniture and two undertaking shops, two wholesale liquor stores and bottling establishments four clothing stores, three dry goods stores, three general merchandise stores, a tea and coffee store, two hardware stores, several grocery stores, a photograph gallery, an express office, a depot, band room, three music teachers with rooms, two dentists, eight physicians, four drug stores, two lawyers, two meat markets, a brass band, Masonic, Odd Fellows, Knights of Honor, and Rebecca Lodges, a skating rink, a public hall and about three thousand inhabitants.

There are two branches of the Tioga railroad and one of the Corning and Cowanesque railroad, leading southward and eastward. The Arnot branch of the Tioga railroad to Hoytville and Morris Run, and the Fall Brook branch of Corning, Cowanesque and Antrim to Fall Brook. Blossburg is one of the most desirable locations for manufacturing in the county.

—M. E. Church organized in 1867.

—Polish Catholic church erected in 1873.

—St. Luke Episcopal church organized in 1867.

—Arbon Lodge I. O. O. F., organized May 20, 1853.

—I. O. O. F., Encampment organized April 13, 1867.

—The 12th Regiment band organized in August 1873.

—Bloss Lodge A. Y. Masons organized March 9. 1865.

—Blossburg Knights of Honor organized July 12, 1876.

—In 1865 the Presbyterian Church purchased by the Baptist.

—Catholic Temperance Association organized August 16, 1874.

—Martin Stratton has been a resident of Blossburg for over forty years.

—Col. Joseph Yonkin has resided continuously in Blossburg since 1836.

—Blossburg has two fire companies and is about to purchase a steamer.

—March 6, 1873, the entire business portion of Blossburg destroyed by fire.

—Christ Church organized 18th of Jan. 1842; no edifice was ever erected.

—Blossburg Register established in 1871, by Harry and Frederic L. Graves.

—Faith Degree Lodge, Daughters of Rebekah organized October 20, 1874

—Mt. Zion Church (Welsh) organized in 1840, erected fine church in 1870.

—Presbyterian Church organized in 1853. James H. Gulick and Hon. Horatio Seymour, prominent contributors.

—Thomas Morgan, an old settler of Blossburg, who died a few years since had been an Odd Fellow for fifty-three years.

—Martin G. Lewis has for several years been chief of the Blossburg fire department. The Lewis fire guard were named in his honor.

—Francis Welch, Esq., who died a few weeks since, at an advanced age, came to Blossburg in 1837, and for nearly thirty consecutive years was acting justice of the peace.

—Blossburg Industrial Register established by John L. Sexton Jr., May 29, 1879, continued two years, when Mr. Sexton retired and the paper was named "Blossburg Register" now owned by F. L. Graves and Charles Ely.

—St. Andrews Catholic Church organized in 1841, with twenty members, Rev. Joseph O'Reily of St. Joseph Church, Susquehanna Co., Pa., first officiating. Coffin Calket, of Philadelphia, and Hon. Horatio Seymour contributed.

Covington Borough.

Covington was organized as a borough by a decree of court of common pleas of Tioga County in the year 1831. It remained a borough for several years and suffered its charter to become void. In the year 1851 it again applied to the court and again was chartered.

Mention has been made in the history of the township of many of the old settlers and will not be here repeated. Among the most prominent citizens in the early history of the borough were Thomas Putman, Edwin Dyer, Stephen Packhard, John S. Hoagland, Thomas Dyer, John C. Bennitt, Elijah Gaylord, O. F. Taylor, Samuel Barber, Phineas P. Cleaver, David Caldwell, Ira Patchen, Elijah Putnam, Peter Keltz, John G. Boyd, Butler Smith, Julius Doane. From 1840 to 1855 Covington was one of the greatest business centres in Tioga County. It was located where the Wil liamson road made in 1792 and the state road completed in 1808, intersected and crossed each other, they then being the two greatest thoroughfares in the county.

Its citizens were enterprising and erected churches, school house, mills, manufactories, hotels, stores, glass works and "Covington Four Corners" were known far and wide. As we have stated in 1851, the borough charter of Covington was renewed. The first burgess under the new charter was Geo. Knox; clerk John Lang; street commissioners Martin Gerould and Elijah Gaylord; treasurer O. F. Taylor; collector Ira Patchen; poormaster Anson L. Johnson.

The chief burgesses have since been George Knox, W. C. Webb, Thomas Putman, John C. Bennitt, Edwin Dyer, H. M. Gerould, Ira Patchen, Leonard Palmer, Perley P. Putman, O. G. Gerould, A. M. Bennett, Jacob Hartman, E. B. Decker, Charles Howland, William Lamkin, Edwin Klock, J. M. Hoagland. Some of these have been elected and served as many as five terms. A. M. Bennett is now the burgess.

Covington borough is situated five miles north of Blossburg, five miles south of Mansfield, twelve miles east of Wellsboro and seven miles southwest of Mainsburg and now contains about eight hundred inhabitants. Within the past three years it has increased in population very materially. The purchase of the window glass manufactory by Messrs. Hirsch, Ely & Co. and the employment of quite a number of men by that company, has been one of the causes which have been instrumental in reviving the borough. The building of a number of fine dwellings and business places together with several industrial establishments have also encouraged and stimulated the business prospects of the borough. It is situated in the center of a good farming country with railroad transportation facilities afforded by the Tioga railroad. There are several churches, a graded school, an Odd Fellows hall, a saw mill and shingle mill, a grist mill, a glass manufactory whose capacity is about 40,000 boxes of glass annually, giving direct employment to about forty men, a fruit evaporator, two hardware stores, one drug store, one jewelry store, three general stores, one bottling establishment of mineral water, a barber shop, a shoe shop, one hotel and several groceries, a harness shop, two gun shops, one wagon makers shop, two blacksmith shops, an express office, depot, post office and reading room, several branches of lodges of Knights of Labor.

—Baptist Sunday school organized January 1st, 1881.

—In 1815, a public school was organized, and in 1816, a school house built.

—First Presbyterian Church organized July 27th, 1841. First pastor Rev. Julius Doane.

—Church of Christ, first known as "Christain" was organized in 1840. Elder Whitehead officiating.

—The Rev. Caleb Boyer held Methodist service, in Covington in the year 1809. The present M. E. Church was erected in 1848.

—In 1841 Prof. Julius Doane and Miss Lucy Putnam established a high school. The building was on the west side of the Tioga river.

—First Baptist Church was organiz d in 1861. It had been known by another name previous to that date. Rev. George Spratt, a native of England officiating in 1839.

—The late Horace B. Clark blew the first glass in Tioga County, Pa., at Blossburg, in the year 1847. He resided for many years before his death, which occurred February, 1884, in Covington.

—Covington Lodge No. 274 I. O. O. F. was instituted August 10th, 1848. The first officers were Theobald Miller, Noble Grand; Ellis Gamble, Vice Grand; George W. Boothe, Secretary; Ira Day, Assistant Secretary; O. F. Taylor, Treasurer. The officers were installed by D. D. G. M. Garreston of Tioga. Members initiated then, Col. N. A. Elliott; Philemon Doud; Lorenzo D. Taylor; Hugh McCabe; Henry Hall and Alonzo Noble. This is the parent lodge for eastern and southern Tioga County.

—Emma Colfax, Rebekah Lodge No. 15, I. O. O. F., was organized Sept. 22, 1869. D. D. G. M., G. M. Butler officiating. Charter members were G. M. Butler; O. G. Gerould; J. C. Bennett; D. S. Irelan, Sr.; A. M. Bennett; C F. King; Joseph Hyland; Lyman W. Kiff; H. G. Levalley; Andrew McIntosh; Edward D. Roberts; David S. Irelan, Jr.; Richard Ashley; Miles G. Lee; James M Everetts; George W. Keltz; Simon Green; L. R. Walker; Stephen F. Richards; L. W. Woodruff; H. A. Fisher; George A. Kinney; Jacob Hartman; Nelson Clemmons; W. S. Holman; George W. Johnson; Lucy Butler; Olive Bennett; Mary Gerould; Maggie Irelan; Frankie Bennett; Julia Keltz; Susan Green; Mrs. S. F. Richards; Susan Roberts; S. C. King; Ella B. Levalley; Mrs. W. Woodruff; Malvina L. Kiff; Ida O. McIntosh; Mrs. Richard Ashley; Martha Lee; Aurelia Walker; Hester A. Fisher.

—Past Grands of I. O. O F., No. 274, have been: Theobald Miller, George W. Boothe, Benjamin Kress, Ira Day, O. F. Taylor, L. D. Taylor, Hugh McCabe, Jacob Whitman, Mathew Skelley, Charles S. Videau, H. Whitman, John L. Lee, John Lang, D. W. Gitchel, Charles Jacques, John C. Bennett, J. B. Husted, A. M. Spencer, Ira Patchen, Thomas Videau, I. P. Keltz, Edwin Dyer, S. L. Barber, L. K. Spencer, S. B. Cochran, T. B. Goodenough, David Caldwell, H. M Gerould, Fred R. Caldwell, William Butler, G. M. Butler, G. Fuller, L. R. Walker, O. G. Gerould, D. S Irelan, Sr., D. S. Irelan, Jr., S. F. Richards, G. W. Keltz, V. O. Spencer, F. M. Spencer, A. B. Brion, H. R. Brion, Jacob Hartman, H. J.

Marvin, J. H. Harmon, J M. Everetts, Miles G. Lee, H. Levalley, George W. Johnson, M. R. Walker, A. M. Bennett, C. F. King, G S. Harding, Nelson Clemmons, V. N. Levalley, G. H. Coe, A. F. Packard, Uri Ferguson, H. Brown, L. S Townshend, G. A. Spring, B. W. Harrison, Sol Blanchard, S. D. Forrest, D. S. LaFrance, E. R. Meeker.

Elkland Borough.

Elkland borough was formed in May, 1850.

The township of Elkland was one of the oldest townships in Tioga County, having been formed in the year 1814, from Delmar. By gradual disintegration it was cut up into various townships, until there remained of its large territory only what is now embraced in the borough of Elkland, and when that borough was formed, Elkland township was absorbed and ceased to exist. Elkland is situated in the very garden of the Cowanesque valley, and surrounded by an excellent farming country. The valley of the Cowanesque broadens at this point, forming a basin of land unexcelled in the county. The Elkland and Lawrenceville railroad, now operated under the management of the Corning, Cowanesque and Antrim Railroad, was completed from Lawrenceville to Elkland, in Sept., 1873, and for ten years remained the terminus of that road. This made Elkland a great shipping and receiving point for localities west of it, up the Cowanesque Valley and into Potter Co., Pa. It stimulated business of every kind. In 1882, the Addison and Northern Pennsylvania R. R. was constructed from Addison and thence westward up the valley to Westfield, thence southward to Pine Creek. This road added largely to the shipping facilities of the citizens of Elkland. The same year the Fall Brook Coal Co., which controlled the Corning, Cowanesque and Antrim road extended their road to Harrison Valley. It contains two hotels, two churchhes, bank, newspaper office, graded school, several industrial establishments, two depots, telephone and two telegraph offices, tannery, number of stores, etc.

—Leander Culver built the first hotel in 1836.

—Col. Lemuel Davenport built the first flouring mill.

—Hon. Benjamin Dorrance died June 26th, 1881, aged 45 years.

—Large quantities of tobacco are raised in and about Elkland.

—The first store was opened in 1824, by John Ryan and Robert Tubbs.

—Joel Parkhurst settled in Elkland, in 1828 and engaged in merchantile pursuits.

—Hon. Geo. Dorrance settled in Elkland, in 1829. Died June 13, 1881, aged 79 years.

—Elkland Furniture Manufactory established in 1883, O. Pattison, superintendent and manager

—One of the most active business men of Elkland, is Mr. C. L. Pattison, son in-law of the late Joel Parkhurst.

—One of the wealthiest citizens of Tioga County, was the late Joel Parkhurst, of Elkland, who died in December, 1881, aged 81 years.

—The elegant graded school building, costing $6,000, was the gift of Joel Parkhurst, Esq., to the school authorities of the borough of Elkland.

—Early settlers of Elkland were, George Dorrance, David Hammond, Lemuel Davenport, Robert Tubbs, Benjamin Tubbs and Leander Culver.

Fall Brook Borough.

Fall Brook Borough was organized from the township of Ward in August, 1864. The borough embraces about six thousand acres of land owned exclusively by the Fall Brook Coal Company. It is situated upon lands whose surface is underlaid by millions of tons of semi-bituminous coal. Its mean elevation above the ocean is nearly 2,000 feet. Its highest point being over 2,300 feet, and its lowest point 1,550 feet.

It is a mining town and contains about two hundred dwellings, a store, mill, hotel, two school houses, whose seating capacity are about 300, two churches, Presbyterian and Catholic, town hall and the necessary schutes, weigh and other offices and shops for the transaction of business. It is connected by railroad with the Tioga & Elmira State Line at Blossburg. It also has telegraphic connections with Morris Run and the Western Union at Blossburg. It contains a population of about one thousand persons, who are engaged in mining, lumbering, etc. The greater portion of its population are employee's of the Fall Brook Coal Company.

—Fall Brook depot finished in 1865.
—Hon. John Magee died April 5th, 1868.
—In 1875 A. J. Owen becomes manager.
—Duncan S. Magee died in February, 1869.
—Doctor Davidson was the first resident physician.
—Population of Fall Brook in 1872 was about 2,000.
—G. A. Backus, civil engineer, died in February, 1864.
—D. W. Knight appointed manager September 24th, 1872.
—Fall Brook Lodge, No. 765, I. O. O. F., May 15th, 1871.
—Fall Brook Library Association organized April 15th, 1873.
—Lewis Clark, outside superintendent, died December 24th, 1872.
—Line of telegraph from Fall Brook to Corning in November, 1864.
—St. Thomas church, Episcopal, organized in 1864; charter obtained in 1867.
—C. E. Halsey becomes store manager in 1864, and continues until 1876.
—Agnes (Rebeckah) Lodge, I. O. O. F., No. 126, organized Nov, 19, 1880.
—Knights of Honor, Fall Brook Lodge, No. 2,506, instituted July 20, 1881.
—"Great Strike" commenced January 1st, 1865, ended May 20th, 1865.
—Fall Brook Hotel completed in May, 1865; cost $15,000; first landlord, Warren Goff.

—Alexander Pollock, senior, was drift master of No. 1 and 2, from 1859 to 1874.

—George Richter, senior, erected a saw mill at the Falls of Fall Brook in the year 1859

—Fall Brook Friendly Society organized May 15th, 1869. This is a beneficial society.

—Patrick Dwrye has been in the employ of the Fall Brook Coal Company thirty successive years.

—Humphrey Brewer and Gustavus A. Beckus were civil engineers and surveyed the railroad route.

—Thomas Reese was the first weigh master of mining wagons; he was assisted by John L. Sexton, Jr.

—The Fall Brook Coal Company consisted of John Magee, Duncan S. Magee and James H. Gulick.

—In the year 1859 a railroad was constructed from Blossburg to the mines at Fall Brook, a distance of about seven miles.

—The first shipping master was John Morse, succeeded by Peter Cameron, Jr., John L. Sexton, Jr., William D. Lynahan.

—James Heron, appointed cashier and store agent in 1860, assisted by O. Pattison, C. L. Pattison and Thomas J. Hall.

—James Heron becomes manager, December 27th, 1867, and continues in that position until his death, September 22d, 1872.

—Presbyterian church organized in the year 1860; church erected in 1867, costing $2,200; Fall Brook Coal Company gave half the amount.

—L. C. Shepard was the first burgess in Fall Brook in the year 1864, and continued to be re-elected until 1871, when he refused longer to serve.

—In 1861 Frank Lewis became manager of the store, and James Heron devoted his whole time to the duties of chief book-keeper and paymaster.

—Catholic church organized in 1873; dedicated church April 26th, 1874; cost of church $2,000, of which amount the Fall Brook Coal Company gave half.

—The first officers of the Fall Brook Coal Company were John Magee, President; John Lang, Secretary and Treasurer; Duncan S. Magee, Superintendent.

In 1861 first school house erected in Fall Brook, and in 1865 another wa built. These proving inadequate, was very much enlarged under directions of John L. Sexton, Jr., secretary of school board

—Humphrey Brewer became manager of the Fall Brook mines in 1862, and occupied that position until his death in December, 1867. He had previously been employed by Magee, commencing work for him in 1854.

—John L. Sexton, Jr., Miss Grace A. Sexton, were employed about seven successive years as teachers in the Fallow school. Miss Bessie Brewer, Mrs. Lucy Cranmer were employed for a long time in the school on Catawissa streeet.

—William Griffiths, drift master of No. 3, from 1861 till 1874 Had been in the employ of the Company since 1855, and continued in their employ until 1880. In 1874 he was sent by the company to take charge of their mines at Clermot, McKean Co., Pa.

—Explorations for coal were commenced by D. S. Magee and his assistants, William Griffiths, Thomas Morgan, John James, Stephen Bowen and others, in the year 1856. These explorations resulted in the purchase of about six thousand acres of land by John Magee of C. L. Ward, of Towanda, in the year 1859.

—In the month of April, 1859, the Fall Brook Coal Company was chartered. The bill for its incorporation passed both houses of the Pennsylvania Legislature, and was vetoed by Governor William F. Packer, March 9th, 1859. The bill of incorporation was passed, his veto notwithstanding, April 7th, 1859, and became a law.

Knoxville Borough.

Knoxville was incorporated a borough, by an act of the legislature and approved by Gov. Wm. F. Johnson, April 19th, 1850, taken from the township of Deerfield. In area it contains about 265 acres. It was named in honor of the Knox's, the pioneer settlers of the township of Deerfield. The first settler within the borough limits was Simon Rixford or Rexford, a revolutionary soldier. He came from Massachusetts and settled near the mouth of Troups creek, in 1799. Knoxville is beautifully located upon the alluvial flats on the north bank of the Cowanesque river, at the point where Troups creek discharges its waters into that river. It is one of the prominent stations upon two railroads, viz: The Addison and Northern Pennsylvania Railroad (narrow gauge) and the Corning, Cowanesque and Antrim Railroad, (standard gauge) and is an active and thriving borough. Its elevation above tide is about 1250 feet. The construction of the two railroads above named within the past three years has added much to its prosperity and wealth.

—Sophia Hale taught school in 1818.
—A good school house erected in 1834.
—1815, Daniel Cummings kept an inn.
—Stephen Colvin, built a hotel in 1822.
—In 1823, Silas Billings built an ashery.
—Daniel Angell built a tannery in 1844.
—Quaker church, erected of logs, in 1812.
—Baptist church, organized March 7, 1868.
—O. P. Beach established a drug store in 1852.
—Christian church, organized October 14, 1865.
—Archibald Knox, built a store in the year 1818.
—A sash factory was built in 1 52, by Henry Seeley.
—In 1826, Silas Billings erected a large framed hotel.
—Jonathan Matteson built a grist mill in the year 1817.
—Peter Roberts, established a blacksmith shop, in 1824.
—John E. White served thirty years as Justice of the Peace.
—There was a small store in the year 1815, owned by Mr. Wing.
—Deerfield Lodge, I. O. O. F., No. 800. instituted June 11, 1872.
—Sons of Temperance, Division No. 359, instituted June 14, 1849.
—A. A. and G. C. Seeley Post, G. A. R, organized July 10, 1875.
—A Free church, open to all christian denominations, erected in 1852.
—A school house erected in Knoxville, in the year 1817, built of plank.
—I. O. O. F., Cowanesque Lodge, No. 332, instituted, March 21, 1849.
—Methodist parsonage erected in 1826. Methodist church erected in 1869.
—Silas Billings and Hiram Freeborn erected a substantial distillery in 1823.
—Silas Billings erected a large grist mill in 1825. Built by John Spicer.
—William Knox, built a log hotel, named "The Rixford House" in 1824.
—In 1818, a cloth dressing and fulling mill was erected, by Daniel Cummings.
—Henry Sherwood now a prominent lawyer at Wellsboro, Pa., was engaged in the merchantile business, in the year 1841. In 1843, he delivered a fourth of July oration.

—Hon. Butler B. Strang, delivered an oration, July 4, 1861.

—A log distillery was built in 1815, by Daniel Cummings and Jonathan Matteson.

—Jonathan Matteson, Alexander Matteson and Joshua Colvin, built a saw mill in 1815.

—Cowanesque Lodge, No. 351, F. A. M., organized, June 24th, (St. Johns' Day.) 1875.

—Ebenezer Seelye, a revolutionary soldier, died, June 3, 1837, aged 81 years, 2 months and 27 days.

—A foundry was built by a firm from Bath, N. Y., in 1851. The business was conducted by John P. Biles.

—Congregational church, organized April 28, 1867, erected a brick church and dedicated the same February 2, 1871.

—Victor L. Beach, Company C., 127th N. Y. Cavalry, died October 30, 1863 aged 23 years, 4 months and 5 days.

—A bank was established in the year 1869, by Morgan Seeley, Vine Crandall and David Coats. It was a private bank.

—The Knox family, who were the pioneers, settled in Deerfield township, a few rods east of the Knoxville borough line.

—Cornelius Goodspeed, settled in Knoxville, in 1813. He was the father of John Goodspeed, the surveyor for the Bingham estate.

—Jonathan Matteson, settled in 1810 within the borough limits. He and his brothers owned what is now the central portion of the borough.

—Rosetta, wife of Silas Billings, died, December 25, 1835, aged 36 years. Abbey, wife of Silas Billings, died, February 15, 1831, aged 27 years.

—Giles C. Seeley, Company F, 86th Regiment, N. Y. Vol., died at Camp Griffin, Virginia, February 21, 1862, aged 18 years, 6 months and 26 days.

—Sergeant Albert A. Seeley, wounded at Gaines Hill, June 27, died in prison at Richmond, Va., July 3, 1862, aged 21 years, 2 months and 15 days.

—Martin Grover, a celebrated public speaker, addressed a mass meeting of Democrats in 1844. Seventy-two yoke of oxen drew a hickory pole from Academy Corners to Knoxville, to the meeting.

—In the year 1822, Silas Billings settled at Knoxville. He was a man of wealth, great business qualifications, energetic and enterprising and did much to advance the interest of Knoxville, the Cowanesque valley and the county of Tioga.

Wellsboro Borough.

In area Wellsboro is the largest borough, except Fall Brook, in the county of Tioga. It was christened Wellsboro in its infancy, in the year 1802, by Mrs. Mary Wells Morris, wife of Benjamin Wistar Morris, the first settler, and sister of William and Gideon Wells, who were pioneers and first settlers in the township now known as Delmar, from which Wellsboro was organized as a borough in the year 1830. Four years after receiving the name of Wellsboro, it was selected as the county seat of Tioga County, which hono rable distinction it has since enjoyed. John Norris was its first burgess. At the time of its organization as a borough, there were only about thirty families within its limits. Five years later, 1835, with all of its prestige as a county seat and borough, there were fifty-nine families, according to the recollection and written memorandum of William Bache, Jr. These consisted of E. Fellows, William Taylor, R. Cole, R. Christianot, B. B. Smith, Samuel Mack, M. Burnside, J. Borst, A. Corey, J. Beecher, S. Bliss, John F. Donaldson, F. Wetherbee, C. Seeley, James Lock, L. I. Nichols, D. Linsey, L. Meek, J. Brewster, J. Hance, E. Jones, J. Gere, —— Horsely, Israel Greenleaf, Elias Spencer (colored), Eben Murray (colored), Ebenezer Jackson, J. L. Robinson, Chester Robinson, John Norris, Samuel Dickinson, —— Bowen, William Bache, Sr., J. Kimball, Mr. Barnes, Doctor Barnes, Mr. Weeden, D. Sturrock, E. M. Bodine, F. Doxtetter, D. Caldwell, J. E. Martin, Josiah Emery, Mr. Barney, Samuel W. Morris, James P. Lowrey, Israel Merrick, O. L. Gibson, U. Cushman, Gates Wilcox, L. Cleveland, G. Cook, Mr. Maase, Dr. Wells, Mr. Whitman, Archibald Nichols, William Norris, Mr. Harris, P. Murray (colored). Wellsboro now contains a population of about three thousand inhabitants, and is one of the richest boroughs in northern Pennsylvania.

—Joseph Fish was the first tanner.

—County poor house erected in 1859.

—M. H. Cobb, founded the *Agitator*, in 1854.

—The *Banner*, established in 1862, by R. Jenkins.

—Harry Sligh was the first child born in Wellsboro.

—Hermaic Society (Literary) organized May 11, 1869.

—Ezekiel Jones was the first blacksmith in Wellsboro.

—In 1842 first Methodist church erected and dedicated.

—William D. Bailey, in 1850, established the *Advertiser*.

—Samuel W. Morris was the first postmaster at Wellsboro.

—Wellsboro and Lawrenceville Railroad completed in 1872.

—In 1874, Wellsboro *Gazette*, established by F. G. Churchill.

—In 1884, the *Advocate* was founded by Charles G. Fairman.

—Plank road built from Wellsboro to Tioga, in the year 1850.

—The *Democrat*, established by Charles G. Williams, in 1867.

—The *Herald of the Union*, established in 1866, by C. C. Keeler.

—In 1865, a division of the Sons of Temperance was organized

—R. Jenkins in 1858 founded a newspaper entitled *The Democrat*

—Tioga Chapter, R. A. M., No. 194, established August 15, 1859.

—Destructive fire in Wellsboro, October 23, 1873. Loss over $100,000.

—The first Court held in Wellsboro was in a log house in the year 1813.

—B. B. Smith, in 1827, established the *Phenix*, changed to the *Herald* in 1838.

—Chester and J. L. Robinson, opened a store in Wellsboro in the year 1834.

—George Travis executed for the murder of Martha Sylva, Jan. 15, 1885.

—Wellsboro Encampment, I. O. O. F., No. 78, instituted April 10, 1848.

—Academy established in Wellsboro in 1817; first principal, James P. Lowrey.

—Wellsboro adopted common schools in 1834-35; Erastus P. Deane employed as teacher.

—Presbyterian church organized February 11, 1843; Rev. Thomas Forster, of Harrisburg, pastor. Rev. J. F. Calkins became the pastor in 1844, and remained over thirty years.

—The Towanda and Barclay Railroad was constructed in the year 1856, from Towanda south westward, to the semi-bituminous coal mines, at Barclay, a distance of sixteen miles.

—The State Line and Sullivan Railroad was constructed in the year 1871. It runs from Towanda to the semi-anthracite coal mines at Bernice, in Sullivan county, a distance of twenty-eight miles. It is now owned by the Lehigh Valley Railroad Company.

TOWNSHIPS.—Albany, Asylum, Armenia, Athens, Barclay, Burlington, West Burlington, Canton, Columbia, Franklin, Granville, Herrick, LeRoy, Litchfield, Monroe, Orwell, Overton, Pike, Ridgebury, Rome, Smithfield, Springfield, South Creek, Sheshequin, Standing Stone, Terry, Towanda, North Towanda, Troy, Tuscarora, Ulster, Warren, Windham, Wyalusing, Wysox, Wells, Wilmot.

BOROUGHS.—Athens, Alba, Burlington, Canton, LeRaysville, Monroe, New Albany, Rome, South Waverly, Sylvania, Towanda, Troy.

POSTOFFICES.—Alba, Allis Hollow, Altus, Aspenwall, Asylum, Athens, Austinville, Ballibay, Barclay, Bently Creek, Big Pond, Birney, Black, Browntown, Burlington, Camptown, Canton, Carbon Run, Cold Creek, Columbia X Roads, Durell, East Canton, East Smithfield, East Troy, Edsallville, Ellwell, Evergreen, Fassett, Foot of Plane, Franklindale, Ghent, Gillett, Granville Center, Granville Summit, Green's Landing, Grover, Herrick, Herrickville, Highland, Homet's Ferry, Horn Brook, Imler Valley, Laddsburg, Leona, LeRaysville, Leroy, Liberty Corners, Lime Hill, Litchfield, Luthers Mills, Macedonia, Marshview, Mercur, Merryall, Milan, Monroeton, Mountain Lake, Myersburg, Neath, New Albany, New Era, North Orwell, North Rome, Orwell, Overton, Parks Creek, Potterville, Powell, Ridgebury, Rome, Rummerfield Creek, Sayre, Sciotaville, Sheshequin, Silvara, Snedekerville, South Branch, South Hill, South Litchfield, South Warren, Springfield, Springhill, Standing Stone, Stevensville, Sugar Run, Sylvania, Terrytown, Towanda, Troy, Tuscarora Valley, Ulster, Warren Center, Warrenham, Wells, West Burlington, West Franklin, West Warren, West Windham, Wetona, Williwana, Wilmot, Windham, Windham Center, Windham Summit, Wyalusing, Wysox.

MEMBERS OF THE HOUSE OF REPRESENTATIVES.—It will be recollected that Bradford county, or rather the territory comprising the present territory of Bradford, was a portion of the county of Westmoreland, under the Connecticut titles and sent members to Hartford semi-annually. The representatives from Bradford were: 1774, Christopher Avery; 1781, Obadiah Gore; Capt. John Franklin; 1782, Obediah Gore. In the years 1813-14, the representative district comprised Lycoming, Bradford, Tioga and Potter counties, and Hon. Henry Welles, was the representative in the Pennsylvania State Legislature. From 1815 to 1819, Bradford and Tioga counties constituted a representative district, and Hon. Samuel McKean, represented Bradford from 1815 to 1819 inclusive. In 1820-22, Simon Kinney represented the district. In the year 1822, Bradford became a separate district and the representative was Hon. William Myer, from 1822 23; then in 1823-24, Lemuel Streator; 1824-28, Constant Mathewson; 1828-29, John LaPorte; 1829-32, John LaPorte, who was speaker in 1832. Two members to the district—1833, Lockwood Smith; 1835-6, Darius Bullock, Isaac Myer. District of Bradford alone—1836-37, Isaac Cooley; 1837-38, George Kinney; 1838-40, David F. Barstow; 1840-41, Stephen F. Pierce; 1841-43, William Elwell. Bradford, two members—1843 45, John Elliott, Irad Wilson; 1845-47, John L. Webb, Victor E. Piollett; 1847-48, Francis Smith, Allen E. Thomas; 1848-49, Charles Stockwell, A. Wattles; 1849-50, Charles Stockwell, Joseph C. Powell; 1850-52, Addison McKean, Henry Gibbs; 1852-54, John Passmore, William E. Barton; 1854-56, Judson Holcomb, Bartholomew LePorte; 1856-58, John G. Babcock, Cullen F. Nichols; 1858-60, O. H. P. Kinney, Thomas Smead; 1860-62, Chester T. Bliss, Henry W. Tracy; 1862-63, Bartholomew LePorte, D. Lilley; 1863-64, Joseph H. Marsh, D. Lilley; 1864-65, Joseph H. Marsh, Lorenzo Grinnell; 1865-66, G. Wayne Kinney, Lorenzo Grinnell; 1866-67, G. Wayne Kinney, James H. Webb; 1867-70, John F. Chamberlain, James H. Webb; 1870-71 Perley H. Buck, James H. Webb, the latter elected speaker. 1871 72, Perley H. Buck, B. S. Dartt; 1872-73, E. Reed Myer, B. S. Dartt; 1873-74, E. Reed Myer, James H. Webb; 1875-77, George Moscrip, Elijah G. Tracy, Uriah Terry; 1877-78, E. Reed Myer, elected speaker; James Foster, John F. Gillett.

PRESIDENT JUDGES.—1812 to 1816, John Bannister Gibson; 1817, Thomas Burnside; 1818 to 1839, Edward Herrick; 1839 to 1849, John N. Conyngham; 1849 to 1851, Horace Willison; 1852 to 1861, David Wilmot; 1861 to 1865, Ulysses Mercur: 1865 to 1874, F. B. Streeter; 1874, Paul D. Morrow.

ASSOCIATE JUDGES.—October 13th, 1812 to May, 1818, George Scott; October 13, 1812 to May, 1837, John McKean; 1818 to 1841, Jonathan Stevens; 1837 to 1845, John LaPorte; 1841 to 1844, Abraham Goodwin; 1845, David M. Bull; 1846 to 1851, Harry Morgan, Reuben Wilber; 1851 to 1856, Myron Ballard, Harry Ackley; 1856, Aaron Chubbuck, John F. Long; 1858, John Passmore; 1861, V. M. Long; 1863, L. P. Stalford; 1866, J. Wilson VanDyke; 1868, Zebulon Frisbie; 1871, Stephen D. Harkness; 1873, Chauncy S. Russell;

ADDITIONAL LAW JUDGE.—Paul D. Morrow, 1870 to 1874.

PROTHONOTARIES.—1812 to 1818, Charles F. Welles; 1818 to 1830, George Scott; 1830-31, Darius Bullock; 1831, Alpheus Ingham, 1831-36, James P. Bull; 1836, Samuel Stra ght; 1836-39, Joseph C. Powell; 1839, David Cash; 1842, Aaron Chubbuck; 1845, Addison McKean; 1848, Allen McKean; 1860, E. O. Goodrich; 1866, William A. Thomas; 1872, Benjamin M. Peck.

SHERIFFS.—1812, Abner C. Rockwell; 1815, John Spalding; 1818, Lemuel Streator; 1821, Joseph C. Powell; 1824, Reuben Wilbur; 1827, Benjamin McKean; 1830, Lockwood Smith Jr.; 1833, John L. Webb; 1836, Guy Tozier; 1839, Ira H. Stevens; 1842, John N. Weston; 1845, John F. Means; 1848, William S. Dobbins; 1851, Chester Thomas; 1854, John A. Codding; 1857, Thomas M. Woodruff; 1860. A. H. Splanding; 1863, James Monroe Smith; 1866, William Griffis; 1869, J. P. VanFleet. 1872, Thomas Monroe Smith; 1875, Andrew J. Layton.

DISTRICT ATTORNEYS.—1850, Thomas Smead; 1853, James Macfarlane; 1856, Paul D. Morrow; 1859, Guy H. Watkins; 1862, George D. Montanye;

1865, William T. Davies; 1868, Warner H. Cornachan; 1871, Joseph B. Read; 1874, John N. Califf; 1877, Isaiah McPherson.

CORONERS. - 1813, John Horton; 1819, John Minier; 1822, Chauncy Frisbie; 1824, John Fox; 1827, John L. Webb; 1837, Aaron Knapp; 1839, Henry J. Salsbury; 1842, Calvin Storms; 1845, John Hatch; 1848, Thomas I. Ingham; 1854, W. W. Easterbrook; 1857, Newall Leonard; 1860, Jeremiah Culp; 1863, Abram Snell, Jr.; 1866, Joseph H. Hurst; 1869, John F. Dodd; 1872, J. B. Geiger; 1875, D. B. Walker;

COUNTY TREASURERS. - 1813, Henry Spalding; 1815, William Means; 1816, Simon Kinney; 1818, Henry Mercur; 1821, Gurdon Hewett; 1823, George Scott; 1824, Andrew Irvine; 1827, J. P. Bull; 1829, Alpheus Ingham; 1830, Andrew Irvine; 1831, William Russell; 1833, Chauncey Frisbie; 1835, D. M. Bull; 1838, John E. Hale; 1839, Charles Stockwell; 1841, William B. Storm; 1843, Leonard Pierce; 1845, Jacob Reed; 1847, James N. Peck; 1849, John Horton; 1851, Benjamin Wilcox; 1853, P. Forbes; 1855, Ezra C. Kellog; 1857, Edward P. Shaw; 1859, William Griffis; 1861, Francis Watts; 1863, Stephen D. Harkness; 1865, J. P. Van-Fleet; 1867, Charles A. Morey; 1869, C. K. Ladd; 1871, William Bunyan; 1875, James C. Robinson.

COUNTY COMMISSIONERS.—1812, Joseph Kinney, Justus Gaylord, William Myer; 1813, Burr Ridgway; 1814, Clement Paine: 1815, Samuel McKean; 1816, Salmon Bosworth; 1816, Nathaniel Allen; 1817, Eliphalet Mason; 1818, Joseph C. Powell 1819, Bartholomew LaPorte; 1820, William Myer; 1821; George Hyde; 1822, Lemuel Streator; 1823, Darius Bullock; 1824, John Taylor; 1825, Theodore Leonard; 1826, Gould Seymour; 1827, Burton Strait; 1828, Churchill Barnes; 1829, Hezekiah Dunham; 1830, Eliphalet Mason; 1831, John L. Webb; 1832, Isaac Cooley; 1833, John Elliott; 1834, Morris Spalding; 1835, Elias Rockwell; 1836, Henry Morgan; 1836, E. S. Goodrich; 1837, Daniel Park; 1838, Ira Stevens; 1839, Myron Ballard, Ira Willson; 1840, Benjamin Buffington; 1841, Edson Aspinwall; 1842, Daniel Brink; 1843, Joseph Turner; 1844, Luman Putman; 1845, Ashbel S. Cranmer; 1846, John H. Black; 1847, Hiram Spear; 1848, Simeon Decker; 1849, Augustus I. Smith; 1850, Sturgess Squires; 1851, Daniel B. Cotton; 1852, Isaac A. Park; 1853, Stewart Smiley; 1854, George H. Bull; 1855, Perley H. Buck; 1856, Dummer Lilly; 1857, Daniel Decker; 1858, Perley H. Buck; 1859, William A. Thomas; 1860, William H Decker; 1861, Isaac Lyon; 1862, Joseph Campbell; 1863, William B. Dodd; 1864, John Beardsley; 1865, Sterne McKee; 1866, William B. Dodge; 1867, John A. Moody; 1868, Asa McKee, Jr.; 1869, John B. Hindes; 1870, E. C. Kelley; 1871, Morris Shepard; 1872, Benjamin Kirkendall; 1873, Abram Snell; 1874, Morris Shepard; 1875, John Baldwin, M. J. Coolbaugh, George W. Kilmer.

COUNTY SURVEYORS—1812, Jonathan Stevens; 1821, Zephon Flowers; 1833, James M. Edsall; 1836, Rowland Wilcox; 1850, Edward G. Nichols; 1853, James A. Paine; 1856, Joseph E. Spalding; 1859, Josiah J. Newell; 1868, Oliver W. Stevens; 1871, Joseph E. Spalding; 1874 George V. Myer; 1877, T. A. Stewart.

MEMBERS OF CONGRESS.—1822-24, Samuel McKean; 1834-36, John LaPorte

1844-50, David Wilmot; 1862-64, Henry W. Tracy; 1664-71, Ulysses Mercur; 1874 76, Joseph Powell; 1876-78 Edward Overton.

JUDGE OF UNITED STATES COURT OF CLAIMS.—David Wilmot appointed in the year 1863.

CONSUL TO WEST INDIES.—Edward H. Perkins appointed in 1862.

SURVEYOR OF THE PORT OF PHILADELPHIA.-E. O'Mara Goodrich appointed in 1869.

Samuel McKean appointed Secretary of the Commonwealth in the year 1829

SURVEYOR GENERAL.—John LePorte in the year 1845.

DEPUTY SECRETARY OF THE COMMONWEALTH.-Elisha S. Goodrich, in 1852.

CHIEF CLERK AUDITOR GENERAL'S DEPARTMENT.—Edward Herrick, May, 1878.

JUSTICE OF SUPREME COURT.—Ulysses S. Mercur, 1872; now Chief Justice.

STATE SENATORS.—1815, Henry Welles; 1829, Samuel McKean; 1830, Reuben Wilbur; 1837, Elihu Case; 1850, George Sanderson; 1856, E. Reed Myer; 1859, George Landon; 1874, Delos Rockwell; 1877, William T. Davies.

First court held in Bradford county commenced January, 1813, John Bannister Gibson president judge, John McKean and George Scott associates, Abner C. Rockwell sheriff, Charles F. Welles prothonotary.

In May, 1770, Rudolph Fox settled at a point near the borough of Towanda.

J. Conrad Weiser, an Indian interpreter, visited (Diahago) Athens, March 29, 1737.

In 1755, Lewis Evans published a map which described the territory embracing Bradford county.

May 20, 1760, Christain Frederic Post preached to the Indians in Bradford county.

Ziesberger, the Moravian missionary, commenced preaching to the Indians in Bradford county in the year 1763.

The Moravian village of Friedenshutten, in Bradford county, was named thus, by the Moravian Synod which convened at Bethlehem, now Northhampton county, in June, 1766.

A monument was erected June 15, 1871, to mark the site of Friedenshutten.

The Susquehanna Land Company was formed in Connecticut, July 8, 1753, the object being to purchase and sell lands now in Bradford county.

About one hundred families had settled within the present limits of Bradford county prior to the revolutionary war.

June 12, 1778, William Crooks was killed by the Indians, the first death at the hands of the Indians upon the north branch of the Susquehanna river during the revolutionary war.

General Sullivan passed through Bradford county with his army against the Indians in 1779.

September, 1778, Col. Thomas Hartley with a small army visited Bradford county to chastise the Indians.

Great floods in the Susquehanna March 15, 1784, October 1786, March 17 1865.

The first lawyer in Bradford County was William Prentice.

Alexander Wilson, the Ornithologist, visited Bradford on his way to Niagara Falls in the year 1804.

The Asylum Land Company, composed of French refugees, was formed April 22, 1794, and purchased large tracts of land in Bradford, Lycoming, Luzerne and Sullivan counties from Robert Morris of Philadelphia. They named their village in Bradford county, Asylum. They were visited by Talleyrand and Louis Phillippe.

Thomas Overton gave the land for the public square at Towanda in the year 1811.

Bradford County Teachers Association organized January 5, 1855, Rev. James McWilliams, President, P. D. Morrow Secretary.

Bradford County Historical Society organized at Towanda, May 4th, 1870. Hon. L. P. Statford, President; Dr. E. P. Allen, Secretary. Officers elected, President, Christopher L. Ward; Vice-Presidents, Dr. Darius Bullock, Hon. F. B. Streeter; Recording Secretary, Dr. E. P. Allen; Corresponding Secretary, Edward Herrick, Jr.; Treasurer, L. P. Statford; Librarian, H. L. Scott.

The Agricultural and Manufacturing Society of Bradford County, incorporated by an act of the legislature in 1820.

Troy Farmer's Club organized January 2, 1875. J. C. McKean, President; G. M. Card, Secretary; A. M. Cornell, Treasurer; A. S Hooker, Reporting Secretary. First fair held October 8th and 9th, 1875.

The Bradford County Bar Association was organized Dec. 17, 1877. President, Elhannan Smith; Vice President, H. J. Madill; Secretary, John F. Sanderson; Treasurer, Henry Streeter.

Bradford County Medical Society was organized in August, 1847. Dr. Samuel Huston, President; Alexander Madill, Secretary.

A printing office was established in Towanda, in 1813.

The *Bradford Gazette* was founded in Towanda, in 1814, by Burr Ridgeway, Gen. Samuel McKean, Gen. Henry Welles and George Scott.

The *Washingtonian* was published in 1815, by Lewis B. Franc.

The *Towanda Republican* was issued in 1826, by Warren Jenkins.

Bradford Argus was first issued by O. P. Ballard in 1829.

The *Bradford Democrat* was first issued in 1836, by Cantine & Hogan.

The *Bradford Reporter* was first issued by E. S. Goodrich, June, 1840.

The *North Branch Democrat* was first issued by Wean Forney in 1850.

The *Towanda Business Item* was first issued August 5th, 1871, by O. D. Goodenough and E. J. Clawson.

The *Bradford Republican* was first issued June 1st, 1875, by Judson Holcomb and T. G. Angus.

The *Towanda Journal* was first issued May 14, 1873, by D. M. Turner.

The *Anti-Masonic Democrat* was published at Troy, in 1830, by O.P. Ballard.

The *Analyzer* was first issued at Troy, by Francis Smith, in the year 1840.

The *New Star* was first issued by O. P. Ballard, at Troy, in the year 1846.

The *Troy Banner* was first issued in 1847, by William C. Webb.

The *Trogan* was first issued in 1850, by Barkley & Messenger.

The *Independent* was issued in 1854, at Troy, by Doctor Johnson.

The *Temperance Banner* was first issued at Troy, by Moses Gustin, in 1855.

The *Troy Times* was issued in 1863, by A. C. Lumbard, now the *Northern Tier Gazette*, edited by A. S. Hooker.

Athens Scribe was issued in 1841, by Owen Worden.

The *Athenian* issued in the year 1841, at Athens, William F. Warner, Edwin C. Marvin, James H Forbes and Ezra O. Long, editors.

The *Democratic Laborer's Advocate* was issued at Athens, March 3, 1843, by Owen Worden and Jason K. Wright.

The *Athens Gazette*, issued in 1855, by Mark M. Pomeroy.

The *Athens Republican* was issued in 1866, by S. Frank Lathrop.

The *Weekly Athens News*, issued in 1868, by D. V. Stedge.

The *Athens Gleaner* was issued March 16, 1870, by Charles T. Huston.

The *Athens Gazette* was issused in April, 1870, by Charles Hinton.

Bradford Democrat was issued Sept. 1875, by Cannon Brothers, at Athens.

The *Athenians* was issued in 1876, by Julius Corbin.

Canton Sentinel was issued in 1871, by C. H. Butts & Son.

Rome Register was issued in 1875, by Cannon Brothers.

Troy Register issued by Frank Loomis, in 1883.

Albany Township.

Albany township was formed in 1824, taken from the township of Asylum. The Fowler branch of the Towanda Creek runs through the township. The Sullivan and State Line Railroad from Towanda to the mines at Bernice also passes through the town, having a station at New Albany. The surface is hilly, but is being brought up to a good state of cultivation. The early settlers were Sheffield Wilcox, Horatio Ladd, Daniel Miller, Ephraim Ladd, Charles W. Ladd, John Ladd, Joseph Langford, Jonathan Fowler, Roger Fowler, Rowland Wilcox, Freeman Wilcox, Sheffield Wilcox, Jr., Edward Warren, Ephraim Granger, Calvin Granger, Dorus Granger, John B. Hinman, Humphrey Goff, Jonathan Frisbie, William Lee, Amzi Kellogg, Archelous Luce, William Miller, John Fogerty, John Nichols, Simeon Chapman, Peter Sterriger, Hugh Cavanaugh, Henry Hibbard, David Sabin. It is bounded on the north by Monroe and Asylum townships, on the east by Terry and Wilmot, on the south by Sullivan county, and on the west by Overton.

—The Wilcox family were Rhode Islanders.

—Louisa Alden taught the first school in 1812.

—Charlotte Wilcox was the first white child born in the township.

—The Ladds, early settlers, were from Tolland county Connecticut.

—The first saw mill was erected in 1820, by Sheffield Wilcox and his relatives.

—The Berwick and Newtown turnpike was constructed through the township in 1818.

—Daniel Miller, one of the first settlers, died October 8, 1856, aged 77 years, 9 months, 2 days.

—Horatio Ladd died January 12, 1850, aged 70 years. He was one of the first settlers in 1801.

—The first death was Ezekiel Ladd July 20, 1803, who was killed at a raising, a timber falling on him.

—A Post of the Grand Army was established at New Albany, June 26, 1877, number of post 72.

—Chauncey Corbin cleared the first farm between the Berwick and Newtown turnpike and the river.

—New Albany Grange Patrons of Husbandry, No 205, Amasa Heverly, first master, F. N. Wilcox, secretary.

—The Universalist Church at Hibbard Hill, was organized in 1844 by Rev. J. P. Sweet, church erected in 1862.

—Horatio Ladd, Daniel Miller, Rowland Wilcox, C. W. Ladd, Freeman Wilcox, Humphrey Goff, were drafted for the defence of Washington in 1814.

—The Baptist Church at New Albany was formed in 1849, church erected in 1879. William McKnown was the first resident minister in 1852, Stephen Harris deacon, John W. Martin clerk.

—New Albany Lodge No 682, I. O. O. F., was organized December 23, 1869, G. W. Burdick Noble Grand, Geooge H. Kendall Vice Grand, S. D. Sterriger Secretary, D. W. Harshberger, Treasurer

—The first permanent settlement was made in 1801, by Sheffield Wilcox and Horatio Ladd, who received a gratuity of seventy-five acres each from Doctor Joseph Priestly, the owner of a large portion of the lands in the township.

Asylum Township.

The township of Asylum was formed in 1814, taken from Wyalusing. The French refugees gave it the name in 1793, who purchased large tracts of land in Bradford, Lycoming, Luzerne and Sullivan counties. It is bounded on the north and east by the Susquehanna river, on the south by Terry and Albany, on the west by Monroe and Towanda. The early settlers were French refugees; among them were Omer Talon, a banker of Paris, M. D. Blacons, M. D. Montule, M. Beaulieu, Dr. Bazzard, of San Domingo, M. Dupetit-Thouars, in all about forty families, who erected a village named Asylum. They remained in the country until about the year 1800, when a large portion of them returned to France.

In 1795, Louis Phillipe afterwards King of France, and Tallyrand visited Asylum.

The early permanent settlers were Stephen Durell, Benjamin Ackla, Richard Benjamin, Amos Bennett, Dea. Ruben Wells, John Shaw, Ezra Shaw, Samuel Gilbert, Charles Homet, Anthony Vanderpool, Isaac Wheeler, Nicholas Johnson, Richard Wheeler, Ambrose Vincent, Henry Cornelius, Samuel Seeley, Samuel Chilson, Jehiel Chilson, Joel Chilson, Robert Chilson, George Chilson, Anson Chilson, William Chilson, Nathan Bailey, Harry Elsworth, John Stringer, Joseph H. Ellis, Solomon Cole, Phillip Fox, Elisha Cole, Abisha Cole, John Cole, Moses Warford, Benjamin Coolbaugh, S. Holden, Jabez Sill, Charles Townley, Richard Townley, Robert Alexander, R. Cooley, Benajah Stone.

—Solomon Cole was the first settler at Macedonia, in Asylum township.

—Stephen Durell, Isaac Wheeler, Henry Cornelius, Samuel Seeley, Solomon Cole, Jabez Sill, Amos Bennett were pioneer settlers in Asylum township and soldiers in the revolutionary war.

—Stephen Durell built a saw mill in 1792 in Asylum township.

—Samuel Seeley, an early settler and a revolutionary soldier, died in 1840, aged 88 years.

—A log school house was erected in Asylum in 1798. The first teacher was William McCarty.

—Isaac Wheeler, an early settler at Asylum, was a drummer boy in the revolutionary war. He drew a pension.

—Anthony Vanderpool came to Asylum in 1790, he died in 1838, aged 99 years. President Martin VanBuren married his niece.

—Charles Homet, an early settler emigrated from France in January, 1793, and settled in Asylum in 1796. He died December 29, 1838, aged 70 years.

Armenia Township.

Armenia township was formed in 1843, taken from Troy and Canton townships. It occupies an elevated position on the western line of the county and forms the water shed between the waters of Sugar creek and the Tioga river. The Tioga rises in the township and flows in a southwesterly course into the township of Ward in Tioga county. Although the lands of the township are situated at an average elevation of eighteen hundred feet above the sea level, still the soil is quite productive and a number of good farms are found in the township. From its elevated position some of the finest landscape views in Northern Pennsylvania are obtained. It is bounded on the north by Columbia township, on the east by Troy and Canton, on the south by Canton and on the west by Tioga county.

Early settlers were: Newton Harvey, George Hawkins, Heman Mc gan, Samuel Avery, Silas E. Shepard, Amasa Wood, Joel Wood, Ne Phinney, Samuel Moore, Joseph Biddle, Alexander Case, John Lyon, Burnham, Daniel Crandall, William Crandall, Andrew Monroe, Ly C. Shepard, Wightman Pierce, William Covert, Abizer Fields, Mason, Robert Mason, James Mason, John J. Reynolds, Timothy John S. Becker, Jacob Y. Dumond, Gasper Webber, C. H. We P. Smith, Lyman Hinman.

—The first school house was built in 1834.

—L. P. Newell erected a saw mill, at Armenia, in 1835.

—Rev. Samuel Salsbury preached first in 1835 in the tow

—The Wesleyan Methodists organized a church in 1845 in 1879.

—The Tioga river rises in Armenia township, and f thence north to Corning, east to Elmira and south t having flowed one hundred and twenty miles, is v source and flowing in the same direction.

—In 1860 there were sixty-two votes cast in t furnished fifty-seven soldiers to the Union arm menia during the war of the rebellion lost the Abner Miller, Barlow Smith, Herrick Welc Rundell, James Whitehead, John H. Dur Knight, Albert Woodworth.

—The first school was established at Athens, in 1788, Ezekiel Root, teacher.

—In 1773, Charles Stewart, Deputy Survey General of the State of Pennsylvania, or Colony, or Proprietaryship of Pennsylvania, laid out lots in Athens.

—Rural Amity Lodge, No. 70, A. Y. Masons, organized in 1798. Officers, Arnold Colt, W. M.; Dr. Stephen Hopkins, S. W.; Capt. Ira Hopkins, J. W. Fourteen original members.

—Athens township, east of the Susquehanna river, was embraced in a purchase made of the Indians at Fort Stanwix, in 1768. The lands west of the river were purchased of the Indians in 1784.

—Guy Maxwell was appointed Justice of the Peace, at Athens, Sept. 1, 1791. In 1796, he removed to Elmira. The late Hon. Thomas Maxwell was born at Athens during the residence of his father there.

—Athens Lodge, No. 165, I. O. O. F., organized March 9, 1846. Reorganized Nov. 2, 1874; J. B. Reeve, Noble Grand; D. W. Tripp, Vice Grand; J. M. Ely, Secretary; A. F. Ovenshire, Treasurer.

—Hon. Samuel J. Atlee, Hon. William Maclay and Francis Johnson, held a council with the Indians, at Athens, in 1784, in behalf of the State of Pennsylvania. They distributed a large number of presents to the Indians, and secured the right of settlement upon the west side of the Susquehanna.

—In 1785, William Maclay, as a Commissioner of Pennsylvania, established a temporary line between New York and Pennsylvania, at Athens. The line was again run by State Commissioners of New York and Pennsylvania, in 1786, and permanently established It commenced about sixty-four miles east of Athens, on the Delaware and continued to Lake Erie.

Alba Borough.

Alba borough was formed 1863, taken from Canton township. It is situated on the line of the Northern Central Railroad, and contains a population of about three hundred inhabitants. It is surrounded by a fine agricultural district. The early settlers were Noah Wilson, Elihue Smead, Caleb Williams, Reuben Case, Reuben Rowley, Elisha Luther, Kilburn Morely, Jeremiah Smith, Samus Rockwell, David Pratt, Levi Morse, Irad Wilson, Robert McKean, David Soper.

—Patty Luther was the first who died in Alba in 1804.

—Martha Wilson taught the first school in Alba in 1806.

—Col. Irad Wilson was the first post master at Alba.

—Noah Wilson was the first settler in Alba, in the spring of 1803.

—The first child born was July 17, 1804, a daughter of Noah Wilson.

—The school was closed in 1806, on account of the eclipse of the sun.

—The first religious meeting was held in 1808, by Rev. Simeon Powers, a Baptist minister.

—Noah Wilson was appointed Justice of the Peace by Gov. Snyder and held the office until 1838.

—Col. Irad Wilson was county commissioner in 1839, and a member of the Pennsylvania House of Representatives in 1843.

—The Baptist organized the first church in 1818. Samuel Rockwell and R. R. Rogers deacons. Church erected in 1818.

—The meaning of the word Alba is white.

—Robert McKean and Martha Wilson, David Soper and Polly Luther were married at the same time, in 1807. The first marriages in Alba.

Barclay Township.

Barclay township was organized in 1867, taken from Franklin. It is bounded on the north by Franklin, on the east by Monroe and Overton, on the south by Overton, on the west by Leroy. It is situated in the highlands in the southwestern portion of the county, about two thousand feet above sea level. The business of mining semi-bituminous coal has been carried on quite extensively since 1856, when a railroad from Towanda, a distance of about sixteen miles was constructed. It was named Barclay in honor of Charles Barclay, of London, England, the owner of lands in the township. The history of Barclay would be the history of the mining companies which have been engaged in mining coal. Several million tons of coal have been mined and shipped to market since the commencement of mining operations. Barclay is a mining village containing about eight hundred inhabitants, who are chifly engaged in mining, or in labor connected therewith. Carbon Run a mining village about two miles west of Barclay, which formerly contained about three hundred inhabitants, is now about entirely deserted, the coal being worked out as is alleged. The coal is let down from the Barclay mountain, by means of an incline to the foot of the plane, from whence it is taken by cars and locomotives to Towanda.

—Mountain Cliff Lodge, Knights of Pythias, was organized April 8th, 1873. First officers were: John Kellock, V. P.; F. M. Miner, C. C.; William Johnson, V. C.; John Noble, K. of R. S.

—Barclay Lodge, No. 807, I. O. O. F., was organized July 12th, 1872. Charles Hutchinson, N. G.; John Deitchburn, V. G.; L. S. Kelder, Sec.; Edward Wheatley, Treas.

—The Barclay Coal Company was organized in 1853, by Edward Overton of Towanda, John Ely and Edward M. Davis, of Philadelphia. Edward Overton, first President; James Macfarlane, General Superintendent.

Burlington Township.

The township of Burlington was one of the original townships in Bradford county, having been formed prior to the organizaiton of the county, in 1786. It is bounded on the north by Smithfield and Ulster, on the east by North Towanda and Towanda, on the south by Franklin, on the west by West Burlington. The township is well watered by Sugar Creek and its tributaries. Its surface is rolling, and the soil well adapted to grazing and agricultural products generally. There are four post offices in the township Highland, Luther's Mills, Burlington, Mountain Lake. The great Indian path from the North Branch of the Susquehanna to the west branch of the Susquehanna, passed through the township. The early settlers were Isaac Dewitt, Abram Dewitt, James McKean, William Dobbins, James Ward, Alexander Campbell, Derrick Miller, Ebenezer Dunbar, Ephraim Swain, Ira Nicholds, Jared Soper, Ezra Brafit, Ephraim Jacque, Ezra Goddard, Luther Goddard, Stephen Ballard, Joseph Ballard, John Ballard, Nathaniel

Ballard, John Clark, Moses Calkins, Jeremiah Taylor, Benjamin Saxton, Jessie Marvin, Jehiel Ferris, John Gammage, George Head, James Campbell, David Campbell, Eliphalet Luther, Col. Lockwood, Nehemiah Allen, John McNean, Joel Calkins, David Miller, William Pratt, Otho a colored man, Samuel McKean, Samuel Wallace, Timothy Hosmer, Major William Judd, John Jenkins John Clark, Champion Scoville, Ebenezer Kendall, Reuben Wilbur, Jehiel Ferris, Jesse Beach, Timothy Beach, Doct. Ira Lee, Oliver Nelson, Lawson Hemengway.

—Burlington borough was established in 1853.

—Burlington was formely known as Juddsburg.

—Jehiel Ferris was the first shoemaker in Burlington.

—The first highway in Burlington was made in 1791.

—Burlington was named after Burlington, Vermont.

—The first school house in Burlington was erected in 1791.

—Ezra Goddard was the first merchant in Burlington, in 1796.

—The first orchard was set out by Ebenezer Kendall, in 1799.

—A number of cases of small pox occurred in 1807, in Burlington.

—Ezra Goddard built the first grist and saw mill in Burlington, in 1798.

—The first settlers of Burlington were from the town of Chemung, N. Y.

—The first Methodist preacher, who visited Burlington, was Rev. Mr. Newman.

—The celebrated Lorenzo Dow, visited Burlington in June, 1806, and preached.

—Charles Carroll, of Carrollton, was a heavy land owner in Burlington township.

—The religious service was held in 1791, by Mrs. James McKean and Mrs. William Dobbins.

—At the first election held in the township of Burlington, there was a wedding, a barbecue, and a dance.

—Burlington Lodge, No. 904, I. O. O. F., was organized March 26, 1875, L. M. Rundell, N. G., P. P. Burns, V. G., N. W. Lane, Sec., R. R. Phelps, Treas.

—Noah Wilson, Nathaniel Allen, James Campbell, James McKean and Eli Case, were the first election board of Burlington. The election was held at the house of Ezra Goddard.

—In 1822, in digging a celler for Gen. Samuel McKean, a stone vault was found, which contained a sketeton of a human being, measuring eight feet two inches in length. A pine tree was growing over the vault three feet in diameter.

—Tom Zack was a Moravian convert, of the Mingo tribe of Indians, and was known as the white man's friend, lived at Burlington, on the Tom Zack Creek. His wife was Betty Montour. His daughter, "White Fawn," was educated by the Moravians, and became a teacher.

—Dr. Ira Lee, an English physician, attempted to introduce vaccination for small pox in 1813, in Burlington, and was compelled to leave the town. The war between United States and Great Britian was then going on, and the inhabitants conceived that Dr. Lee was a secret emissary, employed by the Brisish Governmet to destroy the American people.

—Captain Daniel Dobbins, son of one of the old settlers of Burlington, was in command of a merchant vessel, owned by himself and Mr. Rufus H. Reed, of Erie Pa.; when the war of 1812 occured. He was a t Detroit and was taken prisioner, he was subsequently retaken by Gen. Hull, and again surrendered into the hands of the British, being released he was detailed by General Mead to go to Washington with important dispatches concerning the surrender of Detroit. Upon his arrival at Washington a cabinet meeting was called and he recommended in view of the loss of Detroit, that a naval depot should be established at Presque Isle, in the present harbor of Erie Pa. His suggestion was received with favor, and he was immediately commissioned to enter upon the work of establishing such a depot. He returned to Erie and commenced the construction of gun boats, and in March following, Commodore Perry arrived. Captain Dobbins continued in active service until he had the proud satisfaction of seeing the fleet which he had equipped and manned, commanded by Commodore Perry, victorious in the battle of Lake Erie on the 10th of September, 1814. Thus did a Bradford county citizen contribute towards establishing Erie as a naval port, and the success of Commodore Perry.

Canton Township and Borough.

Canton township is situated in the extreme southwest portion of Bradford county. The sources of Towanda creek, which flows eastward into the North Branch of the Susquehanna, and the sources of the Lycoming creek or river which flows southward into the West Branch of the Susquehanna, are found in this township. The Northern Central Railroad passes through the township from south to north, having several stations in the township. Canton and Alba are boroughs which have been formed from its territory. East Canton, Grover and Minnequa, are villages and post towns. The soil is well adapted to grazing, orchard products, and growing of corn, oats, buckwheat and wheat. Some of the finest farms and farm dwellings and capacious barns in the county are found in Canton. Canton borough stands third in the county as a shipping point for agricultural and other products, and is only excelled by Troy and Towanda. Canton borough is rapidly increasing in wealth and population.

The early settlers were: Rufus Gere, Orr Scoville, Ezra Spalding, Horace Spalding, Jonas Gere, Jonathan Prosser, Alvin Cook, Gershon Gillett, Wilkes Gillett, Zephaniah Rogers, Zephaniah Rogers, Jr., John Newell, Dr. Moses Emerson, Ichabob Sellard, Labon Landon, Benjamin Landon, Major Withey, Ebenezer Bixby, Samuel Griffin, Nathan Roberts, Samuel Griffin, Jr., Joel Bullock, Abram Taber, Jacob Granteer, Isaiah Grover, Benjamin Babcock, Nathaniel Babcock, Samuel Rockwell, David Pratt, Stephen Sellard, Elisha Wilcox, Stephen Strickland, Amos Strickland.

—Ezra Spalding kept the first hotel in 1799.

—Canton borough was incorporated in 1863.

—Orr Scoville built the first framed house, in Canton.

—Samuel Strait opened the first bank in Canton, in 1871.

—Dr. Sylvester was the first regular physician in the town.

—The first settler in the town of Canton, was Rufus Gere, in 1796.

—Zepaniah Rogers built the first grist mill. It was a small concern.

—Canton borough was originally known as "Canton Four Corners."

—Canton was named in honor of a town by that name in Connecticut.

—Samuel Griffin erected the first school house in the township, in 1803.

—Samuel Griffin, an early settler of Canton, was a revolutionary soldier.

—Ezra Spalding, an early settler of Canton, was a soldier of the revolution.

—Miss Emma Seagar taught the first school in 1803, now within Canton borough.

—Loren Kingsbury taught the first school in Canton township, in the winter of 1801 2.

—The early settlers in Canton, had to go to Towanda, Tioga Point, Newtown or Williamsport, for their "store goods."

—Canton Lodge, A. Y. Masons, No 415, instituted March 4th, 1868. C. W. Landon, W. M.; Warren Landon, S. W.; W. W. Whitman, J. W.; B. W. Clark, Sec.

—Minnequa Lodge, No. 374, Knights of Pythias, instituted in April 1871. Theodore Pierce, V. P.; J. A. McNaught, C. C.; E. L. Manley, V. C.; M. R. Doty, K. of R. S.

—Canton Lodge, No. 321, I. O. O. F., organized October 29, 1848. First officers were: William Gosline, N. G.; Dr. W. S. Baker, V. G.; A C. Pickard, Sec.; J. W. Griffin, Treas.

Columbia Township.

Columbia township was organized in 1813, taken from Smithfield. It is situated on the western line of the county of Bradford, adjoining the townships of Sullivan and Rutland in Tioga county. The north and south branches of Sugar Creek run through the township, from west to east. It is bounded on the north by the townships of Wells and South Creek, on the east by Springfield, on the south by Troy and Armenia, and on the west by Tioga county. The Northern Central Railroad touches its eastern borders, and Snedekers, and Columbia Cross Roads are stations in the township on that road. Austinville and Sylvania are villages, the latter an incorporated boro. The soil is well adapted to grazing, and the growing of all kinds of cereals. It is an excellent farming township.

The early settlers were John Ballard, Nathaniel Ballard, Nathaniel Morgan, David Watkins, Oliver Canfield, Joseph Batterson, Jeremiah Chapman, Aaron Bennett, Samuel Lamphere, Phineas C. Morgan, Solomon Soper William Rose, James Morgan, Elnathan Goodrich, Charles Keyes, David Palmer, Ebenezer Baldwin, Abraham Weast, Calvin Tinkham, Carter Havens, John Bixby, Nathaniel Barrett, Samuel Baldwin, Asa Howe, Comfort Peters, Sheldon Gibbs, Phineas Jones, Rev. Joseph Beeman, David R. Hazewell, John P. Gurnet, William Furman, Reuben Nash, Jacob Miller, John Lilly, Michael Wolfe, Oliver Besley, George Moore, Darius Sherman, John McCelland, Asa Bullock, Joseph Gladding, Vial A. Bullock, Thomas Munroe, Henry Harris, Levi Cornell, Peleg Peckham, Kingley Peckham, John Calkins, Moses Calkins, A. M. Wright, Richard Doty, David Watson, Samuel Ingalls, Samuel Hurlburt, Murray Ballard, Ezra Wright.

—The first house erected in the township was by Richard Doty, in 1795.

—Columbia was originally known as Cabot.

—Rev. Mr. Rich was the first Methodist minister.

—The first distillery was built by Sheldon Gibbs.

—Austinville was originally called Morgan Hollow.

—Jared Rowley erected the first grist mill in the town.

—Sylvania was incorporated as a borough May 4, 1853.

—The first death was a child of Capt. Calkins, in 1810.

—The first school house was erected in 1814, by Moses Taylor.

—Darius Sherman was the first blacksmith in Columbia township.

—Peleg Peckham was the first carpenter in the town of Columbia.

—An Equitable Aid Union Lodge was organized at Sylvania, Feb., 1885.

—Charles Keyes, erected the first framed house in the township, in 1808.

—Oliver Besley, brought the first lumber wagon to Columbia, in 1812.

—The first saw mill was erected in 1806, by Samuel Hurlburt and Murray Ballard.

—Laura Watkins born August, 1800, was the first white child born in the township.

—Jacob Miller, an early settler of Columbia, was a soldier in the revolutionary war.

—The first religious society was organized by Rev. Daniel Thatcher, a Presbyterian, in 1800.

—The state road, from Towanda to Wellsboro, was constructed through Columbia township, in 1808.

—The first post office in the town was established in 1818, and known as Sylvania; Reuben Nash, Post Master.

—Sylvan Lodge, No. 926, I. O. O. F. was organized Feb. 1, 1876. The first officers were J. H. Calkins, N. G.; A. M. Card, V. G.; George P. Monroe, Sec.; Peleg Peck, Treas.

Franklin Township.

Franklin township was organized in 1819, taken from Canton, Troy and Burlington. Both branches of the Towanda creek unite within the township. The lands along the valley are very productive. The high or rolling lands are being brought up to a good state of cultivation. The town of Franklin is bounded on the north by West Burlington and Burlington, on the east by Monroe, on the south by Barclay, and on the west by Granville and Leroy. Franklin and West Franklin are small villages and post towns.

The early settlers were David Allen, Stephen Allen, Daniel Allen, Benjamin Stone, Daniel Wilcox, Rev. Thomas Smiley, John Knapp, William Damer, Samuel Wilcox, Absalom Carr, Ezekiel Carr, Widow Jane Lattimer, William Blanchard, Aaron Cook, Daniel Stone, Truman Holcomb, Gilbert Gay, William B. French, Allen Rockwell, Nathan Wilcox, Major Oliver W. Dodge, Burr Ridgway, Horace Spalding, William B. Spalding, Noah Spalding, Stephen Lattimer, Peter Lattimer.

—Mrs. Pladnor died, in Franklin, in 1830, aged 109 years.

—Franklin township was named in honor of Col. John Franklin, of Athens.

—Burr Ridgway settled in Franklin, in 1803, and thereafter established the *Bradford Democrat*, at Towanda.

—David and Stephen Allen, built a grist mill on Towanda creek, in 1796.

—The postoffice was established at Franklin, in 1820. John Knapp, postmaster.

—David Allen and Stephen Allen were taken prisoners at the Wyoming Massacre, and escaped while the Indians were holding a war dance.

Granville Township.

Granville township was organized in 1831, taken from Franklin, Canton, Burlington and Troy. Granville Corners, Granville Center and Granville Summit are villages in the township. The Northern Central Railroad touches its western border, and Granville Summit is a station on that road. The north branch of the Towanda creek passes through the township from west to east. The lands are rolling and well adapted to grazing and the dairy. It is bounded on the north by Troy and West Burlington, on the east by West Burlington and Franklin, on the south by Leroy, and on the west by Troy and Canton.

Its early settlers were: Jeremiah Taylor, Lewis Moffett, Scoville Bailey, David Bailey, Ezra Bailey, Thomas Bailey, Uriah Baxter, Benjamin Saxton, Oliver Nelson, Phillip Packer, Abraham Parkhurst, Charles Butterfield, John Putman, Alvord Churchill, John Pratt, Josiah Vrooman, David Ross, Abijah Ayres, Z. Porter, Avery Clark, Nathaniel Clark, Noah Packard, Giles Avery, Simon Chesley, Peter Shoemaker, Daniel Ferguson, Oliver Bailey, Hugh Halcomb.

—A Good Templars Lodge was organized in 1854.

—The first road was laid out in Granville, in 1802.

—The first death in the township was Mrs. Lewis Moffit.

—Levi Taylor opened the first hotel in the township, in 1849.

—B. F. Taylor opened the first store in the township, in 1849.

—Albert Nichols, erected a large tannery at Granville, in 1857.

—A Lodge of Sons of Temperance, was established, in 1852.

—The first framed house was built by Jeremiah Taylor, in 1815.

—The first school was taught by Miss Delight Spalding, in 1807.

—Adam Inness the celebrated tanner, located in Granville, in 1865.

—Sylvester Taylor was the first white child born in Granville in 1804.

—Granville is one of the finest butter producing townships in Bradford county.

—The first Baptist meeting held in the town, was in 1805, by Rev. Thomas Smiley.

—The first wedding in the township was Hugh Holcomb and Miss Prudence Bailey.

—The first grist mill in the town, was erected by Jeremiah Taylor, Jr., in the year 1820.

—Mail route established through Granville, from East Burlington to Alba, in the year 1827.

—Simon Chesely was an early settler in Granville, and a soldier of the revolutionary war.

—In the year 1832, Dr. Silas E. Shepard, of Troy, organized a Disciple Church, in Granville.

—The "Summit" derives its name from the fact that it is the highest point on the Northern Central Railroad, between Baltimore and Canandaigua.

—Granville was originally known as North Branch, and a postoffice was established in 1827, by that name. In 1831 it was changed to Granville.

—Granville Center Lodge, I. O. O. F., No. 687, was organized December 24th, 1869. Robert Innis, N. G.; M. O. Loomis, V. G.; P. M. Sayles, Sec.; Adam Innis, Treas.

Herrick Township.

Herrick township was formed in 1837, taken from Wyalusing. It is situated in the south-eastern portion of Bradford County, in the highlands east of the Susquehanna river. It is bounded on the north by the town of Orwell; on the east by Pike; on the south by Wyalusing; and west by Standing Stone and Wysox. It was named in honor of Judge Edward Herrick, of Athens, a distinguished lawyer and jurist, who was born October 26, 1787, and studied law in Poughkeepsie, in 1804, with General John Brush. Went to Ohio, was a member of the Ohio Legislature, and during the war of 1812 was a Colonel in command of an Ohio regiment. Came to Bradford County and was admitted to the bar in 1813 In 1818, he was appointed President Judge, by Governor Findlay, of Bradford, Susquehanna, Tioga, Potter and McKean Counties, and remained upon the bench for a period of twenty-one years. He was a life long democrat, and died at Athens, Bradford County, March 7, 1873, aged 86 years.

The first settlers were Zophar Platt, Nathaniel Platt, Jarvis Platt, F. Reed, Asa Matson, Henry Townshend, John Haywood, Ferris Bennett, Elihu Buttles, Isaac Park, Hiram Camp, Robert DePue, James Hinds, Calvin Stone, Reuben Atwood, Charles Squires, Charles Stevens, Micajah Slocum, Ezekiel Mintz, Daniel Durland, Adam Overpeck, Nathan B. Whitman, Henry Wells, James Clark, William Nesbitt, Nathaniel Nesbitt, Alexander Dougherty, James Lee, James Wood, William Hillis, Richard Hillis.

—First school house erected in 1829.

—Isaac Park was the first tanner, in 1819.

—The first settler was Zophar Clark, in 1811.

—The first religious meeting was held in 1829.

—The first death in the township was Daniel Durand.

—Isaac Camp built the first saw mill in the town, in 1822.

—John Haywood was the first blacksmith in the town, in 1817.

—Mathew Wilding and Miss Lydia M. Camp, were married in 1828, the first marriage in the township.

—The Bally bay Irish settlement in Herrick township, was commenced in 1826, by emigrants from Bally bay, Ireland. Among these settlers were William Nesbitt, Nathaniel Nesbitt, Alexander Dougherty, James Lee, James Wood, William Hillis, R chard Hillis.

Leroy Township.

Leroy township was formed in 1835, taken from Canton. It is situated in the south-western portion of the county, near the coal mining region of Barclay. It is bounded on the north by Granville; on the east by Franklin, Barclay and Overton; on the south by Sullivan county; on the west by

Canton. The streams of the township are Towanda creek, and the head waters, of the Schrader. Leroy is quite a thriving village, situated on Towanda Creek. The northern portion of the township is quite productive, while the southern is hilly and mountainous, reaching into the coal measures.

The early settlers were Hugh Holcomb, Sterling Holcomb, Eli Holcomb, Seeley Crofut, Dennison Kingsbury, Elihu Knight, George Brown, Joel Bodwell, Capt. Elijah Rice, Joseph Wallace, Welcome Rice, Peter Gordon, Isaac Chaapel, David Andrews, Truman Holcomb, Isaac Wooster, Luther Hinman, Miles Oakley, George Head, Aaron Cook, Timothy Culver, Alpheus Holcomb, David Wooster, Nicholas Gordon, Henry Segar, David Jayne, Loren Kingsbury, Jesse Morse, Orison Royce, Henry Mercur, John Knapp, Jesse Robart, Henry Knowles, Jeremy Bailey, Samuel McCrancy, Ira Crofut.

—Orison Royce built a distillery in 1802.

—A hurricane occurred in Leroy, in 1794.

—Leroy was christened by Ira Crofut, in 1835.

—The Baptists erected a church in Leroy, in 1855.

—The Disciples erected a church in Leroy, in 1850.

—Hugh Holcomb erected the first grist mill, in 1820.

—The Methodists erected a church in Leroy, in 1857.

—Deacon Seeley Crofut opened the first store in Leroy.

—Martin Holcomb was the first white child born in Leroy.

—Rev. David Jayne taught the first school in the township.

—The first saw mill was erected by Hugh Halcomb, in 1808.

—Aaron Knapp was the first Justice of the Peace in the township.

—Deacon Seeley Crofut organized the first Sunday School in the town, in 1799.

—The McCrancy settlement was made by Samuel McCrancy and Jeremy Bailey, in 1846.

—Hugh Holcomb and Elizabeth Oakley were the first couple married in the township, and Mrs. Holcomb was the first person who died in the township.

Litchfield Township.

Litchfield township was formed in 1821, taken from the eastern portion of Athens. It is bounded on the north by Tioga county, New York, on the east by the township of Windham, on the south by Rome and Sheshequin, and on the west by Athens. The Susquehanna touches its north-western boundry, and Satterlee, Park Bullard and Wappusening creeks water the township. It is principally situated in the high lands, except on the river are some fine alluvial flats. The high and rolling lands are well adapted to grazing, and the dairy, and is being brought up to a state of cultivation.

Its early settlers were Thomas Park, Eleazer Merrill, Hiram Merrill, Solomon Merrill, Eleazer Merrill, Elisha Merrill, Silas Wolcott, Elijah Wolcott, Thomas Munn, Josiah White, Daniel Bush, Henry Kinney, Samuel Kinney, Ruloff Campbell, Samuel Campbell, Alsop Baldwin, Samuel Ball, Christoper Schoonover, Doan Schoonover, David McKinney, Henry McKinney, Henry Hewlett, John Hewlett, Ira Hewlett, Lewis Hewlett, James Brown, William Loomis, Alanson Loomis, John Moore, Joseph Greek, William Cotton, Peter Turner, Richard Struble, Moses Struble, Zenas

Cleveland, Nathaniel Hotchkiss, Joseph Nichols, Russell Marsh, Paul Apgar, Abel Beach, Richard Tappan, John Marks, Lewis Baldwin, Henry Shoemaker, Samuel P. Wolcott, Orson Carner, John G. Nichols, Levi Johnson, Henry Turner, John Van Gorder, David Van Gorder, Jacob Rheinold, Peter Lawser, Conrad Heinman, William Beidleman, Joseph Beidleman, Amos Franklin, William Griffin, Daniel Park, Samuel Park, James Park, Amos Park, Joseph Park, Elijah Park, Benjamin Park, William Drown, Absalom Adams, Joseph Kinney, David Kinney, Lewis Tappan.

—Thomas Park was the first settler in Litchfield.

—Daniel Bush erected the first grist mill in the township.

—James Park was the first white child born in the township.

—Josiah White, an early settler, was a soldier in the war of 1812.

—Baptist Church organized in Litchfield in 1855, with 36 members.

—Zenas Cleveland, an early settler, was a soldier of the war of 1812. He died in 1873, aged 94 years.

—Silas Wolcott, an early settler of Litchfield, was a soldier of the revolutionary war. He died in 1834, aged 78 years.

Monroe Township and Borough.

The township of Monroe was formed in 1821, taken from Burlington and Towanda. Monroeton was incorporated as a borough in 1855. The township of Monroe is bounded on the north by Towanda; on the east by Asylum; on the south by Albany; on the west by Overton, Barclay and Franklin. It is well watered by the Towanda creek and its branches, the Fowler and Schrader, and contains a very fertile and productive soil. Some portions of it is hilly and uneven, but it has been brought under a fair state of cultivation.

Its early settlers were Gordon Fowler, Reed Brockaway, Jonathan Fowler, Roger Fowler, Noadiah Cranmer, John Cranmer, Samuel Cranmer, John Schraeder, John Neeley, Harmon Schraeder, Reese Stevens, William Dougherty, Jacob Bowman, David Gilbert, Timothy Alden, Jared Woodruff, Eliphalet Mason, Gordon F. Mason, Chester Mason, Ebenezer Mason, Andrew Irving, Geo. Irving, Welch Irving, Nelson Gilbert, James Lewis, Amos V. Mathews, Henry Salisbury, Elisha Cole, Anthony Vanderpoel, Russel Fowler.

—Andrew Irving was the first tanner in Monroe township.

—Anthony Vanderpoel built a grist mill, in the township, in 1800.

—The coal was discovered on the Barclay mountain, by Edsall Carr.

—Jared Leavenworth was the first blacksmith to use the Barclay coal.

—The first school was taught in the township, in the year 1801, by Miss Polly Fowler.

—Mrs. Gordon Fowler, planted the first apple orchard, from seeds she brought from Connecticut.

—James Lewis, an early settler, of Monroe, was taken prisoner when twelve years of age, by the French and Indians.

—Evergreen Lodge, No. 163, A. Y. M., was instituted March 1, 1819. The first officers were: Eliphalet Mason, W. M.; Simon Kinney, S. W.; Russel Fowler, J. W.

—Monroeton is a pleasant village, situated at the junction of the Sullivan and State Line Railroad, and the Towanda and Barclay Railroad.

—Eliphalet Mason was an early settler of Monroe, a teacher, Justice of the Peace, Deputy Sheriff, County Commissioner, Register and Recorder. He was the father of Hon. Gordon F. Mason.

—John Schraeder, an early settler, was a Hessian. He deserted from the British Army, in New Jersey, during the revolutionary war and joined the Continental Army, and remained in service until Independence was won.

—"Old Mother Northrup," died in Monroe, in the year 1837, aged one hundred and twelve years, and ten months. She was married when she was about one hundred years old, to Mr. Alexander Howden, a revolutionary soldier. The magistrate performing the service was Samuel Gore, Esq., of Sheshequin.

—Monroeton Lodge, No. 137, I. O. O. F., was instituted at Monroeton, February 12th, 1846. The first officers were: D. C. Salisbury, Noble Grand; E. W. Morgan, Vice Grand; Gordon F. Mason, Secretary; William H. Strickland, Treasurer. The first initiations were: Anthony Mullen, Henry S. Salisbury, William Gosline, Joseph B. Smith, Robert Hunter, Eliphalet Mason, Dr. Samuel Huston, Ira H. Stevens, S. S. Hinman, Peter C. Ward, Elias Mathewson, O. D. Satterlee, O. O. Shipman, Benjamin Wilcox, George Tracy, James H. Wells, Byron Kingsbury, Wilson Rogers, Gordon F. Mason. This was the first lodge of Odd Fellows instituted in the county of Bradford. For years a strong feeling had existed against the formation of secret societies, and especially Free Masons. The introduction of Odd Fellowship was regarded by the uninitiated as being only Masonry revived in a re-organized form, and strong sentiments of opposition to any secret societies was manifested. Many who had been Free Masons joined Odd Fellowship, and together, they turned in a measure, the strong tide of opposition in its favor. Yet they were extremely cautious, and for many years had much to discourage and annoy them. The order however, continued to flourish and increase in numbers and strength, until Odd Fellowship in Pennsylvania stands first in the list of Odd Fellows in the United States. Monroeton has the honor of having the first Odd Fellows Lodge in Bradford county, established within its limits, and Athens, the honor of the first Masonic lodge. It is a subject worthy of remark, that there has never been any rivalry, contention, or disagreement at all between Odd Fellows and Free Masons, notwithstanding, they are two separate and distinct organizations, thus setting an example worthy of imitation by other organizations. They both aim to improve the morals, instruct their members, relieve the poor and needy and spread the mantle of charity in its broadest form.

Overton Township.

Overton township was formed in 1853, taken from Albany, Franklin and Monroe townships. It was named in honor of Edward Overton, of Towanda, who was born in Lancashire, England, December 30, 1795, and came to America in 1815. He had previously studied law in England, and was admitted at the Wilkes Barre, Luzerne county bar, in 1817. Commenced the practice of law at Athens, and removed to Towanda about the year 1820.

He became largely interested in real estate and coal lands, and through his exertions the Barclay Coal mines were developed, and the Towanda and Barclay railroad was constructed. He was the first president of the Barclay Coal Company.

Overton is bounded on the north by Barclay, on the east by Monroe and Albany, on the south by Sullivan county, on the west by Leroy. It is a mountainous and hilly township, and its inhabitants are engaged in farming and lumbering. The settlers are chiefly of Irish and German nativity, and are distinguished for their industry and perseverance. They are fast reclaiming the rugged wilds, and bringing them under cultivation. The obstructions which nature has thrown in the way, are being removed by these energetic settlers.

The early settlers were Daniel Heverly, John Herverly, Christain Heverly, Daniel Heverly, Jr., Henry Heverly, Abner Kissell, Leonard Streevy, Henry Sherman, Jacob Hottenstein.

—Catholic Church was erected in Overton in 1844

—The first settler in Overton was Daniel Heverly.

—Jacob Kissell died in 1812, the first death in Overton.

—Overton village was laid out by Henry Sherman, in 1856.

—Heverlyville post office changed name to Overton, in 1856.

—William Waltman opened the first store in Overton, in 1856.

—The first lot in Overton village was purchased by Moses Mossbacher.

—First white child born in Overton was Amasa Heaverly, April 11, 1817.

—The first framed barn in Overton was built in 1832, by Christain Heverly

—Henry Sherman, one of the early settlers, was the father of twenty-three children.

—The first saw mill in Overton township was erected by Daniel Heverly, Jr., in 1820.

—The first school house in Overton was erected in 1827. Anna Kellogg was the first teacher.

—The first post office was established in 1851, at Heverlyville. Edward McGovern post master.

Orwell Township.

In 1801, Mount Zion township was organized; the Commissioners to fix the boundaries were Ezekiel Hyde, Josiah Grant, William Spalding. In 1802, the name was changed to Orwell. It is bounded on the north by the townships of Windham and Warren; on the east by Warren and Pike; on the south by Herrick; on the west by Rome. Wysox creek, Jerome and Johnson's creeks are its principal streams. It is a very fertile and productive township. There are four post offices in the town, and several small villages and hamlets.

The early settlers were Daniel Russell, Capt. Josiah Grant, Francis Mesusan, Ebenezer Chubbuck, Nathaniel Chubbuck, Ashel Johnson, Zenas Cook, Artemus Johnson, Truman Johnson, Edmund Johnson, Cyprian Allen, Samuel Wells, Capt. Samuel Woodruff, Adrian Manville, Levi Frisbie, Richard Marks, William Johnson, Asa Upson, Theron Darling, Abel Darling, John Pierce, Alpheus Choate, Joel Barnes, William Raney, Libbeus Roberts,

Capt. John Grant, Joel Cook, William Keeler, Mark Mesusan, George Pendleton, William Pendleton, Hamilton Champlain, Noah Shaffee, John Wheaton, Samuel Mathews, Amos Coburn, Ebenezer Coburn, Miles Pierce, Milton Humphrey, Alvin Humphrey, Parley Coburn, James Bowen, Jason Potter, Uri Cook, Chauncey Frisbie, James Newell, Randall Mathews, Henry W. Hind, Ithiel Allis, William Sexton, Jason Chaffee, Jacob Wickizer, Samuel Wheaton.

—The first Temperance Society was organized in 1829.

—The first school was taught in 1803 by Clarissa Woodruff.

—The first death was the wife of Adrian Manville, May 1, 1801.

—Potterville was named in honor of Jason Potter an early settler.

—The first permanent settlement was made in the township by Daniel Russell.

—Joel Johnson born May 18, 1799, was the first white child born in the township.

—Orwell was named in honor of a town in the State of Vermont, from which some of the early settlers came.

—Capt. Josiah Grant an early settler, was a revolutionary soldier, and a cousin to General Ethan Allen. He commanded a company of the Green Mountain boys.

—Capt. Josiah Grant, Capt. Samuel Woodruff, Capt. John Grant, Joel Cook, Ebenezer Chubbuck, George Pendleton, Ashel Johnson, were early settlers of Orwell, and soldiers of the revolutionary war.

—Orwell Library Association was organized in 1812. The first annual meeting of the Association was held Feb. 16, 1813; Thomas Elliott, Chairman; J. M. Piolett, Secretary; J. M. Piolett, Jacob Bell, William Myer, William F. Dinninger, Ashel Johnson, Executive Committee; Doct S. T. Barstow, Librarian and Treasurer.

Pike Township and the Borough of LeRaysville.

The township of Pike was organized in 1813, taken from Orwell and Rush. LeRaysville was incorporated as a borough in 1863, formed from Pike township. The township of Pike is bounded on the north by Warren, on the east by Susquehanna county, on the south by Tuscarora, on the west by Herrick and Orwell. The Wyalusing creek and its tributaries, are the principal streams in the township. The soil is well adapted to grazing and dairy. There are five postoffices in the township. LeRaysville, a borough is the chief village in the township.

Early settlers were: Jacob Fencler, Damon Bostwick, Benazah Bostwick James Rockwell, Seth P. Rockwell, Nathan Abbott, Darius Coleman, Elijah Coleman, Benjamin Abbott. Eleazer Russell, Ephraim Fairchild, William Frink, David Olmstead, Elisha Keeler, John Bradshaw, Capt. Isaac Bronson, Aden Stevens, Nathan Stevens, Samuel Stevens, William Turrell, Samuel Luckey, Abraham Taylor, Salmon Bosworth, Josiah Bosworth, Reed Bosworth, Alba Bosworth, Joseph Bosworth, Daniel Metcalfe, Ezekiel Mowrey, George Mowrey, John Ford, Bela Ford, James Brink, Elisha Coggswell, Joseph Pierce, Thomas Brink, Daniel Bennett, Benajah Bennett, James Brink, William Brink, Jesse Ross, Daniel Ross, Joseph Ross, William Johnson, Adolphus Olmstead, William Buck, Gould Seymour, Isaac Seymour, Andrew Canfield, Isaac Hancock, Edmund Stone, Dr. Baker, Joseph Preston, Elijah Tillotson, James Hines, Samuel Seeley, David Doud, Peter Stephens, Judah Benjamin, Timothy Gaylord, Reuben Wells, Amasa Wells, Jesse Edsall, Reuben Atwood, Joseph Utter, Benjamin Seeley, Mathias Scrivens, Roswell Slater, Ezra Winship, Amos Northrop, Henry Ellsworth, James Ellsworth, Joseph Ellsworth, Jonathan Ellsworth, Joseph Jenkins, Edward Jones, Sr., David Thomas, Sr., Reese Griffith, David Thomas, Jr., David Morris, David Williamson, Phillip Williams, John Williams, Rev. Daniel Jones, Samuel Davis, John Edwards, Jenkins Jones, William Evans, Thomas Jones, Evan Howell, William Howell, John Howell, Thomas Howell, Roger Howell, David Davis, Henry Walters, James Walters, Thomas Walters, Richard Williams, John Morris, Daniel P. Jones, John Davis, John Thomas, Samuel Thomas, Israel Jenkins, John Jones, David J. Thomas, Jenkins Jones, 2nd, David Davis, Thomas J. Thomas, Roger Griffiths, Thomas W. Williams, Dr. William Roberts, Isaac Seymour, Samuel Edsall.

—Alva Bosworth, built a saw-mill, in the year 1805.

—Salmon Bosworth built the first grist mill, in 1819.

—Pike township was named in honor of General Pike.

—Samuel Stevens was the first tanner, in Pike township.

—Elisha Keeler, Sr., the early settler, was a tailor by trade.

—Dr. Baker was the first resident physician in Pike township.

—Salmon Bosworth, was the first blacksmith in the township.

—The first framed house was built in 1808, by Isaac Seymour.

—Elisha Keeler, Jr., opened the first store in 1804, in Pike Township.

—The first wool carding machine was constructed in 1808, by Elisha Keeler.

—LeRaysville was named in honor of Vincent Leray, a French land pro-

—Elisha Keeler, who died in 1794, was the first death in the township of Pike.

—The first school house was erected in 1805. Patty Sill was the first teacher.
prietor of Bradford county.

—The Indian path from Susquehanna to Chenango, at Binghamton, went through the township of Pike.

—James Rockwell built the first brick manufactory in Pike, in Northern Pennsylvania, in the year 1795.

—Newton, in Pike township, was so named by Seth P. Rockwell, when he first located in the township.

—The Welsh settlement, in Pike township, is one of the most thrifty communities in the farming country of Bradford county.

—LeRaysville Lodge, No. 471, A. Y. M., was instituted March 2, 1870. W. S. Heaton, W. M.; S. W. Little, S. W.; William B. Stevens, J W.

—Lerays Lodge, I O. O. F., No. 416, was instituted October 31, 1850. Re-organized, June 9, 1875. Dr. C. S. Dusenberry, N. G.; Stephen Gorham, V. G.; L. P. Blackman, Sec.; John Baldwin, Treas.

—Elisha Keeler, Sr., Capt Isaac Bronson, Ephraim Fairchild, Daniel Bennett, Benjamin Bennett, James Bennett, Joseph Ross, Henry Ellsworth, and Nathan Abbott, were early settlers in Pike township, and revolutionary soldiers.

—Bradford Grange, No. 39, was organized in 1873, by S. W. Buck. Its first officers, were: S. W. Buck Master; G. N. Dewolf, Secretary. The Grange was the first in Bradford county. S. W. Buck, of LeRaysville, was the first District Deputy Grange Master in the county of Bradford, and did much towards establishing granges and interesting the farmers of the county in its behalf. He now holds a position in the office of the Secretary of Internal Affairs, at Harrisburg.

Rome Township and Borough.

Rome township was formed in 1831, taken from Orwell and Sheshequin. Its surface consists of valleys and table lands, under a high state of cultivation. The Wysox and its tributaries are the principal streams of the township, the name given it, Rome, was because it was on the same parallel as Rome, the famous and renowned city of Italy, "who sat upon her seven hills, and from her throne of beauty ruled the world." It is bounded on the north by Litchfield and Windham, on the east by Orwell, on the south by Wysox, and on the west by Sheshequin.

Its early settlers were Nathaniel P. Moody, Enos Moody, Moses Moody, Levi Thayer, Godfrey Vought, Henry Lent, Frederic Eiklor, John W. Parks, Elijah Towner, Enoch Towner, Ezra Towner, Leonard Westbrook, George Murphy, John Hicks, James Elliott, Reuben Bump, Russell Gibbs, Achaitus Vought, Godfrey Vought, Rev. E. C. Taylor, Martin V. B. Moore, Stephen Cranmer.

—Silas Gore was the first blacksmith in Rome, in 1812.

—Godfrey Vought erected the first frame house, in 1804.

—Frederic Eiklor taught the first school in Rome, in 1803.

—The first settler of Rome, was Nathaniel P. Moody, in 1795.

—Burr Ridgway erected the first grist mill in the township, in 1808.

—The first white child born in the township, was Benjamin Moody, in 1798.

—Mrs. Frederic Eiklor, died in February 1800. The first death in the township.

—Henry Lent one of the pioneer settlers, was frozen to death in the year 1801.

—In the early settlement of Rome township, a large amount of maple sugar was made.

—James Lent and Chloe Parks were married in 1803. The first marriage in the township.

—Rev. Elisha Cole, a Baptist minister, held the first religious services in the town, in 1801.

—The first apple trees were set out by Nathaniel P. Moody, in 1798. He also set out fruit trees along the roadside, for the benefit of the boys of the neighborhood.

—Rome Lodge No. 480, I. O. O. F., was instituted September 12, 1853. Reorganized November, 8, 1872, officers H. D. Towner N. G; J. H. Allen, V. G; W. H. Shaw, Sec.

—Rome Lodge No. 418, F. A. Mason, instituted March 9, 1868, L. A. Ridgway, W. M; D. R Woodburn, S. W; E. M. Farrar, J. W; L. L. Moody, Sec; John Passmore Treas.

—Godfrey Vought, Andrus Eiklor and Henry Welt erected the first saw mill in the township, in 1802.

—Nathaniel P. Moody, Elijah Towner and Joseph Elliott were early settlers and soldiers of the revolutionary war.

—Rome Borough situated in the south western portion of the township, was incorporated as a borough in 1861. It is situated upon Wysox creek, surrounded by a rich and fertile country.

Ridgeberry Township.

Ridgeberry township was formed in 1818, taken from the townships of Athens and Wells. It is situated on the northern line of Bradford county, in the northwest portion of the same, adjoining Chemung county, New York. It is bounded on the north by Chemung county, New York, on the east by Athens, on the south by Springfield and Smithfield, and on the west by South Creek. The streams of the township are Benltey creek and its tributaries. The surface of the township is uneven and hilly, but it is under a high state of cultivation. The farmers are prosperous and forehanded, with elegant dwellings, and large and capacious barns.

Its early settlers were Isaac Fuller, Joel Fuller, Samuel Bennett, Adam Ridenbar, Vine Baldwin, George Baldwin, Grisworth Owens, Roswell Goff, Captain Calvin West, John Cummings, Joel Campbell, Benjamin Campbell, Jonathan Kent, James Covell, Silas Campbell, Major Alpheus Gillett, Aaron Marcellus, Elijah Buck, Sturgess Squires, Peter Squires, Joseph Batterson, Elnathan Pierce, John L. Webb, Job Stiles, Ashel Burnham, Abram Westfall, John Sirton, Jonathan Davison, Green Bentley, Samuel Green, Peter Evens, Allen Miner, Cornelius O'Driscoll, Richard O'Connor, James White, John Downs, George O'Leary, Daniel Desmond, John Desmond, Timothy Desmond, Richard Hurley, John Mahoney, Patrick Butler, Daniel Chambers, George Chambers, Thomas Chambers, Daniel Kane, James Crowley, Abial Fuller, David Buck, Kinney Burnham, Lemuel Fuller.

—David Buck cut the first road through to Smithfield.

—Ridgeberry was named by Samuel Bennett, in 1818.

—Sturgiss Squires was the first constable in the town, in 1818.

—The Berwick was constructed through Ridgeberry, in 1820.

—The first framed house was built by Vine Baldwin, in Ridgeberry.

—Centerville and Bently Creek are the two post towns in the township.

—Abiel Fuller erected the first saw mill in Ridgeberry township, in 1826.

—John L. Webb was the first Justice of the Peace, in the township of Ridgeberry.

—Major Alpheus Judd, Job Stiles early settlers of Ridgeberry, were soldiers in the revolutionary war.

—Rev. Roswell Goff, the celebrated Baptist minister, first settled in Ridgeberry township, when he came in from the east.

—Vine Baldwin, an early settler of Ridgeberry, was the first white child born in the Chemung valley, after the revolutionary war.

—Sturgiss Squires, Isaac Fuller, Abiel Fuller, Captain Alvin West, James Covell, early settlers, were soldiers in the war of 1812.

—Bentley creek was named in honor of Green Bently, a revolutionary soldier, who, subsequent to his settlement at Bentley creek, removed to Catharine's Town, N. Y.

Smithfield Township.

Smithfield township was one of the original townships in the county. It is situated west of the Susquehanna river, and west of the township of Ulster, upon rolling lands, which have been brought to a high state of cultivation. Beautiful farms and farm buildings are seen in every portion of the town, with herds of cattle grazing in sweet and luxuriant pastures. It is bounded on the north by Athens and Ridgeberry; on the east by Ulster; on the south by Burlington and West Burlington; on the west by Springfield. The streams of the township are Tom Jack, Brown and Buck creeks.

The early settlers were Isaac Grover, Reuben Mitchell, Abiel Foster, William Baldwin, Ezra Waterman, Zacariah Wheeler, James Satterlee, William Satterlee, Samuel Satterlee, Oliver Hayes, Michael Bird, Timothy Stratton, Samuel Dartt, Jabez Gerould, Phineas Pierce, Joshua Ames, John Pierce, Constant Williams, Solomon Kellogg, Solomon Morse, Nehemiah Tracy, John Bassett, Noah Ford, Elias Needham, Alvin Stocking, S. Stocking, Alpheus Holcomb, Samuel Wood, Ashel Scott, John Scott, Major Jared Phelps, Isaac Ames, Sloan Kingsley, John Phelps, David Titus, Abner O. Ormabee, Zephania Ames, Isaiah Kingsley, Austin Kellogg, Chancey Kellogg, Luman Kellogg, David Forest, Stephen Wilcox, Rufus Halsey, Abner Thomas, Asa Hackett, Asa Farnsworth, William Farnsworth, Stephen Califf, Seth Gates, Daniel Forest, Tarsus Rose, Benjamin Hale, Joseph Ames, David Durfee, Cyril Fairman, Abraham Jones, Asa Allen, Joel Allen, Cromwell Child, Edward A. Child, Ezra Allen, Daniel Allen, George Tompkinson, Conrad Hartman, Nehemiah Beach.

—Isaiah Grover was the first settler in Smithfield, in 1792.

—The first school was taught by Ephriam Gerould, in 1803.

—Phineas Pierce erected the first saw mill in Smithfield, in 1803.

—The first white child born in the township, was in 1795, Reuben Mitchell's.

—The first store in the township was opened in 1833, by Lyman Durfee.

—Reuben Mitchell erected the first framed building in 1803, in Smithfield.

—Reuben Mitchell's child, who died in 1796, was the the first death in the township.

—Smithfield was named in honor of David Smith, who owned the township under the Connecticut title.

—The Gerould family held a re-union in Smithfield, September 15, 1874, and over two hundred relatives were present.

—Solomon Kellogg, an old settler, invented a machine for shearing cloth, which had great influence upon woolen manufactories.

—A Literary Society was organized in 1821, in Smithfield, by Ansel Scott, Buckley Tracey, David Farnsworth, Harry Bird, Darius Bullock.

—A soldier's monument, commemorative of those who lost their lives in the late rebellion, from Smithfield, has been erected at Smithfield Center.

—Smithfield Lodge, No. 928, I. O. O. F., was instituted January 15, 1876. First officers, E. G. Durfee, N. G.; J. L. Vincent, V. G.; O. Gerould, Sec.

—Jared Phelps, Nehemiah Tracey, Samuel Kellogg, Samuel Wood, David Forest, were early settlers of Smithfield, and soldiers in the revolutionary war.

—George Tompkinson, an early settler of Smithfield, was a marine in the U. S. Service, in the war of 1812, on the frigate President, under Commodore Rogers.

—Conrad Hartman, an early settler, was a Hessian soldier, under the British, and taken prisoner at Trenton, December 25, 1776. He became a citizen of the United States.

—Samuel Wood, an early settler of Smithfield, was one of the guards who conveyed Major Andre from North Castle to West Point, when he was under arrrest, during the revolutionary war.

—Smithfield Lodge, No. 428, F. A. M., was chartered September 10, 1868. First officers were A. W. Seward, W. M.; J. O. Gerould, S. W.; H. M. Moody, J. W.; W. E. Voorhis, Treasurer.

—The first church edifice in the township, was erected in 1811, by the Congregational society; Rev. John Bascom was the first minister. Samuel Kellogg, Solomon Morse, Nathan Fellows, were organized in Rutland Vermont, and came as a church to Smithfield in 1801.

Springfield Township.

The town of Springfield was formed in 1813, taken from Smithfield. The town was named by the first settlers in honor of Springfield, Massachusetts. The town is bounded on the north by South Creek and Ridgeberry, on the east by Smithfield, on the south by West Burlington and Troy, and on the west by Columbia. Leona, Springfield and Mill City are villages in the township. The soil is well adapted to grazing and the dairy. The chief pursuit of the inhabitants is farming, and the beautiful fields and well managed farms denote the prosperity of its citizens.

The early settlers were: Capt. John Harkness, Ezekiel Leonard, John Leonard, William Eaton, Abel Eaton, William Harkness, Ichabod Smith, Josephus Wing, James Mattocks, Luke Pitts, Joshua Speer, Stephen Bliss, Oliver Gates, Henry Stever, Amaziah Thayer, Joseph Grover, Gurdon Grover, James Harkness, Joseph Grace, Nehemiah Wilson, Abiel Fuller, Isaac Cooley, Gaines Adams, Samuel Kingsbury, Thomas Pemberton, Samuel Campbell, William Brace, John Parkhurst, David Brown, Charles Phillips, Lemuel White, William Evans, Elam Bennett, Quartius Ely, Amos Sargent, John Sargent, Elisha Fanning, Alexander Kennedy, Charles Burgess, Joseph Brooks, Wakeman Brooks, William Faulkner, Austin Leonard, Charles Satterlee, Hosea Kennedy, John Salsbury, Seth Salsbury.

—Springfield was originally known as Murraysfield.

—John Harkness was the first permanent settler, March 1, 1804.

—The village of Leona, was formerly known as "Leonards Hollow."

—Hannah Morey died in 1809, the first death in Springfield township.

—Sam Huel Campbell erected a distillery in 1810, in Springfield township.

—William Nevins taught the first school in the township, in the year 1808.

—John Harkness erected the first framed dwelling, in 1805, in Springfield township.

—Austin Leonard erected the first saw-mill in the town of Springfield, in the year 1808.

—Prof. J C. Doane, of the Mansfield State Normal School, is a native of Springfield.

—Mt. Pisgah, is in the town of Springfield, is one of the highest points in Bradford county.

—Luke Pitts erected a grist mill, in 1813. The first grist mill in the township of Springfield.

—Hiram Harkness was born, April 20, 1805, the first white child born in Springfield township.

—Abel Leonard and Abigal Leonard, were the first couple married in Springfield township.

—James Mattocks, an early settler, received his commission as captain from Governor McKean, August 3, 1807. He was the first Justice of the Peace, and received his commission from Governor Snyder, February 9, 1810.

South Creek Township.

South Creek township was formed in 1835, taken from Wells and Ridgeberry. The Northern Central Railway runs through the township from south to north, having two stations, State Line and Gilletts. The township is uneven and hilly, but quite well adapted to grazing. The principal stream in the township is South Creek, which runs in a northernly direction, and discharges its waters into the Chemung river. The township is bounded on the north by Chemung county and the state line, on the east by Ridgeberry, on the south by Springfield and Columbia, on the west by Wells.

Its early settlers were Philo Fassett, Asa Gillett, John Morrison, Gideon Andrus, Isaac Baker, Samuel Pettengill, Ezekiel Baker, Hosea Baker, Jesse Moore, George Durnham, N. Y. Glines, Harvey Jones, Elisha Moore, Benjamin Seeley, Solomon Bovier, Hiram Potter, Aaron Stiles, Stephen Stiles, Eben Dunning, Jackeus Thompson.

—Harvey Jones opened a hotel in the township, in 1829

—The first settlers were Jesse Moore and Ezekiel Baker, in 1804.

—Baptist church at Gilletts, in South Creek township, erected in August 1858. Second church erected in 1877.

—Hon. John F. Gillett, of South Creek township, was a representative in the Pennsylvania State Legislature, in the year 1877-78.

—The Elmira and Williamsport railroad was completed through the township in 1854. It is now controlled by the Northern Central Railroad.

—The Elmira and Williamsport Stage route passed through the township with a regular line of coaches. After the construction of the railroad in 1854, these stages were discontinued.

Standing Stone.

Standing Stone township was formed in 1841, taken from Herrick and Wysox. It is bounded on the north by Herrick, on the east by Herrick, on the south by Wyalusing and the Susquehanna river, on the west by Susquehanna river and Wysox. It is one of the oldest settled townships in the county of Bradford, and its name Standing Stone given it by reason of a certain large stone standing in the west bank of the Susquehanna river, has distinguished it from the earliest history of the Susquehanna valley. Settlements were commenced in the present limits of the township, previous to the revolutionary war; under Connecticut titles.

The Lehigh Valley railroad runs through the township from north to south, following the valley of the Susquehanna, and have two stations, Rummerfield and Standing Stone. Along the valley of the Susquehanna the soil is very productive, being a rich alluvial deposit. The soil upon the uplands to the eastward are being cultivated, and are becoming very well adapted to grazing and the dairy. The town is watered by the Susquehanna river, Rummerfield and Fitch's Creeks.

The early settlers were Lemuel Fitch, Simon Spalding, Henry Birney, Anthony Rummerfield, Richard Fitzgerald, Richard Loomis, Walter Walters John Bigelow, Jr. Nathaniel Walters, Stephen Wilcox, Elisha Satterlee, David McCormick, Peter Loop, Walter Westover, Abram Westbrook, William Jackson, Amos Bennett, Silas Beardsley, Theophilus Moyer, Henry Birney, John Hutchinson, Samuel Gorden, Jonathan Stevens, William Houck, Anthony La Fever, Peter Miller, Jacob Primer, (colored,) Cherick Westbrook, Henry Van Curen, David Hawley, David Eicklor, Cornelius Ennis, Levi Ennis, Hiram Gorden.

—Johathan Stevens, an early settler of Standing Stone, served three years in the continental army,

—The lands in Standing Stone township, were among the first grants made by the Susquenanna Land Company in Bradford county, having been sold to David Smith, in 1774.

Sheshequin Township.

Sheshequin township was formed in 1820, taken from Ulster. It is situated on the east side of the Susquehanna, and comprises some of the finest alluvial lands in Pennsylvania. It has become historic grounds on account of its Indian and revolutionary history. The old Indian town of Sheshequin was situated on the west side of the river in the present town of Ulster, but the broad and fertile flats upon the east side now in Sheshequin, early became famous for their productiveness. Sheshequin is bounded on the north by Athens and Litchfield, on the east by Rome, on the south by Wysox and the Susquehanna river, and on the west by the Susquehanna river.

Its early settlers were Gen. Simon Spalding, Joseph Kinney, Benjamin Cole, Col Fordham, Col. Thomas Baldwin, Stephen Fuller, Obediah Gore, Samuel Gore, Arnold Franklin, Col Joseph Kingsbury, Moses Pard, Capt. Jeremiah Shaw, Peter Snyder, Ebenezer Shaw, Daniel Brink, Abel Newell, George Murphy, Stephen Morgan, Daniel Curtis, Henry Hine, Ichabod Blackman, Franklin Blackman, William Ferguson, Ebenezer Franklin, Joseph Franklin, Hugh Rippeth Elijah Horton, William Horton, Joshua Horton, Elijah Horton, Jr., Stephen Horton, Gilbert Horton, Joseph Tuttle, Josiah Newell, Abel Newell, William Webber, John Newell, Joseph Salisbury, Josiah Tuttle, Jonathan Stark, Jesse Smith, Capt. Jabez Fish, Zebulon Butler, Captain Forbes, Harry Spaulding, Capt. Stephen Fuller, Benjamin Clark, Jabez Sill, Elijah Towner, Enoch Towner, John Towner, Daniel Moore, William Kennedy, Hugh Kennedy, Peter Bernard, James Bidlack,

Timothy Bartlett, Samuel Bartlett, Henry Boyce, Jacob Brokaw, Ludowick Carner, Silas Carner, Henry Cleveland, John Deitrick, Christain Brokaw, Zadoc Gillett, Freeman Gillett, William Presher, Edward Griffin, Samuel Hoyt, Samuel Marshall, Thomas Marshall, Josiah B. Marshall, Mathew Rogers, David E. Weed, Earl Masten, Lockwood Curley, David Smith, Samuel K. Gore, William W. Spalding, John C. Van Size. George Killmer, Jeremiah Killmer, James Shores, Peter Snyder, Christain Forbes.

—Obediah Gore opened the first store in Sheshequin, in 1796.

—The first white settlement was made in Sheshequin, May 3 1783.

—Obediah Gore built the first framed house in Sheshequin, in 1787.

—Sheshequin is an Indian name, and signifies "the place of a rattle."

—In 1790, three hundred Indians were encamped on the Sheshequin flats.

—Obediah Gore erected a grist mill, in 1807, the first grist mill in Sheshequin.

—The first marriage was Mathias Hollenback and Miss Sarah Hibbard, April 20 1788.

—Ezra Shaw, an old pioneer in Sheshequin, died in 1871, aged over one hundred years.

—Samuel Kinney, was the first white child born in the present township of Sheshequin.

—Judge Gore and his father were blacksmiths. They were the first persons to use anthracite coal.

—Great floods in the Susquehanna river in 1786, swept over the flats of Sheshequin, and did great damage on the Susquehanna river.

—Simon Spalding, Joseph Kinney, Obediah Gore, Samuel Gore, Captain Jeremiah Shaw, Daniel Moore, Christain Avery, were early settlers of Sheshequin, and revolutionary soldiers

—Col. H. L. Kinney a native of Sheshequin, was the founder of Corpus Christi, Texas, was engaged in the Mexican war, in 1846, and in the Maximillian war was killed at Monterey.

Troy Township and Borough.

Troy township was formed in the year 1815, taken from Burlington. Troy borough was formed from Troy township, by an act of the Legislature of May 14, 1845. The township of Troy is bounded on the north by Columbia and Springfield, on the east by West Burlington, on the south by Granville and Canton, on the west by Armenia. The township and boro of Troy are situated on the head waters of Sugar Creek, on the line of the Northern Central railroad, about twenty-five miles south of Elmira, N. Y. The township is distinguished for its fine farms and the excellent quality of its dairy productions. Troy borough is one of the neatest and cleanest in northern Pennsylvana, and distinguished for its elegant private residences, business places, its public schools and churches, its fire department, its public press, its manufactories, and the enterprise and wealth of its citizens. Its is a half shire and the courts of Bradford county are held semi-annually at Troy. It is also distinguished for being one of the great centers, and shipping points for butter and cheese, of western Bradford.

Its early settlers were Elihu Smead, Aaron Case, Moses Case, Joseph

Wills, Thomas Backer, Samuel Rockwell, Nathaniel Allen. Horace Spalding, Reuben Case, John Barber. Caleb Williams, Samuel Case, Doct Rowley, Uel Porter, John Porter, Reuben Wilbur, Joseph Barber, Thomas Barber, Doctor Almeron Herrick, Major Ezra Long, Silas Rockwell, Luther Rockwell Stephen Palmer, John Ward. Samuel Conant, Adriel Hebard, Timothy Nichols, Elder Elisha Rich, Churchill Barnes, Laban Landon, John Dobbins, Elihu Newberry, Zoroster Porter, Benjamin Oviatt, Isaac N. Pomeroy, Anson Williams, Vine Baldwin, Elihue Case, Abraham Case, James Lucas, Daniel Gregory, John McKean, Allen Taylor, Alfred Parsons, O. P. Ballard, Dummer Lilley, John Cummings, Nelson Adams, George Kress, Doct Silas E. Sheppard, Joseph Morse, Calvin Dodge, James Hickok, Reuben Smead, Laban Bowen, Jonathan Peck, William Dobbins, E. C. Oliver, Daniel F. Pomeroy, Eli Parsons, Seth Paine, Rufus Rockwell, Thomas Paine, Moses Calkins, G. F. Reddington.

—The early name of Troy was Augusta.

—There is a chapter of R. A. M., in Troy.

—The Troy Academy was erected in 1842.

—The first settler in Troy was Elihu Smead.

—The first road through Troy was opened in 1798.

—The first blacksmith in Troy was Caleb Williams.

—Esther Case was the first white child born in Troy.

—John Ward erected the first grist mill in Troy, the site of Long's mill.

—The first house erected in the borough, was built by Timothy Nichols, in 1800.

—Elder Elisha Rich who died in the year 1812, was the first death in the township of Troy.

—Troy was named by Churchill Barnes, who had previously been a resident of Troy, N. Y.

—The first Baptist Church was erected in Troy, in 1808. Rev. Elisha Rich the first minister.

—Ezra Long was the first hotel keeper in Troy, and the first shipper of butter from Troy, in 1840.

—Troy borough is connected by railroad, telegraph, telephone and stage lines with other communities.

—O. P. Ballard, Esq., for many years was one of the most prominent business men in western Bradford county.

—Rev. Silas Shepard an early resident of Troy, visited the Holy Lands and was distinguished as a writer and theologian.

—East Troy is a village situated on Sugar Creek, about three miles east of the borough of Troy, and a center of considerable business.

—Col. I. N. Pomeroy was a celebrated bridge builder, stage proprietor, hotel keeper, banker, and a prominent business man of Troy.

—Hon. Dummer Lilly was a printer, and editor, county commissioner, register, and recorder, and in 1862 represented Bradford county in the State House of Representatives.

—Hon. Reuben Wilbur a prominent and early settler of Troy, was associate judge of Bradford county, sheriff, state senator for two terms, presidential elector, state inspector of prisons, and a life long democrat.

—Trojan Lodge No. 306, F. A. M., chartered January 19, 1857. Elihu Case, W. M; Amasa Greeno, S. W; Jeremiah Adams, J. W.

—The first assessment of property in Troy borough in 1845, showed a valuation of $58,925. The actual valuation is now over $1,000,000.

—Priam Lodge No. 247, I. O. O. F., was instituted August 31, 1847. Frank Smith, N. G; E. W. Hazzard, V. G; W. G. Newberry Sec; C. F. Finch, Treas.

—Troy Farmers Club organized in the year 1874. First officers J. C. McKean, Pres; G. M. Card, Sec; A. M. Cornell, Treas; A. S. Hooker, Reporting Sec.

—The first officers of the borough of Troy were E. C. Oliver burgess, G. F. Reddington, V. M. Long, Frederic Orwan, Layton Runyon councilmen; Allen E. Thomas, Clerk.

—Hon. Delos Rockwell of Troy, one of the most prominent members of the Bradford county bar, was elected by the democrats as state senator, in the year 1874. He led the forlorn hope "and came out victorious," the first democratic senator from Bradford county in many years.

Towanda, North Towanda Townships and Towanda Boroughs.

Towanda was one of the original townships. Towanda village was laid out in the year 1812. North Towanda township was organized in the year 1857.

Towanda borough was incorporated in the year 1828, and additions have since been made to it. It is the county seat of Bradford county, and one of the most flourishing and populous boroughs in Northern Pennsylvania. The Lehigh Valley railroad, the Towanda and Barclay railroad and the Sullivan and State Line railroads have stations in the borough. There are several large manufacturing establishments, giving employment to a large number of men. The borough is finely located upon the west bank of the Susquehanna, and contains a population of about four thousand inhabitants. Towanda is connected with Wysox township and village, which lie upon the east side of the river, by a free bridge. It is thus situated in the center of a rich and productive agricultural country with good railroad facilities. It is destined to become a large and populous borough or city. The history of Towanda borough, Towanda township and North Towanda township is so inseparably connected that they will be treated under one head.

Early settlers were: Ezra Rutty, Rudolph Fox, Elisha Forsythe, Jacob Bowman, John Singer, Casper Singer, Jacob Grantier, Silas Scoville, Orr Scoville, John Smith, Joshua Wyeth, Daniel Gilbert, Reuben Hale, Henry Head, Samuel Strickland, William Goff, William Wyeth, Ezra Heacock, Usual Carter, George Alger, Job Irish, Henry Salsbury, John Brown, Horatio Ladd, Ephraim Ladd, William Myers, William Means, Adam Conley, Ebenezer B. Gregory, Harry Spalding, Gurdon Hewett, Nathaniel Betts, Burr Ridgeway, Lemuel Streator, Edward Benjamin, Andrew Irvine, Andrew Trout, David S. Barstow, Dr. John N. Weston, Hon. George Scott, Dr. Charles Whitehead, Henry Mercur, Jesse Woodruff, Ethan Baldwin, Hiram Mix, Dr. Caleb W. Miles, Miller Fox, Hon. Joseph C. Powell, Capt. Nicholas R. Hentz, David F. Barstow, William H. Foster, Jonas Smith, Nathan Smith, Daniel Guthrie, Isaac Foster, Rufus Foster, Abiel Foster, Osias Bingham, Frank Watts, Nehemiah Mills, Nathan Coon, Martin Stratton, Samuel F. Means, Edward Overton.

—Towanda is 741 feet above tide.

—Great fire in Towanda, March 12, 1847.

—Near Towanda was located an Indian burial ground.

—John Singer built a mill, in Towanda, in the year 1800.

—Ezra Rutty was the first permanent settler in North Towanda.

—Towanda has been known as Overton, Meansville and Canewood.

—The Naiad Engine Company, No. 2, was organized, April 24, 1855.

—Andrew Irvine built the first brick house in Towanda village, in 1828.

—Henry Mercur father of Hon. Ulysses Mercur, came to Towanda, in 1810.

—The Franklin Steam Engine Fire Company, was organized, April 8, 1854.

—Mantua Hook and Ladder Company, No. 4, was organized in March, 1871.

—Jacob Bowman, settled in Towanda, previous to the revolutionary war.

—The first school house in North Towanda, was erected in the year 1813.

—Christopher L. Ward, became a resident of Towanda borough in 1838.

—The new court or second house at Towanda, was built, in the year 1850.

—Towanda Lodge, Knights of St. Crispin, No. 370, was instituted in 1871.

—Dr. Charles Whitehead was the first resident physician in Towanda, in the year 1824.

—Rev. Miner York, was the first Presbyterian minister, who settled in Towanda township.

—Towanda Postoffice was established in the year 1810. Reuben Hale was the first postmaster.

—Burr Ridgeway established a newspaper in Towanda, in the year 1813 Democratic in politics.

—William Means was the first settler within the present limits of Towanda borough in the year 1784.

—James Catlin, an early resident of Towanda, became a distinguished landscape and portrait painter.

—Towanda Gas and Water Company, was incorporated in 1859. Gas was first furnished in Towanda, in 1870.

—Linta Steam Engine Fire Company, No. 3, was organized, Sept. 28, 1857, was incorporated in May, 1871.

—Washington Camp, Towanda, No. 190, Patriotic Order of Sons of America, was established in the year 1873.

—Capt. Nicholas R. Hentz, came to Towanda, in the year 1830. Was captain in the French army, under Napoleon, from 1806 to 1815.

—Hon. James T. Hale, who was born in Towanda township, October 14, 1810, became a distinguished lawyer, jurist and member of congress.

—The first Post of the Grand Army of the Republic, in Bradford county, was established at Towanda, June 17, 1867, with H. A. Frink, commander.

—Towanda Lodge, No. 290, K. of P., was chartered, April 6, 1871. H. S. Clark, V. P.; H. J. Madill, C. C.; G. H. Horton, V. C., A. D. Harding, K. of R. S.

—Rudolph Fox was the first permanent settler in Towanda township, and it is believed in Bradford county, having made a settlement before the revolutionary war, in May, 1770.

—Bradford Lodge, No. 167, I. O. O. F., was instituted July 1st, 1846. William Elwell, N. G.; Stephen Pierce, V. G.; Charles Reed, Sec.; O. R. Taylor, Treas.

—Hon. Joseph Powell, of Towanda, was elected member of Congress in the year 1874, as a democrat. The first democratic member in the district for many years previous.

—The Indian name Towanda, signifies: "Where we bury the dead." Conrad Weiser, the Indian interpreter however, claimed that it meant, "fretful or tedious" and was an Iriquois word.

—The Towanda Union Lodge, No. 108, A. Y. Masons, was chartered April 3, 1807. Horatio Grant, W. M.; Amos Mix, S. W.; Ebenezer Smith, J. W.; Josiah Grant, Treasurer; George Scott, Secretary.

—Bradford Encampment, No. 41, I. O. O. F., was instituted at Towanda, August 27, 1846. William Strickland, C. P.; D. C. Salsbury, H. P.; E. W. Morgan. S. W.; G. F. Mason, J. W.; S. H. Stevens, Scribe.

—Elizabeth Fox, the daughter of Rudolph Fox, afterwards wife of William Means, when a girl of thirteen years of age, remained alone in a bark cabin in Towanda township, six weeks, with no nearer neighbors than Wilkes-Barre, nearly eighty miles distant.

—Hon. Christopher L. Ward, of Towanda, had the finest private library in the State. It consisted of over sixteen thousand volumes, upon every conceivable topic. After his death, his daughter Mrs. Ellen Ward Miller, purchased it of the estate and presented it to Lafayette College, Easton, Pennsylvania. A noble and generous act.

—Hon. Joseph C. Powell was an early settler in Bradford county; was county commissioner in 1818-19 20, sheriff in 1821-22-23, prothonotary in 1836-37 38-39, and member of the state house of representatives in the year 1849. He died in the year 1854, aged 68 years.

—The Susquehanna Collegiate Institute, of Towanda, was incorporated, May 13, 1850. The first faculty was: Rev. Samuel F. Colt, A. M., Principal; Rev. James McWilliam, A. M., Ancient Languages; Charles R. Coburn, Mathematics and Normal School; Miss Margaret Kennedy, Preceptress; Miss Fanny Biles, Assistant and Teacher of Music.

—Hon. Christopher L. Ward, late of Towanda, was one of the most prominent public men in Northern Pennsylvania, an eminent lawyer, a gentleman of rare literary acquirements, a large owner of coal lands, and a prominent democrat. He died in 1870. The township of Ward, in Tioga county, Pennsylvania, is named in his honor.

—Hon. William T. Davies, was born in Wales, in the year 1831, came to Bradford county, in the year 1833, taught school in the years 1856-60, admitted to the bar in 1861 and was commissioned captain that year, and served two years in the Union army, returned, was elected district attorney of Bradford county, in 1863, and is now serving his second term as State senator.

—Miller Fox, who died recently, at an advanced age, at Towanda, was a son of Deacon John Fox, an early pioneer, was a civil engineer, and laid out the Corning and Blossburg railroad. He was much ridiculed when he asserted that the time would come when one hundred thousand tons of Blossburg coal would annually pass over the railroad. He lived to witness his prediction verified ten-fold. A million tons now annually is mined and shipped over the route.

—General William Patton became a resident of Towanda, in the year 1823. He was a justice of the peace, district attorney, clerk of the State and United States Senate. The latter position he held for twenty-five years. He was captain and major-general of militia, president of the Bradford county historical society, and a conspicuous and influential democrat. He died in Towanda, in the year 1878, aged 79 years.

—Hon. John LaPorte, son of Bartholomew LaPorte, one of the French Refugees, was county auditor, member of the State Legislature and speaker of the Pennsylvania House of Representatives, served two terms in Congress, judge of the county and surveyor-general of the State of Pennsylvania from 1845 to 1851. He was one of the old vanguards of democracy. Laporte, the county seat of Sullivan county, is named in his honor.

—Hon. David Wilmot, late of Towanda, was born in the year 1814, studied law and came to Towanda about the year 1838. In 1844 was elected to Congress, serving three terms, president judge of Bradford district nine years, United States senator two years, was chairman of the national convention that nominated Abraham Lincoln, and was appointed United States judge of the court of claims in the year 1863. He was the author of the "Wilmot Proviso." He died, March 16, 1868, aged 54 years. Upon his tombstone are these words: "Neither slavery nor involuntary servitude shall ever exist in any part of said territory, except for crime, whereof the party shall first be duly convicted."

Terry Township.

Terry township was formed in 1859. It is bounded on the north by Asylum township, on the east by the Susquehanna river and Wilmot township, on the south by Wilmot, and on the west by Albany and Asylum. It is a peculiarly shaped township, its principal lines running in a northeast and southwestern direction, forming a similar figure to a key stone placed between the township of Wilmot and Asylum. Terrytown is situated in the northeastern portion of the township, on the banks of the Susquehanna river and New Era, situated in the south western portion of the township are villages and post towns of the township. Along the Susquehanna river settlements were early made, and the land well cultivated, while back from the river lumbering was carried on extensively for years. The timber being removed the lands are now being cleared and cultivated with a fair degree of success.

The early settlers were Benjamin Budd, Johnathan Terry, Stephen Durell, Joshua Terry, Nathaniel Terry, Nathan Terry, Israel Parshall, John Horton, Lebbeus Gardner, Parshall Terry, Uriah Terry, William Terry, Oliver Dodge, Edmund Dodge, George F. Horton, Edmond Horton, J. L. Jones, Charles Homet, Isaac Schoonhover.

—There is an Odd Fellows' Hall at New Era.

—The French refuges built a house near New Era, in Terry township, to receive the King and Queen of France, during the French revolution. The house was erected about the year 1795.

—Uriah Terry was a teacher and poet.

—Parshall Terry erected the first grist mill, in 1794.

—Major Oliver Dodge was an early settler at Terrytown.

—Uriah Terry was the first white child born at Terrytown.

—Benjamin Budd erected a log house in Terrytown, in 1774.

—There were five brothers named Dodge, in the battle of Bunker Hill.

—Major John Horton Sr., built the first framed house in Terry township.

—Union Church or Tabernacle erected at Terrytown, in 1852, open to all evangelical organizations.

—"Terry Castle" an old landmark, a double two story hewed log house was for many years an object of interest.

—Jonathan Terry, was the first permanent settler in Terry township, and the founder of the village of Terrytown, in 1787.

—Major John Horton Sr., built the first framed barn in Terry township, in 1805. He done service in the revolutionary war. He settled in Terrytown in the year 1792.

—Hon. Uriah Terry was the democratic member of the Pennsylvania House of Representativeg, in 1875 and 1876, the only democratic member elected in Bradford county in many years.

—Major John Horton Jr., was Justice of the Peace for many years, a merchant, Captain and Major in the milita, county treasurer of Bradford county, and one of the prominent and influential democrats of the county. He was borne in 1793, and died in 1867.

—Jonathan Terry was commissioned Justice of the Peace, by Gov. Simon Snyder, in the year 1812, and continued in office until the year 1821, when he resigned, and was succeeded by Uriah Terry. The office of Justice of the Peace was held by the Terry family for four successive generations.

Tuscarora Township.

Tuscarora township was formed in 1830, taken from Wyalusing. It is situated in the south eastern portion of Bradford county. Its surface is hilly and uneaven, but well adapted to grazing and the dairy. It is bounded on the north by Pike, on the east by Susquehanna county, on the south by Wyoming county, on the west by the Susquehanna river and the township of Wyalusing. There are several small lakes in the township, in the highlands, and the streams are Tuscarora, Little Tuscarora and Stephens' creeks. The Susquehanna river touches its western border.

The early settlers were Joseph Wharton, Elihue Hall, Elihue Hall Jr., Jacob Gray, D. D. Gray, Thomas Morley, Stephen Beeman, Edward Coggswell, Elisha Coggswell, James Black, Harry Ackley, Jacob Huff, Reuben Shumway, Stephen Bowen, Williank Clink, Daniel Johnson, Jeremiah Lewis, Chester Wells, Oliver Sisson, Julius Coggswell, Joseph C. Town, John Clink, Benjamin Hurlburt, Amos Hurlburt, John Maxfield, Dr. Ebenezer Beeman, Alpheus Crawford, Daniel L. Crawford, David Lacey, Emanuel Silvara, Burrows Dowdney, Abiel Keeney, David Dare, Jacob Huff, Daniel Merritt, Martin Lyon, Moses Rowley, Stephen Richards, Israel Stark.

—The first white child born in the township was Marinda Coggswell, in 1811.

—The first death was Oliver Sission, in 1809.

—Rev. D. D. Gray settled in Tuscarora, in 1815.

—Tuscarora was originally known as "Spring Hill."

—Ludd Gaylord built the first saw mill in the township, in 1818.

—The first settler of Tuscarora was Joseph Wharton, in 1775.

—Jacob Huff, an early settler, was a soldier in the revolutionary war.

—Elisha Coggswell, an early settler, was a soldier of the war of 1812.

—Rev. John Hazzard was the first resident minister in Tuscarora, in 1813.

—The Lehigh Valley railroad touches the southwest corner of Tuscarora township.

—John Morely and Orilla Coggswell were married in 1816, the first marriage in the township.

—Rev. Bela Coggswell was about fifty successive years pastor of the Free Will Baptist church at Tuscarora.

—Bela Coggswell an old settler of Tuscarora township, commenced preaching when he was only sixteen years of age.

—Silvaraville Lodge No. 887, I. O. O. F., was instituted Nov. 11, 1874. First officer, J. J. Culver, N. G.; William Christain, V. G.; E. L. Taylor, Sec.

—The township derives its name from the fact that at the mouth of Tuscarora creek, an ancient village of the Tuscarora tribe of Indians existed.

—Silvaraville in Tuscarora township is named in honor of Emanuel Silvara, a native of Portugal. When Silvara was a lad he attempted to smuggle his passage from Portugal to America, was discovered and sold into service by the captain of the vessel. After serving three years he came to Tuscarora and commenced life, being scarcely able to speak a word of English. He prospered and became one of the prominent citizens of the town.

Ulster Township.

Ulster was one of the original townships and was formed previous to the organization of Bradford county. It is bounded on the north, by Athens, on the east, by the Susquehanna river, on the south, by North Towanda and Burlington, on the west by Smithfield and Burlington. It is situated on the west bank of the Susquehanna, embracing some very fertile and productive lands upon the river flats, and fine grazing and dairy farms upon the uplands. Ulster, a village in the township, on the line Lehigh Valley railroad, is located upon the site of an ancient Indian village. Milan is a village also upon the line of the railroad and a station.

The early settlers were Captain Benjamin Clark, Nathaniel Hovey, Solomon Tracy, Adriel Simons, Eli Holcomb, Capt. Isaac Cash, David Cash, Abram Parmeter, Chester Bingham, Osias Bingham, W. Rice, Elijah Granger, Thomas Overton, Abraham Brokaw, Leonard Westbrook, Joseph C. Powell, Joseph Smith, Lockwood Smith, Ezekiel Curry, Ezekiel Curry Jr., Abraham Minier, William Lockery, Joseph Lockery, Jeduthan Simons, Peter McAuley, George A. VanDyke, Simons C. Hovey.

— An epidemic fever prevailed in Ulster in 1803.

—Captain Benjamin Clark, Adriel Simons, Solomon Tracey and Captain Isaac Cash, were early settlers of Ulster and did service in the revolutionary war.

—Great flood in the Susquehanna, in 1786.

—Lorin Kingsbury taught the first school in Ulster.

—Eli Holcomb built the first saw mill in Ulster, in 1817.

—Captain Benjamin Clark built the first house in Ulster, in 1785.

—Capt. Benjamin Clark, was the first permanent settler of Ulster in 1785,

—Five-hundred shad were caught at a single haul with a seine, in the river at Ulster in 1810.

—Old Sheshequin was the original name of Ulster. Ulster was named by the Susquehanna Land Company.

—The Pennsylvania, New York Canal Railroad, now under the control of the Lehigh Valley Railroad Company, was constructed through Ulster in 1868.

Warren Township.

Warren township was formed in 1813, taken from Orwell and Rush. It is situated in the northeastern portion of Bradford county, and is bounded on the north by the state of New York, on the east by Susquehanna county, on the south by the township of Pike, on the west by Orwell and Windham. The surface is uneven and broken, but the lands are quite well adapted to grazing and the dairy. The Wappasenning creek and its tributaries are the principal streams in the township.

The early settlers were: James Bowen, William Arnold, William Harding, Thomas Gibson, Ebenezer Coburn, Jonathan Coburn, Clement Corbin, Seneca Allen, Ebenezer Lee, Roswell Lee, Henry Billings, Parley Coburn, Azariah Spalding, Arnold Armstrong, Jeremiah Dewing, Luther Buffington, Livingston Jenks, Capt. Leonard Case, Nathan Young, Richard Merrill, Thomas Corbin, Jacob Burbank, Samuel Griswold, Hezekiah Billings, Oliver Cooper, Abel Prince, Joseph Prince, George Pendleton, Robert Lee, Alfred Allen, Charles Sutton, Robert Sutton, Isaac VanBrunt, Samuel Mason, Lewis Barton, Samuel F. Mapes, John Pendleton, Preserve Buffington, Andrew Dewing.

—Warren was originally known as "Martell."

—Noah Bowen built the first grist mill, in 1802.

—The first school was taught by Robert Lee, in 1807.

—Theda Corbin, was the first death in the township.

—William Arnold froze to death, in the winter of 1803.

—The first church erected, was by the Presbyterians, in 1832.

—Livingston Jenks, opened the first store in Warren, in 1810.

—Rev. Salmon King, was the first Presbyterian minister in Warren.

—An epidemic prevailed in Warren, in 1814. A number of deaths occurred.

—There was a beaver's dam on the Wappasenning, when the first settlers came to Warren.

—Amos Coburn built the first framed house, and at its completion, had a "house warming," in 1814.

—Warren was named in honor of General Joseph Warren, who was killed at the battle of Bunker Hill.

—Capt. George Pendleton, an early settler of Warren, was captain of a war sloop, in the war of 1812.

—In 1804, there were only fourteen taxables in the township. There are now 329, with about 1,400 inhabitants.

—James Bowen, William Arnold, William Harding, Thomas Gibson, settled in Warren, simultaneously, in 1798.

—There are four postoffices in the township, viz: South Warren, Warren Center, Warrenham and West Warren.

—Benedict Arnold, son of William and Elizabeth Arnold, was born in the year 1800, was the first white child born in Warren township. Claim is made that Harry Bowen, son of James Bowen was born a few days earlier than Benedict Arnold.

Wells Township.

Wells township was formed in 1813, taken from Smithfield. It is bounded on the north by the New York State line; on the east by South Creek; on the south by Columbia; on the west by Tioga County, Pa. It is situated in the extreme north-west portion of Bradford County. Seeley Creek rises in the township and flows northward and eastward into the Chemung River, and Mill Creek rises in the town and flows west into the Tioga River, in Tioga County, Pa. The surface is broken, but well adapted to grazing and the dairy. There are three post-offices in the township. The Tioga and Elmira State Line Railroad touches its north-western boundary.

Its early settlers were Rev. John Smith, Austin Reeder, Vincent Reeder, Lemuel Gaylord, Solomon Judson, Ithamar Judson, Silas Waldron, John Osgood, John Osgood, Jr., Isaac Judson, Samuel Edsall, Adam Seeley, Thomas Osgood, Shuabel Rowley, Shuabel Rowley, Jr., James Rowley, Jonathan Rowley, Benjamin Seeley, Squire Hyde, George Rowley Peter Rowley, William Ingalls, Samuel Ingalls, Thomas Warner, Truman Warner, James Warner, Hiram Warner, James Gordon, Ralph Bovier, David Griswold, Peabody Keys, Peter P. French.

—Wells was named in honor of General Henry Wells.

—Mrs. Lemuel Gaylord taught the first school, in 1802.

—The first permanent settler was Rev. John Smith, in 1792.

—Peter P. French built the first saw mill in Wells township, in 1824.

—William R. Wilson, son of an early settler, was in the Mexican war, in 1846.

—Mary Reeder, daughter of Vincent Reeder, was the first death in the township.

—The first post-office was established in 1826, Peter P. French was the first post master.

—Wells township sent one hundred and thirteen soldiers into the union army during the late rebellion.

—Shuabel Rowley, Jr., an old settler, was justice of the peace in Wells township for twenty-two years.

—Shuabel Rowley, Solomon Judson, Thomas Warner, were early settlers and soldiers in the revolutionary war.

—Gersom Davis, of Wells, and his eight sons were in the union army during the late rebellion; his sons names were Lewis, Edson, Charles, Thomas, John, George, William, Samuel.

—Rev. Joel Jewell preached twenty-five years in the township of Wells.

—Nathan Shepard, Sr., William S. Ingalls, Shuabel Rowley, Jr., John Fitzsimmons, Strong Seeley, Amos Baker, William Osgood, Theopolis Moore, Israel Moore, Partial Mapes, Searles Barrett, Jesse Edsall, Richard Edsall, Joseph Capron, Thomas Ferguson were early settlers and soldiers in the war of 1812.

West Burlington Township.

West Burlington was formed in the year 1855, taken from Burlington, It is bounded on the north by Smithfield and Springfield, on the east by Burlington, on the south by Franklin and Granville, on the west by Troy. Mill Creek and Sugar Creek are the principal streams of the township. Its surface is rolling and undulating, and the soil is well adapted to grazing and the dairy. West Burlington is a small village and post town, located in the southern portion of the township, in the valley of Sugar Creek, on the stage road between Troy and Towanda. The chief pursuit of its inhabitants is agriculture.

For early settlers etc., see Burlington.

Wilmot Township.

The township of Wilmot was formed in 1859, and named in honor of Hon. David Wilmot, a distinguished lawyer, member of congress, and author of the famous "Wilmot Proviso." It is bounded on the north by the Susquehanna river and Terry township, on the east by Wyoming county, on the south by Sullivan county, on the west by Albany township. It is a very rich and productive township, and embraces a large quantity of alluvial lands, with very desirable table lands.

Its early settlers were Thomas Keeney, Richard Keeney, Joshua Keeney, James Anderson, James Quick, Phillip Painter, Phillip Wycks, Leonard Lott, Christopher Schoonover, Joseph Schoonover, Solomon Schoonover, Nathan Beeman, Timothy Beeman, Judson Beeman, John Brown, Deidrick Vanpoel, Webster Seymour, Silas F. Andrus, William Brindle, John McCoy, Joseph Preston, James Ellsworth, Joseph Ingham, Ephraim Barnes, Eliphalet Marsh, Simeon Marsh, Ebenezer Horton, Gideon Baldwin Jr., Abram Rosekrans, Samuel Gordon, John Gamble, John Kennedy, John Morrow, James Morrow, James Gamble, William Nesbit, Stephen Preston, Ignatius Wilson, Allen Wilson, Edward Winslow, Nathaniel Nesbit, Robert Stranger, Simeon Rockwell.

—Simeon Rockwell was the first school teacher.

—Edward Stranger was the first who died in the township.

—Thomas Keeney was the first white settler in Wilmot in 1786.

—The snow in the month of April 1807, fell five feet deep.

—There are three post offices in the township, Sugar Run, Elwell and Wilmot.

—Silas F. Andrus built the first grist mill and saw mill, in 1793.

—Elwell village was named in honor of Judge William Elwell, a former distinguished member of the Bradford county bar, but now president judge of Columbia county, Pa.

—The Elwells', Morrows', Gambles' and Inghams' were prominent and distinguished families in Wilmot township, who have made their mark in the history of the county.

Windham Township.

Windham township was formed in 1813. It is bounded on the north by Tioga county, New York, on the east by the township of Warren, on the south by Orwell and Rome, and west by Litchfield. The principal streams in the township, are the Wysox creek, which flows in a southwest direction and discharges its waters into the Susquehanna river, at Wysox, in Bradford county, and the Wappasenuing, which flows in a northwest direction and discharges its waters in the east branch of the Susquehanna, in Tioga county, New York. The surface of the township is broken and uneven, but generally well adapted to grazing and the dairy. Some very fine farms are to be found in the township. There are four postoffices in the township, and several small villages.

The early settlers were: Philo Brainard, Darius Brainard, Jeptha Brainard, Henry Brainard, Jeptha Brainard, Jr, Daniel Doane, Seth Doane, Joseph Doane, Stephen Smith, Joseph Webster, Gerard Smith, Rensselaer Moon, Jonah Fox, Thomas Fox, Russell Fox, Rev. David Short, Reuben Short, Lyman Winchester, Nathan Spalding, Augustus Hughling, Jonathan Pease, Edmund Russell, Parley Johnson, Amos Verbeck, Benjamin Shoemaker, Caleb Wright, James Mapes.

—Stephen Smith, was the first settler in Windham.

—Benjamin Shoemaker, kept the first hotel, in 1805.

—There were only two horses in the township, in 1815.

—Philo Brainard, settled in Windham, in the year 1801.

—Caleb Wright, erected a grist mill, on the Wappasenning, in 1812.

—Porley Johnson, was the first blacksmith in the township, in 1809.

—Darius Brainard, built the first framed house in Windham, in 1808.

—Jeptha Brainard, an early settler, was a soldier in the revolutionary war.

—Philo Brainrad, built the first saw mill, in 1802, in Windham township.

Wyalusing Township.

Wyalusing was first organized in 1790, twenty years previous to the formation of Bradford county. It is located upon the east shore of the Susquehanna river, near the south-eastern limit of Bradford county, and is bounded on the north by Herrick; on the east by Tuscarora; on the south and west by the Susquehanna river. The lands of the township are extremely fertile and productive; none better can be found in the commonwealth. The township is historic ground, the former home of the red man, and the site of their ancient villages. Settlements were made by white men upon its fertile flats previous to the revolutionary war. It was in this township that the Moravians established a mission among the Indians, and erected a church, laid out and built a village in 1765. In 1768 the Indians in their treaty with the commissioners of Pennsylvania, sold these lands occupied by these Indians and missionaries, and on the 11th of June, 1772, they vacated their village and removed to Ohio. In 1871, a monument was erected by the Moravian Historical Society, inscribed in a suitable manner, to mark the spot where a hundred years before, the red men and their families were taught by the Moravians the christian religion, and where the remains of many of their number were buried. Delegations were present from Bethlehem, Nazareth in Northamton county, Litz in Lancaster county, and from New York and Philadelphia to witness the ceremonies upon that occasion.

The inscription upon the monument upon its northern face is: "To mark the site of Friedenshutten. (M'chwehilusing.) A settlement of Moravian Indians between 1765 and 1772."

The eastern face reads: "This stone was erected on the 15th day of June, in the year of Redemption, 1871, by members of the Moravian Historical Society."

Western face reads: "And my people shall dwell in a peacable habitation and in sure dwellings and in quiet resting places."

The south face reads: "Remember the days of old, consider the years of many generations; ask thy Father and He will show thee; thy elders and they will tell thee."

The early settlers were Thomas Brown, Joseph Elliott, Henry Elliott, Isaac Hancock, Wareham Kingsley, Nathan Kingsley, Robert Carr, Stephen Beckwith, Sherman Buck, Amos Bennett, Richard Benjamin, Benjamin Ackley, Gideon Baldwin, Humphrey Brown, Gideon Baldwin, Jr., Thomas Lewis, James Wells. Cyrus Wells, Reuben Wells, Amasa Wells, Guy Wells, Justus Lewis, Benjamin Stalford, Peter Stevens, Daniel Sterling, Justus Gaylord, Justus Gaylord, Jr., Abraham Bowman, Robert Lattimer, Ambrose Gaylord, David Shoemaker, Samuel Gordon, Joseph C. Town, John Hollenback, James Anderson, Isaac Hancock, Judah Benjamin, Thomas Brink, Daniel Turrell, David Lake, Zackariah Price, David Lake, Job Camp, Jonas Ingham, William Dalton, Amos Hurlburt, Hiram Buck, Thomas Oviatt, Eleazer Price, Demmon Price, Asa Flint, Elijah Camp, Thomas Gardner, Francis Gardner. Benjamin Crawford, Nathan Winton, Humphrey Brown, Timothy Gaylord, Jabez Chamberlain, Gilbert Merritt, Daniel Merritt, Hezekiah Merritt, Alexander P. Biles, Lewis Biles, Simeon Marsh, Stephen Chalott, Elias Vaughan, John Taylor, John Hollenback, Peter Stevens, Jonas Ingham, Charles F. Wells, Nehemiah Main, Miles Bunnell, Nathaniel Parks, Zackariah Price, Bascom Taylor, Amos York, John Elliott.

—Nathan Parks was struck by lightning in 1804.

—In 1794 salt was worth ten dollars per barrel in Wyalusing.

—Benjamin Ackley was the first blacksmith in the township.

—Justus Gaylord opened the first store in Wyalusing in 1796.

—Samuel Gordon erected the first grist mill in Wyalusing, in 1793.

—Joseph C. Town erected the first saw mill in Wyalusing, in 1796.

—The first temperance society was organized in Wyalusing, in 1829.

—James Hines erected a distillery, in 1800, the first in the township.

—Browntown, Camptown and Wyalusing, are villages in Wyalusing.

—John Dalton murdered Amos Hurlburt in Wyalusing, in June, 1803.

—Wyalusing is an Indian word and means "Good Hunting Grounds."

—The first Sunday school in Wyalusing was organized by Eleazer Price, in 1818.

—The post office was established at Wyalusing, in 1801, Daniel Sterling, post master.

—John Hollenback was the first man to float lumber out of Wyalusing creek in 1801.

—Guy Wells an early settler was Justice of the Peace, in Wyalusing, for twenty-five years.

—The early settlers of Wyalusing were driven from their homes in 1778 by the British and Indians-

—The Lehigh Valley Railroad passes through the township, following the valley of the Susquehanna.

—Upon one square mile in Wyalusing were four families whose aggregate number of children amounted to sixty.

—May 20th 1760, Christian Frederic Post preached to the Indians at Wyalusing, the first religious service in Bradford county.

—Wyalusing Lodge, No. 503, I. O. O. F., was instituted, April 14th 1854. Its first officers were Joshua Burrows N. G.; Hiram Elliott, V. G.; L. W Camp, Sec.; Harrison Black, Treas.

—John Elliott, a son of an early settler, was a captain and division quartermaster in the militia, justice of the peace for twelve years, served two terms in the Pennsylvania legislature, county commissioner and a staunch and influential democrat. He died in 1876, aged 84 years.

—July 4th, 1801, was the first celebration held in Wyalusing, of American Independence, John Hollenback presided, and Jonas Ingham delivered an address. Uriah Terry prepared an ode on the death of Washington, music was arranged for the ode and it was sung by Polly Sill. A barbecued bear furnished the meat for the occasion.

—Wyalusing is the residence of Rev. David Craft, the teacher, minister and historian. No one who has ever lived in the Susquehanna Valley has done more than Mr. Craft to preserve the facts and incidents connected with the settlement of the Valley and Bradford county than he. He has, while ministering to the members of his congregation acceptably for so many years, found time to search out and publish facts which were fast becoming forgotten, and place in an enduring form, a chronicle of events connected with the pioneer settlement of the county and its various townships. He delivered an exhaustive and eloquent address at the dedication of the Sullivan monument in August, 1879, near Elmira, N. Y., to commemorate the battle at Newtown, and his pen has ever been busy in recording past events as they were brought to light by his unceasing diligence and research, and preserving them for the benefit of the present and future generation. Already has he erected a monument to his own memory of historical facts, and reminiscences upon whose shaft the inscriptions will be read by generations yet unborn, with pleasure and delight. All honor to Rev. David Craft, of Wyalusing.

Wysox Township,

The township of Wysox was formed in 1795. It is now bounded on the north, by Rome township, on the east, by Orwell, Herrick and Standing Stone, on the south, by the Susquehanna river, on the west, by the Susquehanna river and Sheshequin. The soil is highly productive. The streams of the township are Susquehanna river and Wysox creek. The Lehigh Valley Railroad passes through the township. Meyersburg and Wysox are post towns and villages in the township.

The first settlers were Isaac Van Valkenburg, Herman Van Valkenburg, Sebastian Strope, Isaac Strope Roswell Franklin, Benjamin Clark, Jehiel Franklin, Job Irish, Jesse Allen, Ralph Martin, Moses Coolbaugh, Ashahel Roberts, William Coolbaugh. John Hinman, James Lewis, Aaron Dean, Adam Mann, Nathaniel Moyer, John Parks, Moses Moody, Willard Green, Adrian Manville, Wilbur Bennett, Robert Bennett, Joshua Shores, Stephen Strickland, Jacob Strickland, Israel Atherton, Theopholis Moyer, Zackariah Price, Jacob Myer, William Myer. Nathaniel Heacock, Amos Mix, Burr Ridgway, Naptalea Woodburn, Elijah Tracey, Elisha Whitney, J. W. Piolett, Doctor Seth D. Barstow, Stephen Pierce, Shepard Pierce, Samuel Coolbaugh.

—The 4th of July was celebrated at Wysox in 1801.

—The first school was taught by Isaac Strope in 1790.

—Wysox is an Indian word, and signifies "Canoe Harbor,"

—Moses Coolbaugh was the first Justice of the Peace in 1800.

—Theopholis Moyer built the first framed house in Wysox, in 1800.

—John Hinman erected a saw mill in 1793, the first in Wysox township.

—The Strope family, early pioneers, were taken prisoners by the Indians.

—The name by which Wysox was known under the Connecticut title, was Claverack.

—Roswell Franklin, an old settler in Wysox built the first house in Cayuga county, New York.

—J. W. Piolett was a captain in the French army under Napoleon, and came to America in 1801.

—Sebastian Strope, John Strope, Roswell Franklin, Jesse Allen, Joshua Shores, Nathaniel Heacock, Amos Mix, Elisha Whitney, early settlers of Wysox and soldiers in the revolutionary war.

—Hon. Victor E. Piolett, a distinguished farmer and prominent citizen resides at Wysox. He has represented the county in the State Legislature and held other responsible positions, He has been a life long Democrat.

—Hon. E. Reed Myer, of Myersburg, in Wysox township, has several times represented Bradford county in the State Legislature, been speaker of the House. He has been a prominent and influential Republican in Bradford county.

CHEMUNG COUNTY, NEW YORK.

Chemung county, New York, was formed from the western portion of Tioga county, by an act of the legislature March 29, 1836.

At that time it consisted of the townships of Big Flats, Catlin, Catharine, Cayuta, Chemung, Dix, Elmira, Erin, Southport and Veteran. In the year 1854, Schuyler county was formed, and the townships of Dix and Catharine taken from Chemung.

Since that time, as will more fully appear in the histories of the townships, the remaining townships have been divided, so that the townships now are Ashland, Baldwin, Big Flats, Catlin, Chemung, Elmira, Erin, Horse Heads, Southport, Van Etten and Veteran.

The county of Chemung is bounded on the north by the counties of Schuyler and Tompkins, on the east by Tioga county, N. Y., on the south by the Pennsylvania state line, and on the west by Steuben. The Chemung river enters the county from the west, in the town of Big Flats, about eight miles north of the Pennsylvania state line, and running easterly and south-easterly through Big Flats enters the town of Elmira, and passes through the center of the city of Elmira, thence southerly through the town of Southport, and along the eastern line of Ashland, enters and runs through the town of Chemung, and passes out of the county and state, into Bradford county Pennsylvania.

The valley through which this river runs is one of the most fertile, productive and beautiful in the state of New York. It was originally inhabited by Indians of the six nations, who occupied its productive lands, planted cornfields and set out orchards, erected their rude huts or habitations along the banks of the Chemung and its tributaries, spending their time in cultivating the soil, hunting and fishing, or making war upon weaker tribes, and the white men of the south and east.

Settlements were made by white men in the county of Chemung soon after the close of the revolutionary war. Who the first actual settler was in the county is a question which has recently been discussed. Some claiming that William Wynkoop, William Buck, Daniel McDowell, Joseph Bennett, Thomas Burt, Enoch Warren and Enoch Warren, Jr., were the first settlers, and others holding to the long conceded claim that Col. John Hendy was the first white man who erected a cabin, planted and harvested a crop within the present limits of the county of Chemung. We have not the space to enter into an argument upon this subject, contenting ourselves with the reflection that a few brief months of priority in the settlement of the county will not add to or detract from the courage, hardihood, enterprise and manly spirit of the early pioneer.

It was a daring and heroic act, to enter the territory at the time that either Col. John Hendy or Mr. Wynkoop and his associates did, so soon after the destructive raid and incursion of Gen. Sullivan and his army in 1779, and so soon after the treaty of peace in the year 1783, between the American Colonies and Great Britain, and while the rival claims of the Indians, the states of Massachusetts and New York were yet pending, covering a territory immediately upon the western limits of the county, and particularly so, when it will be recollected that the valley of the Chemung leading into the valley of the Wyoming was the gateway or pass, that for years had been so watchfully and zealously guarded by the Indians of the six nations.

For ninety years the Penns of Pennsylvania had been gradually crowding the Indians northward, from the lower Delaware, Schuylkill and Lehigh, on to the lower Susquehanna and Juniata, and from the Juniata and lower Susquehanna to the upper waters of the latter river, the west and north branches. For forty years Northumberland, the Kingdom of Shikellemy, was guarded and watched by that Indian soveriegn; but in 1768 he retired to the Tiadaghton (Pine Creek), and in 1784 the state of Pennsylvania by treaty retired the Indians from the Tiadaghton and Tioga Point, the latter their great stronghold, and it was therefore under all the circumstances narrated, a daring and dangerous undertaking for white men to settle in the valley of the Chemung. All honor then to these early pioneers, who laid the foundation for the present happiness and prosperity of the inhabitants of Chemung county. Do not let a few months or years of priority in settlement detract from the honor and glory which should be awarded to the early settlers.

The county of Chemung is unsurpassed by any inland county in the state in railroad facilities. The New York Lake Erie and Western; The Northern Central; The Lehigh Valley; The Tioga, Elmira and State Line; The Delaware Lackawanna and Western, and the Utica, Ithaca and Elmira Railroads center in Elmira, and reach out east, west, north and south through the county. Agriculture receives great care and attention from its inhabitants, wheat, corn, oats, potatoes, barley, tobacco, meat cattle, and orchard and garden products are grown in abundance. The raising of fine horses, meat cattle and sheep also is carried on profitably.

The first Circuit Court held in Chemung county after its organization was held May 16, 1836. Hon. Robert Monell presiding with associates, Hon. Joseph L. Darling, Jacob Westlake and Guy Hulett. Elijah Sexton, of Veteran, was foreman of the first grand jury.

The first Court of Common Pleas was held commencing July 12, 1836. Hon. Joseph L. Darling presiding. Associates, Jacob Westlake, James Hughson, Guy Hulett and Simeon L. Rood.

The first proceedings in the Surrogate's Court was had June 3, 1836. Lyman Covel, Surrogate.

The first board of Supervisors for the county of Chemung, convened at Spencer, in Tioga co., April 2, 1836, at the house of H. Miller. Members present, Samuel Minier, of Big Flats; Timothy Wheat, of Catlin; Jacob Swartwood of Cayuta; John G. Henry of Catharine; Green Bennitt of Dix: John W. Wisner of Elmira; Albert A. Beckwith, of Southport; Asahel Hulett of Veteran. John W. Wisner of Elmira was chosen chairman; Robert C. Hammill clerk.

County Clerks office was erected in the year 1836-7. Commissioners to build the office were Lyman Covell, Charles Orwin, Elijah Sexton, who reported the building completed Nov. 14, 1837.

Present court house was erected in 1862. Cost $20,458.34. Commissioners of construction, Hon. Hiram Gray, Hon. Ariel S. Thurston, Anson C. Ely, Esq.

The present county jail, erected in 1872, cost $56,926.16.

At a special meeting of the supervisors of the county of Chemung held Oct. 21, 1836. It was voted to direct the superintendents of the poor to purchase a farm at a cost of not exceeding $3,000. From this beginning has arisen the county poor house and farm of Chemung county. It is situated at Breesport, six miles east of the village of Horseheads.

The Chemung canal and feeder was completed in 1833.

The New York, Lake Erie and Western Railroad was chartered April 24, 1832. Completed to Elmira in 1848.

The Elmira and Williamsport R. R. now under the management of the Northern Central R. R., completed to Elmira, in 1854.

The Elmira and Jefferson R. R., now under the control of the Northern Central R. R., completed in 1849.

The Lehigh Valley R. R., completed to Waverly, January 1st, 1868, and they commenced running trains over the N. Y. L. E. & W., R. R. Co.'s track to Elmira, in 1870.

Utica, Ithaca and Elmira Railroad was completed in 1875.

The Tioga & Elmira State Line R. R., completed and opened in Nov. 1876.

Delaware, Lackawanna & Western R. R., completed in 1883.

Chemung county Medical Society, organized May 3, 1836. Physicians present, Lemuel Hudson, Asa R. Howell, Nelson D. Gardiner, John Payne, Erastus L. Hart, Nelson Winton, Thesus Brooks, Horace Seaman, H. M. Graves, W. E. Boothe, F. Demorest, Uriah Smith, Z. H. Monroe. They met at the house of E. Jones. Dr. Lemuel Hudson was chosen chairman Dr. Howell, Secretary, and a committee consisting of Doctors Paine, Hart, Demorest, Winton and Howell on constitution and By-Laws.

Homeopathic Medical Society of Chemung county organized Feb. 5, 1861. Present, Drs. P. W. Gray, N. R. Seeley, T. B. Sellen, H. S. Benedict, W. H. Whippey, J. L. Corbin.

Eclectic Medical Society of the Southern Tier organized July 10, 1874.

Chemung County Bible Society organized in 1828. In January 1839 Simeon Benjamin was elected president.

Chemung county Teachers Association organized in 1850.

Post Offices in Chemung County.—Big Flats, Breesport, Catlin, Chemung, Chemung Centre, Elmira, East Elmira, Erin, Hendy Creek, Hicks Horse Heads, Kendall Station, Lowman, Millport, North Chemung, Owens Mills, Park, Pine Valley, Post Creek, Pine City, South Erin, Seeley Creek,

Southport, Sullivanville, Swartwood, Van Ettenville, Wellsburg, Webbs Mills, West Elmira.

Chemung county Agricultural Society organized 1841. Re-organized 1853.

ASSEMBLYMEN OF CHEMUNG COUNTY.—1837 Jacob Westlake, 1838 Hiram White; 1839 Jonathan P. Couch; 1840 Guy Hulett; 1841 Jefferson B. Clark; 1842-3 Samuel G. Hathaway, Jr; 1844 S. Hazen; 1845 Peter McKey; 1846 Abraham Primmer; 1847 William Maxwell; 1848 Geo. W. Buck; 1849 Alva Nash; 1850 Philo Jones; 1851 Samuel Minier; 1852 James B Van Etten; 1853 Hiram W. Jackson; 1854 John M. Randal; 1855 Orrin Robinson; 1856 Jefferson B. Clark; 1857 William T. Hastings; 1858 John Haggerty; 1859 Peter Wintermute; 1860-61 Lucius Robinson; 1862 Tracy Beadle; 1863 Charles Hulett; 1864-5 William T. Post; 1866 Henry C. Hoffman; 1867 George W. Buck; 1868 Edmund Miller; 1869-70 Edward S. Patrick; 1871-72 David B. Hill; 1873 Seymour Dexter; 1874 Edmund Miller; 1875 Jeremiah McGuire; 1876 Edmund Miller; 1877 Hosea Rockwell; 1878 George M. Beard; 1879 John Banfield; 1880 Henry C. Hoffman; 1881 Henry C. Hoffman; 1882 Orville P. Dimon; 1883 Jeremiah J. O'Connor; 1884-5 Jonas S. VanDuzer.

JUDICIARY—SUPREME COURT.—1847-59 Hiram Gray, Justice of the 6th., Judicial district, comprising the counties of Broome, Chemung, Chenango, Cortland, Delaware, Madison, Otsego, Schuyler, Tioga, Tompkins.

CIRCUIT COURT.—1846-7 Hiram Gray, Judge.

COMMISSIONER OF APPEALS.—1870-75 Hiram Gray.

JUDICIAL—COMMON PLEAS AND GENERAL SESSION.—1836-43 Joseph L. Darling, first judge; 1844-46 James Dunn, first judge; 1846-47 Joseph L. Darling, first judge. Judges, 1836-40 Jacob Westlake, Guy Hulett, James Hughson, Simeon L. Rood; 1841-46 William T. Jackson, William H. Wisner, John Crawford, Eli Banks; 1846-47 George W Miller, Samuel Boyer, J. A. McKey, J. L. Darling, Horace Ogden.

COUNTY COURT.—County Judges, 1847-50 John W. Wisner; 1850 Aaron Konkle; 1851-55 Ariel S. Thurston; 1856-59 Theodore North; 1859-60 H. Boardman Smith; 1860-64 Elijah P. Brooks; 1865-68 Gabriel L. Smith; 1869-78 Thomas S. Spaulding; 1878 Seymour Dexter, present incumbent.

JUSTICES OF SESSIONS.—1850-51 Nelson Hotchkiss, Patrick Quinn, Almon Beecher; 1852-3 Guy Purdy, Minor T. Broderick; 1854 John N. Beers, Nelson Colegrove; 1855 Alanson Owen, Peter Blauvelt; 1856 Robert Cassady Jason P. Woolever; 1857 Jason P. Woolever, Charles Patchen; 1858 Noble Weller; 1859 Robert Cassady; 1860 John Swartwood, Hiram Roushy; 1861 O. H. Lewis, Walker V. Personius; 1862 M. A. Burt; 1862-63 John C. Hathorn; 1863 J. A. McKey; 1864 Andrew Gere, Noble Weller; 1865 Jesse Rosencrans, John A. McKey 1866; John S. Gunterman, Noble Weller; 1867 John A. Carey; 1867-69 Moses Cole; 1868 A. A. Harrington; 1869 S. A. Palmer; 1870 John L. Sexton; 1870-71 John A. Carey; 1871 James C. Swartwood; 1872 John L. Sexton; Henry H. Worden; 1873-4 Elisha H. Knapp; 1874 John L. Sexton; 1875 James H. Price, John A. Carey; 1876 7 C. L. Tenbrook, Elijah Rugar; 1878-79 Charles Evans, John W. Dilmore; 1880 Samuel M. Carr; 1881 John Miller; 1882-3 Lorin Grace; 1884 James C. Swartwood.

SURROGATES.—1836-40 Lyman Covell; 1840-42 James Dunn; 1844-46 B.

B. Paine. At the latter date the duties of the office were assigned to the county judge.

DISTRICT ATTORNEYS.—1836-41 Andrew K. Gregg; 1841 Hiram Gray; 1841-44 D. C. Woodcock; 1844 William North; 1845-47 Elijah P. Brooks; 1848-50 Erastus P. Hart; 1851-55 Edward Quin; 1856 Archie Robertson; 1857-59 S. B. Tomlinson; 1860-65 John Murdock; 1866-68 Erastus F. Babcock; 1868 John T. Davidson; 1869-71 Robert Stevens; 1872-74 Walter L. Dailey; 1875-77 Sylvester S. Taylor; 1878 Archie Robertson; 1879 J. Sloat Fassett; 1880 John B. Stanchfield present incumbent.

SHERIFFS.—1836-37 John Jackson; 1837-40 Albert A. Beckwith; 1841-43 Samuel Minier, 1844-46 William R. Judson; 1847-49 William Shellenger; 1850-52 William Thompson Reeder; 1853-55 Daniel F. Pickering; 1856-8 William M. Gregg; 1859-61 Henry Baker; 1862-64 William Halliday; 1865-67 Edwin M. Howell; 1868-70 Jud Smith; 1871-73 George O'Hanlon; 1874-76 Allen Cooper; 1877-79 Edmund O. Beers; 1880-82 Levi D. Little; 1883 Geo. E. Stanley, present incumbent.

COUNTY CLERKS.—1836 8 Thomas Maxwell; 1838-40 Isaac Baldwin; 1841-6 Simeon L. Rood; 1847 9 Green M. Tuthill; 1850-5 A. F. Babcock; 1856-8 Richard Baker; 1859-61 U. S. Lowe; 1862-4 S. B. Tomlinson; 1865-7 George Bennitt; 1868-70 Robert T. Stewart: 1871-6 John G. Copley; 1877 C. Hamilton Baker; 1878 Alexander C. Eustace; 1878 Theodore G. Smith; 1881-3 Alexander C. Eustace; 1884 Archie E. Baxter, present incumbent.

COUNTY TREASURERS.—1836-43 Thomas Maxwell, 1843 6 Lyman Covell; 1847-8 E. B. Carpenter; 1849-51 Riggs Watrous; 1852-4 Nelson W. Gardiner; 1855-7 John N. Elmore; 1858-60 Stephen McDonald; 1861-3 William T. Post; 1864 James H. Loring; 1865-7 Elish H. Cook; 1867-79 Jesse L. Cooley; 1880-2 William J. Lormore; 1883 J. L. McDowell, present incumbent.

SCHOOL COMMISSIONERS.—1842-5 Nathan Tidd; 1846 Alonzo I. Wynkoop. At this time the office was abolished but revived again under a general law in 1856. 1856-9 Philo B. Dailey; 1859 Thomas K. Beecher; 1860-2 James McMillan; 1862 Isaac S. Marshall; 1863 Jesse McKinney; 1864-6 Isaac S. Marshall; 1867-9 John G. Copley; 1870-2 Charles K. Hetfield; 1873-5 Jonas S. Van Duzer; 1876-8 Robert P. Bush; 1879-81 Jonas Van Duzer; 1882-4 Chas. K. Hetfield; 1885 Arthur P. Nichols, present incumbent.

SUPERINTENDENTS OF THE POOR.—1836-40 Wyatt Carr; 1836-38 James Van Etten; 1836-39 George Coryell; 1838-41 John A. McKey; 1839-40 William Van Duser; 1840-41 Lyman Covell; 1841-42 Jonathan P. Couch; Abram Striker, Joel Heller; 1842-44 Timothy S. Satterlee; 1842-46 Horton Huston; 1843-6 F. Hager; 1844 6 E. B. Carpenter; 1846-8 D. W. Frost, Silas Breese; 1846-8 Hiram White; 1847-8 W. W. Bennett; 1847-9 David A. Degroff; 1849-50 Joseph L. Darling; 1849-51 John M. Robinson; 1850 Hiram W. Atkins; 1851 James M. Van Duzer: 1852 54 Guy C. Hinman; 1855-7 C. C. Humphrey; 1858-60 Jesse Barnes; 1859-74 Joseph Rodburn; 1875-76 John M. Griffin; 1877 John P. Breese; 1878 Alfred Strader; 1880 A. Strader; 1882-3 Elliott Griggs; 1884 Eugene Atkins, present incumbent.

COMMISSIONERS OF LOANS, U. S. DEPOSIT FUNDS.—1843 Thomas Maxwell; 1852 E. Jones, George V. Hitchcock; 1854 Jason P. Woolever; 1855 S. B. Tomlinson, Abram Minier; 1857 Frank Collingwood; 1859-69 D. W. C.

Curtis, Alonzo I. Wynkoop; 1870-2 Jason P. Woolever, William Sharp; 1873-4 G. Smith Carman; 1873-8 Paul Collson; 1880 [Paul Collson, W. R. Hammond; 1883-4 Paul Collson, Nathaniel Owen.

COMMISSIONERS OF EXCISE.—1857-8 Lyman Covell; 1857-60 James M. Va Duzer; 1857-62 George W. Buck; 1859-65 Henry Thompson; 1861-6 M Humphrey; 1862-8 Lyman Covell; 1862-6 John Ross; 1864-71 Step Owen; 1866-71 Luther Caldwell; 1868-71 Harry J. Bentley.

CHAIRMEN OF BOARD OF SUPERVISORS.—1836-7 John W John G. McDowell; 1839 Philo Jones; 1840 John G. Alonzo I. Wynkoop; 1843 Thomas S. Andres; 1844 1847 George W. Buck; 1848-50 William R. Judson; 1 1852-4 John N. Beers; 1855 James Griswold; 1856 1857-8 Jason P. Woolever: 1859-60 Samuel G. Hatha W. Buck; 1864 Robert C. Wilson; 1865 Israel Mc Miller; 1867 Geo. W. Buck; 1868 71 Edmund Cuddeback; 1874 Jud Smith; 1875 Dennis H. Swe 1878 John Brown; 1879-80 O. P. Dimon; 1881 Den S. McCann; 1883 Alexander H. Parke; 1884 Mil

CLERKS OF THE BOARD OF SUPERVISORS.—1 1837-42 Philander Norton: 1843-6 Albert F. Bab man; 1848-9 Albert F. Babcock; 1850-4 J. Baldwin. Jr; 1856 J. B. Moore: 1857-64 Jes Dumars; 1866 Jesse L. Cooley; 1867 Samuel C. 1869-74 Royal R. Soper; 1875-8 Hiram B. F

MEMBERS OF CONGRESS.—1837-9 Hiram Gr 1849-51 William T. Jackson; 1871-3-7 H. Arnot, Jr.

PRESIDENTAL ELECTORS.—1852 John Judson.

GOVERNOR.— Lucius Robinson 1877-9

LIEUTENANT GOVERNOR.—David B. H

COMPTROLLER.—Lucius Robinson 186

CANAL COMMISSIONER.—Charles Cook

CANAL APPRAISER.—Elijah P. Brook

STATE ASSESSOR.—Ariel S. Thurston

DELEGATES TO CONSTITUTIONAL C Tracey Beadle, Elijah P. Brooks, 186

MEMBER TO CONSTITUTIONAL Con

SECRETARY OF CONSTITUTIONAL C

STATE SENATORS.—1840-3 Andre Guinnip; 1858-9 Alexander S. Di Sloat Fassett.

Elmira City and Town.

The town of "New Town" was formed from the town of Chemung April 10, 1792. In 1808 it was changed to Elmira. But the name of "New Town" clung to it for many years thereafter. It comprised at its organization all the territory now comprised of the towns of Southport, Big Flats, Horse Heads, Catlin, Veteran, Erin, Van Etten and the townships in Schuyler, of Dix, Catharine, and Cayuta, which were detached from Chemung county to form Schuyler in 1854. We know of no better plan to give the reader an idea of the small number of inhabitants then within the territory named, than by appending the names of the tax-payers and settlers, then in the town of New Town. For brevity sake we will omit the columns, stating the amount of tax levied, and the number of acres, and personal effects upon which the tax was laid, our object being solely to show the names of the pioneers who resided in "New Towr," now Elmira, in 1794. The names of the taxpayers were. John Acmody, Lewis Abraham, Charles Annis, Charles Annis, Jr., Augustus Barber, Phineas Bower, Joel Bower, John Brees, George Bloom, Ebenezer Bartlet, Caleb Baker, Solomon Bovier, Thadeus Bennett, Ephraim Bennet, Henry Baldwin, Green Bentley, Abraham Bennet, Michael Bennet, Ezekiel and Sarah Brown, Jonathan Brown, Hains Bartlet, Thomas Baldwin, Isaac Baldwin, William Baldwin, Benjamin Bailey, James Broderick, Lanader Barns, Silas Beers, Ezekiel Beech, Peter Barlow, David Culver, Daniel Coreyell, Michael Coreyell, Abraham Coreyell, Stoddard Conklin, Thomas Cronover, Phineas Catlin, Israel Catlin, Zebulon Cady, Daniel Cruger, John Cortright, James Camron, Mathew Carpenter, Joshua Carpenter, John Dow, Levy Doty, Benjamin Dusenberry, Tunis Dolson, Stephen Dolson, John Durham, Jacob Durham, Samuel Edsal, Nathaniel Fairchild, John Fitzsummonds, John Fitzsummonds, Jr., Isaiah Funston, Asa Gildersleeve, Sewel Gilbert, Otheniel Gilbert, Elijah Griswold, David Griswold, James Green, William Gardner, Joseph Gray, Widow Olive Gardner, Stephen Gardinghouse, Nicholas Gale, Caleb Gardner, Solomon Gardner, George Gardner, Samuel Hendy, James Henry, John Hendy, Thomas Hendy, Benjamin Hathaway, Frederick Hines, Benjamin Hines, Abner Hatfield, Cornelius Hopper, Lebius Hammond, Josiah Hammond, Ammeriah Hammond, Henry Houser, Lazerus Hammond, John Jennings, William Jennings, William Jenkins, Phillip Jordan, Enoch Kinyon, John Kent, Widow Phebe Kent, Abner Kelsey, John Konkle, Andrew Kinyon, Nathaniel Landen, Cornelius Lowe, Samuel Lewis, William Laton, John Love, Christian Loop, Peter Loop, Cornelius Lowe, Jr., James Lownsberry, Samuel Ludlum, William McFarthing, John McGraham, Thomas McClure, John McClure, George Mills, William McCormick, Garret Miller, John McHenry, David McCormick, Joseph Miller, Abraham Miller, Abraham Middaugh, Samuel Middaugh, John Mitchel, James Mitchel, James Mitchel, Jr., Richard Mitchel, Ezra Meed, Selah Mathews, Vincent Mathews, Mathew McConnel, John McConnel, Samuel McConnel, Joseph McConnel, Alexander Miller, John Miller, John Morris, Peter Minthorn, Christian Minier, David Parshall, Amos Park, Israel Parshall, David Powers, Benjamin Pearce, John Parkhurst, Jacob Peck, Samuel Reeder, Cornelius Roberts, Jonathan Rockwell, James Rockwell, Ezra Rowley, Daniel Sullivan, John Sayres, James Sayres, Ebenezer Sayres, Henry Smith, Daniel Smith, John Smith (at Lake), Silas Sergeant, William Sutton, James Seeley, Caleb Smith, Caleb Seeley, Timothy Smith, John Smith (Seeley Creek), Adam Seeley, Nathaniel Seeley, Conrade Smith, Jacob Stull, Ashkanar Shappee, John Sly, Michael Sly, Michael Shoff, Nathaniel Seely, Jr., Adam Sly, Henry Sterrett, Jonathan Silsbie, John Stoner, John C. Smith, Selah Satterly, Conrade Smith, Jr., Robert Sterrett, Justice Stephans, Adam Stephans, Orris Taylor, Samuel Tuttle, Ephraim Taylor, Jacob Teeple, Lebius Tubbs, Samuel Tubbs, John Tubbs, Lebius Tubbs, Jr, Joel Thomas, Gamaliel Townshend, Abraham Townshend, Nathan Teal, Aaron Thomas, James Thornton, Henry Tower, Peter Vandevanter, Thomas Whitney, John Winkler, Joseph Wyckoff, Elijah G. Wheeler, John Wiers, Cornelius Westfall, Walter Waters, Clark Wynance, (Winans). Abner Wells, Abner Wells, Jr., Henry Wells, George Rankin, Brinton Paine, John Gauf, (Goff), Jacob Emmonds, Phineas Culver, Walter Waters, Jr., Christian Schott, Benjamin Littleton, Frederick Warner.

(*Signed*,)

TIMOTHY SMITH,
PHINEAS CATLIN,
JOHN CONKLE. } Assessors.

TIOGA COUNTY, ss:

To Nathan Teal, Collector of the Town of New Town:—You are hereby commanded to collect of and from all and every one of the person and persons named in the assessment, contained in the last column of said assessment and opposite to their respective names, and to pay it to the Treasurer of said county of Tioga, on or before the first Tuesday of February then next. And in case any person or persons shall neglect or refuse to pay the sum or sums opposite their respective names in said assessment, then and in such case, you are hereby authorized and required to levy on the same by distress and sale of the goods and chattels of the person or persons, who ought to pay the same and if the goods and chattles so distrained shall be sold for more than the amount of such sum opposite their respective names, in said assessment and charges of distress and sale, then the overplus shall be returned to the owners of such goods and chattles, and this shall be your warrant. Given under our hands and seals at Union, in the county aforesaid, this twenty-eighth day of June, 1794.

[Seal.] EMAN'L CORYELL,
[Seal.] PHINEAS BENNET,
[Seal.] GEORGE HARPER,
[Seal.] EPH'M FITCH,
[Seal.] DANIEL HUDSON,
[Seal.] ABNER KELLEY,
[Seal.] JOHN WELCH,
[Seal.] DAN'L MCDOWELL, } Supervisors.

The expedition of General Sullivan in 1779, and the treaty with the Indians at New Town, in 1791, had attracted the people of the various states to this locality, and settlers came in rapidly from Pennsylvania and the eastern states. The opening up of the Pultney estate by means of a highway from Northumberland, Pa., via the Lycoming and Tioga valleys to

Bath, Canandaigua, Geneva and Mount Morris, and the navigation of the Susquehanna and Chemung with small boats or canoes, enabled the settlers from the south to reach New Town early in the history of the developement of southern and western New York.

Settlers also reached New Town via of Albany, Cooperstown, the Chenango and east branch of the Susquehanna, or by way Utica, Fort Stanwix, the Cayuga and Seneca Lakes, so that by the year 1800, New Town was quite a bustling little village, and by the year 1808, it had become so elated with its prosperity, that it assumed the name of Elmira, in honor of one of its fairest daughters. As early as 1798, New Town commenced dividing up her estate. In that year (1798) the town of Catharine was formed from New Town, March 9, 1798. This township embraced the lands upon the inlet of Seneca Lake, and the rolling lands for miles on either side of it. In 1822, April 16, she gave her daughter Big Flats a start in life; and the same day, viz, April 16, 1822, she started another daughter upon the high road to prosperity, Miss Southport. Her daughters began to grow liberal and in 1823, Catlin township was formed from Catharine, April 16. Twelve years later her grand daughter Catlin started the township of Dix on the road to prosperity, April 17, 1835. The town of Veteran was the gift of Catharine, April 16, 1823.

Elmira for a number of years cultivated her large domain, erected school houses, academies, colleges, churches, built villages and hamlets, constructed canals and railroads, so that in 1854 the town of Horseheads was formed from her northern portion. In 1828 Elmira village was organized; Stephen Tuttle, President; Theodore North, Charles Orwan, Lyman Covell, William Maxwell, Trustees; Hiram Gray, Clerk. Its charter was remodled and amended from time to time, according to the increase in wealth and population, when in April, 1864, it obtained a city charter Its first Mayor was John Arnot, Jr., April 24, 1864, succeeded by John I. Nicks, two terms, E. N. Frisbie, two terms, Stephen McDonald, Patrick H. Flood, two terms, Luther Caldwell, John Arnot, Jr., Howard M. Smith, Robert T. Turner, Granville D. Parsons, Alex. Diven, David B. Hill, Stephen T. Arnot, Henry Flood, present incumbent.

—A petition was presented, June 3, 1793, by Amos Park, James Cameron, Nathaniel Seeley, Jr., Henry Sterrett, Peter Loop, Jr., Nathaniel Teal, James Seeley, John Crabtree, to the grand lodge F. & A. M. of New York, for the the establishment of a lodge at New Town, which application was granted, June 28, 1793, under the name of Union Lodge, No. 30. The first meeting of the lodge was held at the house of John Konkle, in the village of New Town, (now Elmira,) August 26, 1793. Present, Amos Park, W. M; James Cameron, S. W; Nathaniel Seeley, Jr., J. W; Peter Loop, Jr., Sec.; John Konkle, Treasurer; Nathaniel Teal, Tiler; James Seeley, member; Abiel Frye, Vistor. William Dunn the first sheriff of Steuben county, in 1796, was the first person initiated into Union Lodge, No. 30. The above named officers were installed at Canandaigua, August 22, 1793, by a convention of past masters. The lodge increased in numbers and influence until the Morgan excitement, and in 1828 suspended work, and resumed again October 9, 1843, under a new dispensation.

—Orphans Home established in 1864.
—State Reformatory completed 1878.
—Hiram Gray was born July 20, 1801.
—Ariel S. Thurston born June 10, 1810.
—Elmira Sangerbund organized in 1856.
—July 25, 1873, death of Hon. A. W. Randal.
—Elmira Farmers Club organized Dec. 14, 1869.
—James Dunn, died May 1, 1877, aged 75 years.
—John Arnot settled in Elmira, in the year 1819.
—William Dunn built the first grist mill, in 1799.
—Thomas Pattinson died Feb. 20, 1838, aged 52.
—Daniel Cruger opened the first store, in Elmira.
—Daniel Pratt, died January, 1877, aged 71 years.
—Asher Tyler, died August 1, 1875, aged 77 years.
—Levi J. Cooley, died June 4, 1874, aged 73 years.
—John Konkle, died May 30, 1828, aged 72 years.
—Thomas Perry, died June 2, 1836, aged 60 years.
—John Davis, died April 10th, 1847, aged 74 years.
—Chemung is an Indian name and signifies Big Horn.
—Andrew Gregg, died October 8, 1807, aged 74 years.
—Aaron Konkle, died October 10, 1861, aged 75 years.
—Lake street bridge across the river, was built in 1823.
—Hon. Thomas Maxwell, was born February 16, 1792.
—May 9, 1878, re-organization of the U. I. & E. R. R.
—Mrs. Jane Fitzsimmons died April 21, 1836, aged 44.
—Gen. Vincent Mathews was the first lawyer in Elmira.
—The failure of the Bank of Chemung, March 22, 1878.
—Independent Hose Co. No. 3, organized in April, 1866.
—May 8, 1873 bill for the Reformatory passes the senate.
—October 24, 1878, public test of the paid fire department.
—The Main street Bridge Company was organized in 1853.
—Great fire in Elmira December 23, 1866. Loss, $400,000.
—Eureka Engine Company No. 5, organized Dec. 11, 1854.
—Simeon Benjamin, died September 1, 1868, aged 76 years.
—Dr. Joseph Hinchman, died July 23, 1802, aged 40 years.
—Banking House of Francis G. Hall organized May 1, 1865.
—Young Men's Christain Association was established in 1858.
—Ann, wife of John Konkle, died in May, 1839, aged 77 years.
—Elmira Lodge No. 113, A. D. O. H., chartered Jan. 29, 1862.
—Elmira Driving Park Association incorporated April 13, 1871.
—Dr. Joseph Henchman was the first physician, locating in 1794.
—May 21, 1873, street cars commence running to Eldridge Park.
—Nathaniel Seeley built the first framed house in Elmira, in 1792.
—The Indian name of Elmira was Kan-e-we-ola, (head on a pole).
—Elmira was the rendezvous for soldiers during the late rebellion.
—Elmira Chapter No. 17, A. D. O. H., chartered August 12, 1867.
—Royal and Select Masters as Excelsior Council No. 6, organized in 1855.
—Ancient Jewish Order, *Kesher Shall Barsell*, organized January 18, 1871.

—The *Sunday Telegram* issued April, 1879.
—The *Sunday Tidings* established in 1883.
—The *Elmira Whig* was established in 1828, by James Durham.
—William Baldwin, died June 25, 1842, aged 74 years and 10 days.
—The Home for Orphans Children formally opened June 28, 1877.
—St. John's German Catholic Church erected in 1867, Cost $6,000.
—February 27, 1873, Benjamin Vail celebrated his golden wedding.
—Hon. Samuel G. Hathaway, Jr., died April 16, 1864, aged 54 years.
—Hon. William Maxwell, son of Guy Maxwell, died in the year 1858.
—St. Patricks Total Abstinence Soceity was organized April 27, 1873.
—John Gregg, died August 5, 1843, aged 75 years, 7 months and 7 days.
—Esther, wife of Andrew Gregg, died December 2, 1807, aged 75 years.
—The *Sunday Times* was established, in January, 1878, by D. T. Daily.
—August 19, 1874, the *Husbandman* was established by the Farmer's Club.
—Charles Fairman, the editor of the first daily paper in Elmira, died 1884.
—Mrs. Lydia, wife of Stephen Tuttle, died March 15, 1824, aged 86 years.
—First Methodist Episcopal Church organized in 1814, by Rev. G Lanning.
—Elmira Iron and Steel Rolling Mill Co. was chartered August 7, 1860.
—Major General Mathew Carpenter, died October 6th, 1839, aged 81 years.
—March 13, 1869, the *Saturday Evening Review* was issued; it continued two years.

—The *Leader*, a weekly paper, was issued in February 1874, James S. Thurston, Manager.

—The *Free Press* was established in April, 1879, and after running about three years was merged into the *Gazette*.

—In 1851 C. Chauncey Burr and Herman Burr purchased the *Democrat* and edited a daily named the *Daily Kanlon*.

—The first daily paper published in Elmira was the *Elmira Daily Repub lican* by S. B. & C. G. Fairman, June 1st, 1846.

—In January, 1847, a paper was established called the *Chemung Democrat*. In 1851 a daily edition was issued by Julius Taylor.

—The *Daily Bazoo* was issued in the fall of 1877, by E. C. George. In the spring of 1878 the name was changed to *Evening Herald*.

—May 30, 1850, R. R. R. Dumars and P. C. VanGelder issued the *Elmira Daily Press*. In 1864 it was merged with the *Daily Gazette*.

—On the 3d of November, 1853, Fairman's *Advertiser* was issued. From this small beginning arose that gigantic establishment known as the Advertiser Association.

—The first newspaper was *The Telegraph*, Bemble & Murphy, in 1815. The *Vidette*, by William Murphy, in 1818. The *Tioga Register* was established by Job A. Smith, in 1822. In 1828 the title was changed to the *Elmira Gazette*.

—The *Elmira Republican* was established, in 1829, by William Murphy, and edited by Chauncey Morgan. The office was subsequently purchased by Ransom Birdsall.

—On September 25, 1854, Young American Fire Company was organized, George Sherman, foreman, William E. Rutter Jr., Secretary, John Good rich, Treasurer.

—The first steam fire engine was purchased Jan. 19, 1864. Cost $4,000.

—Elmira Female College was opened for the reception of students, October 1855.

—Grant B. Baldwin, died January 24, 1840, aged 47 years, 10 months and 6 days.

—In 1830 Miles Covell, Jonn Arnot, Abraham Riker appointed Fire wardens.

—October 1, 1873, fires first lighted in the blast furnace of the Rolling Mill Co.

—Fire Company No. 3 organized August 21, 1848. John M. Robinson foreman.

—Hook and Ladder Company organized in 1844. Thomas Pattinson foreman.

—Zion M. E. Church (African) was built in 1870. Rev. S. H. Thompson first pastor.

—In 1797, Newtown was visited by Louis Phillips, he "put up" at the Kline House.

—Catharine, wife of Gen. Mathew Carpenter, died October 28th, 1830, aged 65 years.

—Patriotic Sons of America organized April 15, 1878, as Washington Camp, No. 2.

—First National Bank was organized 1863. Simeon Benjamin, President. Capital $100,000.

—Bank of Elmira organized in 1853, David H. Tuthill, President, Anson C. Ely, Cashier.

—The project for the Masonic Temple in Elmira, first made public March 23, 1873.

—The first chief engineer was appointed June, 1839. Silas Haight received the appointment.

—In 1865, the *Elmira Advertiser* and *Elmira Gazette* joined the New York Associated Press.

—The Corner Stone of the Masonic Temple, laid with great ceremonies, September 5, 1878.

—Fire Company No. 2, organized June, 1844. George Pattinson, foreman, Ed. Covell, secretary.

—Young Men's Benevolent Catholic and Total Abstinence Society organized August 25, 1872.

—Mercy, relict of William Dunn, and wife of John Davis, died April 8, 1847, aged 76 years.

—William Dunn, first sheriff of Steuben county, died in Elmira, February 17, 1805, aged 40 years.

—Ancient Order of United Workmen was instituted April 20, 1878, known as Elmira Lodge, No. 150.

—Farmers' and Mechanics' Bank organized in 1876, Lewis M. Smith, President, H. L. Bacon, Cashier.

—Elmira Fire Department chartered April 1859. Trustees, A. S. Clark, F. Collingwood, Riggs Watrous, B. F. Herrick, William P. Donnell, O. A. Drury, F. C. Steele, Washington Marsh, B. F. Hancock.

—Free Will Baptist Church organized July 30, 1869. Rev. Schuyler Aldrich first pastor.

—Myrilla, wife of Grant B. Baldwin, died July 6, 1866, aged 73 years, 8 months and 22 days.

—Azubah, widow of William Baldwin, died April 1, 1847, aged 78 years, 3 months and 22 days.

—St. Patricks Church erected in 1871. Dedicated Dec. 13, 1875. Rev. J. J. Bloomer, first pastor.

—Bank of Chemung organized in 1849. Simeon Benjamin, President, Dr. Tracey Beadle, Cashier.

—May 19, 1873, State Fair election to bond the city of Elmira for $50,000 to erect permanent buildings.

—Peggy, wife of William Hoffman, died November 11, 1805, aged 20 years, 10 months and 16 days.

—Patrick Ronan was elected the first chief engineer of fire department under the city charter of 1864.

—Jewish Synagogue erected in 1863. First trustees; Joseph Gladkie, H. Straus, I. Sellner, S. Sittenfield.

—Dr. Elias Satterlee was accidently shot on the 11th of November, 1815, in the gun shop of Charles Ornan.

—German Evangelical Church organized Nov. 8, 1874. Rev. M. Losch first pastor. Church erected in 1876.

—Dr. Elias Saterlee was a surgeon in the war of 1812, in the regiment which was commanded by Gen. Carpenter.

—Southern Tier Savings Bank organized March 19, 1869. Solomon L. Gillet, President, James S. Thurston, Treasurer.

—In September, 1779, General Sullivan's army celebrated the declaration of war by Spain against Great Britain, at Elmira.

—January 31, 1873, a resolution passed the Canal Board to abandon the Chemung Canal, between the river and north branch.

—The first shovel full of dirt was cast by Col. John Hendy, in Elmira, in the construction of the Chemung canal, in the year 1829.

—Southern Tier Council No. 16, Royal and Select Masters, organized Feb. 24, 1860, under dispensation, warrant granted June 5, 1860.

—The lands in and about Elmira were first surveyed by Gen. James Clinton, Gen. John Hathorn and John Cantine, State Commissioners.

—March 23, 1874, the Elmira House on Water street and other buildings burned. The Elmira House was an old land-mark. Loss, $250,000.

—In 1796, there were three divisions in Elmira known as Wisnerburg, Dewittsburg and Hendytown. In a few years these local designations became obsolete.

—Madison Avenue Second Baptist Church organized April 26, 1872, First pastor Rev. E. F. Crane. Board of trustees, J. Wood, J. Wormley. Thomas Bennett, J. J. Smithers, J. F. Rudy, J. R. Braydon, Lewis Hill.

—May 14th, 1851, President Fillmore, and Daniel Webster, visited Elmira, while on the excursion, when the celebration of the completion of the Erie railroad was held. They remained over night at the Rathbun house, then known as the Brainard house.

—November 21, 1833, $200 was appropriated to purchase a fire engine. The engine was a "Goose Neck." Erastus Goodrich was the first foreman.

—St. Omers Commandery, dispensation issued May 1852, to T. C. Edwards Com.; E. L. Wentz, Genl.; Henry G. Rice, C. D; warrant granted June 4, 1852.

—John Kline, died April 23, 1837, aged 77 years, 3 months and 3 days. Elizabeth, his wife, died September 21, 1846, aged 75 years, 6 months and 14 days.

—Grace Episcopal Church was incorporated in 1864. First rector, Charles T. Kellogg. Wardens, Harvey Luce, B. P. Beardsley; present edifice erected Nov. 1869.

—During the late rebellion, eleven thousand nine hundred and sixteen rebel prisoners were received at Elmira, of that number two thousand nine hundred and fifty died.

—The first telegraph office was opened in Elmira, in 1844; The line ran from Elmira to Ithaca, and was owned by Cornell, Sage & Co., one of the first in the United States.

—In 1852, the Elmira Gas Light Co. was incorporated; capital, $50,000; President, Mathias H. Arnot; Secretary, Stephen T. Arnot; Treasurer and Superintendent, S. T. Arnot.

—SS. Peter and Paul Church was organized by Rev. John Sheridan, in that year 1842. In 1857 a brick church was erected, and on the 19th day of July consecrated. Cost $50,000.

—The first church of the Baptist denomination was May 16, 1829. First pastor Rev. P. D. Gillets. First deacons were John Weir, Jr., David Howell. First clerk, William Lowe.

—The Elmira Water Works Co., organized April, 1869, Alex. S. Diven, President; George M. Diven, Vice-President; Alex Diven, Treasurer: John M. Diven, Secretary; John H. Levitt, Superintendent. Capital, $50,000.

—The Elmira Farmers' Club was organized December 14, 1869, by Geo. W. Hoffman, William A. Armstrong, James McCann, Charles Heller, Lewis Fitch, Samuel A. Chapman, Seely P. Chapman, John Bridgeman, Samuel Carr and Daniel E. Howell.

—In 1872, the city of Elmira expended $120,000 in the erection of two iron bridges across the Chemung river, one on Main street and one on Lake street. Subsequently appropriated $30,000 more. The total cost of the two bridges was $149,324, or $676 less than the appropriation.

—Second Presbyterian Church organized Dec. 27, 1860, Rev. David Murdock, first pastor. Church completed and dedicated June 13, 1862. The first trustees were E. L. Hart, David H. Tuthill, Ariel S. Thurston, Lyman Covell, B. M. Partridge, Robert Covell, Jr.

—First Protestant Episcopal services held in Elmira, by Rev. B. F. Onderdonk, May 16, 1832. Church edifice completed in 1836, and was consecrated by Bishop Onderdonk August 21, 1837. Rector, Rev. Richard Smith. Wardens, Harvey Luce, Dorris Hatch. Vestrymen, S. S. Lawrence Damon Hatch, Charles S. Vogel, Levi J. Cooley, Stephen Lewis, George Kingsbury, Ransom Birdsall, Samuel H. Maxwell. Clerk, P. R. K. Brotherson.

—Callisophia Literary Soccity organized in 1856. Its motto is "*Per aspera, ad asterea,*" through difficulties to the stars. Its first officers were President, Fidelia M. Belcher; Vice President, Julia Kellog; Secretary, M. J. Covenhoven; Reporter, Lida Chase.

—Park Church, Congregational, was began May 15, 1845, organization completed January 3, 1846. Rev. F. W. Graves, first pastor. The church and society built a lecture room on Baldwin street, in 1848. The present stone edifice was open for service October 10, 1875. Rev. Thomas K. Beecher pastor. Rev. Thomas K. Beecher commenced his ministry in Elmira, June, 1854.

—Royal Arch Masons, Chapter No. 42, was instituted April 4, 1815, by the authority of Ezra Ames, Grand High Priest of the Grand Chapter of New York, to Elias Satterlee, High Priest; John Cherry, King; Thomas Maxwell, Scribe and Companion; Samuel Tuthill, John Hughes, Solomon L. Smith, Platt Bennett, Amos Park and John Knox. First meeting of Chapter, July 3, 1815. Present, Elias Satterlee, Solomon L. Smith, Thomas Maxwell, Nathan Teal, James Cameron.

—Ivy Lodge, No. 397 F. & A. M. was organized Nov. 22, 1855. Thomas C. Edwards, Master; Lewis E. Bonney, Senior Warden; Theodore North, Junior Warden. Original members, T. C. Edwards, Gabriel L. Smith, William Thompson Reeder, William Dundas, William Lee, L. E. Bonney, Theodore North, James Suffern, C. F. Gosper, S. Cassada, Stephen T. Arnot, George Congdon, H. F. Sweetzer, S. B. Elliothorpe.

—Post masters of Elmira. 1801 John Konkle; 1809 Aaron Konkle; 1822 Grant Baldwin; 1835 Thomas Maxwell; 1841 Ransom Birdsall; 1843 Levi J. Cooley; 1849 Henry M. Mathews; 1853 Daniel Stevens; 1861 Daniel F. Pickering; 1867 William T. Post; 1869 Charles G. Fairman; 1877 Daniel F. Pickering; 1881 H. B. Berry; 1885 E. F. Babcock, present incumbent.

—Elmira Mechanics' Society organized in 1834. First officers were Charles Aman, Pres; Abraham Riker, Vice Pres; Ransom Birdsall, Sec; Francis Collingwood, Treas. Directors, J. A. Smith, Sylvester Munger, William R. Judson, John C. Roe, Levi J. Cooley. Prudential Committee, Francis Smith, William Williams, Hunt Pomeroy, O. Birdsall, Daniel Stephens, Henry Potter, Archibald Heggie.

—First Fire Company was organized in Elmira Nov. 20, 1830. Members, Erastus Goodrich, David H. Tuthill, Brinton Paine, William Vial, John L. Shockey, A. Beardsley, C. Howell, George Kingsbury, R. F. Seabury, Isaac Roe, John Gregg, Solomon L. Gillett, James Hill, William Foster, Elijah Jones, George Burnett, Peter Brotherson, Benedict Satterlee, Isaac Wood, Henry Potter, Benjamin C. Wickham, Charles Miller, William Williams, Asa Willard, Daniel Stephens, Miles Covell, John Arnot, Elijah Briggs, John Selover, Jacob Shockey.

—First Odd Fellows Lodge was instituted Oct. 11, 1844, by D. D. G. Master M. R. Wright, assisted by William P. Pew and Horace King, at Ithaca, New York, and known as Chemung Lodge No. 127. The charter members were Frederic Leach, George P. Tyler, D. C. Mallory, E. J. Horn, R. B. Sharpstein. First officers Richard B. Sharpstein, N. G; E. J. Horn, V. G; B. C. Mallory, Sec.; George P. Tyler, Treas.

—Samuel Riker died August 24, 1881.

—May 10, 1881, Major Archie N. Devoe, died.

—John Arnot, died Nov. 17, 1873, aged 80 years.

—C. C. Atkins, died August, 1876, aged 61 years.

—Benjamin Vail, died July 12, 1873, aged 74 years.

—Silas Haight, died January 25, 1874, aged 62 years.

—William Hoffman, died July 4, 1867, aged 90 years.

—Died August 28, 1853, Silas Billings aged 63 years.

—Mrs. Fannie Satterlee Purdy, died in 1880, aged 74.

—David H. Tuthill, died in July, 1878, aged 65 years.

—Damon Hatch, died at an asylum near Canandaigua.

—Died March 31, 1883, Hon. Samuel Partridge, aged 92.

—Jefferson Burr Clark, died March 29, 1877, aged 63 years.

—Col. John Hendy, Jr., died August 25, 1876, aged 83 years.

—Judge John W. Wisner, died April 24, 1852, aged 51 years.

—Uri Bartholomew, died November 8, 1878, aged about 47 years.

—"Aunt Mary McLaughlin," died January 25, 1875, aged 90 years.

—Gen. William M. Gregg, died September 2, 1881, aged about 66 years.

—Harriet Arnot, widow of John Arnot, died Dec. 6, 1877, aged 73 years.

—Riggs Watrous, died July 12, 1873, aged 63 years, 2 months and 25 days.

—July 8, 1881, Charles M. Beecher died. He was editor of the *Advertiser*.

—Dr. Jotham Purdy, an old and prominent physician of Elmira, died Augest 11, 1858, aged 59 years.

—Dr. Edwin Eldridge, the founder of Eldridge Park, died December 16, 1876, in the 64th year of his age.

—Tom Talliday, better known as "all right" and "all wrong," died February, 1873, aged about 70 years.

—Mrs. Lydia T. Reynolds, daughter of Samuel Tuthill, died in Wilkes-Barre. Her remains were brought to Elmira for interment.

—Fort Hill Encampment I. O. O. F., No. 86, was instituted Feb. 13, 1846, by P. C. P., P. H. Thompson. Charter members, D. C. Mallory, Philo E. Brown, Washington Thurman, Sylvester H. Reynolds, Isaac H. Reynolds, James P. Taylor James Mathews.

—William Dunn, son of William Dunn, the early pioneer, and brother of Judge James Dunn, died at Elmira December 6, 1856, aged 54 years. He was at a fire which occurred on Water street near the Lake street bridge, when a burning cornice fell and struck him in his breast, resulting in his death a few hours afterwards.

—Couer De Lion, No. 7, Knights of the Red Cross of Constantine, was established Oct. 7, 1872, by John S. Bartlett, Sov.; James M. Shoemaker, Viceroy; Frank E. Cleveland, Prelate; John D. Williams, Sen. Genl.; George Whitmore, Junior Genl.; Emmon T. Walker, Standard Bearer; Benjamin P. Fenner, Perfect; David S. Dorr, Sentinel; Joseph E. McWilliams, Recorder; Sutherland Dewitt, Treasurer; Charles H. Richards, Herald; Stephen B. Sargent, Martin V. B. Bachman.

—Chemung Canal Bank organized in June, 1833. Capital $200,000. John G. McDowell, President; Lyman Covell, Vice President; William Maxwell, Cashier; Directors, John G. McDowell, William Maxwell, Lyman Covell,

Horace Mack, Elijah H. Goodwin, Levi J. Cooley, Jacob Westlake, John Jackson, Miles Covell, Augustus S. Lawrence, John Arnot, Mathew McReynolds, Hiram Gray. In about ten years thereafter a majority of the stock passed into the hands of the late John Arnot.

—Second National Bank was organized December 14, 1863, and was a continuance of the Elmira Bank in 1853, whose president was the late D. H. Tuthill. Officers at the time of the organization were Henry M. Partridge, President, William F. Corey, Cashier. It is now owned chiefly by the Pratts.

—Lyman Covell, one of the most prominent pioneers in Chemung Co., was born April 16, 1795. He was sheriff of the county, when it was yet embraced in Tioga; for many years a leading merchant; was president of Chemung Canal Bank; superintendent of the poor; frequently supervisor of the township; county treasurer; U. S. Marshal; president of the village of Elmira; first surrogate of Chemung county, besides filling other honorable positions with fidelity. He is one of the old vanguards of democracy.

—New Town Lodge I. O. O. F., No. 254, instituted Oct. 30, 1846, by D. D. G. M., D. C. Mallory. Charter members, Edward Covell, William L. Gibson, William Woodward, James P. Taylor, Elias Colburn, Samuel C. Gibson, Jacob Daniels, J. W. Chapman, George W. Brown, Rev. Philo E. Brown, John J. Brees, Richard P. Thurber, Peter C. Beckwith, Amos Fenton. Officers, Edward Covell, N. G; William L. Gibson, V. G; William Woodward, Sec; James P. Taylor, Treas.

—May 7, 1878, was an event which will be long remembered by the citizens of Elmira. The volunteer companies composing the fire department upon the evening of that day had their last parade. For a half century, fifty years to a day, the volunteer fire companies had guarded and fought the fiery element. They had commenced their labors when Elmira was a small village of a few hundred inhabitants, and had increased in number, as the country village, town and city had grown in importance, and on that evening they assembled in line, paraded the streets, and with many a tear silently coursing down their cheeks, quietly surrendered to the city authorities their engines, hose, hooks, ladders and all the paraphanalia in their possession, to be thereafter under the control of the paid fire department of the city of Elmira. *Sic transit gloria.*

—General Alexander S. Diven is one of the old landmarks of the legal fraternity. He was born in Catharine, N. Y., February 15, 1809; studied law with Hiram Gray, and was admitted to the bar when he was about twenty-three years of age. He was prominently connected with the project of building the Erie Railroad, the Elmira and Williamsport Railroad, and every other project calculated to benefit the city of Elmira and the county of Chemung. He has represented the county in various political positions, was prominent member of Congress when the late rebellion commenced, and in 1862, assisted in raising the 107th Regiment, N. Y. Volunteers, and went into active service as its Lieutenant Colonel and led it at the battle of Chancellorville. In May, 1863, he took charge of the rendezvous for troops at Elmira; in August, 1864, was still farther advanced, being commissioned assistant provost marshal for the northern district of New York. He has recently retired from the active duties of life to enjoy his ripe old age.

—Elmira is splendidly located; the Chemung river passes through it from west to east; the Newtown creek washes its eastern side and the valley widens on the Chemung, and northward towards the Seneca Lake, to receive its thousands of busy inhabitants. Elmira has not grown into a city with that phenominal celerity which characterizes some of the cities of the west; but her growth has been steady, conservative and sure. From its very earliest history it has been favored with a class of enterprising and far seeing inhabitants, who have not depended upon the local trade of the valley of the Chemung to support her in her onward course to distinction, but through her business men has reached forth, secured the construction of the Chemung canal, which opened a source of transportation to Seneca Lake, central New York and to Albany on the Hudson, thence to the great metropolis of the state, and later her citizens played a distinguished part in the construction of the New York and Erie Railroad; the Elmira and Jefferson, the Elmira and Williamsport, (the two latter now under the control of the Northern Central); the Utica, Ithaca and Elmira Railroad; the Tioga and Elmira State Line Railroad; the Lehigh Valley; the Delaware, Lackawanna and Western; and even forty years ago in the construction of the Elmira, Southport and State Line Plank Road, and at every stage of her history her citizens have manifested that determined purpose of making Elmira the central point of population, trade and industry. Her capital has assisted in the developement of coal and iron mines, and the building of railroads to transport their products to their doors; it has built up schools, academies, colleges, churches, fostered social intercourse, and erected temples, Masonic and Odd Fellows, wherein to meet; has secured protection against fires; provided her people with water and gas, and built a rich and prosperous city; made thousands of beautiful farms, and erected elegant and substantial dwellings, where about ninety years ago was a wilderness. Surely the citizens of to-day can look back upon old New Town of 1792 and congratulate themselves upon the appearance of Elmira in 1885.

Ashland Township.

The town of Ashland was formed by an act of the legislature in 1867, taken from Southport. The principal village in the township is Wellsburg, and a station on the N. Y. Lake E. R. R., Lehigh Valley, and D. L. & W. R. R. It contains some of the finest alluvial soils in the valley.

The township has become famous on account of the battle which was fought within its limits in 1779. A monument was erected in 1879, and dedicated with great and appropriate ceremonies. Among the distinguished persons present upon that occassion were Gen. William T. Sherman, Governor Harry M. Hoyt and staff of Pennsylvania, and the Governor of New Hampshire, George W. Clinton, of Buffalo, nephew of Dewitt Clinton, Hon. Hiram Gray, and thousands of other distinguished citizens. Addresses were made by Hon. Ellis H. Roberts, Rev. David Craft, of Wyalusing, Pa. Gen. Sherman, Gov. Hoyt, Gov. Rice, and George W. Clinton, Hon. Hiram Gray, a poem recited by Ausburn Towner, Hon. Guy H. McMaster, and a letter read by Hon. Hiram Gray from Hon. Horatio Seymour, in fact it was a great event in the history of Chemung valley.

Inscription upon the monument:

NEAR THIS SPOT
ON SUNDAY THE 29th DAY OF AUGUST, 1779,
THE FORCES UNDER JOSEPH BRANT WERE MET AND DEFEATED BY THE AMERICANS UNDER THE COMMAND OF
MAJOR GENERAL JOHN SULLIVAN.

Early settlers, Green Bentley, Abner Wells, Henry Wells, Ebenezer Green, Henry Baldwin, Jacob Comfort, Abner Kelsey, Jesse Carpenter, John Hillman, Caleb Baker, Isaac Baldwin, Samuel Middaugh, James McKean, John Hillman, Wilkes Jenkins, Ferdinand Coffee, Thomas Keeney, David Burt, Nathan Roberts.

The first town meeting held for the town of Ashland was held at the "Wellsburg Exchange" in the village of Wellsburg, May 14, 1867. Officers elected were Richard C. Lockwood, supervisor; William E. Halstead, town clerk; Lyman Lowman, Hiram Roushy, justices of the peace; Alfred Searles, George Rodgers, commissioners of highways; Reuben E. Moss, John Fincher, overseers of the poor; William Hanmer, collector; James Carpenter, Israel O. Scudder, assessors; Wliiam Hanmer, Roswell R. Moss, William Woodhouse, Michael Roushey, Lawrence Mathews, constables.

—The first school house was erected in 1803.

—The first death was Stephen Kent March 21, 1791.

—First saw mill was built by Isaac Baldwin, in 1799.

—The first house was built by Green Bentley, in 1789.

—The first school was taught by Caleb Baker, in 1803.

—Cultivation of tobacco in Ashland commenced in 1858.

—The first tavern was keep by William Baldwin, in 1798.

—The first church was erected by the Baptist society, in 1812.

—The first store was opened by Abner and Henry Wells, in 1791.

—Green Bentley was the first settler in 1788. He was a revolutionary soldier.

—The first supervisor of the town of Ashland was Richard C. Lockwood, in 1867.

—The first birth was that of Eunice, daughter of Abner Kelsey, March 16, 1789.

—Jud Smith was supervisor for several terms, sheriff of the county in 1867, and chairman of the board of supervisors in 1874.

—Christ Episcopal Church organized in 1869, during the ministry of Rev. William T. Hitchcock. Church erected in 1869, and consecrated in November 1870.

—Wellsburg was named in honor of Henry Wells, an early settler. It was organized under a special act of the legislature, August 28, 1872. Its first officers were, President, James P. O'Brien; trustees, William Hanmer, Benjamin Herman, William C. Halstead; treasurer, Hiram W. Young; collector, Stephen B. Herman; inspectors of election, Mathew Fincher, William C. Halstead. It is a brisk and active village, containing about seven hundred inhabitants. The village is surrounded by a splendid agricultural district, and is the center of considerable trade.

—The Wellsburg Baptist Church known by various names, was organized

Sept. 2, 1785, Rev. Roswell Goff was established as minister, Feb. 3, 1791. In 1812, a church was erected. The first trustees were Abner Wells, Stephen Brown, Jesse More, Henry Wells, Jacob Comfort, David Burt.

—Methodsit Episcopal Church was organized in 1839. Class Leader, Henry Watson; Members, Henry Watson and Clarrissa his wife, Jerusha Comfort, Elizabeth Brown, Leslie Brown, Betsey Brown, Silas Simpkins, Elizabeth Simpkins, Jesse Simpkins and wife. First minister, Rev. Charles Davis, church erected in 1849.

Baldwin Township.

The town of Baldwin was formed by an act of the Legislature, April 1856, taken from the town of Chemung. The first election was held May 6, 1856, at the house of Daniel R. Harris. Officers elected: William H. Little, supervisor; Johnson Little, town clerk; Daniel R. Harris, commissioner of highways; William R. Drake, William McCumber, Jeremiah McCumber, justices of the peace; Schuyler Smith, collector; Holly Westbrook, John Bright, Willis Jenkins, Schuyler Smith, constables; Timothy J. Smith, overseer of the poor; Robert R. Hammond, inspector of election. The township was named in honor of the early settlers of Chemung, Thomas and Waterman Baldwin.

The early settlers were: Charles Granger, Warren Granger, Henry Tice, Jason Hammond, Elisha Hammond, James Hammond, David Hammond, Robert Hammond, Cornelius Hammond, Charles Dunn, Jeremiah McCumber, John Collson, Stephen Inman, Alphonso Lathrop, Jesse Brooks, Josiah Brooks, Daniel Higgins, John Blandon, Gilbert Salnave, Isaac Brown, Levi Little, Abram Brewer, Paul Whittaker, James Cooper, John Cooper, Simeon Kent, Harris Haywood, Phineas Blodgett, Francis Drake.

—Elijah Ruger carried the first mail in 1846.

—Allen Cooper was elected sheriff, in 1874.

—Levi Little built the first framed house, in 1835.

—Daniel R. Harris, kept the first tavern, in 1845.

—Elisha Hammond built the first saw mill, in 1828.

—Dr. J. W. Moore was the first physician, in 1836.

—The Methodists held services in the town, in 1818.

—John Blandon built the first framed barn, in 1818.

—The first postmaster was Anthony Collson, in 1846.

—Charles J. Hutchins, built the first grist mill, in 1875.

—The first death was that of Thomas Weaver, in 1820.

—Charles Granger built the first house, in Baldwin, in 1813.

—John Tuthill, Jr., taught the first school, in the year 1819.

—Miles Covell and Jacob Tice, opened the first store in 1840.

—The first school house was built in Baldwin, in the year 1821.

—The Union church was the first church edifice, erected in 1852.

—John Collson brought the first wagon into the township, in 1817.

—Henry Tice, an early settler, was a soldier of the revolutionary war.

—The first marriage was Nicholas Patterson and Miss Anna Tice, in 1818.

—In 1866, John S. Gunterman was justice of sessions. Robert Cassada, in 1856-59.

—Simeon Hammond was the first child born in the town, in the year 1815.

—Baldwin sent one hundred and sixteen soldiers into the Union army, during the rebellion.

—Elisha Hammond, William Hammond, Levi Little, Paul Whitaker, James Cooper, early settlers, were soldiers of the war of 1812.

—Union church, erected in 1852. Free to all denominations. Seven trustees were appointed, one from each church and three from the people. Cost $1,100. Rev. David Murdock preached the dedicatory sermon.

—North Chemung Grange, 227, organized in July, 1874. Its first officers were: Miles S. Nixson, master; J. Collson, Jr., overseer; N. Cooper, steward; E. M. Little, assistant steward; G. S. Little, lecturer; William R. Hammond, secretary; John E. Smith, treasurer.

—North Chemung church, organized in 1818, with the following members: Jesse Brooks and wife, Henry Tice, Huldah Tice, Susan Collson, Abigal Fox, Mrs. Sally Baldwin, Miss Fanny Dunn, Jason Hammond, Mary Hammond. Jesse Brooks, class leader. Rev. Mr. Berge was the first circuit preacher.

Big Flats Township.

The town of Big Flats was formed from the town of Elmira, at the forty-fifth session of the legislature of the state of New York, approved by Dewitt Clinton, Governor, April 16, 1822. It is bounded on the north by the town of Catlin; on the east by Horseheads and Elmira; on the south by the town of Southport; on the west by the county of Steuben. The principal stream in the town is the Chemung river, with Woodruff, Gardiner, Winters and Sing Sing creeks as its tributaries. It derives its name on account of the broad and alluvial flats within the township. Big Flats is a village in the town, with a Presbyterian, Episcopal, Baptist and Methodist churches, a hotel, four stores, a graded school, a Masonic hall, a grist and saw mill, two blacksmith shops, several groceries, a cigar manufactory, and contains about three hundred inhabitants. The New York, Lake Erie and Western Railroad, and the Delaware, Lackawanna and Western Railroad pass through the town from east to west, each railroad having a station, telegraph office, etc. The Chemung Canal Feeder, which is now abandoned, passed through the center of the town from east to west, and for many years was the scene of a large and profitable commerce. In the early history of the town, lumbering was carried on quite extensively; but now the people are almost exclusively devoted to the pursuit of farming—much attention being given to the cultivation of tobacco.

Early settlers were Christian Minier, Tunis Sterrett, Caleb Gardiner, George Gardiner, John Winters, Robert Miller, Roswell Goff, Eleazer Owen, John Goff, John Bennett, Abram Bennett, Clark Winans, William Miller, Comfort Bennett, Elisha Brown, Uzel Goble, Gersham Livesay, Charles Frye, John Silsby, Joel Rowley, Joseph Rowley, Nathan Rowley, John F. Delaney, John L. Sexton, Abram Minier, Frederic Vaughan, a soldier of the revolution, Nathan Mundy, Reuben M. Mundy, Charles Beard, Simon Hawes, Cornelius Lowe, Jr., familliarly known as Uncle Cornelius Lowe, Roswell Goff, Jr., Benjamin Whitney, David Reynolds, David VanGorder,

Sr., John Emmons, Jonathan Boyer, Martin Hammond, Noah Hawley, Calvin Hawkins, Squire Starks, Abram Scofield, John C. Scofield, Daniel Scofield, Lewis Scofield, Henry Fuller, Darius C. Bennett, Telman N. Bennett, Ami Carrier, John Pound, Joseph Pound, Jacob Vantassel, Levi Middaugh, a soldier of the revolution who died, aged 103 years, John Mead, John Riker, Nathan Sanders, James Cooper, Abram Wilmarth, Ebenezer Snow, George Snriver, Jonathan Kent, Aaron Cook, James McNulty, Hezekiah Mead, Amos Rowley, Hugh Miller, Thomas Buck, Salmon Rowley, John Huey, Peter Mead, James Hughson, Tunis Dolson, George Bucher, Henry McCormick, Levi Lovell, Hezekiah Beebe, Abel Keys, Daniel E. Brown, Benjamin Farwell, Andrew McNulty, Jacob Dorn, Aries Hodge, Hezekiah Beebe, William Ellis, Daniel Downing, James Jackson, better knows as "Hickory Jackson," William H. Reeder, Lewis Edminster, Aaron Edminster, John Mead, Elihu Chapman, Joseph Rhodes, Alfred Frye, Joseph Chandlers, George Reeser, Jacob Reeser,. William Hooker, John S. Miller, James DeArmand, Charles Reynolds, Nathan Reynolds, David Van Deren, Elihu Chapman, Daniel Hagar, Doct. Thesus Brooks, Edmond Brace, Phillip Boyer, Samuel Boyer, Samuel Wormley, John Wormley, Daniel Downing, John M. French, Col. VanValin, Hezekiah Woodruff, Erastus Beard, Silas Mills, Henry Farr, Patrick Haggerty, Coleman Olmstead, John J. Barton, Josiah Truesdale, Giles M. Allard, John White, Talcott White, William White, Frederic Wolcott, Henry Minier, Samuel Minier, Ira Minier, Sr., Harry Gobel, Joseph Dates, William Wass, Daniel Lord, John Blowers, Jeffrey Beardsley.

—The first post master was Robert Miller.

—Cornelius Lowe died in 1853, aged 80 years.

—Joel Rowley died July 4, 1854, aged 80 years.

—Tunis Dolson was the first who died in the town.

—Nathan Mundy died May 16, 1847, aged 77 years.

—Robert Miller was appointed justice of the peace, in 1816.

—Eleazer Owen was appointed justice of the peace, in 1819.

—Clark Winans built the first brick house in the town in 1812.

—Levi Lovell, an old pioneer, died Nov. 11, 1861, aged 74 years.

—The first tobacco for market, was raised by Curtis Elmer, in 1850.

—Hon. John Haggerty represented the county in assembly, in 1858.

—The first school house was erected in 1814; Noah Hawley, teacher.

—Reuben M. Mundy, a prominent farmer, died Jan. 3, 1862, aged 69 years.

—George Shriver the first merchant in the town died in 1861, aged 85 years.

—John L. Sexton was elected coroner for the county before it was divided in 1835.

—Doctor Corbett Peebles has practiced medicine in Big Flats for the past 48 years.

—John Huey was killed by the cars at Corning, September 1, 1854, aged 63 years.

—Christian Minier was the first settler in the township. He died in April, 1831, aged 91 years. His wife Christiana Minier, died September 26, 1826, aged 87 years.

—William Applegate and Catharine Minier, was the first couple married in the town.

—Hugh Miller, one of the pioneers of the town, died September 22, 1826, aged 86 years.

—John Brown, better known as Deacon Brown, was appointed justice of the peace, in 1823.

—John Brown, one of the first deacons in the Baptist Church, died in 1866, aged 77 years.

—Christian Minier, Jr., born in the year 1790, was the first white child born in the town.

—The first church organization was the Baptist, in 1807; Rev. Roswell Goff first minister.

—George Shriver was appointed justice of the peace, in 1822, before the county was divided.

—Captain George Gardner, son of Caleb Gardner, built the first framed tavern in the town in 1807.

—Doct William Woodward has practiced in Big Flats over 40 years, and Doct T. W. Read for 30 years.

—John Huey opened a store about the year 1815. George Shriver, afterwards a prominent farmer, was his clerk.

—Abraham Minier, father of the late Hon. Samuel Minier, was killed by the falling of a tree, in 1827, aged 45 years.

—The first distillery was built by Aaron Cook, in 1809. He died by the bite of a rattle snake, July 29, 1825, aged 57 years.

—Amos Rowley was the first person buried in the Robert Miller grave yard, now Big Flats Cemetery, June 5, 1809, aged 39 years.

—Comfort Bennett, an early settler of Big Flats and the wealthiest farmer in Southern New York, died Aug. 12, 1864, aged 83 years.

—Lauren A. Tuttle, and William A. Tuttle, under the firm of L. A. Tuttle & Co., were about thirty consecutive years in business as merchants at Big Flats.

—Thomas Borland was killed by the bursting of a circular saw, used upon a pile driver, in driving piles for the road bed of the Erie railroad Nov. 15, 1840, aged 32 years.

—Doct William Woodward was the first town superintendent of schools of Big Flats, and was succeeded by John Roblyeer, John L. Sexton, Jr., and Doct Theopolis W. Read.

—The pastor of the church erected in 1818, was Rev. Roswell Goff. He died in 1825, before the second church was built in 1828. Rev Philander D. Gillette was the pastor in 1828.

—The early merchants of Big Flats were John Huey, James DeArmand, Charles Reynolds, Samuel Boyer, Caleb L. Gardiner, John M. French, Ebenezer Roberts, Abram Minier, Joel Rowley.

—The Methodist church was erected in 1865. Services however had been held previously for many years. Rev. William Sanders was stationed at Big Flats and held services in the old Episcopal Church from 1843 to 1846. Other ministers had preceded him, among them Rev. Mr. Vaughan in 1837-8-9.

—There have been three school houses in the village of Big Flats. The Robert Miller log school house, erected in 1815, the red school below the village erected in 1837, and the present one erected in 1853.

—In the year 1810, the first Masonic Lodge was organized. Daniel E. Brown was W. M.; George Gardiner, S. W.; Benjamin Farwell, Tiler. Mr. Farwell recently died at Painted Post, at a very advanced age.

—Hon. George Gardner, died May 3, 1848, aged 76 years. He was a member of assembly, in the old county of Tioga, before the county of Chemung was formed. In his day he was the most wealthy and prominent citizen of Big Flats.

—Samuel Minier was sheriff of Chemung county in 1841-3, represented the county in the assembly in 1851, and was many times elected supervisor. He represented the town of Big Flats in the board of supervisors as early as 1833, before Chemung county was formed.

—Judge James Hughson was a member of the legislature from Dutchess county in 1829, and made a strong and eloquent speech in favor of building the Chemung canal. He came to Big Flats in 1832, and was appointed one of the judges of the court of common pleas, in 1836, and remained in office until 1840. He died at Big Flats in August 1858, aged 70 years.

—William Mapes, a revolutionary soldier, died April 1, 1856, aged 103 years. In August 1871 a monument was erected to his memory by the citizens of Big Flats and surrounding towns, and on the 5th day of August, 1871, the monument was unveiled in the presence of a large concourse of people. John L. Sexton, Jr., of Fall Brook Pa. delivered an oration upon the occasion.

- John L. Sexton erected the first steam saw mill in the town, the first in the county, and it is believed to have been the first in the state. This saw mill was stolen from Sexton and taken to Canada. The party who had stolen it becoming involved in that country, stole it away from his creditors and to escape capture, the engine and boilers were thrown into Lake Ontario at Sacket Harbor.

—The first Presbyterian Church was organized in 1825. Church erected in 1829-30. Dedicated by Rev. David Harrower, of Lindley Steuben co N. Y. The building committee was Benjamin Farwell, Eleazer Owen, Nathan Reynolds, Robert Miller, Charles Frye, John Winters, Clark Winans and David Reynolds. The builder was William H. Reeder, father of the late William Thompson Reeder. Mr Reeder had associated with him in the work, his brother Austin Reeder of Pennsylvania.

—St Pauls Episcopal Church was organized in 1830, and a church erected in 1833 4. Trinity Church, of New York, contributing quite a sum towards its erection. Rev. Mr. Gilbert was the first rector. In 1851 the church was sold to the Baptists. The church was re-organized in 1861, with Lauren A. Tuttle, Senior Warden; Archibald H. Gates, Junior Warden; Vestrymen. William Woodward, William A. Tuttle, John Haggerty, Andrew J. Bennett, Abram D. Huey, Ogden T. Tuttle, Jeddiah Stowe, A. B. Steele. A church was erected in 1861, costing $6 000.

—The first Baptist church was erected in 1818, and stood near the late residence of Morris Bennett in Sing Sing. In 1828 a church was erected which stood near the present residence of Joseph R. Lowe, Esq., that is about one hundred rods north east of it. In 1851 this church was abandoned, and the Episcopal Church which stood upon the Gardiner estate, west of the residence of John Minier, was purchased and removed to the place where it now stands and was remodled in that year by William L. Gibson, of Elmira, and occupied by the congregation in September, 1851. The first church erected in 1818, was purchased by the late Comfort Bennett, Esq., removed to his old homestead and used as a granary during the remainder of his life.

—Free Will Baptist church was erected about the year 1849, near the residence of the late George Shriver. It was the result of a dissension in the Baptist church, during the ministration of Rev. Benjamin R. Swick, in the years 1847-8-9. The dissension was caused by the excommunication of Abraham Bennett, one of the founders of the church, for being a Free Mason, and also the excommunication of Capt. David B. Brown and William S. Minier, for being Odd Fellows. At that time the regular Baptist church founded by Goff and Gillette had over five hundred members, residing in various portions of the town on Martin's Hill, Hawes Hill, Sing Sing, in the village of Big Flats, Hooker's Hill, Reeser's Hill and at Bennett's school house now in the town of Corning. Rev. S. T. Aldrich, was the first pastor of the Free Will Baptist church. Another portion of the regular Baptist church purchased the Episcopal church edifice, as before stated, in the village of Big Flats, remodled it, abandoning the old church near the residence of Mr. Joseph R. Lowe.

Catlin Township.

Catlin was organized, pursuant to an act of the Assembly, April 16, 1823, approved by Governor Joseph C. Yates, taken from the town of Catharine. The first election was held May 13, 1823, at the house of Uzal Dickerson. Horace Tupper was elected supervisor; George Lewis, town clerk. The town is bounded on the north by the town of Dix, in Schuyler county, east by the town of Veteran, south by Horseheads and Big Flats, and west by the town of Orange, in Schuyler county, and Hornby in Steuben county. It occupies an elevated position between the valley of Catharine creek and the valley of Post creek.

Early settlers were: John Martin, Jacob King, Charles King, Aaron Davenport, Benjamin Cure, Erastus Beard, Horace Tupper, Edward Beebe, Derias Wood, Andrew Phineas, William Rowley, Abel N. Sweet, Dennison Herrick, James J. Smith, Jacob Bucher, William Haines, Benjamin Lewis, Uzal Dickerson, John P. Cornell, Peter Ostrander, Orange Hubbell, Ebenezer Close, William Locey, Elder Thomas Sheardown, Alanson Owen, Jeduthan King, David Johnson, Jonathan Woodruff, Mathias Backer, Benjamin Cure, Jr., James Wheeler, John I. Kimball, Stephen B. Munn, Willis Savory, Washington Savory, William Masters, Widow Mary Gould, Abram Kimball, Elijah Shoemaker, a soldier of the revolution, Cladius Townshend, Lucius Tracy, Alanson G. Everetts, Peter Miles, Dewitt C. Talmage, —— Weatherby, Timothy Wheat, Ira Cole, Abram Primmer, Miller Shoemaker, William Teeter, Moses VanOrder, Jacob Steinmetz, Preserved Cooley, Thomas McCarty, Samuel Sterling, Lewis Thompson, Johnson Carter, Abel Buckley, Seth Rice.

—The first school house was built in 1820.

—The first death was Horace Tupper, in the year 1827.

—Jacob Harman was the first blacksmith, in the year 1837.

—The first saw mill was erected tn 1827, by James Wheeler.

—Miss Eunice Bartram was the first teacher of schools in 1820.

—The first log house was erected by John Martin, in the year 1816.

—The first marriage was Benjamin Cure, Jr., to Miss Betsey Doty, in 1826.

—The first tavern was built in the year 1825, by Jacob Bucher, on Post Creek.

—The Chemung Canal was constructed within a few rods of its eastern line, in 1833.

—John Ostrander was the first carpenter, and built the first grist mill in the year 1827.

—The Elmira and Jefferson railroad, now controlled by the Northern Central, touches the eastern line of Catlin, was constructed in 1849.

—The Syracuse, Geneva and Corning railway, constructed in the year 1877, touches its western border, in the valley of Post Creek.

—Hon. Abram Primmer represented the town several times as supervisor, and in the year 1846, represented the county of Chemung, in the assembly of the state.

—The first justice of the peace was Horace Tupper, appointed by the Governor, Joseph C. Yates, in the year 1823. Samuel Sterling, John Crawford and Lewis Thompson were appointed the same year.

—The first road was laid out in the year 1823, between Post Creek and Martin's Hill. The old Sullivan or Catharine highway, touching the eastern border of the town was laid out many years previous to this.

—The principal streams of Catlin, are the Sing creek and Post creek, flowing southward and discharging their waters into the Chemung river, Post Creek, at Corning and Sing Sing creek, in Big Flats. Johnson creek and one or two smaller streams rise in the town and flow eastward into the Catharine creek, the inlet of Seneca Lake.

Chemung Township.

The town of Chemung was formed March 22, 1788, as a town in Montgomery county, and elections held for the years 1788, 1789, 1790, the latter year Daniel McDowell acted as town clerk. On February 15, 1791, by an act of the Legislature, the boundaries were changed when the county of Tioga was formed from the county of Montgomery. On the 5th day of April, 1791, an election for town officers was held at the house of George Hornell, in Chemung. Brinton Paine, Bezaleel Seely, John Miller, inspectors. Officers chosen, Abner Kelsey, supervisor; John Konkle, town clerk; Brinton Paine, Bezaleel Seeley, Lebbeus Hammond, commissioners of highways; Conrad Smith, Jr., constable and collector; Christian Loop, John Parkhurst, Daniel Dewitt, James Cameron, constables; Joseph Hinchman, Phineas Catlin, Caleb Baker, assessors; Abraham Miller, William Jenkins, Samuel Seeley, Thomas Keeney, Elijah Buck, Thomas Baldwin, Brinton Paine, Cornelius Lowe and Caleb Gardner, fence viewers; David Burt, Thomas Baldwin, William Jenkins, pound keepers; overseers of the highways, Epenetus Owen, 1st district; Elijah Drake, 2d district; Thomas Bald win, 3d district; Joshua Carpenter, 4th district; Pheneas Catlin, 5th district; Thomas Hendy 6th district; Elisha Brown, Big Flats district; Abner Hatfield, on Seeley Creek.

Early settlers were: William Wynkoop, Joel Thomas, Anthony Rummerfield, Ezekiel Brown, Jacob Shineberg, Christian Loop, Ashkenaz Shappee, Isaac Baldwin, Abisha Marks, Elias Middaugh, Thomas Keeney, Daniel McDowell, Samuel Beidleman, Jacob Kress, Waterman Baldwin, Stephen B. Leonard, Joseph Bennett, Enoch Warren, Enoch Warren, Jr., Ebenezer Green, Jacob Lowman, James Wilson, Israel Parshall, Uriah Wilson, David Burt, Justus Bennett, Benjamin Wynkoop, John Hillman, Joseph Decker, Samuel Westbrook, Jonathan Griswold, John Squires, Abijah Batterson, Jacob Kress, Elijah Buck, Johnson Miller, Uriah Wilson, Thomas Baldwin, Dr. Hovey Everett, Jesse Carpenter, Thomas Burt, Abraham Bennett, James Wilson, Ebenezer Green, Joseph Drake, Moses Depue.

Chemung is the mother township of the county, and formed the original territory of the entire present limits of the county, besides that of the township of Dix, Catharine, Montour and Cayuta, in Schuyler. This was at its formation in 1788. In 1791 its limits were curtailed and in 1792, when the town of Newtown was formed it was still more lessened as will be seen by reference to the history of that township. It was within its original limits that the great battle between the army of General Sullivan, and the British and Indians occurred in August, 1779. The Chemung river passes through the township forming a valley rich in alluvial soils. Its early settlers were men of mark, several of them had been soldiers and officers in the revolutionary war. Others were distinguished civilians and brought with them intelligence and enterprise. The McDowell's, the Baldwin's, the Buck's, the Lowman's, the Wynkoop's, the Carpenter's, gave the town of Chemung a lasting and permanent reputation in the history of the early settlement and developement of the county.

—Elijah Buck kept the first store.
—Ashel Buck was the first lawyer.
—Chemung Grange, organized May, 1874.
—Dr. Hovey Everett was the first physician.
—Samuel Walker was the first school teacher.
—Moses Dewitt was the first surveyor in 1787.
—Elijah Buck was the first postmaster, in 1810.
—Erie railroad, completed to Chemung, in 1849.
—Asa Parshall erected the first brick house, in 1829.
—Henry Teater carried the first mail through the valley.
—Major William Wynkoop built the first framed house.
—William Wynkoop kept the first hotel or tavern, in 1788.
—Sergeant Elijah Buck, died in the year 1830, aged 81 years.
—Jefferson Burr Clark was a member of assembly, in 1851-56.
—Paul Colson was commissioner of loans, from 1873 till 1880.
—Capt. Daniel McDowell, died in the year 1808, aged 44 years.
—Hon John G. McDowell, died January 1, 1866, aged 72 years.
—Noble Weller of Chemung, was justice of sessions, in 1858-64-66.

—Major William Wynkoop, died in the year 1827, aged 74 years.

—The first death in the town was William Bosworth, in the year 1790.

—Nathaniel Goodspeed was the first commissioner of highways in 1788.

—Chemung Valley Lodge, No. 350, F. & A. M., organized June 8, 1855.

—Guy Maxwell and Eleanor VanSteinberg, were the first couple married.

—Henry Baker of Chemung, was sheriff of Chemung county, from 1859 to 1861.

—Joseph Batterson drove the first stage. He was subsequently killed by the Indians.

—During the war of the rebellion there were one hundred and fifty-three men enlisted from the town.

—Samuel Beidleman, located on his farm in the year 1787. He was from Easton, Northampton county, Pa.

—The first child born in Chemung, was Morris Catlin, the son of Israel and Diantha Catlin, in the year 1790.

—At a town meeting held April 3, 1792, a bounty of forty shillings was voted to pay for every wolf killed in the town.

—Vine Baldwin, an old pioneer, in the town of Chemung, was the first white child born west of the Allegheny mountains.

—The soldiers of the revolutionary war who were pioneers in Chemung, were: Major William Wynkoop, Sergeant Elijah Buck, Captain Daniel McDowell, Israel Parshall, Thomas Keeney, Jacob Kress, Waterman Baldwin, Thomas Baldwin, Samuel Beidleman, Moses Depue.

—Hon. John G. McDowell, of Chemung, son of Captain Daniel McDowell, was appointed judge of the court of common pleas, for Tioga county, in 1821, elected to the assembly in 1829, senator in 1831, was the first president of the Chemung Canal Bank, and was appointed a commissioner of loans, by Gov. W. L. Marcy. He was one of the foremost men in the county, and a life-long democrat.

—Hon. George W. Buck, son of one of the old pioneers, was member of assembly in the year 1848 and 1867. In 1848 he was a commissioner to appraise damages caused by the construction of the New York and Erie railroad. He filled many civil positions.

—The first religious society was formed by the Baptist, in 1789, by Rev. Roswell Goff. His remains are buried in the northeastern portion of Big Flats, in a small grave-yard, about one hundred rods north of the home of the late George Shriver. He was the pioneer Baptist clergyman in the counties of Chemung, Tompkins, Schuyler and Steuben.

—First M. E. church was formed in the year 1819. The first meeting was held in the school house, at Wynkoop's creek, Rev. Horace Agard, presiding elder. Rev. William H. Pearn was the first resident minister. The original members were: Jerry Holland and wife, James Ribble and wife, Epenetus Owens and wife, Phillip McConnell and wife, Joseph Swain and wife, Nancy Floyd, Katie Floyd, Treadway Kellogg, Betsey Swain, Julia Wynkoop, Stephen Vanderlip and wife, William Kellogg and wife.

—The first court of common pleas, for the county of Tioga, was held at the house of George Hornell, in Chemung, in 1791, in the month of June, and in January, 1792. Hon. Abraham Miller of Chemung presiding, with three associate judges and one justice. James McMasters, sheriff; Thomas Nicholson, clerk; Vincent Mathews, David Woodcock, David Powers, attorneys. In 1792, Abram TenBroeck, Peter Loop, Samuel M. Hopkins and John Wickham were admitted as attorneys.

Erin Township.

Erin was formed by an act of the legislature of New York, passed March 29, 1822, and approved by Governor Dewitt Clinton, taken from the town of Chemung. It is situated in the highlands, in the north eastern portion of the county, and its surface is broken and uneven with several valleys through which flows Newton, Baldwin, Jackson and Wynkoop creeks. The soil is quite well adapted to grazing, and some very fine farms are found in the township. It is bounded on the north by Cayuta, in Schuyler county, on the east by Van Etten, on the south by Baldwin, and on the west by Horse Heads and Veteran. The Utica, Ithaca and Elmira railroad passes through the center of the town from west to east.

At an election held pursuant to law, on the third Tuesday of May, 1822, at the house of John Banfield, the officers elected were, Alexander McKey, supervisor, Arden Austin, town clerk; Daniel Vaughan, Thomas Baker, Ebenezer Brown, assessors; John A. McKey, Jared Patchen, David Swartwood, commissioners of highways; John Tuthill, Robert McDowell, William D. Steward, commissioners of common schools; Alexander McKey, Arden Austin, Francis Banfield, inspectors of common schools; John Tuthill, Robert McDowell, overseers of the poor; Varnum McDowell, constable and collector; Thomas Baker, John Banfield, fence viewers; John Banfield, pound keeper.

The first tax-payers were Alexander McKey, John McKey, John Tuthill, John Tuthill, Jr., Green M. Tuthill, Allen Hurlburt, David Harrington, Ransom L. Wade, Eli Sommers, Ira Simmons, Julius Simmons, Abraham Shoemaker, Daniel Swartwood, Isaac Shoemaker, Abraham Swartwood, David Swartwood, Jonah Osborn, Joseph McIntyre, William McIntyre, Brewster Goldsmith. Thomas Lewis, Christopher Hedges, Christopher Hedges, Jr., Farrel Hedges, Robert McDowell, William Hoyt, Daniel Decker, Varnum McDowell, Thomas McDowell, Francis Banfield, Michael Robinson, Joshua Clark, Thos. Baldwin, John Boyer, James Relyea, Oliver Relyea, John Hollenback, Anthony Hollenback, Henry Hollenback, James Hollenback, Abram Elston, Phillip Thomas, James VanHouter, Thomas S. Van Houter, John Banfield, Daniel Curtis, GabrielCurtis, David Jackson, William Groom, John W. Watkins, Lewis Catlin, John Elston, Nathaniel Campbell, Mathew N. Norris, Richard Walker, Jared Patchen, Ephraim Bennitt, Daniel Bennitt, Jeddiah Bennitt, Caleb Curtis, Daniel Howell, Elias Billington, James Bishop, Henry Clear, Morris Dean, John Walker, Charles Chapman, Herman Sawyer, Horace Sawyer, Smith Paril, Nicholas Paril, Robert Park, Alexander Park, Jacob C. Swartwood, David Park, Jeremiah Jared, James Vaughan, John B. Andrews, Arden Austin, Cornelius Westbrook, Andrew H. Everett, Samuel Vaughan, James Boyer, Joseph Bennett, Silas Valentine, Zackariah Valentine, John McMillan, Isaac Van Tyle, Joseph Mills, John Hartgrove, Levi Decker, James Decker, Isaac Brown, William Brown, Silas Brown,

Joseph Frost, Daniel Vaughan, Henry Decker, Benjamin Smith, William Smith, Elijah Shoemaker, Isaac Shoemaker, Jeremiah Barnes, John Cooper, John Burrows, W. D. Stewart, Robert Stewart, James McMillan, James McMillan, Jr., George R. McMillan Elihu Everett.

—John Mitchell kept the first tavern.

—Arden Austin was the first surveyor.

—The first school house was built in 1818.

—Basil Sperry built the first house, in 1815.

—Basil Sperry harvested the first crop, in 1816.

—Mrs. Basil Sperry was the first who died in Erin.

—Joseph Rodburn built the first grist mill, in 1855.

—The first teacher in Erin was Robert Stewart, 1818.

—Thomas Baker built the first framed house, in 1825.

—Dr. James McMillan was the first resident physican.

—James H. Rodburn established the first store, in 1867.

—The first church erected was by the Presbyterians, in 1836.

—James and Joseph McMillan built the first saw mill, in 1824.

—Green M. Tuthill was county clerk in 1847-9, deputy sheriff 1838-40.

—Erin was bonded for $30,000 to help construct the U. I. & E., R. R. in 1874.

—In 1844, Hon. S. Hazen, of Erin, represented Chemung county in the assembly.

—Isaac Boyer, John Hollenback, David Caywood, John Thomas were soldiers of the revolutionary war.

—Robert Stewart done distinguished service during the war of the rebellion, and was elected county clerk in 1868.

—Baptist Church of Erin was organized in 1864. Rev. Mr. Whitney was the first minister, church erected in 1871,

—John A. McKey was superintendent of the poor, justice of the sessions two terms, county coroner, supervisor, justice of the peace.

—Jason P. Woolever represented the township several times as supervisor, commissioner of loan, in 1854, justice of sessions and justice of peace.

—The M. E. Church was organized in 1827. Rev. James Taylor was the first local preacher. The original members were Jeremiah Barnes and wife, C. C. Humphreys and wife, Joshua Baker and wife, Cornelius Becker and wife, James Baker and wife.

Horseheads Village and Township.

Horseheads was made historic in the annals of the revolution on account of its being the spot where General John Sullivan, in 1779, killed his worn out horses, on his return from his expedition against the six nations. It also has been distinguished for being the spot where some of the earliest pioneers in Chemung county erected their rude log houses, and commenced the work of clearing the forest and transforming the wilderness into farms rich in agricultural products. It has always enjoyed since the organization of the county in 1836, the notoriety of being the great center, where county conventions of all parties have been held, the political Mecca, where candidates and friends have assembled, where political slates have been made and broken, where promises have been given, and afterwards denied or ignored, the theatre upon whose stage the political actors have played their parts publicly, while behind the scenes were wire pullers who were manipulating the wires, causing the actors to play their parts automaton like, while those who made no public display of their designs were carrying out a special programme, not advertised on the bills. All these things have transpired in Horseheads, giving her a name to be long remembered by those who have been upon the political stage or behind the scenery. Horseheads has also been distinguished as a great social center, four hundred couples assembling in two halls, and enjoying the innocent and healthful excercise of dancing. Its citizens have been enterprising, establishing churches, schools, lodges, aiding in the construction of canals and railroads, and otherwise demeaning themselves with distinction as citizens of the great state of New York.

The village was first incorporated as Fairport, in May 1837, and in 1845 by an act of the legislature it was designated as Horseheads, and in 1885 was changed to North Elmira.

The town of Horseheads was formed from Elmira, Feb. 8, 1854, and on the 14th day of the same month an election was held at the house of Waterman Davis for town officers. Samuel H. Maxwell was elected supervisor; Ebenezer Mather, town clerk; Hiram S. Bentley, superintendent of common schools; David Edwards, Joel Heller, George H. Taylor, justices of the peace; John Ross, Lewis Carpenter, Daniel Bennett, assessors; Joseph Rodburn, commissioner of highways; David P. Breese, collector; William Reynolds, Abner K. Shappee, overseers of the poor; David P. Breese, A. D. Loomis, Moses P. Breese, Asa J. Jackson, Hiram H. McConnell, constables; Lewis H. Turner, Zeno Carpenter, John C. Jackson, inspectors of election.

Horseheads is bounded on the north by Catlin and Veteran, east by Erin, south by Elmira, and on the west by Big Flats. The Utica, Ithaca and Elmira, R. R., the D. L. & W. R. R., the N. C. R. R., and the N. Y. L. E & W. R. R. pass through the township. The principal stream is Newtown creek, which flows from the northeast, and thence south through the town. It is one of the most fertile and productive townships in the county.

Early settlers: Samuel Tubbs, Phineas Stevens, Lebbeus Hammond, John Breese, Asa Gildersleeve, John Winkler, David Powers, Chistopher Van De Venter, Jonathan S. Conklin, Jonas Sayre, Ebenezer Sayre, John Sayre, Vincent Conklin, Brinton Paine, Morderica Rickey, John Ten Brook, Gersham Livesay, John Jackson, Darius Bently, Paris Green, Rev. James Taylor, Joseph McConnell, John McConnell, Daniel Carpenter, Richard Hetfield, Levi Maxwell, Josiah Maxwell, David Shappee, William Rockwell, John C. Wannamaker, John Hathorn, Nathan Teal, Alexander Miller, William Seeley, Jacob Westlake, Stoddard Conklin, Capt William Hull, Abel Shute, Benjamin Smith, Charles W. Dunn, Caleb Bentley, Henry Wisner, John Parkhurst, George Payne, Charles Maxwell, Holmes Hutchinson, Silas Clark, William Hastings, Sr., George Whiteman, Peter Hastings, Theodore Valleau, Benjamin Westlake, James Taylor, Obediah Thorne, Orris Eddy, Israel Boyer, A. Scoonover, John N. Barbour, John Acmoody, Silas Breese, Willis Sayre, Walter Dailey, Sr., Samuel Westlake, John Westlake.

—John Breese erected a log house in 1789.
—Solomon More built the first tannery in 1808.
—The first tavern was opened by Vincent Conklin.
—Pioneer Hose Company, organized December, 1873,
—The first saw mill was built by Nathan Teal, in 1804.
—The first death was Susannah Conklin, March 3, 1793.
—The first grist mill was erected in 1798, by John Breese.
—Horseheads Fire Department, incorporated June 2d, 1876.
—Sarah Breese born Feb. 18, 1789, was the first child born.
—The first church was erected in 1832, by the Presbyterians.
—The first school was taught by Miss Amelia Parkhurst, in 1793.
—The Chemung *Patriot*, a weekly paper established by J. T. Bradt.
—In 1855, the boundaries of the village of Horseheads were enlarged.
—Rev. Daniel Thatcher, a presbyterian, preached in Horseheads, in 1801.
—The first marriage was that of William Dunn and Mercy Sayre, in 1790.
—William T. Hastings, from Horseheads, represented Chemung county in 1857.

—In 1855, Samuel C. Taber issued a weekly newspaper entitled "*The Philosopher.*"

—*Horseheads Journal*, a weekly newspaper, was issued May 15, 1866, by Clizbe & Hinton.

—In 1856, *The Chemung County Republican* a weekly newspaper was issued by Florus B. Plimpton, Esq.

—Great fire in Horseheads August 12, 1862. Almost the entire business portion of the village was destroyed.

—Horseheads Chapter, R. A M., No. 261, was instituted April, 1871. Charter members R. P. Bush, M. P.; Calvin Eddy, E. K.; S. A. Palmer, E. S.

—The Presbyterian Church was organized Feb. 8, 1832, with twenty-four members. Theodore Valleau, Hector Sayre, Myron Collins were the first elders.

—Horseheads Steamer and Hose Company, No. 1, was organized August 22, 1873, with John W. Lovell, foreman of Steamer; Richard Donovan, foreman of Hose.

—Hon. Jacob Westlake, of Horseheads, was an assemblyman in 1833, before the county of Chemung was erected. He was the first assemblyman from Chemung county, in 1837.

—Acme Hose Company, No. 2, organized November 14, 1877. Chas. Whitney, Foreman. Frederic F. Herrick, Recording Secretary; Edward H. Fleming, Financial Secretary; Darius Smith, Treasurer.

—In 1854 the Horseheads Building Association was organized. Comfort Bennet, Pres; Willis B. Sayre, Vice President; Hiram S. Bentley, Secretary, Charles Hulett, Treasurer. The company erected a large brick block in 1855, which was destroyed by fire in 1862.

—Methodist Episcopal Church was organized in 1815. Benjamin Westlate local preacher. Among the first members were Benjamin Westlake, Samuel Westlake and wife, Hannah Shute, James Taylor and wife, William F. Hull and wife, Obediah Thorne and wife, David Holmes and wife, Lanah Westlake, Phillip Smith.

—George Bennett was county clerk in 1864-7.

—William R. Breese built the first store in 1855.

—Joseph Rodbourn built the first grist mill in 1860.

—Walter L. Dailey was the district attorney, in 1872-4.

—Baptist church organized in 1828, as a branch of Horseheads.

—Peter Wintermute, of Horseheads, member of assembly in 1859.

—Joseph Rodbourn was superintendent of the poor for many years,

—Albert A. Beckwith, of Horseheads, was sheriff from 1837 to 1840.

—Post office established at Breesport in 1852; Warren Lincoln, postmaster.

—William T. Reeder, of Horseheads, was sheriff of Chemung county in 1849-52.

—Horseheads free school established October 11, 1865. Academic department added in 1877.

—Chemung County bank was established at Horseheads by William T. Hastings, Nov. 1855. Capital $50.000.

—St. Peter's and St. Paul's Catholic church erected in 1865, by Rev. Father Cavanaugh—consecrated in 1866.

—John Jackson, of Horseheads, was sheriff of Tioga county, in 1834 to 1837, and of Chemung county from 1837 to 1840.

—Chas Hulett was member of the assembly in 1862. Member of the Baltimore and Charleston National Conventions, in 1860.

—Methodist Episcopal, Breesport class, was organized in 1839; Isaac VanGorden, leader. Church erected in 1852; Rev. M. Beach minister in charge.

—Horseheads Lodge, No. 364, F. A. M., organized Feb. 1, 1855, James A. Christie, W. M.; O. D. Chatfield, S. W.; James Barlow, J. W.; Adam L. Staring, Treas.; Hiram S. Bently, Sec.; John Bachman, S. D.; John N Beers, J. D.

—Horseheads Grange, No. 105, organized February 18, 1873, H. M. Van Duzer, Master; Chas. K. Hetfield, Overseer; James McQueen, Treas.; J. F. Westlake, Sec.; Mrs. Samuel Marshall, Ceres.; Mrs. Wilson Rickey, Pomona.; Miss Kate Van Duzer, Flora.

—The first canal boat was built by John Jackson, and was ready for launching when the water was first let into the Chemung canal. It was used on an excursion in the celebration of that event, where canons were fired, a band of martial music employed, and a grand time generally had.

—Baptist church, Rev. Roswell Goff and Rev. Philander D. Gillette were the early Baptist ministers, and Goff commenced his labors here and elsewhere as early as 1805; Rev. Gillette about 1825. In April, 1840, a church was organized by Rev. Aaron Jackson. Among the members were deacon Joseph Smith, John Tenbrook, Ebenezer Mather, Increase Mather.

—Protestant Episcopal church was organized in October, 1862, through the efforts of Samuel H. Maxwell, Mrs. Nathan VanDuzen, Mrs. Fanny Sayre, Mrs. A. H. Judson, Stephen Johnson, Rowland Parker. A brick church was erected and consecrated by Bishop Coxe, October 8, 1867; Rev. H. M. Brown, rector.

—Captain Vincent Conklin, of Horseheads, when the bill was pending in the legislature of New York, for the construction of the Chemung canal, took a team, went to Blossburg before there were any bridges across the Canisteo or Tioga rivers, obtained a wagon load of coal, and sent it to Albany in a wagon, for the inspection of the committee upon canals, and legislators generally. Captain Conklin is still living at this time, March 20, 1885.

—Breesport was laid out in 1854, by Azariah Breese. It now contains about seven hundred inhabitants. The Chemung County Poor House is located at this point. The shops of the Utica, Ithaca and Elmira Railroad were located there immediately after the completion of the road. It is the home of Joseph Rodbourn, a prominent business man, who was instrumental in building up the village; was the projector of the railroad, and by his energy, skill and enterprise, it was successfully completed. He was the first president of the road

—Horseheads, for many years under the old militia system of the state, was the place where "General Trainings" were held, in the meadow upon the farm of the late Col. Henry C. Hoffman. A writer speaking of one of these old "General Trainings," says: Across Newtown creek from where I stand, on lands now owned by Col. H. C. Hoffman, was the spot, where from all sections of Chemung county assembled annually the rifle companies and militia to drill according to Scott's Manual. At that time several revolutionary soldiers were living in the county, and quite a large number of soldiers of the war ot 1812, who generally were present and inspired a martial spirit in the breast of the riflemen, militia and officers. The men were then living who had taken part in the battles of Lake Erie, Lundy's Lane, Plattsburg, New Orleans, and the music performed by the martial bands, was the same as played during the triumphs of Commodore Perry, General Scott and the hero of New Orleans. At these general musters the prospective and ideal enemy was the Red Coats or British, and every manouver was studied with an idea of how to parry and ward off the blows, or elude the shot or evade the charge of the English soldiers. Forty-six years ago I stood on this very spot, and with breathless anxiety watched the parade, the drill and military evolutions. There were probably five hundred men drilling, a host, in my youthful mind, sufficient to repel the armies of Great Britain or France. With what eagerness I watched the manouvers of the cavalry, the exercise in the manual of arms, by the infantry and their charges with fixed bayonets, and listened to the shrill blast of the bugle, the inspiring notes of the fife, accompanied with beats in perfect time of the snare and bass drums. These things inspired me with the greatness, strength and powers of the American soldier, and furnished me with topic for elaboration among the less fortunate boys of my neighborhood, when I returned home, for weeks thereafter. It set me to practicing with flail staffs, pitchforks, corn-cutters as imaginary guns, sabers and bayonets, and *Don Quixote* like I was ready to attack any object which came in my way.

Southport Township.

Southport was formed by an act of the legislature, approved by Gov. Dewitt Clinton, April 16, 1822, taken from Elmira, (see session 45, Chap. 121, laws of New York.) A portion of the town was added to the village of Elmira, and in the year 1867 a portion was taken to form the town of Ashland. It is bounded on the north by the city and town of Elmira, on the east by the Chemung river and the town of Ashland, on the south by Pennsylvania state line, and on the west by Caton, in Steuben county.

It contains an area of nearly 29,000 acres. The Chemung river passes along its northern and eastern borders, while Hendy creek and Seeley creek are tributaries of the Chemung, passing from west to east through the town. A large portion of the lands of the township are alluvial flats, and very productive, while the upland portion is susceptible of growing also most excellent crops.

Quite a number of extensive manufacturing and industrial establishments are located within its limits, and several small villages, lying in the immediate vicinity of Elmira city, every product of the farm is readily marketed, and some of the very finest farms in the county are to be found in Southport. The Northern Central Railroad, the Tioga and State Line R. R., and the Erie Railroad pass through the town.

From present indications it will be but a few years hence, before a large amount of the territory of Southport will be absorbed, and become a portion of the city of Elmira.

The first town election was held May 14, 1822, at the house of John Weir, and Solomon L. Smith was elected supervisor; William Wells, town clerk; John W. Knapp, William Jenkins, Samuel Strong, assessors; John L. Smith, Platt Bennett, Samuel Strong, commissioners of highways; William Benson, James B. Goff, Platt Bennett, inspectors of common schools; William Jenkins, William C. Weir, Jacob Miller, commissioners of common schools; John Fitzsimmons, John L. Smith, overseers of the poor; Nathaniel Knapp, collector; Aaron Brown, Nathaniel Knapp, constables; Samuel Strong, John L. Smith, fence viewers; John Weir, pound master; Samuel Middaugh John Bovier, John Fitzsimmons, John Sly, William K. Knapp, Philo Jones, Thomas Comfort, Jeremiah Coleman, overseers of roads or path masters.

Early settlers Judge Abraham Miller, John Miller, John Smith, Timothy Smith, Solomon Bovier, Lebbeus Hammond, William Jenkins, Judge Caleb Baker, Jabez Culver, Lebbeus Tubbs, Samuel Middaugh, David Griswold, Rev. Simeon R. Jones, Philo Jones, Dr. A. G. White, Archibald Marvin, Daniel Beckwith, Peter Stryker, Charles Evans, John McHenry, Nathaniel Seeley, John Fitzsimmons, John Sly, William Benson, James B. Goff, Platt Bennett, Jacob Miller, James Seeley, Elijah Griswold, Silas Billings, Valentine Strouse, Samuel Giles, William Lowe, Partial Mapes, Richard Comfort, Rufus Baldwin, William Jenkins, James Mitchell, Daniel Dalrymple, Adam Seeley, Israel Seeley, Josiah Pedrick.

—C. Hamilton Baker, county clerk in 1877

—The first school house was erected in 1799.

—Second M. E. Church at Webbs' Mills, was erected in 1858.

—Baptist church at Pine City, Southport, dedicated in 1854.

—Silas Billings erected a woolen manufactory, in 1821, with a flax mill attached.

—The first dwelling in Southport was erected by Judge Abraham Miller, in the spring of 1790. He also built a saw mill on a branch of Seeley creek in 1798.

—Ezra Canfield member of assembly, in 1837.
—Richard Baker was county clerk, in 1856-8.
—James Griswold, chairman board of supervisors, in 1855.
—George W. Miller was judge of Chemung county, in 1846.
—Samuel C. Gibson opened a store at Webbs' Mills, in 1845.
—The first grist mill was erected by David Griswold, in 1798.
—Northern Central Railroad shops established in 1867, in Southport.
—Nathaniel Seeley was the first hatter in Southport, and in the county.
—Abraham Miller was appointed the first Judge of Tioga county, in 1791.
—The first Presbyterian church was erected in 1819. Destroyed by fire in 1831.
—Charles Evans was justice of sessions in 1878-79, and 3 terms as supervisor.
—Plank road constructed from Elmira through Southport to State Line, in 1847.
—Philo Jones was member of assembly in 1850. Had been chairman of the board of supervisors in 1839.
—Edmund Miller was chairman board of supervisors, in 1866, 1868, 1871, and member of assembly in 1868, 1874, 1876.
—Caleb Baker was appointed judge in 1810. Had been a surrogate in 1806. Member of assembly 1814-15, and 1829.
—John Miller was appointed judge, in 1807. He had been a member of assembly for the years 1805-6. In 1798 judge of common pleas.

Van Etten Township.

Van Etten was organized April 17, 1854, taken from Erin and Cayuta, and named in honor of John B. Van Etten. The first election was held on 9th of May 1854, and George B. Hall was elected supervisor: John S. Swartwood, town clerk; David Swartwood, James Ennis, Nicholas Richards, assessors; Uri Osborn, Lauren J. Stewart, Seymour Burchard, commissioners of highways; Emanuel Ennis, superintendent of schools; Guy Purdy, justice of the peace; William Campbell, John Swartwood, John S. Ennis, inspectors of election; Benjamin D. Kniffin, H. Vanderberg, overseers of the poor; John Banfield, collector; John Banfield, Asa Nichols, John Swartwood, Cornelius Van Auken, Nelson Woolever, constables; Daniel C. Van Etten, sealer of weights and measures.

The town of Van Etten is bounded on the north by Newfield, in Tompkins county, on the east by Spencer, in Tioga county, on the south by Barton, in Tioga county, and Baldwin, in Chemung county, on the west by Erin, in Chemnng county, and Cayuta in Schuyler. The villages in the town are Van Ettenville and Swartwood, and stations on the Utica, Ithaca, and Elmira R. R., and the Geneva, Ithaca and Sayre R. R. The surface is broken and uneven.

Early settlers; Joel Thomas, Gen'l. Jacob Swartwood, Emanuel Swartwood, Isaac Swartwood, Peter Swartwood, William Ennis, Alexander Ennis, John Ennis, Emanuel Ennis, Benjamin Ennis, James Van Etten, Emanuel Van Etten, Joshua Van Etten, James Van Etten, Jr., Major Samuel Westbrook, James Westbrook, Daniel Westbrook, Joshua Westbrook, John Hill-

David Hill, William Hill, Daniel Decker, Isaac Decker, Levi Decker, Hiram White, David Jayne, Gabriel Jayne, Henry Barnes, Abraham Barnes, Jacob Van Auken, Michael Higgins, Guy Purdy, Solomon White, John Zimmerman, Jonathan Baker.

—Joel Thomas built the first house, in 1795.

—Gen'l. Swartwood kept the first hotel in 1801.

—Mrs. Ann Baker taught the first school in 1803.

—The Utica, Ithaca and Elmira Railroad built in 1874.

—Peter Swartwood opened the first store in the year 1821.

—Gen'l. Jacob Swartwood harvested the first crop, in 1797.

—Geneva, Ithaca and Sayre Railroad built in the year 1871.

—Hon. James B. Van Etten was member of assembly in 1852.

—The first church was the Hedding M. E. Church in the year 1826.

—Gen'l. Jacob Swartwood was the first post-master in the year 1820.

—Hon. Hiram White, represented Chemung county in the year 1838.

—Doctor Charles Murray was the first resident physician in the year 1823.

—Mrs. Elizabeth Allington was the first person who died in the town, in the year 1797.

—Daniel Decker and Nancy Swartwood, were the first couple married in the town in the year 1803.

—Isaac Swartwood built the first saw mill, in 1800, the first framed house in 1802, and the first grist mill, in 1803.

—Gen'l. Jacob Swartwood, was a member of assembly in the year 1828. His colleague was Hon. William Maxwell.

—Mt. Lebanon Lodge, No. 775, F. A. M., was organized July 12, 1877. Amos S. Hixson, W. M.; Alfred Burchard, S. W.; Geo. W. Banfield, J. W.

—O. P. Dimon, has represented the town several times as supervisor, and was chairman of the board of supervisors 1876-7. He was also member of assembly.

—Guy Purdy, was a justice of the peace, justice of sessions, and several times supervisor, town clerk, town superintendent of schools, and a very prominent citizen.

—Van Ettenville was incorporated as a village, Nov. 27th, 1876. First officers were Amos S. Hixson, President; John Banfield, O. P. Dimon, A. B. Clark, Trustees; Sanford Hoff, Treasurer; Isaac Knettles, Collector.

Veteran Township.

Veteran was organized by an act of the Legislature, approved by Governor Joseph C. Yates, April 16, 1823, taken from Catharine. It is bounded on the north by Catharine and Montour in Schuyler county; on the east by Cayuta in Schuyler county and Erin in Chemung county; on the south by Horseheads; on the west by Catlin. It was originally covered with an immense growth of white pine timber, and the Catharine creek which runs centrally through the town from south to the north, furnishes water power for a large number of saw mills which were erected along its banks. The Chemung Canal passed through the township following the valley of Catharine creek, which, after 1833, enabled the lumbermen to get their lumber to the Geneva, Utica, Albany and New York markets. The business of boat building was also carried on extensively, as many as two hundred boats at a time could be seen upon the stocks in the course of construction. By the time that the Elmira and Jefferson Railroad was completed (which also passes through the valley of the Catharine creek), the timber to a great extent had become exhausted. During the lumber excitement rival villages sprang up, viz: Millport and Pine Valley, and great feeling and enthusiasm were at various times manifested. The great thoroughfare leading from Elmira to Seneca Lake also passed through the town, following the valley, where daily stages, loaded with passengers, enlivened the scene. This valley was also distinguished by having been the route which General Sullivan marched his army, in 1779. For many years scarcely any attention was paid to agricultural pursuits; so intent were the people interested in lumbering and boat building. But after the pine trees had been cut down, and there was nothing more to be done in the lumber business, the inhabitants commenced devoting their attention to extracting the pine stumps, clearing the land and raising wheat, corn, oats and potatoes, stocking their farms with neat cattle and sheep, thus presenting to-day a town rich in agriculture.

Early settlers were Green Bentley, Abiard Latten, Elder Ebenezer Mallory, Daniel Parsons, Augustus Lyon, David Coe, Asa Coe, Luther Coe, John Dailey, Hawkins Fanton, Nathan Bedient, Eli Banks, Zackeus Moorehouse, John McDougal, David Banks, John St. John, Myron Collins, James Gifford, Elijah Sexton, Erastus Crandall, Eber Crandall, Allen Kendall, Amos Crandall, Harvey Turner, William VanDuser, John Turner, Morris Hewitt, Welcome Mosher, David Turner, Welcome Mosher, Jr., John L. Sexton, Richard Dearborn, John Egbert, P. S. Tanner, Benjamin Hackney, Ebenezer Longstreet, Horton Frost, Dr. Horace Seaman, Jeremiah Hackney, J. D. Mandeville, Jabez Bradley, Jarvis Langdon, William H. Phillips, Patrick Quinn, William Bentley, B. B. Parsons, Thomas McCarthy, Ransom Latten, Oliver Grecno, Jacob Weller, Caleb Allen, Levi Mallet, Curtis Miles, Uriah Hall, Nathan Botchford, L. Compton, Dederich Shaffer, John Burch, Richard Dilmore, Reuben Tift, Moses Cole, John Denson, Solomon Bennett, Thomas C. Sleeper, Henry Taylor, Sen., Chauncey Taylor, William Duscam, a revolutionary soldier, James M. VanDuser, Henry Hall, Samuel A. Beardsley, William Christler, Sr., Ezra Mallett.

—Daniel Parsons kept the first tavern.

—Elder Mallory cut the first fallow, in 1806.

—The first saw mill was built by Jacob Teal.

—The first school teacher was Simeon Squires.

—Erastus Crandall built the first store, in 1825.

—James T. Gifford built the first tannery in 1825.

—The first road was built by Gen. Sullivan in 1779.

—Dr. Horace Seaman was the first physician in 1830.

—The first church was built by the Methodists, in 1832.

—The first framed house was built by Daniel Parsons in 1805.

—Myron Collins built a cloth dressing and fulling mill, in 1823.

—Elijah Sexton was the first postmaster at Pine Valley, in 1827.

—David Coe and Thomas McCarthy built the first grist mill in 1823.

—The first canal boat in Veteran, was built by Jonathan Thomas, in 1834.

—The first religious services were held by Elder Mallory, in the year 1806.

—Old Oak Lodge, No. 253, F. A. M., organized Jan. 7, 1852. Charles Benson, W. M.

—Moses Cole, a prominent business man, of Veteran, died, June 5th, 1875, in the seventy-fifth year of his age.

—Order of the Eastern Star was organized in 1871. Mrs. Martin Thomas, Matron ; Thomas Dillmore, Patron.

—The Baptist church of Pine Valley was organized Oct. 1867, under the pastorate of Rev. E. C. Rollins. Church erected in 1871.

—John Hulett, a pioneer, died, January 12th, 1847, aged 80 years. He was the father of the late Hon. Charles Hulett, of Horseheads.

—The cholera raged during the construction of the Elmira and Jefferson railroad, in the year 1849. Three hundred and seventy-eight deaths occurred.

—Millport was originally christened Millvale, but after the passage of the bill for the construction of the Chemung Canal in 1829, it was changed to Millport.

—Presbyterian church organized in 1836, Rev. Mr. Jackson was the first pastor. Jarvis Langdon, deceased, of Elmira, (then of Millport,) was the first member admitted to the church.

—A great flood occurred in Catharine creek, in 1857, in the month of June. The banks of the canal were washed away, and lock torn out, and navigation suspended for about a month.

—Elijah Sexton and John L. Sexton, brothers, both erected dwellings upon the spot where General Sullivan encamped, in the year 1779. Elijah Sexton erected his dwelling in 1824 and John L. Sexton in 1829.

—The town of Veteran was the first to fill her quota during the war of the rebellion, and the large number of additional volunteers in the service, more fully confirmed the right to inscribe "Veteran" upon her banners.

—Major Erastus, the friendly rival of Elijah Sexton, the active business man and polished gentleman, died, January 27th, 1872, at an advanced age. The Masonic fraternity turned out and bore his remains to the silent grave, on Sunday, January the 28th.

—Baptist Church of Millport, organized, December 24th, 1844. Rev. Philander D Gillette, was the first pastor. P. S. Tanner, Charles C. Costen, Chauncey Palmer, deacons. Church erected in 1871. Cost $1,000. Dedicated, September 27th, 1871, by Elder J. B. Pixley.

—Mr. and Mrs. John Denton, and Mr. and Mrs. Boston Bement, celebrated their golden wedding, at Millport, December 7th, 1875. P. S. Tanner, Charles C. Costen, Christopher C. Costen and Alfred Tanner, four witnesses to the marriage were present at the golden wedding.

—Veteran Ridge Free Communion Baptist Church, was organized, Nov. 19, 1836, Samuel Dean, first pastor. Members : Joshua Kendall, Ephraim B. Kendall, Jared Strait, Levi Malette, Erastus Andrews, Silas Bates, Philip Aber. In 1840 the society was incorporated. John Turner, Uriah Jacob Weller, trustees.

—Green M. Bentley, a revolutionary soldier, settled in Veteran, in 1798. He also served in the French and Indian war, and from his known character for patriotism, when the town was organized it was called "Veteran," to signalize his valor by being a veteran in war and a veteran pioneer. The village of Millport stands upon a portion of the land that Bentley purchased in 1798.

—Elijah Sexton erected three saw mills, on Catharine creek and he and his sons, Sylvander and Sylvester, for many years carried on the business of lumbering extensively. He also purchased a large tract of timbered lands in the towns of Lindley and Caton, Steuben county, and at Big Flats. He became one of the most prosperous and wealthy men in the town. His eldest son died, in 1839, and Sylvester, in 1844. He died, March 18, 1850, aged 66 years. He was distinguished for his liberality and generosity.

STEUBEN COUNTY, NEW YORK.

The county of Steuben was organized March 8, 1796, taken from the county of Ontario—named in honor of Frederic William Augustus, Baron Steuben, a German soldier and patriot, who came to America and did distinguished service for the colonies during the revolutionary war. Since the organization of the county in 1796, it has been materially lessened in territory. A portion was attached to Allegany county, March 11, 1808, a portion to Ontario, Feb. 25, 1814, a portion to Livingston county, Feb. 25,1814, a portion to Yates in the year 1824, and a portion to Schuyler, April 17, 1854. At the time of its formation it consisted of six townships, viz.: Bath, Canisteo, Dansville, Frederictown, Middletown and Painted Post. As townships the names of Fredrictown, Middletown and Painted Post have been absorbed. Painted Post, however, being retained in a village of that name within the original limits of Painted Post township. Steuben county now contains thirty-two townships, known as Addison, Avoca, Bath, Bradford, Campbell, Cameron, Canisteo, Caton, Cohocton, Corning, Dansville, Erwin, Fremont, Hartsville, Hornby, Hornellsville, Howard, Jasper, Lindley, Prattsburgh, Pultney, Rathbone, Thurston, Troupsburgh, Tuscarora, Urbana, Wayne, Wayland, West Union, Wheeler and Woodhull.

The first court in the county, was convened at Bath, June 21st, 1796. Hon. William Kersey, assistant judge, presiding in the absence of Hon. Charles Williamson, first judge. Judge Kersey was assisted by associates, Abram Bradley and Eleazer Lindsley. The attorneys present were, Nathaniel W. Howell, Vincent Matthews, William Stewart, William B. Vanplanck, David Jones, Peter Masterton, Thomas Morris, Stephen Ross, David Powers. Several of them were non-residents of the county, residing at Canandaigua, Geneva and Albany. William Stewart was district attorney. During the session of the court, George Hornell, of Hornellsville, Uriah Stevens, of Canisteo and Abel White of Addison, were qualified as justices of the peace. At the term of Oyer and Terminer, held during the year 1796, the first grand jury consisted of John Sheathar, foreman, Charles Cameron, George McClure, John Cooper, Samuel Miller, Isaac Mullender, John Stearns, Justus Wolcott, John Coudry, John Devanter, Alexander Fullerton, Amasiah Hammond, John Seeley, Samuel Shannan. There were only two indictments presented, and they were for assault and battery.

William Dunn was the first sheriff of Steuben county, appointed March 31st, 1796. He held the office four years. The court house was erected in the year 1796, was one and a half stories with wings or linto's and made of wood.

THE FIRST SETTLERS.—The first settlers were a hardy and intelligent people, many of them of New England origin, and many from the bordering state of Pennsylvania. The Erwins, the Pattersons, the Stephens, the Magees, were from Pennsylvania. Arthur Erwin, the senior, was form Erwinna, Bucks County, Pennsylvania, he who purchased the township of Painted Post; the Pattersons were from Northumberland county and the Stephens were from Luzerne county, Pa. William Dunn, the first sheriff, was from the south, and John Magee, the distinguished sheriff, banker, contractor, member of congress and railroad and coal operator, was born on the banks of the Lehigh, in Northampton county, Pa. General Charles Williamson, the agent of Sir William Pultney, was an Englishman. He founded Bath in 1792, and did many things to advance the settlement of Steuben, Ontario and other sections of western New York. Steuben county was in what was known as the "Genessee country," and the land of the Painted Post, and attracted settlers from almost every state in the Union. No particular locality therefore, can claim pre-eminent honors in the settlement of the county We shall refer more particular to the early settlers in the various township sketches.

MEMBERS OF ASSEMBLY OF STEUBEN COUNTY.—Before Steuben county was organized from Ontario, Col. Eleazer Lindsley, from Lindley, was a member of the assembly in 1792, and in 1796 Col. Charles Williamson, of Bath, was also a member. When the county was formed in 1796, Col. Williamson was elected for the county of Steuben. Since that time the members have been: 1798. Charles Williamson; 1799, Charles Williamson; 1800 Charles Williamson; 1804, James Faulkner; 1805, John Wilson; 1806, John Wilson; 1807, John Wilson; 1808, George Hornell; 1809, Henry A. Townshend; 1810, John Knox; 1811, John Knox; 1812, Jacob Teeple; 1813, Jacob Teeple; 1814-15-16, Daniel Cruger; 1817-18, William B. Rochester; 1819 John Dow; 1820, John Dow; 1821, John Dow; 1822, Grattan H. Wheeler; 1823, George McClure, William Woods; 1824, George McClure, Grattan H. Wheeler; 1825, John Kennedy, James McBurney; 1826, Daniel Cruger, Grattan H. Wheeler; 1827, Paul C. Cook, George McClure; 1828, Dugald Cameron, William Woods; 1829, Randall Graves, Henry Phœnix; 1830, Andrew B. Dickinson, Josiah Dunlap; 1831, Paul C. Cook, Josiah Dunlap; 1832, Edward Howell, John McBurney; 1833, William Hunter, William Kernan; 1834, Joshua Healy, William Kernan; 1835, Jeremiah Baker, Joshua Healey; 1836, Lemuel B. Searles, Henry Shriver; 1837, Henry G. Cotton, John I. Poppino, Benjamin Smead; 1838, Samuel Griggs, David Hall, Manning Kelley; 1839, Andrew G. Chatfield, Abram Lybolt, Johnson N. Reynolds; 1840, Richard Brower, Andrew G. Chatfield, Abram M. Lybolt; 1841, Andrew G. Chatfield, William S. Hubbell, Samuel A. Johnson; 1842, Aaron W. Beach, Francis E. Erwin, Ziba A. Leland; 1843, Morris Brown, Francis E. Erwin, Ziba A. Leland; 1844, John Jamison, Asa McConnell, Jeffrey Smith; 1845, William C. Rogers, Ansel C. Smith, Jacob VanValkenburg; 1846, Andrew G. Chatfield, Otto F. Marshall, William C. Rogers; 1847, Hiram Chapman, William Diven, William

Hunter; 1848, Abel Kendall, John G. Messereau, Alexander H. Stephens; 1849, Abram J. Quackenboss, John G. Messereau, John K. Hale; 1850, Edwin F. Church, Ferral C. Dininy, James Alley; 1851, Charles G. Higby, James M. Miles, Joel Cavungton; 1852, Robert B. VanValkenburgh, Benaziah P. Bailey, Nathaniel M. Perry; 1853, Dryden Henderson, John McBurney, Henry H. Bouten; 1854, John F. Williams, Benaziah P. Bailey, Obediah Stevens; 1855, Seth B. Cole, Sylvester Smith, Peter C. Ward; 1856, Goldsmith Denniston, Albert C. Morgan, Harlo Hakes; 1857, R. B. VanValkenburgh, George T. Spencer, Solon O. Thatcher; 1858, R. B. Van Valkenburgh, Washington Barnes, William B. Jones; 1859, Abel Eveland, Wickham R. Crocker, John T. Plato; 1860, Daniel Gray, W. R. Crocker, Lorenzo M. Rider; 1861, Daniel B. Bryan, Jeffery Smith, Redman S. Davis; 1862, Daniel B. Bryan, Henry Sherwood, Samuel M. Alley; 1863, John W. Taggart, Henry Sherwood, Horace Bemis; 1864, William E. Bonham, Alexander Olcott, J. Harvey Stephens; 1865, William E. Bonham, Alexander Olcott, Horace Bemis; 1866, William B. Boyd, Amaziah S. McKey, Frederic M. Kreidler; 1867. William B. Boyd, Christian Minier; 1868, John F. Little, Lyman Balcom; 1869, Monroe Brundage, Samuel Mitchell; 1870, James G. Bennett, John Davis; 1871, Thomas M. Fowler, James B. Murdock; 1872, Thomas M. Fowler, Stephen F. Gilbert; 1873, Stephen D. Shattuck, Charles F. Houghton; 1874, Stephen D. Shattuck, Lewis C. Pierson; 1875, William B. Ruggles, Jerry E. B. Santee; 1876, William B. Ruggles, Jerry E. B. Santee: 1877, Azariah C. Brundage, George R. Sutherland; 1878, Azariah C. Brundage, George R. Sutherland; 1879, John W. Davis, Russell M. Tuttle; 1880, John W. Davis, Russell M. Tuttle; 1881, Charles S. Longwell, Russell M. Tuttle; 1882, Allen A. VanOrsdale, Orange S. Searles; 1883, Andrew B. Craig, Orange S. Searles; 1884, George E. Whiteman, Andrew B. Craig; 1885, George E. Whiteman, Charles D. Baker.

SHERIFFS OF STEUBEN COUNTY.—William Dunn, March 31, 1796; John Wilson, March 3, 1800; Dugald Cameron, Feb. 22, 1804; Jacob Teeple, Feb. 16, 1808; Howell Bull, March 22, 1810; Cornelius Younglove, March 25, 1811; Thomas McBurney, March 7, 1812; Benjamin Wells, Feb. 23, 1813; Lazarus Hammond, March 2, 1814; George McClure Feb. 28, 1815; Henry Shriver, March 2, 1819; John Magee, Feb. 19, 1821; John Magee, Nov., 1822; John Kennedy, Nov., 1825; Alva Ellas, Nov., 1828; George Huntington, Nov., 1831; John T. Andrews, Nov., 1834; Henry Brother, Nov., 1837; Hiram Potter, Nov., 1840; Hugh Magee, Nov., 1843; Henry Brother, 1846; Oliver Allen, 1849; Gabriel T. Harrower, Nov., 1852; Lewis D. Fay, Nov., 1855; Orange Seymour, 1858; Edwin B. Kasson, 1861; William N. Smith, Nov., 1864; Willis E. Craig, Nov., 1867; William B. Boyd, Nov. 1870; Holland B. Williams, Nov., 1873; Franklin B. Sherwood, Nov., 1876; Erastus P. Higgins, 1880; Esek Page 1883.

COUNTY CLERKS.—George D. Cooper, March 31, 1796; Henry A. Townshend, Feb. 11, 1799; John Wilson, March 21, 1807; Henry A. Townshend, Feb, 8, 1808; Dugald Cameron, Feb, 16, 1810; John Wilson, Feb. 13, 1815; Edward Howell, March 19, 1821; John Metcalfe, Nov., 1822; David Rumsey, Nov., 1829; William H. Bull, Nov., 1832; William Hamilton,

Nov., 1838; Paul C. Cook, Nov., 1844; Philo P. Hubbell, Nov., 1850; Charles W. Campbell, Nov., 1853; Samuel M. Alley, Nov., 1856: Orson Mosher, Nov., 1859; Oscar J. Averill, Nov., 1862; Allen A. VanOrsdale, Nov., 1865; Nirom M. Crane, Nov. 1868; Henry Faucett, Nov., 1871; Archibald E. Baxter, 1874; Lucius A. Waldo, 1877; Archie E. Baxter, 1878; William Warren Wilson, 1881; Jacob H. Lansing, 1884.

COUNTY JUDGES.—Charles Williamson, March 31, 1796; William Kersey, Jan. 29, 1803; James Faulkner, Feb. 16, 1804; Samuel Baker, Jan. 18, 1813; Thomas McBurney, April 15, 1816; James Norton, Feb. 7, 1823: George C Edwards, Jan. 13, 1826; Ziba A. Leland, Jan. 9, 1838; Jacob Larrowe, April 17, 1843; William M. Hawley, Jan. 30, 1846; David McMaster, June, 1847; Jacob Larrowe, Nov. 1851; David McMaster, Nov., 1855; Washington Barnes Nov. 1859; Guy H. McMaster, 1863; George T. Spencer, 1871; Guy H. McMaster, Nov., 1877.

JUSTICES OF THE SUPREME COURT.—Thomas A. Johnson, of Corning, from April 7, 1847, to Nov. 1873; Hon. David Rumsey, of Bath, from 1873 up till his death; Hon. George B. Bradley, of Corning, from 1882——

DISTRICT ATTORNEYS.—The office was created in April, 1801. William Stewart, appointed March 2, 1802; Daniel W. Lewis, March 9, 1810; William Stewart, Feb. 12, 1811; Vincent Mathews, March 12, 1813; Daniel Cruger, April 17, 1815; Daniel Cruger, June 11, 1818; John Cook, Feb. 19, 1821; Henry Welles, Oct. 22, 1824; Edward Howell, Feb. 7, 1829; B. W. Franklin, June, 1834; Edward Howell, June 21, 1836; Lazarus H. Read, March 4, 1840; Andrew G. Chatfield, Dec. 2, 1845; Morris Brown, June 20 1846; Alfred P. Ferris, elected June, 1847; Robert L. Brundage, Nov., 1850; Joseph Herron, Nov., 1853; John Maynard, Jan. 7, 1856; Christopher John McDowell, Nov. 1859; Harlo Hakes, in Novr, 1862; John H. Butler, 1865; Alphonso H. Burrell, Nov., 1871; Ellsworth D. Mills, Nov., 1874; re-elected again in 1877.

MEMBERS OF CONGRESS.—Daniel Cruger, Bath, N. Y., 1817, one term; William Woods, Bath, 1823, one term; John Magee, Bath, 1827, two terms; Grattan H. Wheeler, Wheeler, 1831, one term; Edward Howell, Bath, 1833, one term; John T. Andrews, Bath, 1839, one term; William S. Hubbell, Bath, 1843, one term; David Rumsey, Jr., Bath, 1847, two terms; Robert B. VanValkenburgh, Bath, 1861, two terms; Charles C. B. Walker, Corning, 1873, one term; John N. Hungerford, Corning, 1875, one term.

The Chemung canal feeder was completed in the year 1833.

The Erie Railroad was completed to Corning in the month of Dec., 1849. Entirely completed and opened from Piermont on the Hudson to Dunkirk on Lake Erie, in May, 1851.

The Corning and Blossburg Railroad completed from Corning to Blossburg, in the year 1840.

The Conhocton Valley Railroad constructed in the year 1852.

The Syracuse, Geneva and Corning Railroad completed in the year 1876.

The D., L. & W. R. R. completed in the year 1883.

In the year 1831, the Crooked Lake Canal was finished.

In 1852, a plank road was constructed from Corning up the Conhocton Valley.

In 1882, the Addison and Northern Pennsylvania Railroad was constructed from Addison, Steuben county, N. Y., to Gaines, Tioga county, Pa., a distance of forty miles.

The *Bath Gazette* and *Genesee Advertiser*, the first newspapers published in Steuben county, were issued under the patronage of Gen. Charles Williamson, in January, 1796, by William Kersey and James Eddie. To give briefs of the newspapers subsequently published in the county, would require a volume. Steuben county has been prolific in newspaper enterprises.

In the year 1830, January 19, a great convention was held in Bath, in relation to the Pultney estate.

Robert Campbell, Jr., elected Lieutenant Governor, Nov. 2, 1858.

Hon. Stephen T. Hayt, of Corning, elected canal commissioner, Nov. 6, 1866.

Daniel C. Howell, of Bath, appointed Superintendent of State Banking Department, Feb 3, 1870.

Hon. Daniel Cruger, of Bath, elected speaker of the Assembly Jan. 30, 1816.

Hon. James E. Jones, appointed captain of the Port of New York, Jan. 1869.

From the organization of the county from 1796 to 1846 a period of fifty years, surrogates were appointed. Since 1846, the county judges have performed that service. For the first fifty years the surrogates in Steuben county were Stephen Ross, March 31, 1796; Henry A Townshend, March 24, 1800; George McClure, March 25, 1805; John Metcalfe, April 6, 1813; James Reed, April 8, 1815; Samuel Baker, April 10, 1817; William Read, March 20, 1821; James Brundage, March 28, 1823; William Woods, Jan. 8, 1827; Robert Campbell, Jan 31, 1835; David Rumsey, Jan. 24, 1840 Ansel J. McCall, Feb, 3, 1844.

Post offices, Addison, Addison Hill, Adrian, Avoca, Bath, Bennett's Creek, Big Creek, Blood's Depot, Bradford, Buena Vista, Cameron, Cameron Mills, Campbelltown, Canisteo, Caton, Canisteo Center, Corning, Cooper's Plains, Curtis, Cohocton, Doty's Corners, East Campbell, East Woodhull, East Troupsburgh, Erwin, Erwin Center, Goff's Mills, Greenwood, Gibson, Hammondsport, Haskinville, Hedgesville, Hornby, Hornellsville, Howard, Jasper, Kanona, Lindleytown, Merchantville, Mitchellville, Neils' Creek, North Cameron, North Jasper, North Urbana, Perkinsville, Painted Post, Pultney, Rikers' Hollow, Risingville, Savona, Sonora, South Addison, South Bradford, South Cameron, South Dansville, South Howard, South Pultney, South Troupsburgh, Stephens' Mills, Swale, Towlesville, Troupsburgh, Wallace, Wayland Depot, Wayne, Wayne Four Corners, West Union, Wheeler, Wileysville, Woodhull, Young Hickory.

Steuben County Medical Society, organized in 1818. Doctor Warren Patchen was its first president.

Steuben County Homeopathic Medical Society, was organized May 25, 1867. First president, Doct. A. Dewolf of Bath.

Hornellsville Academy of Medicine, organized Dec. 17, 1873. Dr. J. W. Robinson first president.

Steuben Farmers' Agricultural Society, organized at Bath, June 1, 1841. First president, Otto Marshall. A society has subsequently been organized which has large and commodious buildings. This society was organized in 1853.

Soldiers Home at Bath completed and dedicated, in 1879.

Vine Culture commenced near Hammondsport, in 1855 by Judge Jacob Larrowe and Orlando Shepard.

Pleasant Valley Wine Company, organized in 1860.

Urbana Wine Company, organized in 1865.

Lake Keuka Wine Company, organized in 1878.

August 1, 1846, Capt. William E. Shannon of Bath, with his company, left Bath to engage in the Mexican war.

About 3,000 citizens of the county of Steuben, enlisted in the service of their country, in various regiments, during the war of the rebellion.

Steuben county with its nine hundred thousand acres of land, two thirds of which are under cultivation, the rich alluvial soils of its valleys, its vast agricultural and manufacturing products, its railroads, villages and prospering towns, its public schools, and academies of learning, its charitable institutions, its churches and lodges, the ability of its public press, and the enterprise and wealth of its citizens make it one of the most important counties in the empire state.

Addison Township and Village,

The township of Addison was formed April 6, 1808. It had previously been known as the township of Middletown. The township of Addison was greater in area at its formation than now, portions of it having been detached to form the township of Troupsburgh, in 1808; Cameron, in 1828; a portion of Woodhull, in 1828; a portion of Rathbone, in 1856, and Tuscarora, in 1859. It is located on the north and south sides of the Canisteo river, in the second range of townships north of Pennsylvania state line. Its principal streams are the Canisteo river, the Tuscarora and Goodhue creeks, the two latter being tributaries of the Canisteo river; the Tuscarora creek discharging its waters into the river, from the south, in the corporate limits of the village of Addison, and the Goodhue from the north about two miles east of the village. Along the valleys of the Canisteo and Tuscarora, the soil is rich and alluvial, and under a good state of cultivation. The highlands on the north and south sides are being cultivated, and are producing fair crops of wheat, oats, corn and potatoes, and most excellent crops of grass. For many years the business of lumbering was carried on extensively

Addison, the chief village of the township, was incorporated in 1854, and is one of the most active business villages in the county. It is the center of a large trade, for the towns lying south and south-west of it. It is the largest of any of the villages on the Canisteo river, with the exception of Hornellsville. It is situated on the north and south banks of the Canisteo river, connections being had by two substantial iron bridges. It contains two banks, two newspaper offices, several fine churches, an academy or graded school, two railroad stations, those of the New York, Lake Erie and Western Railroad, and the Addison and Northern Pennsylvania Railroad Co., a foundry and machine shop, a sash and blind manufactory, a large steam flouring mill, a chair manufactory, a boot and shoe manufactory, and a full compliment of dry goods stores, furnishing stores, groceries, saloons and hotels.

First settlers—It is believed by many that Samuel Rice was the first settler in the township, in 1791. Soon thereafter settlements were made by Reuben Searles, Lemuel Searles, John Martin, George Goodhue, Oliver Miller, Abel White, James Benham, Asahel Stiles, Elisha Gilbert, William Wombaugh, Samuel Colegrove, John Wyman, William B. Jones, Stephen Dolson, Jonathan Tracey. The Canisteo valley was one of the great haunts of the Six Nations, one of their war paths and trails led out of the valley near the village of Addison, up the Tuscarora creek, and over into the valley of the Cowanesque, to where the present borough of Elkland is situated, a distance of only about twelve miles by this path, and twenty-four via the valley of the Canisteo, Tioga and Cowanesque, and when the early white settlers came into Addison, or upon the Canisteo, they found quite a number of Indians still lingering in the valley.

At an election, or town meeting, held at Middletown, (now Addison) the first Tuesday in April, 1797, the officers elected were Supervisor, Reuben Searles; Town Clerk, Oliver Miller; Assessors, George Goodhue, John Wyman, John Martin; Constable, Lemuel Searles; Poor Masters, Jonathan Tracey, Asahel Stiles; Commissioners, John Martin, George Goodhue, Stephen Dolson; Collector, Lemuel Searles; Commissioners of Schools, Abel White, Jonathan Tracey and Oliver Miller; Path Masters, Reuben Searles, Jr., James Benham; Fence Viewers, Elisha Gilbert, Silas Morey; Pound Master, Reuben Searles.

—Academy burned in October, 1856.

—Addison Academy established in 1847.

—Baptist Church organized May 6, 1869.

—Union Free school organized in March, 1868.

—Addison "burrying ground," laid out in 1808.

—William Wombaugh built a grist mill, in 1806.

—James Birdsall was the first lawyer in Addison.

—Methodist Episcopal Church organized, in 1835.

—George Goodhue built the first saw mill, in 1794.

—Addison Chap. R. A. M., chartered Feb. 9, 1854.

—St. Catharine's Catholic Church organized in 1854.

—A bridge across the Canisteo river, was built in 1798.

—The Erie railroad was completed to Addison, in 1849.

—Addison and Elkland plank road constructed in 1851.

—Addison Lodge No. 285, I. O. O. F., instituted in 1847.

—First services by the Episcopals held in Addison, in 1847.

—Ancient order United Workmen organized Sept. 14, 1876.

—In 1819, township voted a bounty of ten dollars on wolves.

—Canisteo Lodge I. O. O. F., No. 345, instituted Feb. 19, 1873.

—Addison Lodge No. 118 F. and A. M., chartered June 4, 1847.

—Presbyterian Church organized in Addison, in September, 1832.

—Boot and shoe manufactory established by George W. Farnham, in 1878.

—Dr. Fredrick Wagner located in Addison, in 1830. He was the first physician.

—Post office established at Middletown, now Addison, in 1804.

—Iron bridge across the Canisteo river erected in 1870. It cost $10,000.

—Sash and blind manufactory established by Rufus Baldwin and others, in 1851.

—Foundry and Machine shop established in 1846, by E. J. Horn and Stephen Lewis.

—William Baskins Jones kept one of the first hotels on the north side of the Canisteo river.

—In 1831, William B. Jones carried the mail in a two horse coach from Addison to Painted Post.

—In the year 1814, four school districts were formed. June 26, 1818, one more district was formed.

—Capt. James H. Mills raised a company in 1862, which was attached 107th regiment N. Y. S. Vol.

—The Addison and Northern Pennsylvania R. R., was completed from Addison to Gaines, Pa., in 1882.

—Addison Merchant and Custom Flouring Mills erected by David Curtis, of Painted Post and James S. McKay of Campbell, in 1852. They are now owned by the heirs of David Curtis and Thomas Paxton.

—May 4, 1803, Elisha Searles, Elisha Gilbert, Robert Martin, Lemuel Benham licensed to keep Public Inns. Board of excise, John Knox, Reuben Searles, Abel White. The price charged each Inn-keeper was $5. for the use of the town.

Avoca Township.

Avoca was formed from the townships of Bath, Cohocton, Howard and Wheeler, April 12th, 1843. It is bounded on the north by Cohocton township, east by Wheeler, south by Bath. and west by Howard and Cohocton. The Rochester branch of the New York Lake Erie and Western R. R., passes through the township in a north westerly and south easterly course. The Cohocton river flows through the township, receiving several tributaries. The soil of the township is in the valleys alluvial, and upon the hillsides and uplands are clay and gravel, with a mixture of loam and is quite productive.

The earliest settler was from Pennsylvania, in Wyoming valley. His name was William Buchanan. He and his son Michael came on upon the recommendation of Genl. Charles Williamson in the year 1794, and kept a public house. It was known for many years as the tavern at the eight mile tree. Mr. Buchanan set out an orchard in 1795, some of the trees growing to an enormous size, and which are now alive. This eight mile tree or tavern, was on the Williamson road to Genesee. Soon after the settlement of Buchanan, other settlers came in, among them were James McWhorter, Hugh McWhorter, George Moore, James Moore, Gershom Towner, Finley McClure, Joel Collin. A few years after this or by 1815, there were Asa Phillips, Abram Towner, Oliver Rice, Samuel Burnham, Allen Smith, Eleazer Tucker, John Donahe, Jonathan Tilton, Daniel Mackensie, William Moody, John Van Buskirk, James Davis, Henry Smith, Richard Van Buskirk, James Babcock. In that portion of Avoca taken from Howard in it formation, among the early settlers of that locality were William Goff,

Henry Kennedy, Timothy Parkhill, William Allen, Israel Baldwin, Charles Robords.

—There are now three churches in the village of Avoca.

—Henry Kennedy erected the first saw mill in the year 1809.

—First religious services in Avoca, were held in Buchanan's barn.

—The second hotel in the town was erected in 1808, by Joel Collins.

—The death of Michael Buchanan, in 1807, was the first in the township.

—The first merchants in Avoca were Alonzo and George Simons, brothers.

—Avoca village is an active little place of about seven hundred inhabitants.

—There were about fifty Indian huts in the town when the early white settlers first located.

—Avoca was named by Sophia White, in honor of Thomas Moore's "sweet vale of Avoca."

—Anna Parker was the first school teacher, in the year 1796. Susan Collier was the next teacher.

—Henry A. Loucks was the first supervisor of the town, in the year 1843, and Oliver Rice the first justice of the peace.

Bath.

Bath was settled in the spring of 1793, by General Charles Williamson, agent for the Pultney estate, who had purchased about one million, two hundred thousand acres, now embraced in Steuben and other counties adjoining. At that time (1793) there were a few settlers at Painted Post, and a few on the Canisteo river, but all southern and western New York can be truly said was a vast wilderness. Possessed of ample means General Williamson commenced with great zeal and activity to populate this vast manor, and to this end, established a printing office, erected stores, hotels, mills, constructed roads, built boats to ply upon the Seneca and Crooked lakes, and did everything in his power to spread the fame of his possessions in the wilderness of southern and western New York. He had reached Bath via. a road cut and made through the wilderness from Northumberland, Pa., up the West Branch, to where the city of Williamsport is located, thence up the Lycoming and over the Laurel Ridge mountain, to where the present village of Liberty, in Tioga county, Pa., now stands. There erecting a Block House, or station, thence down to the head-waters of the Tioga, to where Blossburg is situated, thence down the Tioga river to Painted Post and up the Conhocton river to Bath, the Eldorado.*

*Mr. Williamson held this vast estate in secret trust for Sir William Pultney, an English Baronet, and Mr. Williamson being a member of the New York State Legislature, secured the passage of an act, in March, 1801, enabling an alien to hold the estate in his own name. Mr. Williamson therefore re-conveyed his trust to the *bona-fide* owners. Mr. Williamson had previously, that is on the 13th day of December, 1800, assigned for the consideration of $300,000, all the bonds and mortgages held by him to Sir William Pultney. In March, 1801, Williamson conveyed 50,000 acres of land in Ontario county, twenty lots in the city of New York, 1,784 acres of land in the county of Otsego, 1,200 in the town of Unadilla, 1,400 in the county of Herkimer, 9,000 acres in the county of Montgomery, 41,108 in the county of Chenango, 5,000 acres in Gerundigat township, 600 in the township of Galena in Cayuga county, and *all* lands held by the said Williamson in the State of New York. Sir William Pultney, in consideration of the above, indemnified General Williamson for certain claims and indebtedness, which he had contracted as agent for the Genesee Association, prior to April 1st, 1801.

Benjamin and Robert Patterson, brothers, were the pioneers, who conducted General Williamson's party to Bath. In 1793, a number of dwellings were erected. As early as 1796, General Williamson advertised that a grand horse-race would take place, which had the effect to bring the sporting gentlemen from Maryland, Virginia and Southern Pennsylvania, to Bath. He was determined that the new city erected in the wilderness in the land of the Genesee, and Six Nations should become the centre of attraction. When the county of Steuben was organized, in 1796, he caused himself to be appointed first judge of the county, and in 1798 was elected to the Legislature and continued to be elected for three successive years.

Among the first settlers were Dugald Cameron, Charles Cameron, William Dunn, Thomas Metcalfe, Hector McKensie, Andrew Smith, George McClure, James McDonald, Henry McElwee, James Reese, William Kersey, John Wilson, George D. Cooper, Brown Gillespie, Daniel McKensie, John Wilson, Gustavus Gillespie, Robert Campbell, Andrew Smith.

Never was a patron more indefatigable in promoting the general well-being of his settlers, than General Williamson. He dispensed with a liberal hand. He established a weekly mail between Bath and Northumberland via. the Williamson road and paid all the expenses himself connected with it. Bath is one of the six original towns in Steuben county, and was erected March 18, 1796. It covered a very large territory. The townships in part or in whole of Pultney, Urbana, Wheeler, Howard, Cohocton and Avoca have been detached from it.

The first election for town officers was held at the house of John Metcalfe April 4, 1797. The officers elected were: Charles Cameron, supervisor; James Eddie, town clerk; William Aulls, Patrick McKell, Hector McKenzie, commissioners of highways; Gustavus Gillespie, collector; Amos Stone, George Dixon, Abijah Peters, constables; Daniel Cruger, Patrick McKell, overseers of the poor; Amos Eggleston, Joseph McElwee, Jacob Phillips, overseers of highways; Eli Read, Andrew Smith, James McKell, Thomas Streeter, fence viewers; Robert Biggar, Samuel Baker, Samuel Miller, assessors; Samuel Baker, Silas Beers, pound masters; George D. Cooper, John Sheather, Charles Williamson, Benjamin F. Young, commissioners of schools.

The principal stream in the township is the Cowanesque river, fed by a number of tributaries from the east and west. There is a great variety of soil in the township, including the alluvial of the valleys, and the gravel, shale and clay of the uplands. The Rochester branch of the Erie passes through the township, having several stations. The Delaware, Lackawanna & Western railroad also passes through the township.

Kanona and Savona are thriving villages in the township of Bath.

Bath village is situated upon the east and west sides of the Conhocton river and is the county seat of Steuben county. It was incorporated May 6, 1836, and the first election was held June 7, 1836, at the house of A. R. Gould. The officers elected were: Trustees, John D. Higgins, TenEyck Gansevoort, Benjamin Smead, Moses H. Lyon, John T. Andrews; Assessors, Ziba A. Leland, John M. Campbell, Henry Brother; Treasurer, Robert Campbell, jr.; Clerk, Levi C. Whiting; Collector, Elisha Hampstead; Constable, O. W. L. Warren.

Dr. TenEyck Gansevoort was selected as president by the board of trustees.

An act was passed June 20, 1851, by the Legislature, creating a new charter, and provided for an election to be held on the 6th of April, 1852. James Lindsay officiated as clerk under both charters, for a period of twenty nine consecutive years, from 1848 to 1876, inclusive.

The New York State Soldiers' and Sailors' Home, at Bath, Steuben County, N. Y., is the only state institution of the kind in the United States. All other Soldiers' Homes are supported by the National Goverment, with rules of admission that exclude many worthy, disabled veterans. Because of this fact the department of New York Grand Army of the Republic in 1875, initiated the project of a State Home. It was located at Bath, because of the liberal contributions of the citizens of that town, and the warm interest which they took in the enterprise.

The Grand Army raised $100,000, in voluntary contributions, and laid the corner stone of the first buildings in 1877, with imposing ceremonies. The three first buildings were completed in 1878, with accommodations for about 600 inmates, and the trustees then deeded the property to the State, which assumed its support. Since then large additions have been made, the grounds have been beautified, a large and well appointed hospital built, also a head-quartersbuilding, a store, bowling alley, conservatory, and numerous other buildings. Accommodations for over 300 inmates have been built during 1885, and the number of inmates during the coming winter will exceed 1,000.

BOARD OF TRUSTEES.—The Governor, *ex-officio*; The Attorney-General *ex-officio*; Henry W. Slocum, President, Brooklyn, N. Y.; Isaac F. Quinby, Vice-President, Rochester, N. Y.; Jonathan Robie, Secretary and Treasurer, Bath, N. Y.; William F. Rogers, Buffalo, N. Y.; John Palmer, Albany, N. Y.; William E. Howell, Bath N. Y.; Hosea H. Rockwell, Elmira, N. Y.; Jno. F. Little, Bath, N. Y.; Oliver B. Cadwell, Watertown, N. Y.

OFFICERS.—T. G. Pitcher, U S. A., Superintendent; R. H. Gansevoort, Adjutant; J. S. Dolson, Surgeon; C. C. Leavens, Steward.

—Baptist church organized March 16, 1842.

—Rev. David Higgins came to Bath in 1813.

—Presbyterian church organized January 1, 1808.

—Constant Cook died Feb. 24, 1874, aged 76 years.

—George W. Hallack's bank established Jan. 1, 1849.

—Methodist Episcopal church incorporated Sept. 4, 1822.

—Grist mill and saw mill erected in 1794 by Gen. Williamson.

—The New St. Thomas Episcopal church at Bath cost $60,000.

—First school house erected in Bath village about the year 1796.

—John Magee died at Watkins, N. Y., April 5, 1868, aged 74 years.

—Bank of Bath organized in April, 1854. Constant Cook, President; H. H. Cook, Cashier. Dec. 14, 1863, changed to a national bank.

—Through the untiring efforts of Mrs. Elizabeth Hull Townshend, Episcopal services were first held in the Court house at Bath, about the year 1816.

—Ira Davenport died at Bath, N. Y., May 2, 1868, in the 73d year of his age. He founded the "Davenport Home" for orphan girls.

—Dugald Cameron was first post-master at Bath in 1800. He has had twenty-two successors.

—Charles Williamson Dunn, born in Bath, 1794. First white child born in the Conhocton valley. His father, William Dunn, was the first sheriff of Steuben county.

—July 8th, 1846, Union school established. Adam Haverling donated the land upon which the school building was erected. The building was consumed by fire in 1865.

—Steuben county bank incorporated March 9th, 1832. First board of directors, John Magee, Wm. W. McCay, Reuben Robie, Edward Howell, Constant Cook, James Faulkner, Andrew B. Dickenson, Chauncey Hoffman, Charles Butler, Henry S. Williams, Henry B. Gibson, Ansel St. John, William S. Hubbell.

Bradford.

Bradford township was formed April 20, 1836, taken from Jersey, (now Orange.) It is situated on the eastern line of Steuben county and is bounded on the north by Wayne township, east by Schuyler county, south by the township of Campbell, and west by Urbana and Bath. It is quite an uneven and hilly township, yet quite productive.

The early settlers came in under the patronage of General Charles Williamson, and located on the outlet of Mud Lake. Frederick Bartles and John Harvey, by the assistance of General Williamson erected a flouring and saw mill on the outlet, in the year 1795. They had been located there two years previous In the year 1798 he rafted 100,000 feet of lumber from his place to a southern market. In the year 1800 he filed in the county clerk's office at Bath the following:

"Steuben County:—This fourth day of April, one thousand, eight hun-"dred, started from the mills of Frederic Bartles, on the outlet of Mud Lake, "two arks of the following dimensions: One built by Col. Charles William-"son, of Bath, seventy-two feet long and fifteen feet wide, the other built "by Nathan Harvey, seventy-one feet long and fifteen feet wide, were con-"ducted down the Conhocton, (after coming through Mud creek without ac-"cident,) to Painted Post, for Baltimore. Those arks are the first built "in this county, except one built on the Conhocton, at White's saw-mill, "five miles below Bath, by a Mr. Patterson, Sweeney and others from Penn-"sylvania, seventy feet long and sixteen feet wide, which was finished and "started about the 20th of March, the same year.

"This minute is entered to show at a future day, the first commencement "of embarkation in this (as is hoped), useful invention.

By HENRY A. TOWNSHEND, Clerk of Steuben County."

Among the early settlers of Bradford, the names are re-called of Henry Switzer, Samuel S. Camp, Abram Rosenberg, Thomas Rowles, Michael Scott, Daniel Bartholomew, Capt. John N. Hight, Henry Axtelle, John Schriner, Ezekiel Sacket, Asa Tolbert, George Snell, John Zimmerman, Stephen Edwards, Elias Thomas, Peter Low, David Dennis, James D. Morris, James Longwell, Phillip Morse. John Phelps, Daniel Taylor, Joshua King, Moses Ellas, Jesse Munson, James Woolverton.

The first election was held at the house of John Zimmerman, on the 4th Tuesday in May, 1836. The officers elected were: S. Snell, supervisor; Charles McFane, town clerk; Thomas Rowles, collector; James Woolverton, James Bradley, justices of the peace.

—Baptist church established in 1824.

—The first inn-keeper was John N. Hight.

—South Bradford church, organized July 29th, 1848.

—The first lawyer in the town was Herman Train, Esq.

—In 1827, wheat sold in Bradford, at 50 cents per bushel.

—Methodist Episcopal church in Bradford village, April 26, 1876.

—Bradford is a village in the township and contains about 250 inhabitants.

—The first merchant in Bradford, was Frederic Bartles. He died in the year 1819.

—Henry Axtell, a revolutionary soldier and early settler, located in Bradford, in 1815.

—First Methodist Episcopal church of South Bradford, was erected, February 23, 1847.

—Capt. John Phelps, a revolutionary soldier, aud early settler of Bradford, died in the year 1856.

—Henry Switzer was the first mail carrier. It was carried by him, or under his direction for nearly twenty-five years.

—Jersey Lodge, No. 668, F. & A. M., organized June 12, 1868. John A. Stewart, W. M.; Cyrus M. Merriman, S. W.; Jacob Zimmerman, J. W.

—Order Eastern Star, (Harmony Chapter,) No. 24, organized June 7, 1871. John A. Stewart, W. P.; Nancy T. Goble, W. M.; C. E. Zimmerman, A. M-

—The first school house in Bradford was a log one. In the year 1814. "The Little Academy," erected under the supervision of Jesse Munson and Hiram Merriman, in the year 1852. Among the teachers, Rev. Wm. B. Atwell, D. M. Merriman officiated.

—St. Andrews' church, Bradford, organized June 8, 1851. The officers were: Wardens, Joseph W. Lord, Edgar Munson; Vestrymen, Jesse Munson, Sr., Hosea Longwell, Jonathan Wood, John H. Read, Ezekiel Bordseye, Henry H. Foote, Rufus Munson, Andrew T. Wood,

Canisteo,

Canisteo township was originally known as Williamsburgh. This was when it was in the county of Ontario. But when the county of Steuben was formed from Ontario in the year 1796, it assumed the name of Canisteo, and was one of the six original townships in Steuben county. In point of settlement it is the second in the county. It is the earliest settled township on the Canisteo river, as Painted Post is the earliest on the Conhocton or Tioga.

Canisteo is bounded on the north by Howard, east by Cameron, south by Jasper and Greenwood and west by Hartsville. Much of its original territory has been detached to form new townships. A part went to form Troupsburgh in 1808 and 1818, Hornellsville in 1820, Jasper and Greenwood in 1827. The Canisteo river passes through it from the west to the east, and the New York, Lake Erie and Western R. R. follows the valley of the Canisteo.

The valley of the Canisteo is from half a mile to three-quarters of a mile in width. The flats or bottom lands are very productive The hills on either side rise to the height of about four hundred feet above the valley, where table-lands are found well adapted to grazing and the dairy. The "Canisteo Flats" were when discovered and entered upon by white men, covered with a very heavy growth of wild grass.

EARLY SETTLERS.—In the year 1788, Solomon Bennett, John Jamison, Uriah Stevens and Richard Crossley, from Pennsylvania, entered the upper valley of the Canisteo, from the east, and determined to locate there. In the following year they came on and cut a large quantity of grass, cured it, and otherwise made preparations for a permanent settlement. They were originally from Connecticut and the eastern states, but had settled in the valley of the Wyoming, under the Connecticut title previous to the revolutionary war, and at that time, (1788,) there was likely to be serious trouble between the state of Pennsylvania, and the Connecticut claimants as they were termed, that these gentlemen determined to abandon their lands in Pennsylvania, and begin life anew upon the upper waters of the Canisteo, where the land titles were perfect and no dispute existing. Accordingly in the year 1790, they removed their families and became permanent settlers in Canisteo. They were only the advance guard of others who quickly thereafter followed them. The Bennetts and Stephens in the present limits of Canisteo, and George Hornell in that portion of Canisteo, now within the boundaries of Hornellsville, soon gave an impetus and a fame to the valley of the Canisteo. They ploughed up the rich meadows and sowed them with wheat and planted them with corn, they erected dwellings, built saw and grist mills, and soon found themselves in a land of plenty. We would delight in elaborating the events of that period, but space forbids.

The following are the old settlers: Solomon Bennett, John Jamison, Uriah Stephens, Richard Crosby, Uriah Stephens, Jr., Col John Stephens, Jedediah Stevens, John Redford, Andrew Bennett, Elias Stevens, James McBurney, John Moore, Obediah Ayres, Daniel Upson, Samuel VanCampen, Moses VanCampen, a hero of the revolution, Nathan Hallett, James Hadley and William Stephens.

At an election held in the year 1801, before the town of Hornellsville was organized, at the house of Benjamin Crosby, the officers elected were: Supervisor, Uriah Stevens; Town Clerk, Joseph A. Rathbone; Assessors, Obediah Ayres, Richard Crosby, Nathan Hallett; Collector, Samuel Hallett, Jr.; Overseers of the Poor, James Hadley, Nathan Hallett; Commissioners of Highways, Mathew McHenry, Daniel Upson, Joseph Purdy; Constables, Samuel Hallett, Jr., Samuel VanCampen, Joel Atherton; Overseers of Highways, Christopher Hurlburt, George Hornell, Obediah Ayres, Joseph Coleman, Benjamin Crosby, Samuel Agnew, William Stephens, Benjamin Kenyon, Samuel Hallett; Fence Viewers, George Hornell, Uriah Stephens, Moses VanCampen.

—Nicholas Doughty was the first blacksmith.

—Solomon Bennett opened the first store and hotel.

—Solomon Bennett built the first mill on Bennett's creek, in 1792.

—Foundry and machine shops, H. Carter & Sons, established in 1873.

—Presbyterian church organized in 1836.

—Voorhis planing mill established in 1868.

—Canisteo graded school house cost $6,000.

—Masonic Lodge organized in the year 1814.

—Baptist church organized November 30, 1876.

—In 1808 the bounty on wolves and panthers was $5.

—Methodist parsonage built in 1850. Church in 1857.

—Boot and shoe factory established by L. Allison & Co., 1868.

—*Canisteo Times*, a weekly newspaper, founded Jan. 25, 1877, by S. H. Jennings.

—Olive Stephens, born November 18, 1790, the first white child born in the township.

—Bank of Canisteo established in 1876. Prest., M. Allison, Vice-Prest., L. Allison; Cashier, W. W. Ball.

—Rev. John B. Hudson, a Methodist, preached in Canisteo in the year 1800. A class formed at that time.

—Jedediah Stephens represented Williamsburgh, (now Canisteo,) in the board of supervisors, of Ontario county, at Canandaigua, in 1794.

—Uriah Stevens, Sr., was a soldier in the French and Indian war. He was a native of Connecticut. Uriah Stevens, Jr., was a revolutionary soldier.

—Jeremiah Baker was born in Canisteo April 18, 1791, was the first white male child born in Steuben county. His father lost all his property in the Wyoming valley by the indians and British.

—The village of Canisteo was incorporated in the year 1874. At the first election held under the charter, May 17th, 1883, Lucius A. Waldo was elected president; Mortimer Allison, L. P. Weed, Smith Eason, trustees; Daniel Upson, collector; William H. Mead, treasurer. May 19th, 1873, William Stephens was appointed clerk; Hiram J. Colegrove, police constable; Hiram C. Whitwood, street commissioner.

—The thriving village of Canisteo is located upon the site of an ancient Delaware Indian town, and where stood their famous castle known as "The Kanestio Castle." The town consisted of about sixty hewed log houses or dwellings with stone chimneys. It was the home of At-weet-se-ra. It was destroyed in the year 1764, by one of the Montours, by order of Sir William Johnston.

Cameron Township,

Cameron township was formed from Addison, April 16, 1822. It lies partly in the valley of the Canisteo, and is bounded on the north by Bath, east by Thurston, south by Rathbone and Jasper, and west by Canisteo. It was named in honor of Dugald Cameron, one of the early settlers of Bath. Its northern portion forms the watershed from which flow tributaries of the Conhocton river on the east, and the Canisteo river on the west and south. The land along the valley of the Canisteo is quite productive, as well as that in the uplands of the north and east, and many fine farms are to be found. The New York Lake Erie and Western R. R., passes through its southern limits, having three stations in the township.

Lumbering was carried on extensively for many years, the product of the forest being made into rafts and floated down the Canisteo river. Soon after the construction of the Erie railroad in 1850, the business of rafting gradually began to diminish, until it is now substantially abandoned. The shipping of lumber, bark and shingles is now confined to the railroad.

The early settlers were Richard Hadley, Samuel Baker, James B. Wheeler, Urbane Baker, Amos Caldwell, John Place, John Dean, James Jones, Luther White, Amasa Downs, James Brownell, John Hallett, Elisha Leach, Hirah Chase, Chauncey B. Hubbard, Reuben Drake, Elias Mason, James Knickerbocker, Henry Knickerbocker, Andrew Bates, John Shaw, Hiram Averill, father of Gen. William W. Averill, John French, J. D. Yost, Isaac Santee, Byron French, Joseph Loughrey, Moses L. Pierson, Dexter Pratt, George S. Pierson, Andrew G. Pierson, James H. Miles, Reuben W. Miller, Stephen Baskin, James Swartwood, George Cameron.

The first annual election for town officers was held in February 1823. Elias Mason was the first supervisor.

—Richard Hadley built the first saw mill, in 1811.

—Samuel Baker built the first grist mill in Cameron, in 1816.

—There was an Indian settlement in Cameron, as late as 1804.

—Presbyterian Church erected in the village of Cameron, in 1853.

—Cameron Village Methodist Church, organized in February 1851.

—Rev. John B. Chase, a Baptist minister, preached in Cameron, in 1832.

—Baptist church organized July 11, 1844, under the pastorate of Rev. Moses Rowley.

—Christian Church erected in 1854. First preaching by Rev. John Stocking, in 1831.

—Rev. Abner Chase, a Methodist preached in Cameron in 1812. Church organized in 1834.

—There were 95 citizens of Cameron engaged in the war of the rebellion, in the Union army.

—A branch Methodist Church was erected in 1872, at a cost of $2,500, on South Hill, Cameron.

Campbell Township.

The township of Campbell was organized April 15, 183[illegible]. It is bounded on the north by the townships of Bath and Bradford, on the east by Hornby, on the south by Erwin and Addison. The Rochester branch of the Erie railroad, and the Delaware Lackawanna and Western R. R. cross the township in a north westerly and south easterly direction. The Conhocton river crosses the township in the same direction, and courses as the railroads. The townships contains some splendid alluvial soils in the valley of the Conhocton, and along Meads' Creek, and good grazing and wheat land in the uplands. Some of the finest white pine in Steuben county, was originally found in this town.

The first settlers were. Mead, Joseph Wolcott, Elisha Williams, Samuel Calkins, David McNutt, Robert Campbell, Solomon Campbell, Philo Campbell, Daniel Curtis, Joseph Stevens, Joseph Stevens, Jr., Benjamin Stevens, David Holmes, William Holmes, Jonas Woodward, Jacob Woodward,

Hinsdale Hammond, Seth Hammond, Cyrus Ames, Zalmon Tousey, Robert Bonham, Archibald Campbell, James Faulkner, James Fulton, Frederic Stewart.

The first election for town officers, was held at the house of Samuel Bessley in the year 1832. The officers elected were Daniel Clark, supervisor; Milo Hurd, town clerk; William Stewart, Samuel Cook, Daniel Horton, assessors; John H. Burritt, William Stewart. Selah Hammond, commissioners of highways; Joseph Stevens, Pliny Cobb, overseers of the poor; H. Corbin, Frederic Stewart, Miner Campbell, commissioners of schools; Milo Hurd, Harvey Burritt, Daniel Horton, inspectors of schools; Aden J. Pratt, collector; Aden J. Pratt, John Robbins, Jr., constables; Parley Seamans, Alvin Corbin, justices of the peace. There were fourteen road districts in the town, and the path masters appointed were, district No. 1, Richard Gregory; No. 2, Samuel Bessley; No. 3, Daniel Clark; No. 4, Gilbert Reed; No. 5, Benjamin F. Balcan; No. 6, Alanson Peirce; No. 7, Peter Covenhoven; No. 8, Stephen Boyden; No. 9, Moses Hammond; No. 10, Moses Woodworth; No. 11, Salmon Hunsinger; No. 12, Salmon Dickinson; No. 13, Parley Seamans; No. 14, Hosea Robbins.

—In 1846, a saw and grist mill combined was erected.

—Union Free school house in Campbelltown, cost $4,500. It has three departments.

—Baptist Church of Campbell, organized as a branch of Savona, in 1870. In 1873 church erected.

—The first grist mill in Campbell, was built in 1812, by Gen. John Knox and Archibald Campbell.

—The first school in Campbell, on Mead's Creek, was taught by Rhoda Simmons in a hunter's cabin, in 1817.

—First Presbyterian Church organized January 20, 1812, at the house of Frederic Stewart, church erected in 1833. Rev. B. F. Pratt, of Southport, N. Y., preaching the dedicatory sermon, Thursday Nov. 5, 1833.

—Methodist Episcopal class organized in 1827, services for many years were held in school houses. Church dedicated Jan. 21, 1869, by Rev. Mr. Searles, of Auburn, N. Y. J. P. Knox and J. M. Bemis gave the lot, cost of edifice $2,500.

Caton Township.

Caton was formed on the 3rd day of April, 1840. It had hitherto been known as No. 1, it being the extreme south east portion of Steuben county, and in the first range of townships. It is located upon the highlands south of the Chemung river, and east of the Tioga river, and bounded on the north by the township of Corning, by the Chemung county line, south by the Pennsylvania state line, west by the township of Lindley. The creeks which rise in the township, flow northward into the Chemung river, and westward into the Tioga river.

It is under a good state of cultivation, the inhabitants at present almost exclusively devoting their attention to agriculture. It originally contained large quantities of white and Norway pine, and other valuable timber. But this has been pretty generally removed.

Caton Center a small village located as its name implies, in the center of the township, although small, is a place of considerable business.

Among its early settlers were Simeon Hurd, Joseph Wolcott, Charles Wolcott, Nelson Wolcott, Isaac Rowley, Stephen Hurd, Solomon Tarbox, E. B. Babcock, Edward Robbins, Ephraim Hill, John Gillett, Isaiah Cram, William Brown, George Bucher, Amos Hamlin, Isaac Thompson, Dr. Gregory, Benoni Johnson, Rufus Howe, Arthur Westcott, Frederic Barnard, Samuel Gorton, Samuel Wormley, Jonathan Brown, James Davison, A. B. Breese, Pierce Herrick, Amos Bonham, Russel Stanton, H. D. Smith, Rufus Howe, Thomas Brooks, Amzi English, Thomas Brooks, George Thurber, William Hubbard, Titus Smith.

At the first annual election held for the township of Caton, in Feb. 1840, at the house of Russell Stanton, Amos Lewis was elected supervisor; Orlando Gregory, town clerk; John Gillett, Russell Stanton, Zimri B. Robbins, assessors; Amos Bonham, Joseph P. Brooks, Horace Westcott, commissioners of highways; Abram D. Kinney, Amzi English, Joshua Russell, commissioners of schools; Naboth C. Babcock, Henry L. Babcock, Henry Stanton, inspectors of schools; John Griswold, John Spencer, Poor Masters; Thomas Brooks, collector; Smith Spencer, Josiah B. Bailey, Harvey C. Howe, constables; Israel Woodworth, Jacob Robbins, Geo. Westcott, Naboth C. Babcock, justices of the peace.

—Samuel Wormley kept the first tavern.

—A. B. Breese built the first grist mill, in the year 1830

—Free Methodist Church organized at Barnard's Mills, 1835.

—Presbyterian services held in Caton, in 1824. Church erected in 1833.

—The farmers of Caton township are as thrifty and forehanded, as any in the county.

—Rev. Arthur Westcott was a missionary—preached in Caton from 1835 to 1870.

—Caton Baptist church organized at the house of Judge Nelson Wolcott, August 23, 1832.

—The first Methodists in the town of Caton were William and Martha Hubbard, in 1831. Thomas Wheat formed the first class, in the year 1835. Church erected in 1840.

—William D. Gilbert opened the first store in Caton Center, in 1849. He was the father of Dr. R. H. Gilbert, the projector of the Gilbert Elevated Railroad, in New York.

—William Hubbard organized and was superintendent of the first Sunday-school in Caton. He was an Englishman by birth, and was killed by the falling of a tree, in the year 1840, March 10th.

Cohocton Township.

Cohocton was organized June 18, 1812, taken from Bath and Dansville. A portion of Avoca was taken from it in 1843, and a large portion constituting the town of Wayland, in 1848. In 1874 it received an accession from the township of Prattsburgh. It is bounded on the north by the county of Ontario, on the east by Prattsburgh, and on the south by Avoca and Howard, and west by Wayland and Fremont. The Cowanesque river runs through the township from the northwest to the southeast. It is also traversed by the Buffalo branch of the Erie, and by the Del. L. & W. railroad. It occupies a position near the headwaters of the Conhocton, and is a very productive township. The first town election was held at the house of Joseph Shattuck, Jr., in April 1813. The officers elected were Samuel Wells, supervisor; Charles Bennett, town clerk; Stephen Crawford, John Slack, William Bennett, assessors; Jared Barr, John Woodward, Isaac Hill, commissioners of highways; John Slack, Samuel D. Wills, poor masters; James Barnard, constable and collector; Isaac Parmenter, constable; James Griffis, Thomas Rogers, fence viewers; Path Masters—District No. 1, Samuel D. Wells; No. 2, Seth Kellogg; No. 3, David Reynolds; No. 4, James Griffis; No. 5, Jonas Cleland; No. 6, Jonathan Danforth; No. 7, Stephen Crawford; No. 8, J. M. Drake; No. 9, Elisha Brownson; No. 10, Levi Smith; Samuel D. Wells, Jonas Cleland, Pound Masters.

The early settlers were Joseph Biven, who settled in the northern portion of the township and erected a hotel in the year 1794, then known as the twenty-two mile tree, on the Williamson road from Bath to Genesee. He was one of the employees of Gen. Williamson. Other settlers soon located, among whom were James Woodard, Aruna Woodard, Jonas Cleland, James Cleland, Alvin Talbot, Ezra Parker, Job Briggs, Joseph Chamberlain, Joseph Shattuck, Horace Fowler, Timothy Sherman, James Brainard, Samuel Rhodes, Jesse Atwood, Isaac Morehouse, Charles Burlingham, Richard Hooper, William Walker, Rudolphus Howe, Phillip Cook, David Loomis, Samuel Leggett, Abram Lent, Cornelius Crouch, John Larrowe, Matthew Hatch, Phillip Hatch, Sylvanus Hatch, Jared Barr, James Armstrong, Gideon Potter, Anthony Crosby, Gabriel Dusenberry, Philetus Finch, Joseph Wilkinson, Levi Camberlain.

—I. O. O. F. established in the year 1848.

—Joseph Biven kept the first hotel in 1794.

—Lucius Shattuck built a log tavern in 1810.

—K. of H. No. 944, organized March 9, 1878.

—St. Peter's Catholic Church erected in 1861.

—Ladies Missionary Society organized Apr l 11, 1878.

—The first tannery was built by Wm. Walker in 1816.

—First school house erected in 1810, and was constructed of logs.

—William Waite Warner established the *Cohocton Journal* in 1859.

—Liberty lodge, No. 510, F. & A. M., established January 15, 1851.

—Samuel Hartwell, an early settler, was a nephew of Roger Shuman.

—Sophia Trumbull was the first teacher, in a house built by Jonas Cleland.

—F. N. Drake went to Liberty in 1854, and engaged in the lumbering business.

—North Cohocton Post-office established in 1853. Post-office established at Bloods in 1871.

—Jonas Cleland built the first saw mill in the town in 1808. The iron for it was manufactured in England.

—Methodist Episcopal church of North Cohocton organized in 1816. Church edifice erected in 1846, enlarged in 1868. Methodist Episcopal church of Lent Hill organized in 1831; church erected in 1834.

—Frederick Blood, a native of Germany, kept the hotel in 1805, at Blood's Corners.

—O. S. and L. N. Fowler, the celebrated phrenologists were born in this township.

—H. B. Newell established the *Cohocton Herald* in 1872. It is now published as the *Cohocton Valley Times*.

—The first Methodist church established Feb. 24, 1829, by the efforts of Cyrus Story and Sylvanus Calkins, with Rev. Samuel Bibbins as the first pastor. Chapel erected in 1832.

—Joseph Biven and Sarah Hooker were married in 1798, and was the first marriage in the township. Bethiah Hooker Biven was born in 1800, the first white child born in the township.

—Although the Universalists have held services for many years, a church was not organized till Sept. 19, 1859, and completed and dedicated in 1863, by Rev. J. M. Austin, of Auburn, N. Y.

—St. Pauls Lutheran church established in 1860, under the ministry of Rev. Mr. Strobell. Evangelical (Lutheran) Zion church organized in 1869, Rev. Mr. Beauregaurd was the first pastor.

—The first Presbyterian services held in 1802. Church organized Oct. 8, 1809. Church edifice erected and dedicated in 1830, Rev. Robert Hubbard preaching the dedicatory sermon. Present church edifice erected 1872.

Corning and Corning Township.

Corning was incorporated as a village in the year 1848, taken from the township of Painted Post. The first charter election was held Jan. 12, 1849. The officers elected were, trustees, Horace G. Phelps, Laurin Mallory, James S. Robinson. The first meeting of the board, Laurin Mallory was chosen president, and Thomas Messenger, clerk. When the township was organized, March 31, 1852, it absorbed all the territory hitherto known as Painted Post. To be sure the name was still retained by the village of Painted Post, but that is in the township of Erwin.

The first settlers were Frederick Calkins, Ephraim Patterson, Icabod Patterson, Benjamin Eaton, Eli Mead, John Knox, Benjamin Patterson, Howell Bull, Jared Irwin, Hezekiah Thurber, John Jennings, Ansel McCall, Thomas McBurney, Samuel Wormley, George Wolcott, Stephen Ross, George McCulloch, Fitch Wattles, Jonathan Rowley, Abram Bradley, Phineas Bradley, Enos Calkins, Eliakin Jones, David Hayden, Jonathan Cook, David Trowbridge, Joseph Gillett.

Corning is one of the most prosperous villages in the county of Steuben. Extraordinary railroad facilities afforded; the N. Y. L. Erie, the D. L. and Western, the Corning, Cowanesque and Antrim, and the Geneva, Syracuse and Corning, enable its citizens to obtain cheap and rapid transportation. Its manufacturing and business interests are large. Its schools, churches and lodges, afford ample opportunities for the education of the youth, the spread of religion and the enjoyments of a social nature.

—Corning *Journal* established, in 1846, by Thomas Messenger. In 1851 it passed into the hands of the Hon. Geo. W. Pratt, who still is the editor and proprietor.

—The Gibson mill burned, in 1855.
—Hayt's Flouring Mill, built in 1868.
—Henry Goff came to Corning, in 1862.
—John Herman's died, January 23, 1882.
—Corning Gas Co. incorporated, in 1862.
—Corning was made a half-shire, in 1852.
—F. N. Drake, came to Corning, in 1867.
—A. H. Gorton, born in Corning, in 1828.
—Steam granite works established in 1875.
—C. C. B. Walker, came to Corning, in 1848.
—Glass works established in Corning, in 1868.
—Q. W. Wellington, came to Corning, in 1859.
—Corning Consistory, organized Sept. 14, 1866.
—Corning contains a population of about 9,000.
—The Corning library established Feb. 25, 1873.
—Nelson Somers was an early settler in Corning.
—The Chemung Canal completed to Corning, 1833.
—Col. C. L. Thompson, settled in Corning, in 1850.
—C. C. B. Walker was elected to Congress, in 1874.
—M E. church, of Corning, was organized in 1839.
—Baptist church, of Corning, was organized in 1842.
—Corning Council R. & S. M., instituted June, 1876.
—Hon. George B. Bradley, came to Corning, in 1852.
—Judge Thomas A. Johnson, died, December 5, 1872.
—Ansel J. McCall taught the first school in Centerville.
—Dr. William Tubell was the first physician in Corning.
—Corning Chapter, Rose Croix, instituted Sept. 14, 1866.
—Corning water works completed, in 1872, cost $20,000.
—W. S. Hubbell was born in Corning, January 17, 1801.
—Corning R. A. M. Chapter, chartered February 7, 1866.
—In 1876, J. M. Hungerford was elected member of Congress.
—Corning Council, Princes of Jerusalem, instituted Sept. 14, 1866.
—Dr. Corbett Peebles located in 1842, and was the second physician.
—Corning was named in honor of Hon. Erastus Corning, of Albany.
—Preston & Heerman's foundry and machine shop, established, in 1867.
—A. A. S. Rite, Corning Lodge of Perfection, instituted Sept. 14, 1866.
—Post office established at Corning, in 1841, Maj. S. B. Denton first P.M.
—George W. Fuller, became proprietor of the Dickinson House, in 1865.
—A. B. Dickinson, died in Central America, April 21, 1873. Aged 71 years.
—The present Free Academy was completed, in 1873, at a cost of $70,000.
—In June, 1846, twelve hundred dollars was voted to erect a school house.
—Fall Brook Coal Co., established their machine shops, in Corning, in 1862.
—In the year 1839 the first locomotive passed over the Corning and Blossburg Railroad.
—The Erie Railroad completed to Corning in 1850, with J. A. Redfields as first station agent.
—Col. Williamson erected a hotel at Knoxville, in 1797, which was kept by Ben. Patterson.

—Episcopal (Christ) church, was organized, in April 1841, Rev. Richard Smith, rector.

—Dickinson House, erected in 1850, and took its name from the late Andrew B. Dickinson.

—In 1793 a log grist mill was built on Post creek, near its mouth, by Payne & Henderson.

—Ansel McCall built the grist mill on the sight of the Hammond & Johnson mill, in the year 1804.

—Dr. John Hayt, a lumberman, settled in Corning, in 1833. He was the father of Hon. S. T. Hayt.

—In the year 1839, a bridge was constructed across the river, three miles below the village of Corning.

—Fall Brook Coal Company, opened an office in 1859, in Corning. Their first agent was Andrew Beers.

—Canal collector's office established at Corning, in 1845, Thomas McBurney being the first collector.

—The first bank established in Corning, in 1839, by Hiram W. Bostwick, with P. J. Mallory as cashier.

—Great fire in Corning, in May, 1850. Also one in the spring of 1851. One June 30, 1856 and July 16, 1856.

—The first daily newspaper printed in Corning, was by F. B. Brown, in 1884, and called the *Daily Democrat.*

—In the year 1824, at Centerville, now in the town of Corning, Judge Thomas McBurney laid it out into lots.

—The Second Presbyterian church was established, in Corning in the year 1845, Rev. Horatio Pattingill, pastor.

—The Corning *Sun*, a weekly newspaper, was established in 1853, by Mark (Brick)Pomeroy and P. C. VanGelder.

—John Magee took possession of the Corning and Blossburg Railroad, in 1851, soon after a substantial T rail was laid.

—On the 13th of April, 1859, a special act of the legislature was passed to encourage and promote education in Corning.

—St. Mary's Catholic church was organized, in 1849, Father Sheridan, pastor ; on the 10th of June, 1866, the corner stone of the present church was laid.

—Corning Company organized in 1835. Among its members were Erastus Corning, Joseph Fellows, Watts Shuman, Bowen Whiting, Wm. A. Bradley, L. J. Gillis.

—The *Corning Democrat*, established in 1850, with the Rev. Ira Brown as editor. He was succeeded by his son Frank B., who still edits it in conjunction with a daily.

—The first public school opened in Corning village, in 1839, with Miss May Bonham as teacher. The late Thomas S. Johnson was the first president of the school board.

—Painted Post Lodge, No. 117, F. A. M., organized July 4, 1808, John Knox, W. M.; Ben Patterson, S. W.; Solomon Campbell, J. W.; Thomas McBurney, Treas.; Samuel Colgrove, Sec.

—Corning is 291 miles from New York city ; from Buffalo, 142 miles ;

Rochester 94 miles; Hornellsville 42 miles; Bath 20 miles; Dunkirk 168 miles; Blossburg 41 miles; Elmira 18 miles.

—The first load of coal from Blossburg, over the Corning and Blossburg railroad, arrived November 9, 1859. The engine drawing the train was called the Chemung. The engineers name was John Graham.

—Payne's Foundry, established in 1840, by Mills & Osborn. In 1845 it was purchased by B. W. Payne, P. J. Mallory and John M. French, of Rochester. In 1847, Alex Olcott became associated with Mr. Payne.

—The State erected an arsenal in Corning, in 1851, and in 1873 it was sold to the Catholic church for a convent and nunnery.

—The first Presbyterian church, of Corning, was organized at Knoxville, in the year 1810, under the name of the Presbyterian church, of Painted Post. The same church organization erected a church in Corning in the year 1842. In the year 1867, the present edifice was erected at a cost of $36,000, Rev. Clement Heckman was the pastor in 1812.

—Fire department, organized Jan. 9, 1851, with Rescue Fire Co. No. 1, Rescue Hose Co. No. 1, Rough and Ready Fire Co. No. 2, Rough and Ready Hose Co. No. 2. In 1857, Alliance Hook and Ladder No. 1, was organized. In 1862 the fire department was incorporated. The first foreman of Rescue Fire Co., No. 1, was Daniel C. Compston. Thomas W. Adams was the first foreman of Hose No. 1. Rough and Ready Fire Co. No. 2, had for its foreman, Alexander Olcott. John Bullmer, was the first foreman of Alliance, No. 1. Alfred Jones was the first president of the Fire Department, with George W. Pratt, secretary.

Dansville Township.

Dansville township was organized in March 1796. Much of its territory was taken from it in forming the townships surrounding it, leaving it without any inhabitants in 1804. In 1812, parts of Howard and Cohocton were taken from it, a part of Wayland in 1848, and a portion of Freemont in 1854; a portion of the township was in 1822 added to the town of Sparta in Livingston co., and in 1834, it received an accession from the town of Cohocton. It occupies an elevated position between the waters of the Cohocton and Canisteo, the streams flowing north, and finding their outlets in the Gulf of St. Laurense, and south in Chesepeake Bay. It is bounded on the north by the county of Livingston, on the east by the township of Wayland, on the south by Freemont and Hornellsville, and on the west by the county of Allegany.

Among the early settlers were Isaac Sterling, Osgood Carlton, Jehial Gates, Charles Oliver, Joshua Healey, Elisha Robinson, Joseph Phelps, Josiah Pond, Joseph Cobb, Martin Smith, Newman Bell, John Robbins, David Demery, Arad Sheldon, Silas Brookins, Jesse Churchill, Nathaniel Brayton, Thomas Brayton, T. Alword, William S. Lemon, John Faulkner, Chauncey Day, Rufus Stone, John Brial, Alexander Fullerton, Jacob Vanderventer, Frederick Barnhent, Henry Cruger, Thomas MacWhorter, John Robinson.

The first election was held at the house of Samuel Faulkner, April 4; 1797, Isaac Vanderventer, James Faulkner, overseers of highways; David Fuller, collector. In 1799, Daniel P. Faulkner was elected supervisor; James

Hooker, town clerk; William Phoenix, Amariah Hammond, James Porter, commissioner of Highways; Alexander Fullerton, William Porter, John Phoenix, assessors; Frederick Barnent, constable and collector; James Hammond, path master; William Porter, overseer of the poor; Amariah Hammond, and Frederick Court, fence viewers.

—Rogerville Union Seminary erected in 1852.

—Humphrey Stevens settled in Dansville in 1822.

—An Evangelical church erected on Oak Hill, in 1864.

—Universalist Church was erected at Rogerville in 1852.

—Dr. Thomas M. Bowen settled in the township in 1819.

—William C. Rogers opened a store at Rogerville, in 1829.

—In 1806, Isaac Sterling opened the first tavern in Dansville.

—Charles Oliver organized a company of militia, in April 16, 1861.

—Log Church erected in 1819. In 1862, a new church was erected.

—In 1834, cholera appeared in Dansville, eighteen persons dying from it.

—In 1824, wheat was hauled to Rochester and sold for 40 cents per bushel.

—William S. Lemon from Harrisburg, Pa., settled on Canaseraga creek, in 1816.

—James P. Lemon was the first white child born in the town of Dansville, March 1, 1816.

—The first Baptist meetings were held at Beechville, at the log school house, in 1819.

—The first Methodist meeting held in the town, was at the house of George Butler, in 1817.

—The first barrel of salt brought into Dansville, was exchanged for 14 bushels of oats.

—In June 1816, James Jones and Miss Polly Shaw were married, the first in the township.

—In 1811 school was opened with James Jones as first teacher, the school house stood near Doty's Corners.

—Rufus Fuller built a saw mill in April, 1816, and in 1820, a grist mill. The mill was carried away by a flood in 1823.

—January 29, 1811, Nathaniel Rochester, manumitted two negro slaves, (Benjamin) about 16 years old, and (Cassandra) about 14 years old.

—Settlements made on Oak Hill, in 1816, by Moses Hurlburt, Joshua Williams, Daniel Griswold, George Grisworld, Hubbard Griswold, William C. Rogers, Thomas C. Buck, George Butler, Joshua Woodward.

Erwin Township and Village of Painted Post.

The township of Erwin was erected July 1, 1826. Lindley was taken from it in 1837, and a portion of Corning added on to it 1856. It is bounded on the north by Campbell and Hornby, on the east by Corning, on the south by Lindley, on the west by Addison. The Conhocton river flows through the township from the northwest, the Tioga river from the south, and the Canisteo from the west, uniting near the village of Painted Post, in the township, and forming the Chemung river. The Rochester and Buffalo branches of the Erie and the Delaware, Lackawanna & Western railroads pass through it. It contains some of the finest alluvial soils in the county. Within this township, at the village of Painted Post, the first settlements were made in Steuben county. The township was named in honor of Arthur Erwin, who on the 18th of July, 1789, purchased 23,040 acres of land, now comprising the town of Erwin, at that time known by the name of Painted Post. The first white man who made a settlement after the discovery of the celebrated painted post in 1779, by a detachment of Gen. Sullivan's army, was William Harris, an Indian trader, who established a trading post there in the year 1786. When Augustus Porter Frederick Saxton surveyed these tracts into townships, in the year 1789, the only white persons within the present limits of Steuben county, were Mr. Harris, and his son William and Mr. Mead who lived at the mouth of Mead's creek, and Mr. Goodhue, who lived hard by Painted Post. While the surveyors were yet at work Col. Arthur Erwin, from Erwina, Bucks county, Pa., purchased for £1,400 sterling, the land heretofore alluded to and immediately thereafter settlers came in, purchased lands and located in the town. The fame of Painted Post, in the land of the Six Nations, was spread by every soldier in Gen. Sullivan's Army, and the soldiers of the continental army, generally. Among the settlers who came after, were the sons of Col. Arthur Erwin, Samuel, Francis and Arthur, David Fuller, Benjamin Patterson, Robert Patterson, John E. Evans, Abner Trowbridge, Edmund C. Cooper, David Cook, Eldad Mead, Ben Eaton, George Young, Samuel Mulholland and Samuel Cook.

—David Fuller kept the first hotel.

—Empire Block was built in 1841.

—John E. Evans taught the first school.

—In 1850 the M. E. church was erected.

—In 1860 the Baptist church was erected.

—John E. Evans was the first town clerk.

—Several of the citizens were drafted in 1812.

—In 1840 the first Presbyterian church was erected.

—Union Graded School, built in 1868. Cost $14,000.

—In 1850 the Erie railroad was completed to this place.

—In 1803 Capt. Samuel Erwin removed to Painted Post.

—In 1822 Francis Erwin erected a two-story frame hotel.

—September 2, 1850, a Lodge of F. & A. M. was instituted.

—In 1852 the Buffalo and Conhocton railroad connected here with the Erie.

—The village of Painted Post was laid out in 1833, and incorporated July 18, 1860.

—The first newspaper was the Painted Post *Gazette*, established in 1846, by a Mr. Fairchild.

—In May, 1848, the Painted Post *Herald* was established, by Ransom Burnett and B. M. Hawley.

—In the year 1851, the Bank of Cayuga Lake was removed to Painted Post. Its capital was $50,000.

—In 1824 John Wygant cut out the sheet-iron Indian, which for many years hung on the painted post.

—In 1822 Capt. Samuel Erwin erected the first frame store, and rented it to the late John Arnot, of Elmira.

—In 1848 A. H. Erwin, F. E Erwin, I. P. Bennett and H. S. Brooks erected a foundry and machine shop.

—In 1870, the Painted Post *Times*, was established by William C. Bronson, H. C. Hegman and S. H. Ferenbaugh.

—In 1849, the late Arthur Erwin built the large two-story frame building and rented it to the district for one hundred dollars per annum.

—In 1855 a plank road company was formed, entitled The Corning, Painted Post, Cooper's Plains and Monterey Plank Road Company.

—The great "pumpkin flood" occurred in 1817, another great flood in 1833, which was surpassed by a flood on the 10th of November, 1857.

—The first saw-mill at Painted Post was erected by Isaac Gray, in 1832, and in 1846 this mill passed into the hands of Fox, Weston & Bronson.

—Painted Post derives its name from a post erected over the body of Andrew Montour, who was mortally wounded at the battle of Freeland's Fort, in Pennsylvania. The post stood on the bank of the Conhocton river, and was stained with juices of wild berries. Montour was a half-breed Indian and was a son of Queen Catherine.

—August 21, 1880, a new painted post was erected. There were about 2,000 people present. Addresses were made by T. F. Minier, of Painted Post, Judge Guy H. McMaster and Ansel J. McCall ,of Bath and John L. Sexton, jr., of Blossburg.

The officers of the day were President, General Francis E Erwin; Vice Presidents, John M. C. Patterson, Willis J. Savory, Benjamin Farwell, David Curtis, Lyman Balcam, Alson Pearce, Peter Conover, of Erwin, Benjamin Stevens, George W. Campbell, of Campbell, A. H. Gorton, George W. Pratt, S. T. Hayt, James McBurney, Henry Goff, Jones Wolcott, of Corning, Theodore Mercereau, Beadley Lindsley, S. M. Morgan, of Lindley, A. J. Stanton, Daniel Conover, William Dunlap, of Hornby, John E. Wolcott, of Caton, G. T. Harrower, of Elkland, George Haverling, Ira Calkins, of Bath, Wm. Wombaugh, of Tucarora, A. H. Erwin, H. A. Jones, Henry Baldwin, of Addison, W. E. Bonham, Hornellsville. Reception Committee, Sidney B. Howell, W. S. Hodgsman, Charles Iredell, A. B. Hurd and E. H. Smith. Marshall, Major Charles J. Fox. Assistant Marshall, Fred Weston.

Fremont Township.

The town of Fremont was organized November 17, 1854, taken from Hornellsville, Dansville, Wayland and Howard. It is bounded on the north by Dansville aud Wayland, on the east by Cohocton and Howard, on the south by Hornellsville and Howard, and on the west by Hornellsville and Wayland. It is situated on the highlands between the valleys of the Conhocton and Canisteo.

Its first settlers were: Job B. Rathbun, Abel H Baldwin, Thomas Buck, Salmon Gates, Elisha G. Stevens, David Dunbar, Jeremiah Carrington, Solomon Conderman, Jacob Conderman, Lemuel Harding, Elisha Strait, Jerry Kinney, George Nutting, Barnet Brayton, Henry Cotton, Leonard Briggs

Alexander Kelley, James Rider, William Haskins, William Holden, Gideon Maynard, Stephen Holden, Daniel Upson, Silas Benjamin and Byron Harlow.

—Miss Lydia Everett taught the first school.

—Fremont is noted for its cheese factories.

—Oliver Harding, an early settler, was a revolutionary soldier.

—Daniel Upson killed the last elk seen in the township, in 1818

—The first death in the town was Mrs. Amos Baldwin, December 12, 1815.

—Job B. Rathbun was the first settler in the town of Fremont. He came in 1812.

—Daniel Upson built the first saw-mill in the town, in 1816, and in 1819, the first grist mill.

—The name Fremont was conferred on the township by Elisha G. Stevens, in honor of Gen. John C. Fremont.

—The Wesleyan Methodists organized a class in the year 1831. Church erected in 1876. Dedicated by Rev. L. N. Stratton.

—The first M. E. meeting was held by Rev. David Dunham, in Byron Harlow's house in 1828. In 1831, Rev. Cyrus Story formed the first class.

—Rev. William A. Fenn an Advent preacher, held services in 1870. Thirty persons were converted, and in 1871 a church was erected and dedicated.

—Elisha G. Stevens went into the township in 1834, purchased the Upson mills, and was the first supervisor in 1855. The postoffice is known as Stevens Mills.

—Evangelical church, held its first meeting at the house of Jacob Conderman in 1828, conducted by German pastors, from Pennsylvania. Church built in 1860, and dedicated in July of that year, by the Rev. John Wagner.

—The first marriage in the town was John A. Buck to Rebecca Baldwin, daughter of Abel H. Baldwin, August, 24, 1815. Charles E. Buck, born November 12, 1816, was the first white child born in the township.

—The first town meeting was held in Fremont, February 13, 1855. Officers elected: Elisha G. Stevens, supervisor; Franklin Dartt, town clerk; Jason Ranger, Salmon Gates, Ebenezer H. Grayson, justices of the peace; Randall F. Beecher, Isaac Haskin, Morrison Harding, assessors; Herman Culver, Norman Eldridge, William Haskin, commissioners of highways; James R. Babcock, collector; Cornelius Conderman, overseer of poor; Derrick Goss, Joshua W. Palmer, Caleb Bullock, inspectors of election; John Eldridge, Henry J. Pawling, George Bartholomew, Thomas McAdams, constables; J. S. Green, town sealer. George Collins, Jr., was appointed town superintendent of schools.

Greenwood Township.

The town of Greenwood was formed January 24, 1827, taken from Troupsburg and Canisteo. In 1845, West Union was taken from Greenwood, and in 1848 a portion of Jasper was annexed to it. It is situated in the southwestern portion of the county, one township north of the Pennsylvania state line. It is bounded on the north by Hartsville, on the east by Jasper, on the south by West Union, and on the west by Allegany county. Its chief stream is Bennett's creek, which flows north and empties into the

Canisteo river near Canisteo village. Its first permanent settlers were Alexander H. Stephens and Ansan Robinson, in 1821. Among its other early settlers were Jacob Manning, Denis Sandford, Eleazor Woodward, Seba Norton, Stephen Powell, Enoch Ordway, Ezra Lovejoy, Hiram Putnam, John H. Hoyt, Joseph Bachelor, Josephus Bachelor, Guy Wardwell, Levi Davis, David Foot, Benjamin F. Brundage, Daniel McCormick, Henry Young, George Updyke, Benjamin Edwards, William Atkins, Abram Williamson, Daniel Rickey, John J. Dutcher, John Rogers, Hiram Benger, Enos Smith, Samuel Mallory, John Balsby, Ezra Stephens, John H. Smith, John H. Stephens, Phineas Stephens, Richard Krusen, Joseph Crossing, Randal Pease, Aden Lewis. William Brown, Timothy Terpeting, James Bess, William Bess, John Potter, Timothy Holloway, Elisha Sandford, Robert Richards, Nathaniel Richards, Enos Mead, Alvin Mead, William Burrows, Ezekiel Benger, James McCormick.

The first town election was held at the house of Levi Davis, March 6, 1727. The officers elected were Levi Davis, supervisor; Anson Cook, town clerk; David Murray, Randal Pease, Uriah F. Stephens, assessors; Richard Krusen, Uriah Ingley, Aden Lewis, commissioners of highways; Jacob Manning, James Bess, overseers of the poor; Abram B. Olmstead, Joseph Bachelor, Thomas Johnson, commissioners of common schools; Francis Strang, Josiah Haywood, Moses Clausen, inspectors of schools; John H. Stephens, collector; John H Stevens, Ira S Mills, constables; path masters, John J. Holt, John Stevens, Amos Lewis, Jr., Landen Lewis, Francis Pilgrim, Amos Labar, Enos Mead, John Krusen, William M. Blair. Sylvanus Strang, William Crampton, Joseph Davenport, Seba Norton, John Matteson, A. V. Olmstead.

—The Wesleyan Methodist church class, organized in 1860.

—The name Greenwood was given it by Hon. Alexander H. Stevens.

—Greenwood is celebrated for paying for a railroad that was never built.

—In the year 1825, Levi Davis built a log tavern, the first "inn" in the township.

—David Foote and William Ferguson opened a furniture and coffin factory, in 1830.

—Ezekiel Benger discovered a salt spring, in 1830, where salt was boiled for many years.

—The first Christian church, organized February 19, 1876, and church erected in 1879.

—James McCormick made the first firkin of butter that was shipped for market, in 1835.

—Benjamin F. Brundage in the year 1830, erected a carding machine and a cloth dressing manufactory.

—Alexander H. Stevens and J. Uriah Stevens erected the first grist mill in the township, in the year 1822.

—The Universalist church, organized 1851, and a church erected and dedicated in 1852, by Rev. E. Francis.

—In 1827, Levi Davis erected the first pot and pearl ashery; seven hundred bushels of ashes were required for a ton of potash. A ton of potash was worth about ninety dollars.

—In 1828 Joshua L. Chapman carried the mail on horseback, from Greenwood to Canisteo and Hornellsville.

—In 1825, Levi Davis opened the first store. The first postoffice in this township, was at this store in the year 1828.

—The M. E. class formed in 1827, under the leadership of Enos Mead. A church erected and dedicated September 14, 1876.

—Daniel McCormick, an irishman, from the county Antrim, Ireland, erected a grist mill in the southern part of the township, in 1832.

Hartsville Township.

Hartsville was organized Feb. 7, 1844, taken from Hornellsville. It is bounded on the north by Hornellsville, on the east by Canisteo, on the south by Greenwood, on the west by county of Allegany. It occupies an elevated position west of the Canisteo river, and the main branch of Bennett's creek.

Its early settlers were Joseph Purdy, Jesse Palmetur, Perry Potter, Andrew Potter, William D. Burdic, Daniel P. Carpenter, Frank Powell, William Hudson, John Granger, R. G. Martin, Joseph Hood, James Thompson, James Howell, John Martin, William Allison, Casper Van Buskirk, Simeon Baker, Robert Hemphill, Benjamin Cook, David Cook, Oliver Pettibone, Jonathan Pettibone, Solomon Pettibone, Lewis Clark, Othniel Call, Micah Kennedy, Francis Kennedy, Joseph Alma, Thomas Stout, David Alger, Daniel M. Stevens.

The first election for town officers was held at the house of Erastus S. Beard, on the 1st Tuesday of March, 1844. The officers constituting the election board were, Christopher C. Purdey, Sidney Frisbee, Calvin Withey. The officers elected were Charles N. Hart, supervisor; Erastus S. Beard, town clerk; James Beard, Johnathan Pettibone, Eleazer Sage, assessors; Silas Palmetur, Jonathan B. Purdy, Reuben W. Millard, Henry Acker, justices of the peace; Israel Adams, Edmond Cook, Levi C. Henry, commissioners of highways; David S. Whiting, Russel Amedon, overseers of the poor; Silas Palmetur, superintendent of schools; John Van Buskirk, collector; Robert Hamphill, Calvin Withey, inspectors of election; Samuel H. Burdic, Barny Henckley, Chester F. Whiting, constables; Casper Buskirk; sealer of weights and measures; path masters, William Allison, David S. Whiting, Uriah F. Stevens, Oliver Pettibone, Nathan Neff, Peter Henckley, Elisha Potter, David Call, Reuben Milliard, Burton H. Saunders, Ebenezer Martin, Benjamin Hall, Silas Tolls, David Alger, John Holt, S. S. Fenton.

—Cheese factories are numerous.

—First Baptist Church, organized in Nov. 1838.

—In 1827, Daniel P. Carpenter built the first saw mill.

—Joseph Purdy was the first actual settler in the township, in 1810.

—John Hood, one of the early settlers, was an officer of the war of 1812.

—Seventh-day Baptist Sunday school class, organized by Hiram P. Burdic in 1836.

—Hartsville was named in honor of Charles N. Hart, one of its principle business men.

—Seventh-day Baptist Church organized in 1847, church erected in 1856.

—Charlotte, daughter of Ebenezer Martin, died in 1823, and was the first death occurring in the place.

—In 1828, a log school house was erected, and Miss Z. A. Purdy, daughter of Joseph Purdy, taught the first school.

—First M. E. Church organized in June, 1825, church erected 1870, and dedicated by Rev. B. I. Ives. Cost $3,400.

—Sarah Ann Carpenter daughter of Daniel P. Carpenter, was the first white child born in the township, in Jan. 1823.

Hornby Township.

Hornby was organized Jan. 27, 1826. It was taken from the town of Painted Post, and named in honor of John Hornby, a prominent English landholder. In the year 1831, the town of Campbell was formed from it, and in 1842 a portion of it was attached to the town of Orange, now in Schuyler county, New York. It is bounded on the north by Schuyler county, on the east by Chemung county, on the south by Corning, and on the west by Campbell. It is in the highlands, east of the Conhocton river and the valley of Post creek.

Its early settlers were Asa Nash, Uriah Nash, Edward Stubbs, Ezra Shaw, Samuel Adams, Jesse Underwood, Jesse Platt, John Robbins, Amasa Stanton, James S. Gardner, Chester Knowlton, Aden Palmer, Hiram Gardner, Benjamin Gardner, John St. John, Isaac Goodell, Aaron Harwood, John Sayre, Jacob Goodsell, Andrew B. Dickinson, Theodore Hendrick, Fredalious Ferenbaugh, Thomas Oldfield, Samuel Lilly, W. W. Cole, Benjamin Lewis, Jr., Isaac LaFevre, Alonzo Gaylord, James W. Holmes, John Dickinson, Josiah Wheat, Milo Hurd, Pliny Cobb, Jonathan Kimball, Rice Nash, Elijah Robbins.

At an election held in 1826, at Dickinson store, A. B. Dickinson was elected supervisor; Josiah Wheat, town clerk; Hiram Gardner, collector; Alonzo Gaylord, John Fellows, Milo Hurd, justices of the peace; A. B. Dickinson, Josiah Wheat, Alson Pearce, inspectors of election: Alonzo Gaylord, assessor; Amasa Stanton, commissioner of highways; Hiram Gardner, constable.

—Jane C. Leach taught the first school.

—Isaac LaFevre built the first grist mill.

—Andrew B. Dickinson opened the first store, in 1824.

—The first hotel in the township was kept by Ezra Shaw, in 1817.

—Theodore Hendrick, one of the pioneers, was born in Massachusetts, in 1792.

—Samuel Lilley, one of the pioneers, was born in Northumberland Co,, Pa. Aug. 7, 1793.

—A. M. E., Class was organized at the house of Abel R. Palmer, by James Hall, in 1828.

—In Sept. 14, 1831, a Presbyterian Church was organized, and in 1852, a church edifice was erected.

—The Wesleyan Methodist Church was organized in 1843, Rev. Simeon Hall, first pastor. In March, 1877, a church edifice was erected.

—The Syracuse, Geneva & Corning R. R., passes through it, having a station at Ferenbaugh.

—A. B. Dickinson bought his goods at Newburg on the Hudson, and brought them to Hornby in wagon.

—Lorena A. Hendrick, daughter of Theodore and Charlotte Hendrick, was the first white child born in Hornby, Jan. 19, 1818.

—The Baptists held services in 1824, and in 1840, a church was erected at Hornby Forks. Amasa Stanton, Jacob Underwood, trustees.

—Andrew B. Dickinson, one of the early settlers, served two terms in the State senate of the state, and during Lincoln's administration, was appointed Minster to Nicarauga.

Hornellsville Township.

The township of Hornellsville was formed April 1st, 1820, and was taken from Canisteo. The town of Hartsville was taken from it in 1844 and a portion of the town of Fremont, in 1854. The first town meeting was held in March, 1821, at the house of Martha Hornell, and the following officers were elected: Ira Davenport, supervisor; John R. Stevens, town clerk; John Hurlburt, George Hornell, James Harding, assessors; William B. Bostwick, collector; Elijah Stevens, Stephen Webb, poormasters; Stephen Kuhn, Asa Upson, Samuel Harding, commissioners of highways; Christopher Hurlburt, Arbin Kennedy, George Hornell, inspectors of schools; James Taggart, William Stephens, Amos Graves, school commissioners; William B. Bostwick, David Whitney, William Webb, constables; Amasa Thatcher, Justice Harding, William Stephens, Jr., fence viewers.

The original purchase of the lands embraced within the limits of Hornellsville, was made August 8, 1798, by a company of twelve persons who at the same time also purchased the land in the townships of Canisteo and Hartsville. The twelve lots into which the town of Hornellsville was divided by the original purchases were assigned as follows: James Hadley, No. 1; John Jamison, No. 2; Arthur Erwin, No. 3; Christian Kriss, No. 4; Joel Thomas, No. 5; Uriah Stephens, jr., No. 6; John Stevens, No. 7; William Wynkoop, No. 8; Uriah Stephens, sr., No. 9; Solomon Bennett, No. 10; Elisha Brown, No. 11; Solomon Bennett, No. 12. George Hornell, after whom Hornellsville was named, settled there in 1794, and purchased three thousand acres of land, erected a hotel, a saw mill, and a grist mill, and for nearly twenty years was one of the most prominent and distinguished men in the valley of the Canisteo. The village of Hornellsville was incorporated June 28, 1852. The first election for officers was held Aug. 30, 1852, when John H. Little, Thomas Snell, J. T. Wilbur, Richard Durbin, William C. McCormick, were chosen trustees; George Alley, Hiram Bennet, Rufus E. Holmes, assessors: Horace Bemis, clerk; Martin Adsit, treasurer; James Fogel, pound master. At a meeting of the board John H. Lillie was chosen president.

In 1866, a new charter was obtained, which went into effect in 1867. The village is now divided into six wards. The early settlers were George Hornell, Mowry Thatcher, Richard Crosby, Reuben Crosby, —Hough, Oliver Harding, Moses Van Campen, Nathaniel Thatcher, Elias Stephens, Elijah

Stephens, Judge Hurlburt, Nathan Crory, Stephen Webb, Samuel Woolever, Joel Atherton, William Hyde, John P. Ryers, Elias Ayres, Seeley Van Scoter, John Pitts, Captain Abbott, William Sharp, David Woolever, Andrew Hendershott, John Meeks, Peter Best, Samuel Hathaway, Thomas Bennet, Matthias Reed, John Beattie, Jonathan L. Nicholson, Dudley Robinson, William R. Stevens, Samuel Jones, Nathaniel Finch, Nathan Osburn, Hugh Magee, James Dyke, James Taggart, Truman Botswick, Erastus Lewis, Augustus Newell, Thomas J. Reynolds, Martin Adsit, Andrew L. Smith, Dugald Cameron, Abram Minier, Henry Minier.

—Oliver Harding was a soldier in the continental army.

—Judge Hurlburt was the first surveyor in Hornellsville.

—George Hornell, was a member of the legislature, in 1808.

—First Methodist Episcopal church, was organized in 1830.

—Dr. Samuel Olin, was a physician in Hornellsville, in 1828.

—The Erie railroad shops now cover over six acres of ground.

—The first Erie railroad shop was built in 1849, and enlarged in 1850.

—The first post master in the town of Hornellsville was George Hornell.

—A Union Sunday school was organized by George Hornell, Jr , in 1820.

—Hornell Library, established June 1, 1868, it now contains about 8,000 volumes.

—The first Presbyterian church organized in the village of Hornellsville, July 10, 1832.

—The First Baptist church was organized October 7, 1852. Rev. Thomas S. Sheardown, pastor.

—The public schools of Hornellsville, are now organized under a special act of the legislature.

--November 19, 1851, Edwin Hough published the first issue of the *Hornellsville Tribune*.

—James Taggart, Asa Upson and Stephen Coon, were the first school commissioners, in 1821.

—The Hornellsville and Canisteo lodges were maintained during the Morgan Anti Masonic excitement.

—Christ Episcopal church organized into a regular parish, March 6, 1854. Rev. James Robinson was the first rector.

—There are several F. A. M., Lodges, one Chapter, and a Commandry in Hornellsville, besides an I. O. O. F., lodge.

—The Tories and Indians in 1778, cut pine trees and made the canoes which carried them down the river to the massacre of Wyoming.

—George Hornell in the year 1800, built the first ark ever run on the Canisteo river. The ark was loaded with wheat, and went to Baltimore.

—George Hornell built the first saw mill at Hornellsville, in 1798. He also built a large store house, situated on the east bank of the Canisteo, for the reception of grain.

—The first school in Hornellsville was established under the patronage of George Hornell, in 1810. It was taught by Miss Sarah Thatcher.

—In 1806, Hall and Elsworth of Geneseo, sent from Hornellsville an ark loaded with three hundred barrels of pork, a large quantity of cheese, and a quantity of venison hams.

—The first school house erected by the inhabitants of the village of Hornellsville, was made of hewed logs, and erected in 1818, and the first teacher was Dudley Miller.

—The first National Bank of Hornellsville, was organized November, 1863, by Martin Adsit, of Hornellsville, Ira Davenport, Constant Cook, Ira Davenport, Jr., Henry H. Cook of Bath.

—St. Ann's Catholic church was organized by Father Benedict Bayer, in 1845, his parish then extended from Friendship, Allegany county, to Corning, N. Y., and from Rochester, south to the Pennsylvania state line.

—Hornellsville is the most populous village in the county of Steuben. It is situated near the head of the Canisteo valley. The Erie railroad branches at this point, one branch going direct to Buffalo, and the other to Dunkirk. It is the terminus of the Susquehanna division of the Erie. It contains about 8,195 inhabitants. The shops and yards of the Erie railroad company are located here.

—Ira Davenport was the first merchant in the village of Hornellsville, in 1815. He came with a single wagon load of goods from Harpersfield, Delaware county, N. Y. His store was a framed building, 18x20. Mr. Davenport's next store was the first brick building erected in Hornellsville.

—Masonic meetings were held at Hornellsville, and Canisteo as early as 1812 or 13. In January 1814, Evening Star Lodge met for installation of officers, Joel Redfield was installed as W. M; Wm. Higgins, P. M; John Ayres, Past Senior Warden. Brethren present Andrew Simpson, W. M; Timothy Perry, S. W; John Stephens J. W; James Jones, Nathaniel Thatcher, William Mulhollen. Visiting brethren, Andrew Morris, Uri Stephens, William Hyde, Samuel O. Thatcher, Elias Perry, Samuel Lenox, and Samuel Darby. Extra lodge called, William Stephens, petition and deposite paid, John R. Stephens, petition and deposite paid, William B. Jones, petition and deposite paid, Timothy Russell, petition and deposite paid, William Stephens, balloted for and accepted, John Stephens, balloted for and accepted, William Stephens, John R. Stephens, William B. Jones initiated.

Howard Township.

The township of Howard was formed June 18, 1812, taken from Bath and Dansville. A portion of it was taken to form Avoca, in 1843, and a portion to erect Fremont, in 1854. It occupies an elevated position on the ridge dividing the valleys of the Conhocton and Canisteo, and is one of the best agricultural towns in the county. It is bounded on the north by the townships of Fremont, Cohocton and Avoca, on the east by the township of Bath, on the south by the township of Canisteo, and on the west by the township of Hornellsville. The streams of the township flow eastward into the Conhocton river, and westward into the Canisteo river.

Among its first settlers were Abraham Johnson, Charles McConnell, Alkali Bennet, Samuel Baker, Reuben Smith, Abram Smith, Joel Bullard, Abel Bullard, Daniel N. Bennett, Jacob Bennett, Job R Rathbun, Wm. Allen, John Hoagland, Henry Kennady, William Goff, Russell Burlison, Seth Rice, Jonas Rice, Jonathan Ketchum, Isaac Bennett, Thomas Bennett,

Benjamin Bennet, Hamilton Parkhill, John Stephinson, David Walker, Andrew Baker, James Stewart, George Stewart, Richard Towle, Reuben Hammond, Joseph C. Lane, Isaac Brasted, Oliver Parkhill, R. F. Ferris, Simeon Baker, David Rathbun, Jabez Beebe, Randal Graves, Calvin Graves, Calvin Whitwood, Simeon Bacon, Rufus Halsey.

At the first town meeting held, April 1813, at the hotel of Simeon Bacon, it is reported that the first supervisor elected was Thomas Bennett. From its organization in 1813, no records can be found until the year 1823. In that year Israel Baldwin was elected supervisor; and Rufus Halsey, collector.

—Howard Academy erected in 1835.

—In 1835, the First Baptist church was erected

—Presbyterian church erected in Howard, in 1834.

—Henry Kennady erected the first saw mill, in the township.

—Jonatham Kitchen built the first frame tavern in the township.

—The first settlement was made in the town of Howard, in 1806.

—Baptist church organized in the village of Howard, Feb. 6, 1826.

—Dr. Baker was the first regular physician in the town of Howard. He settled there in 1817.

—Isaac Bennet erected a small log tavern in 1813, and Benjamin Bennett erected a double hotel about the same time.

—Randall & Calvin Graves opened the store in the township of Howard. It was the only store in the township until 1831.

—Wm. Goff built the first grist mill erected in Howard, in 1813. The place where it was erected has since been known as Goff's Mills.

—The ladies of Howard, during the rebellion, formed a Ladies Aid Society, for the purpose of aiding the National Sanitary Commission.

—During the rebellion a war committee was appointed by the citizens of the township, consisting of Aaron McConnell, Alonzo Graves and Albert T. Parkhill.

—During the rebellion John R. Parkhill, Alonzo Graves, Alkali Bennett, Andrew Stewart, were appointed committee, to see that none of the families of the soldiers that enlisted suffered for the necessaries of life.

Jasper Township.

The town of Jasper was erected Jan 24, 1827. Taken from Canisteo. It occupies an elevated position in the southwestern portion of the county. The streams of the township flow south easterly and north westerly into the Canisteo river. It is bounded on the north by Canisteo, on the east by Cameron and Woodhull, on the south by Troupsburg, and on the west by Greenwood. Its surface is uneven and hilly, some of the highest points reaching an elevation of 2,000 feet or more above the level of the sea.

Among its early settlers were Nicholas Prutsman, Sr., Andrew Craig, Sr., Andrew Murphey, Sr., John Murphey, Andrew Moor, Andrew Simpson, John G. Marlatt, Gideon Marlatt, Sr., Mathias Marlatt, Thomas Fenton, Uzal McMinds, Oliver Pease, Robert Sharp, Guy Wardwell, Wm. F. Gardner, Henry Whiteman, Richard Winship, Sylvester Winship, Samuel Dennis, Moses Dennis, Ephram Woodward, Joshway

Sargent, Thomas Whiting, Enock Ordway, Abram Marlatt, Gideon Marlatt Jr.

The first town meeting was held at the house of Andrew Simpson, the first Tuesday in March, 1827. Officers elected were Andrew Craig, supervisor; William Hunter, town clerk; Uzal McMinds, Oliver Pease, Sr., Samuel Dennis, assessors; Jonathan Schouck, collector; John G. Marlatt, Elijah Peake, Benjamin Hilliker, commissioners of highways; Stephen Towsley, Ira Smith, overseers of the poor; Harvey Phoenix, Enock Ordway, Joseph Dutton, commissioners of schools; Ira Simpson, Jonathan R. Prentice, William Hunten, inspectors of schools; Lewis Fenton, Philip Brotzman, Jonathan Schauck, constables; path masters, J. G. Marlatt, Ira Smith, Barnabus Kinney, Joseph Dutton, Isaac Wardwell, Israel Osgood, Alvah June, Benj. Hilliker, Jahial Wood, Ebenezer Spencer, Jedediah Tolbut; fence viewers, John G. Marlatt, Stephen Towsley, Philip Failing. At the November election Oliver Pease, Stephen Towsley, Ira Smith, Samuel Dennis were elected justices of the peace.

—Amand Smith was the first school teacher.

—Methodist Episcopal meetings were held in 1818.

—Harvey Pheonix, opened the first store in the town.

—Samuel Dennis established a cheese factory in 1874.

—Andrew Craig, Sr., settled in the township, in 1810.

—William Gardner was the first post master in the township.

—John G. Marlatt was the first settler at Marlatt Corners, in 1811.

—Enock Ordway organized the first Sunday school in Jasper, in 1825.

—Nicholas Prutsman, Sr., was the first settler in the township, in 1807.

—Samuel Dennis was the first settler in the Hampshire Settlement, in 1824.

—The first Presbyterian church organized October 29, 1829. Church erected in 1844.

—The first settlement in the northwestern part of the town, was made by Guy Wardwell, in 1822.

—William F. Gardner, Henry Whiteman, Richard Winship, settled in the southern portion of the town, in 1821.

—Wesleyan Methodist church organized in March, 1871, at the Gulley school house. Church erected in 1875. Cost $1,800.

—Baptist church erected in 1834, but not entirely finished until 1840. In June 1817, Rev. Samuel Bigelow, baptized fourteen persons.

Lindley Township.

The town of Lindley, originally spelled Lindsley, was organized May 12, 1837, taken from Erwin. It is bounded on the north by Erwin, on the east by Caton, on the south by the Pennsylvania line, and west by Tuscarora. The Tioga river passes through it centrally, from south to north. Along the valley of the Tioga river is to be found in the town of Lindley, some of the finest alluvial lands in the county of Steuben. The hills or uplands east and west of the valley, are being rapidly settled, and becoming productive

—Joseph Miller taught the first school in the township, in 1793.

—Methodist Episcopal church organized at Erwin Centre, in 1850.

—The first Baptist church was organized in Lindley June 13, 1841.

—The Free Methodist church organized in 1866, church edifice erected in 1867.

—There are three regular, and one flag stations, on the line of the C. C. & A. R. R., in the township.

—Frederick Heckart, and Abner Thurber were early settlers, and prominent in the affairs of the town for many years.

—In 1814, a company of soldiers from Baltimore, Maryland, on their way to Buffalo camped in the orchard of Robert Patterson.

—M. E. Class formed at Lindley, Dec. 13, 1876, and the Centennial M. E. Church, was commenced and the edifice completed Nov. 15, 1877.

—For many years before their death Benjamin Patterson, Benjamin Harrower, Albert C. Morgan, were prominent business men of the town.

—Independent church of Lindley organized May 20, 1375. May 22, 1878 church was changed from an independent church to a Baptist church.

—The first post office in the township was at Judge Lindsley's house, and in 1830, it was at the store of Lyon & Morgan, Albert Morgan being postmaster.

—Rev. David Harrower, father of Benjamin Harrower, and grandfather of Col. G. F. Harrower, was an early settler, and a distinguished minister of the Scotch Presbyterian church.

—Capt, Isaiah A. Jones, was an early settler of Lindley, and married Rachel, daughter of Robert Patterson, the pioneer. He was severely wounded in a fight with a bear on Averill Hill, in 1817.

—The first annual town meeting was held in the school house at Erwin Centre, Feb. 6, 1838. The officers elected were Benjamin Harrower, supervisor; Chauncey Hoffman, town clerk; Silas Cooke, William Seelye, Jonas Davis, justices of the peace; Ansel C. Smith, William Lindsley, Jeremiah Upham, assessors; G. A. Ryerss, Thomas Clark, Benjamin Patterson, commissioners of highways; Michael R. Thorp, A. B. Lindsley, James Mersereau, school commissioners; D. P. Harrower, T. L. Mersereau, school inspectors; Benjamin Patterson, Jeremiah Mulford, overseers of the poor; William A. Lindsley, Richard Marks, Abner Collins, Royal Vamilea, constables; W. A. Lindsley, collector.

The old settlers of the town were Eleazer Lindsley, Samuel Lindsley, Eleazer Lindsley Jr., Dr. Ezekiel Mulford, Ebenezer Bachus, Capt. John Seelye, David Cook, David Payne, Robert Patterson, Hezekiah Kinney, Isaiah J. Jones, Rev. David Harrower, Theodore Mersereau, Benjamin Harrower, Samuel Patterson, Benjamin Patterson, Silas Cook, Jeremiah Upham, Frederick Heckart, A. C. Morgan, Thomas Clark, Elam Watson, William Seelye, Abner Thurber, Dr. Orton, Joseph Miller, John P. Ryerss, E. F. Tremaine, Julius Morgan, James Ford, Hiram Middlebrook, Charles Miller, Joshua Russell,

—Col. Eleazer Lindsley, of New Jersey, settled in the township in 1790, purchasing several thousand acres of land. He was an officer in the revolutionary war. He was accompanied to Lindley, by about forty persons. He was elected a member of the state legislature of New York, in 1793, before the county of Steuben was formed, and while it was the county of Ontario. He died in 1794, and the township was named in his honor.

—Robert Patterson settled in Lindley in 1804, having previously settled at Painted Post in 1797. He purchased in Lindley one thousand acres of land, and cleared up a fine farm upon the alluvial flats. He was a soldier of the revolution and in company with his brother Benjamin, conducted the English and German emigrants under Genl. Charles Williamson, from Northumberland, Pa., over the mountains to the valley of the Tioga and to the Pultney estate at Bath, in 1792. He lived to see the construction of the Corning and Blossburg railroad completed, and the locomotive to pass through his farm, and traverse the valley where fifty years before he had assisted in constructing a highway through the wilderness of northern Pennsylvania and southern New York. His fine estate was divided among his children, Benjamin Patteson, Samuel Patterson, Polly Cook, and Rachel Jones.

Prattsburg Township.

Prattsburg was formed from the township of Pultney, April 12. 1813, and the first town meeting held was in March, 1814, at which Joel Pratt was elected supervisor. The township is located upon the northern line of the county of Steuben, and is bounded on the north by Italy and Naples, in Ontario county, east by Pultney, in Steuben county, south by Wheeler and Urbana, and west by Avoca and Cohocton. The lands of the township were purchased on commission, June 6, 1802. from Robert Troup, chief agt. of the Pultney estate, by Capt. Joel Pratt of Columbia county, N. Y., and Wm. Root of Albany, N. Y.

The early settlers were, Capt. Joel Pratt, Uriel Chapen, Jared Pratt, Daniel Buel, Harvey Buel, William Curtiss, Pomeroy Hull, Rev. John Niles, Enock Niles, Samuel Tuthill, Salisbury Burten, Rufus Blodget, Jesse Waldo, Judge Hopkins, Ebenezer Rice, Robert Porter, Gamaliel Loomis, Samuel Hayes, Abiel Linsley, Moses Lyon, Asher Bull, Roban Hillis, Aaron Bull, Henry Allis, Cyril Ward, Theodore Brown, Aaron Cook, Warham Parsons, Stephen Prentis, Michael Keith, Thomas Ryker, William Drake, Burrage Rice, Elam Bridges, James F. Judson.

—The first burrying ground was laid out in 1806.

—Rev. John Niles, settled in Prattsburg, in 1803.

—Masonic lodge organized in Prattsburg, in 1820.

—Aaron Bull, kept the first hotel, (built of logs) in 1806.

—Rev. B. Foster Pratt, was installed as pastor, in Jan. 1838.

—Four schools were in operation in the township, prior to 1812.

—First Congregational church of Prattsburg, was erected in 1808.

—Prattsburg lodge, No. 583, F. and A. M., instituted July 7, 1865.

—First religious service held in the town was by Rev. John Niles, in 1803.

—First Sunday school in the town was organized by Judge Porter, in 1816.

—A post route was established from Geneva, via Prattsburg to Bath, in 1808.

—Capt. Joel Pratt, came into the township in 1799. In 1800, he cleared over 100 acres of land, and sowed the same to wheat, when it was harvested and threshed, he took it to Baltimore, and sold it for nearly $8,000.

—The first framed building erected in the town was by Joel Pratt, in 1804.

—Dec. 12, 1872, Paul C. Howe issued the first number of the *Prattsburg News.*

—The first Methodist Society was organzied in Prattsburg, in 1829, and a chapel built.

—A frame barn erected by Jared Pratt, in 1804, was used as a place for public worship.

—The First Baptist church organized in Prattsburg, in 1821, and in 1822, a log church was erected.

—Franklin Academy of Prattsburg was chartered Feb. 23, 1824. Rev. William Beardsley, principal.

—Rev. James H. Hotchkin, became pastor of the Congregational church, Aug. 16, 1809, which continued for 30 years.

—The village of Prattsburg was incorporated Dec. 7, 1848. Addison Ainsworth, Abram I. Quackinbush, and Whiteman Smith, were appointed the first inspectors, to hold the first election.

Pultney Township.

The town of Pultney was organzied in 1808. It is situated in the northeast corner of the county of Steuben, on the western shore of Crooked Lake, and is bounded north by Yates county, on the east by Crooked Lake on the south by Urbana, and on the west by Prattsburg.

The first town meeting was held on the first Tuesday of March, 1808, at the house of Jesse Waldo, the officers elected were Uriel Chapen, supervisor; Aaron Bull, town clerk; Aaron Cook, Elias Hopkins, Nathan Wallis, assessors; William Curtiss, collector; Saulsbury Burten, and Daniel Bennett, overseers of the poor; Samuel Hayes, John Hopkins, Shadrach Norris, commissioners of roads; John Ellis, Gamaliel Loomis, George Raymond, Cornelius Lounsbury, Josiah Allis, fence viewers; Herman Emmons, William P. Curtiss, constables; Shadrack Norris, Joel Pratt, Jr., pond masters; path masters, Cornelius Lounsbury, Solomon Daker, John Ellis, Isaac Spaulding, Asa Brown, Aaron Bordin, James Stone, John Kent, Reuben Hall, John Black, Daniel Bennett, Isaac Pardy, Joel Tuthill, Asa Cooper, Josiah Allis, Martin Hayes, Stephen Prentis, George Wrenchin, William Rowley.

Among the early settlers, John Van Camp, David Thompson, Samuel Miller, G. F. Fitzsimmons, John Black, James Simons, George Simons Shadrach Norris, Samuel Wallis, Nathaniel Wallis, John Ellis, William White, James Dailey, Erastus Glass, Harmen Emmons, Seth Pierce, Elias Hopkins, Cornelius Lownsbury, Thomas Hyatt, Stephen Stratton, Benjamin Bridges, John Hathaway, John Prentiss, Josiah Dunlap, John N. Reynolds, Daniel Sheldon, Elijah Kent, Seth Weed, David Hobart, John Lay, James Bentley, Lovitt H. Edget, Anson Cogswell, Daniel Northrop.

—J. W. Prentiss was the pioneer grape culturist in the town of Pultney and in 1857, large vinyards were planted by other parties, which soon developed into a great industry.

—The Pultney village is situated in the northeastern portion of the town.

—South Pultney is a hamlet in the southern portion of the town.

—Pultney contains an area of 20,140 acres, over 16,000 of which are under cultivation.

—Shadrack Norris, one of the pioneer settlers of the town, was a revolutionary soldier.

Rathbone Township.

Rathbone was organized March 28, 1856, taken from Addison, Cameron, and Woodhull. It is bounded on the north by Cameron and Thurston, on the east by Addison, on the south by Tuscarora and Woodhull, on the west by Woodhull and Cameron. The Canisteo river passes through the township, from the northwest to the southeast. The Erie railroad passes through it, in the valley of the Canisteo. The soil in the valley is alluvial and very productive, wheat, oats and corn, are raised profitably, besides large crops of tobacco. Many years ago it was quite a centre for the manufacture of white pine lumber, hewing of square timber, cutting spars, and rafting the same down the Canisteo to a southern market. General Ransom Rathbone, who settled in the township in 1842, and in whose honor the town, was named, gave impetus to the business of lumbering. He erected mills stores and a hotel, and during his lifetime was one of the most prominent men in the central Canisteo valley.

At an election held May 6, 1856, at the house of David A. Fulmers, William R. Rathbone was elected supervisor; Geo. W. Young, town clerk; Israel Horton, Stephen G. Loyd, justices of the peace; Edwin L. Peckham, superintendent of common schools; Lucius Parker, commissioner of highways; George Northrup, Jonathan Brumley, Uri Scofield, assessors; George Barber, George Harrington, George B. Davis, Charles Reynolds, Timothy T. Brooks, constables; Abram Rogers, James Northrup, overseers of the poor; Seth Whitmore, William P. Barron, Ira Boyer, inspectors of election; Samuel Edmons, collector; Samuel Mitchell, town sealer; the town board was C. H. Cool, George C. Loyd, George W. Young and Seth Whitmore, Jr.

The early settlers were; Abel White, Solomon Tracy, Benjamin Riggs, Peleg Cole, Martin Young, Moses Powers, Jacob Cook, Zeno Sellick, John Helmer, Daniel Hubbard, Jonathan Rowley, Thomas Allen, Isaac Merrill, Seth Cook, Rolland Sanders, Samuel Miles, Jacob Cole, Lewis Crawford, Thomas Mayberry, Zephaniah Townsend.

—Abner Chase, a minister, preached in Rathbone, in 1812.

—In 1831, an M. E. Class was formed, Jacob Cole, class leader.

—An M. E. Class was formed at the Cole school house, in 1847, Jacob Cole, class leader.

—The store of H. W. Rathbone, and the Good Templars hall was destroyed by fire, in 1853

—Martin B. Young, Capt. James Young, A. H. Kinney, Harvey Bergett, were prominent business men in the town, at the time of its formation.

—In 1845, a Methodist church was built, then in the township of Cameron, but the subsequent formation of Rathbone, placed this church in that town.

—An M. E. church, was erected in Rathboneville, in 1850. The ground was donated by General Ransom Rathbone. Trustees, James H. Miles, Lewis H. Bridgeman, Ira Martin, Lewis Crawford, Martin B. Young, J. H. Loper, Willliam D. Smith.

—Maj. William R. Rathbone, son of Gen. Ransom Rathbone, received a thrust from the assassin's knife, while intercepting the murderer of Abraham Lincoln.

Thurston Township.

Thurston was formed from Cameron, Feb. 28, 1844. It is bounded on the north by Bath, on the east by Campbell, on the south by Addison and Rathbone, and on the west by Campbell. It was named in honor of William B. Thurston, one of the principal land holders of the town. It is situated between the dividing ridge of the Conhocton and Canisteo valleys. At an election held at the house of Joseph Cross, April 2, 1844, Joseph Cross was elected supervisor, Noble H. Rising, town clerk; John S. DePue Henry Briggs, Peter D. Edsel, Arnold Payne, justices of the peace; Henry Rising, James L. Ostrander, Fenner Eddy, assessors; William Jack, Amos Fluent, Jared Goodsel, commissioners of highways; Stephen Wakeman, Abijah Youmans, overseers of the poor; John S. Eddy, collector; Oliver Stewart, Oliver Baker, James A. Booth, Jefferson Moore, Nathan Stephens, constables; Warner A. Aldrich, Samuel R. Creveling, Aaron R. DePue inspectors of election.

Early settlers:—Luke Bonny, Wm. Smith, Anderson Carpenter, Amos Dickinson, Harvey Halliday, Jacob Parker, John Fluent, John Stocking. B. Fluent, Harlo Smith, Moses Depue, Stephen Aldrich, Warner M. Aldrich, Stephenson Rugsley, Wm. Jack, James Jack, Samuel Fiske, Amos Fiske, Ethias Fiske, Boralis Fiske, Seth Cook, Arnold Payne, M. O. Keith, John Vandermarker, Henry Forburg, William Hawley, Fenner Eddy, Paris Wheelock, John Corbett, Edwin Merchant, Harley Searse, James Jerry, Jobh Richmyer.

—Fenner Eddy erected a tannery in 1832.

—Edwin Merchant, 1805 built a saw mill.

—Rev. Buel Parker preached in Thurston, in 1814.

—The first school was taught by Caroline Vinan, in 1818.

—A Masonic lodge was established, and E. P. Mulford the first W. M.

—In 1842 a church was erected and made free to all church denominations.

—In 1853, Joseph Turbell erected a large saw mill in the valley of Risingville.

—An M. E. class was organized at Merchantville in 1850. Church erected in 1861.

—Post office was established at Risingville 1853, and Noble H. Rising post master.

—Bonny Hill is named in honor of Luke Bonny, the first settler of the township. He settled there in 1813.

—Christian Church of Thurston was first organized in the town of Bath, March 26, 1836, by Rev. G. A. Hendrick, and on March 20, 1842, during the pastorate of Rev, E. Fleming, it was transferred to West Hill, in Thurston

—The Christian church was erected at Merchantsville, in 1852. Cost $600; Trustees, Edwin Merchant, M. O. Keith, John Roycel.

—M. E. meetings were held near Risingville at the school house, in 1841. A Methodist class was organized in 1850, and a church erected in 1864.

—The Goodhue pond, situated in the southeastern portion of Thurston, and the northwestern portion of Addison, is a body of pure water over a half a mile long, and about one quarter of a mile wide. It was stocked with black bass in 1873.

Troupsburg Township.

The township of Troupsburg was formed from Middletown (now Addison), Feb. 12, 1808. Greenwood and a portion of Jasper were taken off in 1827, and the greater portion of Woodhull in 1828. Troupsburg is bounded on the north by Jasper, on the east by Woodhull, on the south by Pennsylvania, and on the west by West Union. The streams of the township flow northeast into the Canisteo river and south into the Cowanesque river. Some of the highest lands in the county are in this township, reaching an elevation of nearly 2,500 feet above the level of the sea. At the first annual election, held at the house of Daniel Johnson, in March, 1808, Daniel Johnson was elected supervisor; Samuel B. Rice, town clerk; Stephen Dolson, Brown Gillespie, Elijah Cady, assessors; Uri Martin, William Wooley, Nathaniel Mallory, commissioners of highways; R. Sears, constable and collector; Daniel Johnson, poor master; Elijah Cady, 2d poormaster; Caleb Smith, fence viewer; Domady Prison, Peter Cady, overseers of highways.

Early settlers:—Ebenezer Spencer, Daniel Johnson, Lemuel Benham, A. B. Reynolds, Lewis Hays, Jonathan Rodgers, George Martin, Nathaniel Mallory, David Smith, James Carpenter, John Miller, Samuel Cady, Harry B. Reynolds, Samuel Griggs, Orange Perry, Joshua Sluiter, Jesse Weldon, Marsena Cummings, William Card, Lyman Dodge, Rufus Gilbert, Griffin Rodgers, Rufus Fuller, David Simpson.

—Quakers held meetings in the year 1816.

—The regular Baptist services were held in a barn, by Rev. J. B. Chase, in 1836.

—Troupsburg was named in honor of Robert Troup, agent for the Pultney estate.

—Free Will Baptist church, organized in 1850. Rev. B. F. Mack was the pioneer preacher.

—Abner Thomas taught school in Troupsburg in the winter of 1809, and was succeeded by Sarah Thacher.

—Through the instrumentality of Rev. N. S. Reynolds, an academy was erected in the town of Troupsburg.

—Baptist church at Troupsburg, June 3, 1874, was dedicated by Rev. M. S. Reynolds. Cost of church, $3,000.

—The East Troupsburg Baptist church, erected and dedicated Nov. 4, 1875, by Rev. Gustave Anderson. Cost of church, $3,000.

—M. E. Church Class organized in Chenango settlement, in the year 1846. by Rev. Luther Northway, and Henry Bates, class-leader. During the pastorate of Rev. E. B. Thomas a church was built, at an expense of $2,000.

Tuscarora Township.

Tuscarora township was formed from the southern portion of the township of Addison, Dec. 13, 1859. It occupies an elevated position between the vallleys of the Canisteo, Tioga and Cowanesque, its streams running northward into the Canisteo river, eastward into the Tioga river, and westward into the Cowanesque river. The Addison and Northern Pennsylvania railroad runs through the township from the northeast to the southwest, ascending its highlands from the valley of the Tuscarora Creek, and winding around its hills and descending into the valley of the Cowanesque, at Elkland, Pennsylvania. The construction of this road reflects great credit upon the energy of its projectors. The town, although broken by ravines, and abrupt declivities, is under a fair state of cultivation. At the first annual election for town officers, held at the house of Oliver Moore, Feb. 14, 1860, by Jos. Manley, Stephen Coon and Charles W. Robinson, election board. The township officers elected were: Jesse W. Rowley, supervisor; George W. Webb, town clerk; Phillip W. Perkins, commissioner of highways; Lorenzo Wettenhall, Joseph Oakden, Lansing Hand, assessors; Archibald Manley, Albert W. Wells, Charles Hill, inspectors of election; Myron M. Manley, James Lemunyan, Charles W. Robinson, justice of the peace; G. H. Freeman, collector; Cicero Wettenhall, Amos Tobias, Geo. Thomas, constables. Tuscarora is bounded upon the north by the townships of Rathbone and Addison, on the east by Lindley, on the south by the Pennsylvania state line, and west by Woodhull.

Early settlers:—Its first settlers were William Wombaugh, Amos Dolph, John Towsley, Jesse Rowley, Samuel Colegrove, Daniel Strait, Daniel Strait, jr., Asahel Thomas, Joseph Gile, John C. Orr, Joseph Orr, Daniel Burdick, Andrew Crowl, Rev. David Short, Warren Northrup, Benedict Northrup, John Webster, Rev. Aaron Baxter, Alfred Nichols, James Sprague, M. Taft, David Hart, Samuel Mack, Enoch Mack, A. Alba, Orrin Swan, Samuel Smith, Justus Wright, Simeon Freeman, Joseph Manley, Zelos Toles.

—Addison Hill M. E. church dedicated Oct. 15, 1874.

—Jesse Rowley settled in the township in the year 1804.

—Daniel Strait, who settled at Straitsburg, Tuscarora township, was a revolutionary soldier.

—Quite a number of the early settlers of Tuscarora (then Addison) were from the county of Chenango, N. Y.

—Free Communion Baptist church constituted July 5th, 1829, by Rev. Aaron Baxter. Church erected in the year 1847.

—William Wombaugh was the first settler. He became very wealthy. In the year 1806 he built a grist mill and saw mill on Tuscarora creek.

—Methodist Episcopal church erected in the year 1849. Previous to that time services had been held in private houses and in school houses.

—Jemima Rowley, daughter of Jesse Rowley, was the first white child born in the township. She was born in Feb., 1806.

—William Wombaugh, jr., built a woolen factory on Tuscarora creek, in the year 1842. It worked 250 spindles and gave employment to thirty or more persons.

—Plank road from Addison via Tuscarora to Elkland, completed in the year 1851. Abandoned Sept. 15, 1878. It was a great public convenience for many years.

—Methodist Episcopal Class formed in Tuscarora in the year 1833. Among the members of that class were Richard Finch and wife; Seth Wixon and wife; Stephen Coon and wife; William Wixon, class leader.

Urbana Township and Hammondsport Village.

Urbana was formed from the township of Bath, April 17, 1822. A portion of it was re-annexed to Bath in the year 1839, and at the same time a portion of Wheeler was attached to Urbana. Urbana contains some of the most productive lands and some of the most delightful scenery in Steuben county. It was among the earliest settled townships in the county. It is distinguished for its extensive vineyards and wine cellars, the intelligence and hospitality of its citizens. It is bounded on the north by Pultney and Prattsburgh, on the east by Wayne and Bradford, on the south by Bath, and west by Bath and Wheeler. The first town election was held in Pleasant Valley, on the fourth Tuesday in March, 1823. Henry A. Townshend was elected supervisor; Lazarus Hammond, town clerk; Andrew Layton, H. Griffith, Abraham Brundage, assessors; Obediah Wheeler, Reuben Hall, Abraham Brundage, commissioners of highways; Caleb Rogers, collector; Caleb Rogers, Daniel Kingsley, William H. Ennis, constables; Samuel Baker, William Read, overseers of the poor: William Reed, Edward Townshend Franklin Baker, commissioners of schools. Path masters: Abraham Brundage, Samuel Baker, John Walters, Cornelius Younglove, William Read, John Brundage, Noah Griffith, Robert Harrison, John Daniels, Reuben Hall, Simon I. Jacobus, John Plane, John Richardson, Andrew Layton, Isaac Noble, Stephen Douglas, Isaiah Webster, Erastus Webster, John Loder, Simon Ingersoll, James Harrison. The office of path master or overseer of roads was one of the most essential and important offices in the town. It was to the energy, ability and good judgment of these officers that much of the prosperity and future settlement of the town depended. To have good roads was the key to the rapid development of the township. At the same time John Walters, Abraham Brundage Reuben Hall were chosen fence viewers, and William Baker, pound master.

Early settlers:—William Aulls, Thomas Aulls, Samuel Baker, Richard Daniels, Amos Stone, William Read, Eli Read, John Sheathar, John Faulkner, James Brundage, Abraham Brundage, Cornelius Younglove, Lazarus Hammond, George McClure, James Sheathar, Darius Read, Jonathan Barney, Daniel Bennett, Abram Depuy, David Hutches, Samuel Drew, Derrick Brink, Joseph Rosenkrans, Jonathan Easton, Henry Schoonover, John Daniels, Samuel Townshend, John Phillips, Obediah Wheeler, John Walters, Reuben Hall, Andrew Layton, Henry Griffith, Daniel Kingsley, Caleb Rogers, Noah Griffiths, Robert Harrison, Isaac Noble, Isaiah Webster, Erastus Webster, Caleb Chapman, Israel R. Wood, Edward Townshend, Franklin Baker.

—Hammondsport academy erected in 1858.

—Bank of Hammondsport, established in 1878.

—John Randel built a brick store, in the year 1852.

—William Hastings & Co. were prominent merchants.

—Urbana Lodge, F. & A. M., chartered June 17, 1879.

—Meridith Mallory erected a grist mill, in the year 1836.

—Caleb Chapman kept the first tavern at North Urbana.

—Capt. John Sheathar built the first saw mill, in the year 1797.

—The first steamboat upon Crooked Lake was the Keuka, in 1835.

—Samuel Baker, jr., was the first white child born in the township,

—John Phillips died in the year 1794, the first death in the township.

—Lazarus Hammond purchased the Sheathar property, June 9, 1807.

—Eliphalet Norris taught the first school in Pleasant Valley in the year 1795.

—The first school house in the village of Hammondsport was built in the year 1827.

—Gen. George McClure built the first grist mill at Cold Spring, in the year 1802.

—Cold Spring valley was occupied by General George McClure, in the year 1802.

—In 1831, Gen. George McClure built a saw and plaster mill at Hammondsport.

—St. James Protestant Episcopal Church, organized June 15, 1829. Church erected in 1832.

—Capt. John Sheathar, the original settler at Hammondsport, was a revolutionary soldier.

—Henry A. Townshend purchased Gen. McClure's Spring Valley mills, in the year 1814.

—Jonathan Barney and Polly Aulls were married in the year 1794, the first marriage in the township.

—In the year 1831, the Crooked Lake canal was completed, which gave a great impetus to business at Hammondsport.

—Rev. Ephraim Sandford preached the first sermon in the township, at the house of Judge Samuel Baker, in the year 1795.

—The first sail vessel upon Crooked Lake was "The Sally," built for th purpose of carrying wheat in 1803. Gen. McClure was the owner.

—William Aulls, or Reading, Pa., was the first permanent settler in the township, in the year 1793, and Samuel Baker, Richard Daniels and Amos Stone were the next in the same year (1793.)

—Samuel Baker was also the first settler in Tioga county, Pennsylvania. in the year 1786, and resided there until he went to Urbana, in 1793. He was a revolutionary soldier and a native of Connecticut.

—Hammondsport Fire Department, organized in April 1871, with Jacob VanAuken, Chief Engineer; Almon H. Eggleston, first assistant; William Benner, second assistant.

—The Hammondsport Company was formed in 1831. Among its members were: Thomas W. Olcott and others of Albany; Judge Whiting, Charles Butler and William Dezang of Geneva. This company purchased extensive property of Judge Hammond and William Hastings Esq.

—Presbyterian Church of Hammondsport organized Sept. 14, 1831. Judge Hammond gave a lot, and William Hastings erected a church and presented it to the society.

—Corner stone of New St James Church laid by Bishop Coxe, April 18, 1876. Consecrated June 12, 1877, by Bishop Coxe. Cost $10,000, value of Rectory and Glebe $3,000.

—Gen. George McClure was the most enterprising man in his day, of any of the distinguished citizens of Steuben. He built mills, purchased thousands of bushels of grain, converted them into flour, bought all the surplus pork, etc., built arks, and ran them laden with flour, pork, and lumber, to a southern market, and erected the first store house at Hammondsport, in 1803.

—Officers of St. James Episcopal Church, at its organization in 1829, were Henry A. Townshend, John Powers, Wardens; Lazarus Hammond, Cornelius Younglove, Ezekiel B. Pulling, Israel R. Wood, John Mitchell, Jr., Zelotus Knapp, Vestrymen; Rector, William W. Bostwck. The organization was witnessed by Mrs. Elizabeth H. Younshead, Charles N. Tuttle, Rev. William W. Bostwick, John Powers, and H. A. Townshend. Church erected and dedicated by Bishop Onderdonk, Aug. 27, 1833.

Hammondsport is a beautiful village in the town of Urbana, situated at the head of Crooked Lake, or Lake Keuka, a splendid sheet of water twenty miles long and from one to one and a half miles wide. A narrow guage railroad connects Hammondsport with Bath, and a line of steam pleasure-boats ply between Hammondsport and Penn Yan, at the foot of the lake. Hammondsport is situated in the center of one of the greatest wine-producing sections in the United States. It was incorporated in the year 1856, re-chartered in 1871.

Wayland Township.

The township of Wayland was organized April 12, 1848, taken from Dansville and Cohocton. It is situated in the extreme northwest portion of Steuben county, and is bounded on the north by the county of Livingston, east by the township of Cohocton, south by Fremont and Dansville, and west by Dansville and Livingston county. Its western line bordering upon Dansville, is a series of irregular lines, resembling saw teeth, or a flight of stairs. Its surface is made up of beautiful rolling and highly cultivated lands. Two small lakes are found within its limits. The Rochester branch of the Erie passes through the northeastern portion of the town.

At an election held for the purpose of choosing its first officers at the house of C. Patchin, May 2, 1848. W. Patchin, Jr., John Hess, Myron M. Patchin, D. C. Ward, town board. John Hess was elected supervisor; Myron M. Patchin, Amos Knowlton, Chauncey Moore, Gardner Pierce, justices of the peace; Samuel W. Epley, town clerk; R. M. Patchin, David Poor, David Brownson, assessors; H. H. Hess, superintendent of schools; Stephen C. Phillips, Westley Doughty, F. E. Day, commissioners of highways; George Karcher, Gideon Moon, Joseph Fronk, constables; John Hamlin, sealer of weights and measures.

Early settlers: Adam Zimmerman, Thomas Bowles, John Hume, —Bowen,

—Hicks, Thomas Begole, Solomon Brownson, James Brownson, Elisha Brownson, Isaac Willie, Osgood Carlton, Solomon Draper, Demas Hess, Samuel Draper, Benjamin Perkins, Walter Patchin, John Hess, Peter Shafer, Robert S. Miner, Erastus Ames, —— McMillen.

—Adam Zimmerman settled in Wayland, in 1806.

—Doctor Patchin built the first grist mill, in 1822.

—Benjamin Perkins was the first settler in Perkinsville.

—A plank road was built from Patchinville to Dansville, in 1845.

—Doctor Warren Patchin built a hotel near Patchins Mills, in 1824.

—Erastus Ames, a noted Nimrod, settled near Loon Lake quite early.

—Samuel Brownson was the first settler at Loon Lake. He purchased 400 acres of land.

Wayne Township.

Wayne was formed as "Frederickstown" March 18, 1796. Its name was changed April 6, 1808, and named in honor of Gen. Anthony Wayne, a Pennsylvanian, and a distinguished officer of the revolutionary war. It originally consisted of a very large territory, but Reading was taken from it in 1806. Orange in 1813; and Barrington and Tyrone in 1822, and again a portion of it was annexed to Tyrone in 1854. It is bounded on the north by Crooked Lake, (Lake Keuka,) east by the county line, south by Bradford, and west by Urbana and Crooked Lake. Its soil is well adapted to the general agricultural products, peculiar to this county, and especially to the growing of grapes. Some of the most productive vineyards of the United States are in this and adjoining townships.

Early settlers; Zephaniah Hoff, Henry Mapes, —— Widow Jennings, Solomon Wixson, Enos Silsbee, Joshua Smith, John Holdridge, Elijah Reynolds, Ephraim Tyler, Ehpraim Sanford, Jr., Nathaniel Frisbee, Anthony Swarthout, Jabez Hopkins, Aaron Olmstead, John Goble, Thomas Bennett, Gersham Goble, Thomas Margeson, Henry Houck, Israel R. Wood, Joseph Bailey, George Hunter, John Earnest, John B. Mitchell, Sr., Simeon Sackett, John Teeple, John McDowell, William Kernan, Joseph Silsbee, James Silsbee, Abraham Henderson.

—First Baptist Church erected in 1794.

—Jabez Hopkins kept the first hotel at Keuka.

—John Silsbec built the first saw mill in the town.

—John Teeple, a surveyor, settled in Wayne in 1800.

—The Wayne Baptist Church was constituted in 1794.

—Joseph Bailey a revolutionary soldier, settled in Wayne in 1799.

—Solomon Wixson, and Henry Mapes, settled in Wayne, in 1793.

—Aaron Olmstead was an early settler. He made axes and scythes.

—The first vineyard in the town was set out by John Grace, in 1863.

—Enos Silsbee kept the first hotel in the town, and built the first ashery.

—Rev. Roswell Goff preached occasionally at Wayne from 1804 to 1807.

—James Silsbee built the first tannery, and ran the first grist mill by horse power.

—Abram Hendricks, built the first store at Keuka. James Silsbee was the first merchant at Wayne.

—Methodist Episcopal Church organized February 28, 1837. Church erected in 1840.

—Ephraim Sanford from Luzerne county, Pa., a revolutionary soldier, settled in Wayne in 1793.

—William Kernan, father of Senator Francis Kernan, was supervisor of Wayne, in 1817, and 1818.

—Elizabeth Wixson was born in Wayne, Nov. 6, 1793, she was the daughter of Soloman Wixson, and was the first child born in the town.

—John B. Mitchell, an early settler in Wayne, and at one time one of the most extensive business men of the town, died January 14, 1873, aged 71 years.

—Joshua Silsbee, better known as "Yankee Silsbee," the great personator of Yankee character, was a son of John Silsbee, and was born in the town of Wayne.

—St. John's Episcopal Church organized March 25, 1872, by Rev. William Atwill. Presbyterian church purchased and repaired and consecrated by Bishop Coxe, Sept. 2, 1875.

—The Baptist Church at Wayne in 1807 belonged to the Chemung association; in 1811, to the Cayuga association; in 1814, to the Ontario association and in 1818, to the Steuben Baptist association.

—December 24, 1805, a Presbyterian Church was organized by John Lindsley, missionary. Frederic Bartles was the first elder chosen. January 19, 1830, the church of Wayne united with that of Tyrone.

—Francis M. McDowell one of the seven who founded the "Patrons of Husbandry" was born at Wayne, June 12, 1831. He was also one of the firm, who contracted to build the eastern division of the Kansas Pacific Railroad.

Samuel Hallett, one of the most energetic citizens of Wayne, who married Ann McDowell, daughter of Mathew McDowell, Esq., was assassinated at Wyandotte, Kansas, by a discharged engineer, July 27, 1864. Mr. Hallett was a teacher, banker, railroad contractor, and probably done more than any other ten men to secure the building of the Atlantic & Great Western R. R., and the Union and Pacific railway.

West Union.

West Union was formed from Greenwood, April 5, 1845. It is situated in the extreme south eastern portion of Steuben county, in the highlands at the head waters of Bennet's creek, which flows northeasterly into the Canisteo river, and at the head waters of Troups creek, which flows southeasterly, and empties into the Cowanesque at Knoxville, Tioga county Pennsylvania.

The first election for town officers was held at the house of John Hauber, May 6, 1845. The officers elected were David Sherman, supervisor; Moses Forbes, town clerk; Jeremiah B. Millard, Cornelius Rosa, William Olmstead justices of the peace; David Collins, Peter A. McLean, Marsena Cummings, assessors; Jeremiah B. Millard, Jeremiah Ingley, Alvin Chaplin, commissioners of highways; Cornelius Rosa, Henry B. Baker, Jr., Marsena Cummings, inspectors of election; Thomas F. Hubbard, Henry B. Baker, overseers of the poor; Walter B. Olmstead, collector; Walter B. Olmstead, Calvin Clark, William B. Hauber, L. D. Baker, constables.

Early settlers; Jonathan Mattason, John Mattason, David Davis, Abram V. Olmstead, William Burger, Frederic Hauber, Uriah Ingley, Vincent Compton, B. Ingley, William Compton, Vincent Compton, Jr., Adam Young, William Young, Ephraim Young, Henry Young, Daniel Hamilton, David Baker, Stephen Boyd, —— Reed, John Shehan, Dennis Malone, Luke Fox, Phillip W. Failing, —— Bigelow, David Sherman, Alvin Chapin, Alexander Keenan, Charles Rexford, Daniel Rexford, John Wiley, William Fisher, Benjamin Wilkes.

—Uri Stephens taught the first school in the township.

—The first store was opened by Jesse Jones and Dr. C. B. Knight, in the year 1855.

—Jonathan Mattason, John Mattason and David Davis, were the first settlers in the township.

—David Sherman was the first farmer who manufactured cheese for market, in 1841.

—John Wiley, William Fisher and Benjamin Wilkes, erected a saw-mill at Wileyville in 1849.

—A cheese factory which takes the milk from 1240 cows, is located near Rexville, in the township.

—David Sherman was twelve years supervisor of West Union, ten of which were in succession.

—The first child born in the township was Walter B. Olmstead, son of Abram V. Olmstead, Nov. 4, 1823.

—Charles Rexford and Daniel Rexford built the first mill in the township in 1849. They also erected a tavern, the first in the township.

—There are more than one hundred naturalized citizens, chiefly natives of Ireland in the township. They are among the most wealthy and prominent farmers in the township.

—The first religious meeting (Methodist,) was held in the year 1831, at the house of Abram V. Olmstead; William Burger, was the first class leader. Methodist church erected and dedicated in August 1870, by Rev. M. H. Davis. Trustees when church was erected, were Edward Daly, Sylvester Skillman, John Paisted.

—The first Catholic Church erected to accomodate the members of this church, residing in the south eastern portion of the county was in Greenwood, in 1845. A number of the early communicants of this church, resided in the town of West Union. In 1848, Rt., Rev. John Timour. Bishop, visited diocese, and comfirmed a large number of children and adults. In 1875, St Mary's church was dedicated by Bishop Ryan, at Rexville, in the town of West Union. Cost of church $18,000. This church was burned Feb. 13, 1877, and a new church soon thereafter erected, at a cost of $9,000. A parochial residence was also erected. The present membership is over 1,000.

Wheeler Township.

Wheeler was formed from Bath and Prattsburg, Feb. 25, 1820. It was named in honor of Capt. Silas Wheeler, a native of Rhode Island, and a soldier of the revolutionary war, and the first settler of the township. A portion of Wheeler was taken to form Avoca, in 1843, and a portion to form

Urbana, in 1839. It is bounded on the north by Prattsburg, on the east by Urbana, on the south by Bath and Avoca, and on the west by Avoca. The principal streams in the township are Ten Mile creek, and Five Mile creek, tributaries of the Conhocton river. The Conhocton river runs near its southern boundary.

Atthe first town meeting held for the election of township officers, Thomas Aulls was elected supervisor. In 1823, Grattan H. Wheeler was elected supervisor, and in 1824, Thomas Aulls was elected supervisor. From 1824, until 1830, the record of the township election cannot be found. In 1830, Jonathan Barney, was elected supervisor.

Early Settlers:—Capt. Silas Wheeler, Levi Gray, Nathan Rose, William Holmes, Otto F. Marshall, Daniel Marshall, George Renchan, J. C. Overhiser, George Raymond, Jenks Young, Thomas Cuming, Philip Beemer, Uriel Chapen, William Rowley, Daniel Raymond, Andrew Harris, Noah Stephens, Reuben Montgomery, Abram Cranmer, Daniel Raymond, Jonathan Barney, Furmen Gardner, Henry Chichester, Thomas Aulls, Albertus Larowe, Philip Myrtle, Hiram Rose, Albert Wilcox.

—The first school teacher was Uriel Chapen.

—Capt. Silas Wheeler died 1828, aged 78 years.

—Capt. Silas Wheeler set out a nursery, in 1804.

—Capt. Silas Wheeler built the first saw mill, in 1802

—Levi Gray was the first post master in the township.

—October 19, 1831, Central Wheeler Church organized.

—Maj. Jonathan Barney, a captain in the war of 1812, died in 1852.

—William Barney born Nov. 1, 1801, was the first birth in the township.

—Presbyterian church organized August 30, 1825. It consisted of 23 members.

—J. C. Overhiser was the father of eighteen children. He died May 13, 1871, aged 90 years.

—Rev. E. Eggleston, (Baptist) was the first preacher. Rev. Daniel Harriower, (Presbyterian) as a missionery, also held early services in the township.

—Methodist Episcopal Society of Center Wheeler formerly belonged to the Kanona charge. In 1872, a separate charge was organized. Parsonage purchased in 1874.

—Presbyterian Church of Wheeler organized in 1832. Harry Reed, Albert Wilcox, Reuben C. Montgomery, Cornelius Younglove, Otto F. Marshall, Levi Gray, trustees; Thomas Aulls, treasurer; T. W. Hitchcock, clerk.

—In 1832, Samuel Aulls erected a church for the Presbyterian Society of Wheeler. Cost of church $600. In 1867, the society built another church at a cost of $2,000. Dedicated September 7, 1870, by Rev. James M. Pratt.

—M. E. meetings were held early in the settlement of Wheeler, in private houses, and in school houses. In 1845, Joseph H. Tuttle, pastor; John A. Banter, George Banter, George Shepherd, Hiram Rose, John Overhiser, trustees, erected a church at a cost of $800, George Renchan, carpenter.

Woodhull Township and Village.

The town of Woodhull was formed Feb. 18, 1828, taken from Troupsburg and Addison. It derives its name from Gen. Nathaniel Woodhull, a soldier of the revolutionary war. It is bounded on the north by Cameron and Rathbone, on the east by Tuscarora, on the south by the Pennsylvania State line, on the west by Troupsburg and Jasper. It occupies the highlands between the Tuscarora valley, and the valley of the Cowanesque. Asher Johnson was elected supervisor; Jeffery Smith, town clerk; Stephen Kent, collector; Zebulin Tubbs, assessor, at its first election. David Edwards represented the township in the board of supervisors for eleven years, Asher Johnson four years, Christopher Marlatt four years, S. V. Lattimer seven years, in the early history of the township.

Early settlers:—Daniel Johnson, Bethuel Tubbs, Squire Wilkes, Caleb Colvin, Josiah Stiles, Stephen Dolson, B. Patrick, William Martin, Caleb Smith, Joshua Green, Asel Stiles, Henry Martin, L. Clark, Samuel Smith, Levi Rice, Micajah Sherwood, John Stone, Hugh Boyd, —— Hornocker, James Williams, Asel Bears, Worchester Perry, Thomas Hedges, Martin Harding, Andrew Colegrove, Joseph Tubbs, Sylvester Tousey, John Stone, Calvin Searle. Ichabod C. Leech, John Brimmer, Daniel Christeon, Alvinsaey Foote, Jeffrie Smith, Silas H Tubbs, Seth Pierce, Henry Harding.

—A cheese factory was erected in 1874, by Henry Cobb.

—First death was that of a daughter of Stephen Dolson, in 1808.

—Charles Adams started the *Woodhull News*, a weekly newspaper, in 1871.

—Caleb Smith built a saw and grist mill on the Tuscarora creek, in the year 1806.

—Rev. Simeon R. Jones, of Elmira, preached at the house of Daniel Johnson, in 1808.

—A foundry was established for casting farming implements, by Warner & Gardner, in 1844.

—Col. Henry Baldwin, of Addison, erected a large steam flouring mill at Woodhull village, in 1858.

—Free Will Baptist Church services were held at private houses, in 1830, and in 1834, a society was formed.

—Abner Thomas taught the first school in the township, in 1808, in a log school house erected for the purpose.

—Woodhull Academy and Union School was erected in 1868, at a cost of $4,000, Hamilton Marlatt, and Owen B. Baxter, were conspicious in carrying the design into execution.

--A second Free Will Baptist Church was formed February, 1852. A church was erected and dedicated August, 1875, by Rev. S. Aldrich, of Elmira, cost of church $2,000.

—Hon. Henry Sherwood, son of Micajah Sherwood, was born in the township, in January 1824. Mr. Sherwood was elected a member of the legislature, in 1861. He was very active in filling the quota of Steuben county during the war of the rebellion. He was one of the charter members of the Blossburg Coal Company in 1866, and a director of the Erie railway in 1871. He died in July 1875.

—Daniel Johnson was the first settler in the township, in 1804, and 1805, Bethuel Tubbs, Squire Wilkes, Caleb Calvin, Josiah Stiles, Stephen Dolson, B. Patrick, and William Martin.

—Woodhull is a thriving village, containing about 500 inhabitants, situated on Tuscarora creek. There are a Union School, several churches, a number of stores, and it is the centre of a large trade from the township, also from Jasper, Greenwood, West Union, and Troupsburg.

—M. E. Church services were early held in the township, but a church was not erected until 1846. This church was located in Woodhull village. The trustees were Alfred Smith, F. H. Tubbs, C. T. Locke, F. D. Brown, Philo Millard. A second organization was effected in 1848, at Hedgesville, and in 1861, a Union church was erected by this organization and the Presbyterians. Trustees for the Methodist, Joel Eggleston, William Geer. Trustees for the Presbyterians, Thomas Hedges, Wheeler Perry, C. P. Hubbard.

—The Presbyterian Church of Woodhull was organized October 15, 1831 by Rev. Isaac Flaglar, of Hammondsport. The original members were Allen Sheldon and wife, Franklin B. Hubbard, Chauncey P. Hubbard and wife, Obed Hathaway and wife, Catharine Pomeroy, Martin Whiteman, Hannah Gulick, Dorothy Whiteman, Thomas Hedges, Mary Shumway, Hannah Smith, Elizabeth Strond, Lyman Morrell and wife. Allen Shelden and C. P. Hubbard were chosen elders; F. B. Hubbard, clerk. The M. E. Society joined them in erecting a Union Church at Hedgesville, in 1861.

—Woodhull Baptist Church organized Nov. 20, 1835, at the house of John Kent. Among the early members were Seth Baxter and wife, John Kent wife and daughter, Ira Smith and wife, Stephen Kent, Ephraim Wood and wife, Samuel Stone, William Martin and wife, Maria Edwards, Emma Edwards, Philena Marsh, Lucy A. Dodge, Ebenezer Gardner, Samuel Cookes and wife. Stephen Kent, clerk; John Kent, deacon. In June 1849, seventeen members withdrew and formed the Newville church, and in 1858, both churches disbanded, and organized the Union Baptist Church of Woodhull. A church was erected, the pastor Rev. Mr. Marine, working upon it himself as a carpenter.

TIOGA COUNTY, NEW YORK.

Tioga county was formed in pursuance of an act of the legislature of the State of New York, passed Feb. 16, 1791, taken from Montgomery (formerly Tryon county.) The same act contained a section re-organizing the town of Chemung, which had previously been formed in 1788, as a town in Montgomery county. The county of Tioga as formed in 1791, contained the territory now embraced in the counties of Chemung, Tioga and Broome, the county of Schuyler, with the exceptions of the towns of Orange and Tyrone, which were then in Ontario, subsequently Steuben and now Schuyler, all of Tompkins except the town of Groton, and a portion of Lansing, about one third of Cortland county and a large portion of Chenango county. Within the next four years commenced a series of acts lessening the territory of Tioga county. March 5, 1794, an area of about 300,000 acres was taken, consisting of the townships of Hector, Ulysses, Virgil and Cincinnatus, to assist in the formation of Onondaga county. March 15, 1798, Chenango county was formed, taking the large territory originally contained in the township of Greene, Oxford and Jericho, from Tioga county. Broome county was formed March 28, 1806, and a large portion of Tioga was taken, a portion of which was restored to her March 22, 1822. At the same time, March 22, 1822, the townships of Danby, Caroline and Newfield were given to form Tompkins, to take effect in 1823. March 29, 1836, the county of Chemung was formed, thus aggregating one million nine hundred and twenty thousand acres, which she had given away to start out her daughters in a respectable manner, in the management of affairs for themselves. Generous mother! long may her noble act be remembered, and her name "Tioga" be preserved. The county now embraces an area of five hundred and forty-two square miles or three hundred forty-six thousand eight hundred and eighty acres, a territory sufficient to maintain with dignity her public institutions, her churches and lodges, her villages and towns, her poor and disabled, her schools and institutions of learning, her public highways and contribute to the construction of railroads and other necessary improvements.

The name of Tioga, in the Indian dialect means "meeting of the waters," and has been variously spelled and pronounced. As early as 1737, Tioga Point was visited by Conrad Weiser, the Indian Interpreter of Pennsylvania. He found an Indian village at the point, and his orthography is "Diahoga." The townships of Tioga county are Barton, Berkshire, Candor, Newark Valley, Nichols, Owego, Richford, Spencer, Tioga.

PROCESS OF ORGANIZATION.—The act establishing the county of Tioga, Feb. 16, 1791, also provides for the holding of courts, the first to be held at Chemung, (now Elmira) in June, 1791, and January, 1792. Abraham Miller was the first judge, and James McMasters sheriff. For several years after the formation of the county, courts were held at Elmira, and the town of Union, and prisoners were confined in the Montgomery county jail. In the meantime the supervisors of the county were to assemble and levy a tax of £800, for the erection of public buildings.

An act passed Jan. 14, 1793, provided for a half shire, and directed that the building erected at New Town, (Elmira) until further provisions were made should be the jail of Tioga county. March 25, 1794, by an act of the legislature, the loan officers were required to meet at Chenango, and New Town, alternately, and on March 7, 1795, the sheriff was required to reckon his mileage from Nanticooke bridge in Union. March 31, 1801, an act was passed creating two jury districts in Tioga county, and directing that the courts be held in the new court house, at Chenango, and the other at New Town, (Elmira.) On March 20, 1804, the place was fixed for the county clerk's office to be located not more than three miles from Owego village, on the north side of the Susquehanna. The erection of the county of Broome, March 28, 1806, changed the geographical center of Tioga County, and the courts were directed to be held at New Town. In 1810, the county of Tioga, was again re-organized into two jury districts, the erection of Broome county necessitating the change. According to this re-organization, Spencer was created a half shire and a deputy county clerk appointed who should reside within three miles of that place. Elmira remained the other shire, and courts were held alternately at Spencer and Elmira until other wise directed by law. But a law passed March 14, 1818 required the board of supervisors to meet annually at Spencer. February 1817, the sheriff was directed to charge his mileage from Spencer, and the courts were also directed to be held at that place. Against this latter arrangement the citizens of the western portion of the county now comprising the county of Chemung remonstrated, and succeeded in obtaining the passage of an act restoring the two jury districts, and constituting Elmira a half shire. This was effected by an act of the legislature passed March 22, 1822. The eastern jury district o be composed of Tioga, Spencer, Danby, Caroline, Candor, Berkshire and Owego, and the western to comprise the townships of Chemung, Catharine, Cayuta, and Elmira.

At the same session April 16, 1822, the township of Big Flats was formed from Elmira, and Erin from Chemung March 29, 1822, and Southport April 16, 1822, taken from Elmira, thus making seven townships with seven supervisors in the western district and seven in the eastern. In 1823, April 16, the town of Veteran was organized from Catharine, also the town of Catlin at the same time, making nine townships in the western jury district. At the same session Newark was organized April 12, 1823, (by the name of Westville, which name was changed next year to Newark) making eight townships in the western jury district.

The act of March 22, 1822, provided for a court house at Elmira and Owego, and the meeting of the courts alternately at those places. The supervisors were also to meet alternately at Owego and Elmira, thus depriving Spencer of the honors of the half shire. This state of things continued to exist until the formation of the county of Chemung embracing the western jury district, March 29, 1836. Several towns however were formed, both in the eastern district and western district prior to the erection of Chemung county.

The first court erected for the county was at Elmira, and the next at Chenango, now in Broome county. In 1810, an act was passed authorizing the erection of a court house at Spencer. Two acres was donated by Andrew Purdy, as a site. The court house was erected in 1810-11, by Andrew Purdy, for which he was paid $5,000. Samuel Westbrook superintendent of construction. The entire cost of the building was $5,595.60. In 1818, a county clerk's office was erected at Spencer, by Andrew Purdy, in pursuance of an act of the legislature, February 20, 1818; Joshua Ferris Henry Miller, and Abel Hart commissioners to contract the work. The court house was burned in 1821, and the act heretofore alluded to was passed in 1822, creating the eastern and western jury districts, and fixing the places for holding the courts at Owego and Elmira, and aurthorizing the erection of a court house and jail at Owego and Elmira, providing that certain sums should be raised by voluntary subscriptions. Lots for building purposes were also to be conveyed free to the county. Under these provisions John R. Drake, Anson Camp and Charles Pumpelly, were appointed commissioners for Owego or the eastern district, and Stephen Tuttle, Mathew Carpenter and William Jenkins for New Town or the western district after the money had been voluntarily subscribed, and raised by tax. Jail limits were prescribed at Owego, covering an area of 250 acres. An act was passed in 1822, authorizing the trustees of the village of Owego to convey certain lands to Tioga county for court house purposes. About this time a dispute arose in relation to the construction or erection of the county clerk's office at Spencer, between Andrew Purdy and the county authorities, and Richard Townley, Richard Smith, and Luther Gere were appointed arbitrators to adjust the difference. They awarded Mr. Purdy $1,139, which was paid. Thus was provision made for a court house and county jail both at Owego and Elmira, and the wheels of justice continued in motion.

In 1851, a new jail was built at Owego, costing about $6,000. In 1855, a new county clerk's office was erected. In 1868, the court house and jail were condemed, which finally resulted in the erection of a new court house, in the years 1872-3, at a cost of $65,318.90, and the repairing of the jail of over one thousand dollars more. The laying of the corner stone of the new court house was attended with very interesting ceremonies in the presence of a large number of citizens. The masonic fraternity were represented by some of the most distinguished of that order. Hon. John J. Taylor was the orator, and Charles A. Munger, Esq. the poet of the occasion.

Poor House;—An act was passed April 18, 1829, authorizing the construction of a poor house in each of the jury districts, comprising the county of Tioga, and the sum of $3,000 to be raised in each district. A farm was purchased in the eastern district consisting of about sixty acres, in 1836, and soon thereafter erected a poor house thereon. In 1850, a loan was effected of $11,000 toward the erection of a new house. In 1856, a house was erected for the keeping of the insane. In 1866, a stone building was erected at the cost of about $5,000. These buildings are located about three miles north of the village of Owego.

The county of Tioga is bounded on the north by the counties of Tompkins and Cortland, on the east by Broome, on the south by the Pennsylvania state line, and on the west by the county of Chemung, The principal stream of the county is the North East Branch of the Susquehanna, which enters the county from Broome county, in the town of Owego, the south eastern township of Tioga county, and flowing westerly through to the village of Owego, thence south easterly through the township of Nichols, passes out of the county into Pennsylvania on the town line of Barton and Nichols near the village of Waverly. The tributaries of the Susquehanna in Tioga county are Cayuta creek, Ellis creek, Owego creek and its tributaries, and several smaller creeks from the north, and the Appalachian creek and other small creeks from the south. The New York, Lake Erie & Western railroad follows the valley of the Susquehanna and leaves the county at Waverly, having several stations in the county, the principal ones being Owego and Waverly. The Utica, Ithaca & Elmira railroad enters the county in the northern portion, passing through the towns of Spencer and Candor. The Geneva & Sayre railroad leaves Waverly in the county and running out of the county into Chemung, follows close along the western line of Tioga county, and entering the county and passing out of it in the town of Spencer. The Southern Central departs from Owego and runs northerly through Owego township, Newark, Berkshire and Richford, and enters Cortland. The Cayuga & Susquehanna Division of the Delaware, Lackawanna & Western railroad has a line which leaves Owego and runs northward across the north east corner of Tioga township and through the township of Candor, passing into Tompkins county in the town of Caroline. From Spencer a railroad runs north through the township into Danby, thence via Newfield to Ithaca. It will therefore be seen that Tioga county is well provided with railroads. For list of old settlers see the various township histories. The main line of the Delaware, Lackawanna & Western railroad passes through the county.

MEMBERS OF ASSEMBLY for Tioga county have been: David McMasters, 1789–90 (then Montgomery county;) Jonathan Fitch, 1792; John Patterson, 1793; Vincent Mathews, 1794–5; Emanuel Coryell, 1796–98; Benj. Hovey, 1798; Mathew Carpenter, 1799; Samuel Tinkham, 1800; Edward Edwards, 1801; Caleb Hyde, 1801–2, Ashael Wells, 1804; John Miller, 1805–6; Emanuel Coryell, 1808–10; Thos. Floyd, 1811; Henry Wells, 1812: Jabez Beers, 1813; Caleb Baker, 1814–15; Gamaliel H. Barstow, 1816–18; Henry Wells, 1819; Judson Jennings, 1820; Samuel Lawrence, 1821; Jared Patchen, 1822; Matthew Carpenter, Benjamin Jennings, 1823; Grant B. Baldwin, G. H. Barstow, 1824; Charles Pumpelly, Samuel Winton, 1825; Isaac Baldwin, Anson Camp, 1826; G. H. Barstow, David Williams, 1827; William Maxwell, Jacob Swartwood, 1828; Caleb Baker, Samuel Barager, 1829; John G. McDowell, Wright Dunham, 1830; John G. McDowell, David Williams,

1831; Nathaniel Smith, Joel Talmage, jr., 1832; Thomas Farrington, Jacob Westlake, 1833; John R. Drake, George Gardiner, 1834; Green Bennett, George Fisher, 1835; Elijah H. Goodwin, William H. Sutton, 1836.

COUNTY DIVIDED.

Ezra Canfield, 1837; John Coryell, 1838; Wright Dunham, 1839; Thomas Farrington, 1840; Washington Smith, 1841; John McQuigg, 1842; Simon R. Griffin, 1843; Nathaniel W. Davis, 1844; Gideon O. Chase, 1845–6; Charles R. Barstow, 1847; Erastus Goodrich, 1848; Ezra S. Sweet, 1849; Isaac Lott, 1850; James Ely, 1851; William Pearsons, 1852; Thomas I. Chatfield, 1853; Lewis P. Legg, 1854; Carlyle P. Johnson, 1855; Abram H. Miller, 1856; David Reese, 1857; William P. Raymond, 1858; David Earle, 1859–60; C. F. Barber, 1861; Benjamin F. Tracey, 1862; N. W. Davis, 1863; James Thompson, 1864; William W; Shepard, 1865; John H. Deming, 1866; Oliver A. Barstow, 1867, O. P. Kinney, 1868; Lyman Truman, 1869; John H. Deming, 1870; Burnette B. Bignall, 1871: William Smythe, 1872; Jerome B. Landfield, 1873–74; James Bishop, 1875; Eugene B. Gere, 1876–77; J. T. Sawyer, 1878; J. T. Sawyer, 1879–80; Edward G. Nowlan, 1881–2; Jacob B. Floyd, 1883; Myron B. Ferris, 1884; Charles F. Barager, 1885, the present incumbent.

COUNTY CLERKS.—Thomas Nicholson, 1791; Mathew Carpenter, 1792; Thomas Maxwell, 1819; Green M. Tuthill, 1828; David Wallace, 1834; Moses Stevens, 1843–6; Leroy W. Kingman, 1852; Thomas C. Platt, 1858; Horace A. Brooks, 1861; John J. VanKleeck, 1873; John C. Gray, 1876; John J. VanKleeck, 1882, present incumbent.

SHERIFFS.—James McMasters, 1791; Joseph Hinchman, 1795; Edward Edwards, 1799; Guy Maxwell, 1800; John Cantine, 1804; William Woodruff, 1805; William Jenkins, 1806; Jonathan Platt, 1810; Miles Foreman, 1811; Jonathan Platt, 1813; Miles Foreman, 1815; Elijah S. Hinman, 1818; Henry Wells, 1820; Miles Foreman, 1821; William Jenkins, 1822; E. Shoemaker, 1825; Henry McCormick, 1828; Lyman Covell, 1831; John Jackson, 1834;

COUNTY DIVIDED.

Prentice Ransom, 1837; Robert L. Fleming, 1840; Charles R. Barstow, 1843; John J. Sackett, 1846; Nathan H. Woodford, 1849; R. D. Willard, 1852; Samuel Mills, 1855; Daniel L. Jenkins, 1858; Frank L. Jones, 1860; Hiram W. Shoemaker, 1861; Joseph B. Upham, 1864; Lewis W. Truesdell, 1866; Thomas F. Pearl, 1869; C. C. Brooks, 1872; William H. Wrightmire, 1875; Timothy Robertson, 1878; Burr J. Davis, 1881; Charles Rodman, 1884, present incumbent.

COUNTY TREASURERS.—Jonathan Fitch, 1792; Orange Stoddard, 1795; David Pixley, 1798; Samuel Tinkham, 1803; Joshua Ferris, 1804–36.

COUNTY DIVIDED.

John Carmichael, 1837; Daniel Armstrong, 1843; Franklin Slosson, 1846; William P. Stone, 1847; Charles Platt, 1848; Franklin Slosson, 1851; Ezra S. Buckbee, 1854; Gordon C. Manning, 1860; John B. Brush, 1863; Eli W. Stone, 1872; Frederic L. French, 1882, present incumbent.

COUNTY JUDGES.—Abraham Miller, 1791; John Patterson, 1798; John Miller, 1807; Emanuel Coryell, 1810; Gamaliel H. Barstow, 1818; Silas

Hopkins, 1823; Lathrop H. Burrows, 1825; Grant B. Baldwin, 1825; John R. Drake, 1833.

COUNTY DIVIDED.

Stephen Strong, 1838; Alanson Munger, 1843; Charles P. Avery, 1847–55; Stephen Strong, 1856–59; Thomas Farrington, 1860; Charles A. Clark, 1872; Charles E. Parker, 1883, present incumbent.

SPECIAL JUDGES AND SURROGATES.—Charles A. Munger, 1853; Alanson Munger, 1856; William F. Warner, 1859; Alanson Munger, 1862; Charles A. Munger, 1865; Adolphus G. Allen, 1868; James B. Carroll, 1871; J. Newton Dexter, 1872; Jacob B. Floyd, 1875; J. Newton Dexter, 1878.

JUDGES OF COMMON PLEAS.—Joshua Mersereau, John Miller, Elijah Buck, Emanuel Coryell, 1798; Caleb Baker, Phineas Catlin, Lewis Beers, Joseph Speed, Henry Wells, 1810; August Boyer, John Cantine, 1814; Joshua Ferris, Noah Goodrich, Stephen Beers, 1816; Thomas Floyd, 1820; William Jenkins, Jacob Wilsey, Henry Miller, Benjamin Jennings, 1821; Latham A. Burrows, David Williams, John H. Knapp, 1825; John McConnell, 1825; Darius Bentley, J. T. Waldo, 1827; John G. McDowell, John R. Drake, 1828; Joseph L. Darling, Elijah Shoemaker, 1832; George Fisher, 1833; Jacob Westlake, Ira Clizbee, Samuel Barager, 1836.

COUNTY DIVIDED.

Elisha P. Higbee, Arthur Yates, 1838; Clark Hyatt, 1844.

ASSISTANT JUSTICES.—John Konkle, Thomas Floyd, John Robinson, Joel Smith, 1810; John Cantine, Benjamin Wynkoop, Elijah S. Hinman, 1816.

JUSTICES OF SESSIONS under the Constitution of 1846: J. Talcott Waldo, Thomas Yates, 1848–9; G. H. Barstow, Samuel Barager, 1850; J. Talcott Waldo, Israel S. Hoyt, 1851; J. Talcott Waldo, Sylvester Knapp, 1852; Oliver A. Barstow, Samuel Barager, 1853; Gaylord Wilsley, A. F. Carey, 1854; Robert B. Miller, Samuel Barager, 1855–6; Nathaniel F. Moore, John L. Howe, 1857; Nathaniel F. Moore, Thomas Yates, Edwin H. Scoonover, Augustus T. Carey, 1858; Robert B. Miller, Lorain Curtis, 1860; Robert B. Miller, Samuel Barager, 1861; Samuel C. Bidwell, Samuel Barager, 1862: Horace C. Hubbard, Samuel Barager, 1863; William E. Gee, Luther B. West, 1864; Lorain Curtis, Samuel Barager, 1865; Oscar Gleason, John H. Yontz, 1866; Samuel C. Bidwell, William F. Belden, 1867; Herbert Richardson, John H. Yontz, 1868; Herbert Richardson, William F. Belden, 1869; Samuel B. Bidwell, John H. Yontz, 1870; Luther B. West, H. H. Bidwell, 1871; Luther B. West, George Cooper, 1872; Luther B. West, Daniel B. Nash, 1873; Anson M. Kimball, John C. Parmalee, 1874; Daniel B. Nash, John C. Parmalee, 1875; Gershom A. Clark, Robert B. Miller, 1876; Charles F. Curtis, Robert B. Miller, 1877; Daniel B. Nash, Junius Collins, 1878.

SURROGATES—John Mersereau, 1791; Balthazar DeHaert, 1798; William Woodruff, 1802; William Jenkins, 1805; Caleb Baker, 1806; Robert Lawrence, 1808; Isaac S. Boardman, 1820; Robert Lawrence, 1821; C. Baker, 1825; William Maxwell, 1829; Thomas Farrington, 1835.

COUNTY DIVIDED.

Nathaniel W. Davis, 1840, Alanson Munger, 1844. By the provisons of the constitution of 1846 the office of surrogate was abolished in counties with less than 40,000 inhabitants.

JUSTICE OF SUPREME COURT.—John M. Parker, 1859; re-elected in 1867.

DISTRICT ATTORNEYS.—William Stewart, 1796 to 1813; Vincent Mathews, 1813–18; John Tillinghast, 1818; William Maxwell, 1822; Eleazer Dana, 1823: Aaron Konkle, 1826; Andrew K. Gregg, 1835; Stephen Strong, 1836.

COUNTY DIVIDED.

Ezra S. Sweet, 1838; John J. Taylor, 1841; George S. Camp, 1843; Stephen Strong, 1844; Ezra S. Sweet, 1847; Alanson Munger, 1850; Benjamin Tracy, 1853; D. O. Hancock, 1859; Isaac S. Catlin, 1865; D. O. Hancock, 1867; Eugene B. Gere, 1870; Lyman Settle, 1873; Howard J. Mead, 1879, present incumbent.

STATE SENATORS.—Vincent Mathews, 1796; Caleb Hyde, 1804; Gamaliel H. Barstow, 1819; Latham A. Burrows, 1824; John G. McDowell, 1832; Nehemiah Platt, 1841; Nathan Bristol, 1852; Lyman Truman, 1858; Thomas I. Chatfield, 1872.

MEMBERS OF CONGRESS.—John Patterson, 1803; Vincent Mathews, 1809; John R. Drake, 1817; Thomas Maxwell, 1829; Gamaliel H. Barstow, 1831; Stephen B. Leonard, 1835; Stephen Strong, 1845; John J. Taylor, 1853; John M. Parker, 1855; Thomas C. Platt, 1873.

UNITED STATES SENATOR.—Thomas C. Platt, 1881.

MEMBERS CONSTITUTIONAL CONVENTION.—John Patterson, 1801; Mathew Carpenter, 1821; Jonn J. Taylor, 1846; Charles E. Parker, Oliver H. P. Kinney, 1867.

STATE TREASURERS.—Gamaliel H. Barstow, 1825; Thomas Farrington, 1842: Wheeler H. Bristol, 1867; Benjamin F. Traccy was appointed U. S. district attorney, eastern district of New York, in 1866.

POST OFFICES IN TIOGA COUNTY, NEW YORK.—Barton, Berkshire, Campville, Candor, Cattatonk, East Berkshire, East Nichols, Factoryville, Flemingville, Halsey Valley, Hoopers Valley, Jenksville, Ketchumville, Lockwood, Newark Valley, North Barton, North Spencer, Owego, Smithboro, South Apalachin, Tioga Center, Waverly, Weltonville, West Candor, Wilson Creek.

TOWNSHIPS IN TIOGA COUNTY.—Barton, Berkshire, Candor, Newark Valley, Nichols, Owego, Richford, Spencer, Tioga.

The first school opened in Tioga county by David McMasters, in 1796, in Newark Valley.

In 1796, nine hundred and forty-six dollars were raised for school purposes, in Tioga county.

Feb. 20, 1796, the first church was organized within the present limits of Tioga county, and was named the Baptist church of New Bedford. Rev. David Jayne, the first preacher.

Eleazer Dana was the first resident attorney, within the present limits of Tioga county, in 1800.

The Tioga County Medical Society, was formed Oct. 13, 1806, with Doctor John Ross, moderator; Doctor Amos Park, president; Doctor A. Gates White, vice president; Doctor William Benson, secretary; Doctor John Ross, treasurer; Doctors Elias Satterlee and Uriel Bennett, censors. Among the resolutions adopted were: *Resolved*, that there is an orthodox faith in medicine, as well as in theology.

Rev. Horace Agard was the pioneer Methodist circuit minister.

The American Constellation was the first newspaper published in the southern tier counties of New York. It was issued by Leroy W. Kingman and Daniel Cruger, Jr. Its motto was, "Free but not licentious."

There was an Agricultural Society in Tioga county, in 1819. Among the proceedings of the society was a resolution: *Resolved*, that the members of this society appear at the next annual meeting, clothed in the manufactures of our own country. Thomas Maxwell, secretary.

The first temperance society was organized Feb. 22, 1836. Officers; B. B. Curry, president; Dr. L. H. Allen, E. Rainsford, vice presidents; W. H. Platt, secretary; E. W. Warner, treasurer; Cyrus Dana, William Platt, Col. Henry McCormick, B. C. Crandall, A. P. Storrs, executive committee.

Tioga county bar organized in 1800. Some of the most distinguished gentlemen of the state, have either been members of it, or have practiced in the courts.

The first church was erected within the present limits of Tioga county, at Newark Valley, by the Congregational Church, in 1803.

The first M. E. Church was organized at Spencer, in 1809.

The first Protestant Episcopal Church was organized in the town of Candor, in 1832.

The first Roman Catholic Church was organized in the village of Owego, in 1843.

The Tioga County Bible Society was organized at Elmira, Feb. 12, 1823. Officers were James Pumpelly, of Owego, president; Dr. G. H. Barstow, of Nichols; Eleazer Dana, of Owego; James Sayre and Samuel Lawrence, of Elmira, vice presidents; William Maxwell, of Elmira, treasurer; Thomas Maxwell, of Elmira, recording secretary.

Tioga county Teachers Association organized in 1850, re-organized in 1870.

Doctor Ezekiel Lovejoy, was the first to introduce homeopathy, in Tioga county, in 1847.

The Homeopathic Medical Society was organized July 29, 1870, by Drs. Lovejoy, Armstrnog, Hawley, Hunter, Greenleaf, Welsh.

Union, then in Tioga, now in Broome county, was the first post office established on the east branch of the Susquehanna, east of Tioga Point.

NEWSPAPERS.—*The American Constellation*, established Nov. 23, 1800, by Leroy W. Kingman and Daniel Cruger, Jr. In 1803, it was published at Owego under the name of *American Farmer*. In 1805, Stephen Mack purchased the material and issued *American Farmer*, and *Owego Advertiser*. June 15, 1814, Stephen Leonard who had been an apprentice in the office, issued the paper as the *Owego Gazette*.

In March, 1836, the *Owego Advertiser*, was first issued by Andrew H. Calhoun. It went through various hands, until it is now known as the *Owego Times*.

The Tioga County Record was issued Nov. 30, 1867, by Charles H. Keeler. *The Working Man* was established at Owego, Nov. 2, 1877, by M. E. Webster and B. B. F. Graves.

The *Waverly Advocate* was first published Oct. 3, 1851, by Thomas Messenger, as the *Waverly Luminary.* It first appeared as the *Advocate*, Sept. 17, 1852.

Waverly Review was issued the 11 of Feb. 1876, by Ira S Wales, The *Waverly Enterprise* was issued by Frank F. Scudder, Oct. 15, 1867. On the 22 day of November, 1876, it assumed the name of *The Waverly Free Press.*

The first newspaper published in Candor was issued by Clizbee and Mandeville, under the name of *The Candor Press.* The *Candor Independent* was established Oct. 14, 1876, by T. H. Pride.

The *Tioga County Herald* was issued by C. L. Noble, March 4, 1876, at Newark Valley.

The *Owego Free Press* was issued Sept. 2, 1828, by Stephen S. Chatterton.

The Tioga Freeman was issued as a "*Free Soil*," newspaper, by John Dow and Gideon O. Chase, in 1848.

St Nicholas, a monthly magazine was first issued in April, 1853, by a number of young men. It was peculiarly distinguished for its historical informatioo, and literary merit.

The *Owego American* was issued by Andrew H. Calhoun, August 23, 1855 It was the organ of the "Know Nothing's".

The *Awagah Chief* was first issued Feb. 23, 1872, by Horace A. Brooks.

The *Tioga and Bradford Democrat* was issued January 7, 1863, at Waverly by F. H. Baldwin.

The *Waverly and Athens Democrat* was issued in 1867, by D. P. Schultz.

Nathaniel Parker Willis resided near Owego for some years, in Glen Mary.

Charles A. Munger, Mrs. E. A. B. Mitchell, Raphael Pumpelly, Rev. Washington Gladden, William C. Toby, Judge Charles P. Avery, William F. Warner, Dr. D. W. Patterson, Rev. Mark Fibas, have been distinguished for their literary and scientific productions.

Barton Township and Waverly Village.

The town of Barton was organized by an act of the legislature, session Number 47, Chap. 100, March 23, 1824, taken from Tioga. It is bounded on the north by Spencer, in Tioga county, and Van Etten, in Chemung, on the east by Tioga township, and the Susquehanna river, on the south by the Pennsylvania state line, on the west by Baldwin, Chemung and Van Etten townships in Chemung county. The principal village of the town is Waverly, an incorporated village.

The first town election was held the 27 day of April, at the house of Gilbert Smith. Officers elected, Gilbert Smith, Supervisor; John Crotsley, town clerk; Jonathan Barnes, A. H. Schuyler, and William Hanna, assessors; William Crouse, Frederic Parker, John Giltner, commissioners of highways; John Parker, constable and collector; John Hanna, Jr., Seeley Finch, overseers of the poor; Gilbert Smith, Eliphalet Barden, Nathaniel Potter, commissioners of common schools; James Birch, Ely Foster, Joseph Talmage, Samuel Mills, Jonathan Barnes, inspectors of schools; George W. Johnson, Abraham Smith, Joseph Talmage, fence viewers; John Hyatt, Joel Sawyer, pound masters.

The town is broken and uneven as it extends northward from the Susquehanna river. The alluvial flats in the valley of the Susquehanna, and upon Cayuta Creek are very productive, while the highlands are being brought to a fine state of cultivation. The principal streams are the Susquehanna river Cayuta creek, and Ellis creek, the Chemung river washes it southwestern boundaries. Some of the earliest settlements in the county or in the Chemung valley were made in this township, or near it borders. Gen. John Sullivan, and his army passed through the southwest portion of the town, in 1779. It was upon the plain or peninsula between the present village of Waverly, N. Y., and Athens, in Pennsylvania, that the ancient village Diahago was located.

Early settlers;—Ebenezer Ellis, Stephen Mills, John Hanna, James Swartwood, Samuel Ellis, William Bensley, Luke Sanders, Charles Bingham, Layton Newell, Lyon C. Hedges, Phillip Crouse, Justus Lyon, John Manhart, Robert Reed, Silas Wolcott, George W. Buttson, Gilbert Smith, Josiah Crocker, John Hyatt, James Hanna, Eliphalet Barden, Benazah Mundy, Samuel Mundy, Peter Barnes, Peter Hoffman, Selah Paine, Isaac Shepard, John Barker, Jonathan B. Stewart, Jeremiah Adams, Luther Stone, Elias Walker, George Walker, Amos P. Spaulding, Alanson E. Shaw, Ephraim Strong, Doctor Prentiss, Ely Foster, John Shepard, Owen Spalding, Joseph Hallett, Gilbert H. Hallett, Jacob Reel, Richard A. Elmer, Benjamin Aikens, Arthur Yates.

Waverly was incorporated in 1853, and the first election was held March 27, 1854. Officers elected, Francis H. Baldwin, William Gibson, Hiram M. Moore, Peter Dunning, Alva Jarvis, trustees; Squire Whittaker, John L. Sawyer, B. H. Davis, assessors; William P. Owen, collector; Owen Spaulding, treasurer; P. B. Bennett, clerk; Morris B. Royal, Absalom Bowman, W. H. Brooks, street commissioners; David E. Howell, pound Master, Alva Jarvis was chosen president of the board of trustees.

—William Giles was the first lawyer.
—Elias Walker built the first tavern.
—Ebenezer Ellis built the first house.
—The Hotel, was opened in Waverly in 1825.
—Dr. Prentiss was the first resident physican.
—Rev. Valentine Cook was the first preacher.
—Deacon Ephraim Strong was the first teacher.
—George Walker erected the first grist mill, in 1800.
—Erie railroad completed through Waverly, in 1849.
—First Presbyterian church of Waverly, erected in 1849.
—Alva Jarvis opened the first store in Waverly, in 1841.
—Peter Wentz was the first justice in Waverly, in 1854.
—Benjamin Aikens was the first local preacher, in 1805.

—J. E. Hallett suggested the name of Waverly, for the village.

—Alexander Ellis was the first white child born in the township.

—R. O. Crandall, M. D., was the first resident physician, in 1840.

—The village of Waverly was first lighted with gas July 24, 1873.

—Ebenezer and Samuel Ellis built the first saw mill on Ellis creek.

—Deacon Ephraim Strong built the first framed house in Waverly, in 1808.

Josiah Crocker and John Shepard, built a fulling mill, on Cayuta creek, in 1808.

—The piles for the road bed of the Erie railroad, driven through Waverly in 1840.

—The post office was established at Waverly in 1849. Benjamin H. Davis first post master.

—The post office was established in 1812, at Factoryville Isaac Shepard the first post master.

—Grace Protestant Episcopal Church organized Dec. 28, 1853 First rector, Rev. George Watson.

—The first manufacturing establishment in Waverly, was a foundry, built by Hallett and Price, in 1842.

—Waverly Bank organized April 1, 1872, H. T Herrick, president; George Herrick, cashier; H. T. Sawyer, teller.

—Stephen Mills, John Hanna, Luke Sanders, John Hyatt, William Bensley, were pioneer settlers, and revolutionary soldiers.

—The Lehigh Valley, the Erie, the Delaware, Lackawanna & Western, Geneva, Ithaca & Sayre Railroads pass through Waverly.

—Citizens Bank of Waverly incorporated June 18,1874. Capital $50,000. Officers, J. T. Sawyer, president; M. Lyman, Jr., cashier.

—First National Bank organized Feb. 13, 1864. Capital $50.000. R. D. Van Duser, president; R. A. Elmer, vice president; Howard Elmer, cashier.

—The Baptist Church of Waverly, was established in 1865. Trustees, B. B. Clark, A. Lamonte, J. H. Tozer, H. Shriver, J. Hungerford, Henry Hallett.

—Cayuta Lodge No. 35, A. O. U. W., was organized Aug. 19, 1876. Officers were S. D. H. Brown, M. W; R. C. Bennett, recorder; A. Mulock, receiver.

—Waverly Lodge No. 293, Knights of Honor, instituted June 1, 1875. John R. Murray, dictator; Frank P. Harkness, reporter; Charles Sweet, treasurer.

—Manoka Lodge, No. 219, was chartered January 30, 1850. Officers, Silas Fordham, N. G; J. E. Hallett, V. G; L. A. Waldo secretary; William Polleys,, treasurer.

—The first Presbyterian Church of Waverly, was organized June 8, 1847, by a committee of the Chemung Presbytery, consisting of Rev. C. C. Carr, Thurston and Backus.

—Cayuta Chapt. No. 245, R. A. M., was organized Aug. 22, 1869. Officers, O. W. Shepard, H. P.; R. A. Elmer, C. K.; A. J. Van Atta, S.; E. P. Curtis, secretary; Thomas Marsh, treasurer.

—Waverly Lodge No. 407, F. A. M., organized June 3, 1856. Officers, George H. Fairchild, W. M.; Francis H. Baldwin, S. W.; Addison B. Phillips, J. W.; H. S. Davis, secretary; Amos P. Spalding, treasurer.

—Waverly Hook and Ladder Co., No. 2, organized June 12, 1876. Officers, C. J. Bergen, foreman; H. E. Robbins, first assistant; J. S. Cummings, second assistant; H. C. Mersereau, president; George B. Vanvelzer, secretary; D. J. McDonald, treasurer.

—April 15, 1875, the Tioga Hose and Steamer Company, No. 1, was organized. Officers, Frederic M. Snook, president; Col. Mulock, secretary: F. E. Lyford, treasurer; R. J. Crans, chief engineer; J. K. Murdock, foreman; J. B. Bailey, J. F. Buck, assistants.

—Methodist Episcopal Church of Waverly, was organized as a class at Factoryville, in 1828, with Elisha Tozer, leader; Rachel Tozer, Joshua Wilcox, King Elwell, members, subsequently removed to Waverly, erected a church which was dedicated in March 1864, by Bishop Jaynes.

—First Fire Company organized in Waverly, was the Neptune Engine and Hose Company, No. 1, May 24, 1855, J. E. Hallet, foreman; O. L. Deland, Timothy Cassady, assistants; E. W. Atwater, secretary; William Peck, treasurer. Hose Company, A. F. Little, foreman; W. H. Brooks, assistant.

—Shepard Institute, afterward the Waverly Institute, was incorporated in 1856. Trustees, Owen Spaulding, Arthur Yates, Benjamin G. Rice, F. H. Baldwin, Isaac Shepard, R. A. Elmer, Alva Jarvis, William Manners, G. H. Fairchild, R. D. Van Duser. Prof. Andrew J. Lang, was the first principal.

Berkshire Township.

Berkshire was formed by an act of the legislature, session 31, chap. 10, Feb. 12, 1808, taken from Tioga. It is situated in the northeastern portion of the county, and is bounded on the north by Richford, east by Broome county, south by Newark, on the west by Candor, in Tioga county, and Caroline in Tompkins county. It occupies an elevated position, and its surface is diversified by rolling uplands and valleys. The Southern Central railroad from Owego passes through the township. Its early settlers were principally from the New England states, and brought with them the religion, customs, habits and intelligence characterestic of those states. Neat and comfortable, and we might add costly dwellings, fine barns, and well tilled farms are to be seen in the township.

The first town meeting for the town of Berkshire was held March 1, 1808. Ebenezer Cook was moderator; the officers chosen were John Brown, supervisor; Artemus Ward, town clerk; Eben Slosson, Ebenezer Cook, assessors; Henry Moore, Elijah Belcher, poor masters; Noah Lyman, Hart Newell, Samuel Haight, commissioners of highways; Peter Wilson, collector; Peter Wilson, pound master; Jesse Gleason, Adolphus Dwight, constables; Asa Bement, Nathaniel Ford, Asa Leonard, John Bement, Lyman Rawson, Elisha Jenks, fence viewers.

Early settlers;—Elisha Wilson, Capt. Abram Brown, Isaac Brown, Daniel Ball, Eben Slosson, Asa Bement, Daniel Gleason, Asa Leonard, Solomon Leonard, Peter Wilson, Enoch Slosson, Silas Whitney, Ashel

Churchill, Henry Moore, Heman Smith, Samuel Hosford, Artemus Ward, Enoch Williams, Paul Stevens, Ebenezer Persons, Ripley Manning, Consider Lawrence, Ebenezer Cook, Dr. Joseph Waldo, Luke Winship, Josiah Ball, Nathaniel Ford, David Williams, Ransom Williams, John Brown, Abel Hovey, Azel Hovey, Nathaniel Hovey, Jonas Muzzy, John Carpenter, Seth Aikens, Captain William Torrey, Samuel Collins, John Gregory, Ashel Royce, Deodatus Rice, Col. John R. Royce, William H. Moore, Ebenezer Cook, Thomas Paine, Barnabas Manning, John Fellows, Jeremiah Osborne, John Bement, Edward Edwards, Solomon Williams, Elijah Dewey, Adolphus Dwight, Hart Newell, Elijah Belcher, Samuel Haight, George Vickery, Nathan Ide, Timothy Williams, Noah Lyman, Jesse Gleason.

—Thomas Paine was a weaver, in 1802.

—Stephen Ball opened a brick-yard, in 1827.

—Samuel Ripley built a harness shop, in 1818.

—Ebenezer Cook built the first tannery, in 1800.

—In 1804, Isaac Brown built the first framed barn.

—The first store was keep by Joseph Waldo, in 1809.

—In 1829, a Methodist Sunday School was organized.

—David Williams built the first grist mill in the town.

—Jesse Gleason and Miss Mary Adzdell were married Oct. 29, 1800.

—John Brown was the first justice of the peace in the town in 1800.

—Josiah Ball, John Brown and Abram Brown, erected the first saw mill.

—Isaac Brown was the first person who died in the town, April 10, 1797.

—William W. Ball was the first white child born in the town, September, 1794.

—Dr. Joseph Waldo and John Brown, raised the first framed house, in 1806.

—Theresa Moore taught school in Asa Bement's barn in the summer of 1799.

—The first post office was established in 1812, William H. Moore, post master.

—Rev. William Bradford erected the Brookside Family Boarding School, in 1845.

—The first framed school house was erected in the village of Berkshire, in 1807.

—Col. John B. Royce built the first brick house in the town, about the year 1832.

—Isaac Brown and Clarissa Ball were the first couple married in the town, in 1795.

—The first religious services were held in the town by Rev. Seth Williston, about 1800.

—A carding mill was erected in 1806, by Elijah Belcher, Barnabas Manning and Isaac Ball.

—Ebenezer Cook built the first blacksmith shop, and Reese Thomas was the first blacksmith, in 1808.

—Frederic Schaff, settled in Berkshire, in 1838, and died in 1860, at the age of 107 years. He was a soldier of the revolution.

—David Williams and Eleazer Goodrich, were the first justices of the peace, elected by the people in 1830.

—The first settlement in the town was made in the spring of 1791, by Elisha Wilson, Abraham Brown, Isaac Brown, and Daniel Ball.

—The Berkshire Cemetery Association was formed in 1867. H. H. Bidwell, president; George C. Royce, clerk. It is called the "Evergreen Cemetery."

—Judge David Williams an early pioneer, who was judge of Broome and Tioga counties, member of the legislature, died in 1867, aged ninety-two years.

—Heman Smith held Methodist class meeting until the formation of the church, by Rev. George Dunsmore, in 1825. Church dedicated July 4, 1828, by Rev. Gaylord Judd.

Candor Township.

The town of Candor was formed pursuant to an act of the legislature, session 34, February 22, 1811, taken from the town of Spencer. It is situated in the northern portion of the county, and is well watered by numerous springs and creeks. It is bounded on the north by Danby and Caroline, in Tompkins county, on the east by Berkshire, Newark and Owego, on the south by the town of Tioga, on the west by Spencer, in Tioga county, and Danby in Tompkins county. Owego creek is the eastern boundary. The Utica, Ithaca & Elmira railroad, and the Delaware, Lackawana & Western railroad, passing through the township, afford the citizens the opportunity of shipping their products either east or west, north or south.

At the first town election held March 5, 1811, at the house of Captain Abel Hart, the officers elected were Joel Smith, supervisor; Asa North, town clerk; William Scott, Orange F. Booth, Samuel Smith, assessors; Nathaniel Sackett, Seth Baker, Charles Taylor, commissioners of highways; Truman Woodford, constable and collector; Abel Hart, Asa North, overseers of the poor; Eldad Pickett, Daniel Parks, constables; Joseph Delind, Charles Taylor, Eli Bacon, Job Judd, fence viewers; Thomas Parks, James McMaster; Ezra Smith, pound masters; Jacob Harrington, Seth Bacon, Osias Woodford, Joseph Kelsey, Daniel Cowles, George Allen, Reuben Hatch, William Taylor, Joseph Scoonover, Thomas Baird, Daniel H. Bacon, Jacob Clark, Alexander Scott, path masters.

Early settlers:—Elijah Smith, Collins Luddington, Thomas Hollister, Job Judd, Daniel Bacon, Joseph Boothe, Orange F. Boothe, Israel Mead, Joel Smith, Jr., John Gridley, Elijah Hart, David Whittlesey, Abel Hart, Daniel H. Bacon, Samuel Hart, Harvey Potter, Jacobus Shenick, Elisha Forsythe, Thomas Parks, Daniel Parks, Hiram Williams, Capt. Eli Bacon, Seth Bacon, William Bates, Richard Ellis, Selah Gridley, Jacob Clark, Christian Hart, Ezra Smith, Dr. Joel Talmage, Jacob Wilsey, Joel Robinson, John Whitley, Aaron Whitley, Elisha Blinn, Beriah Strong, Caleb Galpin, Ebenezer Lake, Moses Grimes, Eldad Pickett, Nathaniel Sackett, Jacob Harrington, Thomas Evans, James McMaster, Samuel Barager, Bissell Woodford, Osias Woodford, Sylvester Woodford, Dr. Horatio Worcester, Phillip Case, Rev. Seth Williston, Sidney Hayden, Joseph Delind, Rodolphus Durkee, Asa North, William Scott, Ebenezer Woodbridge, Joseph Scoonover, Daniel Cowles, Joseph Baird, Russell Gridley, Austin Thompson.

—The first church was erected in 1818.

—Rodolphus Durkee built the first tannery.

—The first store was opened by Phillip Case.

—The first physician was Dr. Horatio Worcester.

—Noah Barber built the first brick house, in 1836.

—The first settled minister was Rev. Daniel Loring.

—The first church organized was the Baptist in 1802.

—The first brick was made by Sidney Hayden, in 1835.

—Ithaca and Owego Turnpike built through Candor in 1809.

—William Mead was the first white child born in Candor, in 1796.

—Grange No. 203, organized May 1874. A. H. Krum, first overseer.

—Elijah Hart and David Whittlesey, built the first grist and saw mill.

—Abel Hart was the first blacksmith, and built the first blacksmith shop.

—Population of the town of Candor in the year 1800, was 135, and 23 voters.

—The first religious services were held in a barn, in 1797, by Rev. Seth Williston.

—Candor Free Academy was established in 1864. Prof. Denson was the first principal.

—Candor Lodge No. 411. F. A. M., instituted June 1856. Jonathan B. Hart, first master.

—Lodge 542, Knights of Honor, organized March 21, 1877. H. F. Booth first dictator,

—The first Sunday school was held in 1820. Mrs. Betsey Thomas and Harvey Potter were the teachers.

—Thomas Hollister kept the first tavern in 1795. He also built the first framed house, and set out the first orchard.

—The first school house in Candor was built in 1798. Joel Smith the first teacher, and also the first justice of the peace.

—Lewis Wheeler, Ephraim Personeus, John Lane, Capt. Daniel R. Parks Capt. Eli Bacon, Thomas Hewett, Wait Johnson, Phineas Judd, were soldiers of the war of 1812.

—The Ithaca and Owego railroad was chartered Jan. 28, 1828. Completed April 18, 1834. It passed through Candor. It was among the first railroads constructed in the state.

—First National Bank of Candor was chartered March 30, 1864. Capital $50,000. President Norman L. Carpenter; John J. Bush, cashier. On the night of Dec. 17, 1868, it was robbed of $30,000.

—The Congregational Church of Candor was organized June 29, 1808. First members were Ebenezer Sanford, Rhoda Sanford, Asa North, Laura North, Eli Bacon, Sarah Bacon, Job Judd, Osias Woodford, Theda Woodford, Orange F. Boothe, Sylvester Woodford, Truman Woodford, Thomas Gridley, Joel Smith, Abel Hart, Timothy North. In 1833, it was changed to the Presbyterian Church.

—Mount Olive Lodge F. A. M., No. 353, was chartered in 1823. Its first officers were Jacob Wilsey, W. M.; Dr. Joel Talmage, S. W.; Abner Beers, J. W.; Dr. William Bacon, secretary; ——Holley, Tiler. The first initiations were Daniel Bacon, Stephen Seymour.

—Job Judd, Capt. Joel Smith, Israel Mead, Thomas Gridley, Capt. Thomas Parks, Hiram Williams, Bissell Woodford, Elias Williams, Aaron Whitley, were pioneer settlers in the town of Candor, and were soldiers in the war of the revolution.

—The Baptist Church was organized May 1, 1802. Members were Lewis Mead, Lavina Mead, Jasper Taylor, Catharine Taylor, John Bunnell, Hannah Bunnell, George Lane, Sarah Lane, Peter Garbet, Sarah Garbet Abram Everett, Deborah Everett, Samuel Stewart, Alvin Steward, Elizabeth Jacobs.

—St. Marks Protestant Episcopal Church was organized April 23, 1832. Rev. Lucius Carter, first rector; Seth Bacon, William Bacon, wardens; Daniel Bacon, Harvey Abbott, William Hand, Richard H. Sackett, Samuel Barager, Stephen F. Smith, Thomas Buell, Harvey Smith, vestrymen.

—Methodist Episcopal Church was organized in 1827, at the house of Jared Smith, members; Judge Samuel Barager and wife, Mr. James Smith and wife, Mrs. Hannah Gilbert, Thomas Hewett and wife, George Hubbard and wife, A. Hubbard and wife, Mrs. Asaph Colborn, Jared Smith and wife, Rev. John Griffin, the first minister.

Newark Valley Township.

By an act of the legislature, session 46, chapter 153, passed April 12, 1823, the town of Westville, taken from the town of Berkshire was created, and by an act of the legislature, session 47, chapter 109, passed March 24, 1824, the name Westville was changed to Newark, and in 1862, again changed to Newark Valley. The town is situated in the central eastern portion of Tioga county, adjoining the Broome county line. It is bounded on the north by the town of Berkshire, in Tioga county, on the east by Broome county, on the south by Broome county, and the town of Owego, in Tioga county, on the west by the town of Candor, in Tioga county. The east branch of Owego creek runs through the township from north to southwest, and is also traversed in like direction by the Southern Central Railroad. It contains several villages, the most populous of which is Newark Valley, a village of about 1,000 inhabitants. Jenksville and Ketchumville are post villages in the township.

At an election held March 2, 1824, at the house of Otis Lincoln, Solomon Williams was elected Supervisor; Beriah Wells, town clerk; Francis Armstrong, Ebenezer Pierce, Benjamin Waldo, assessors; Henry Williams, William Richardson, Otis Lincoln, commissioners of schools; Benjamin Walton, William B. Bement, George Williams, inspectors of common schools; Anson Higbe, Abram Brown, Reuben Crittenden, commissioners of highways; William Slosson, constable; Lyman Legg, collector; Peter Willson, Ebenezer Robbins, overseers of the poor; Joseph Benjamin, sealer of weights and measures.

Early settlers:—Elisha Willson, Capt. Abram Brown, Isaac Brown,

* Daniel Ball, Peter Willson, Esbon Slosson, Asa Benment, Daniel Gleason John Carpenter, John Ruey, Enoch Slosson, Mrs. Beulah Brown, Joseph Brown, Levi Bailey, Joseph Hosford, Mrs. Mary Willson, Abram Johnson, Edward Edwards, Jonathan Edwards, Henry Moore, Jonas Muzzy, Michael Jenks, Laban Jenks, Elisha Jenks, Captain Scott, Thomas Baird, Stephen Williams, Jr., Henry Williams, Oliver Williams, Daniel Churchill, Amos Draper, Ripley Manning, Parley Simons, Joel Gaylord, Jonathan Hedges, Ezekiel Rich, Otis Lincoln, Dr. Joseph Waldo, Timothy Williams, Stephen Williams, Sr.

—Enos Slosson kept the first store in 1800.

—Dr. Joseph Waldo was the first physician.

—The first carpenter was Stephen Williams, Sr.

—Otis Lincoln was the first tanner in Newark Valley.

—Jonas Muzzy felled the first tree on West Owego creek.

—Enos Slosson was appointed the first post master, in 1812.

—Asa Bement and Elisha Willson erected a grist mill, in 1797.

—The Tioga county *Herald* was first issued March 4, 1876, by C. L. Noble at Newark Valley.

—The Free Will Baptist Church was organized in 1816. Rev. John Gould the first minister.

—The Baptist Church of Newark Valley was organized Oct. 27, 1857. Rev. D. F. Leach was the first stated minister.

—The Alpha Methodist Episcopal Church was organized at Jenksville, in 1852. Rev. Mr. Salisbury was the first misister.

—A Congregational Church was organized at West Newark, in 1822. Rev. Zenos Riggs, was the first minister and preached in barns.

—Newark Valley is composed of a portion of what was early known as "The Boston Ten Towns," and was re-surveyed by Walter Sabin, assisted by Capt. Abram Brown, Amos Patterson, David Pixley and Elisha Willson, in 1790.

—David A. Shepard organized the first Methodist Episcopal Society, in 1831. Though prior to this there was occasional preaching by missionaries, and circuit ministers. The society consisted of seven members; Selecta Williams, Minerva Collins, Mary Ann Ruey, Eperience Clark, Munson Clark, Jehial Dean and wife. Rev. Moses Adams was the first stated minister.

Nichols Township.

Nichols was organized pursuant to an act of the legislature, session 47, chapter 100, March 23, 1824, taken from Tioga. It is situated on the south side of the east branch of the Susquehanna river, adjoining the Pennsylvania state line, opposite the town and village of Owego, and is bounded on the north by the Susquehanna river, on the east by Owego township, on the south by Pennsylvania, on the west by the Susquehanna. It contains the villages of Nichols, Hoopers Valley, Wappassening and Canfield Corners.

---

* A portion of these early settlers names also appear in the list of early settlers in Berkshire township.

The alluvial flats along the valley of the Susquehanna are very productive while the uplands are being brought under a good state of cultivation.

Early settlers:—Ebenezer Ellis, Pelatiah Pierce, Stephen Mills, James Cole, John W. Launing, John Eveland, Frederic Eveland, A. Van Gorder, Leonard Van Gorder, Benjamin Van Gorder, Dennis Sullivan, George Walker, Emanuel Coryell, Isaiah Jones, Benjamin Bass, John Emmons, Caleb Wright, Stephen Dodd, Jonathan Platt, Col. Richard Sackett, Lewis Brown, Miles Foreman, Major John Smyth, Benjamin Lownsberry, Ziba Evans, Jonathan Hunt, Jonathan Pettis, John Annabel, Joseph Annabell Joseph Morey, Daniel Lanning, John Russel, Daniel Shoemaker, Nicholas Shoemaker, Isaac Sharp, David Brakes, Henry Dunham, Dailey Dunham, Isaac Dunham, George Kirby, John Howell, Joseph White, Joseph Morey, John McCarty, Gamaliel H. Barstow, Oliver A. Barstow, Daniel Pearl, —— Williamson, —— Palmer, Judge Chubbuck, Thomas Pearshall, Gilbert Pearshall, Ira J. Parks, Elijah Cole, Wright Dunham, Elijah Shoemaker, Ezra Canfield, Joseph Utter.

—Post office was established in 1812.

—The first school house was built in 1799.

—Jonathan Platt kept the first tavern, in 1799.

—Nehemiah Platt built the first brick house, in 1830.

—The first store was opened by Judge Barstow, in 1814.

—The first house was erected by Pelatiah Pierce, in 1787.

—The first church erected was the M. E. Church, in 1822.

—The first grist mill was erected in 1794, by Caleb Wright.

—The first framed house was built by Dr. Barstow, in 1814.

—The first steam saw mill was built by George Kirby, in 1833.

—The first crop of wheat was sown by John Emmons, in 1791.

—Nichols graded school organized with an academic department in 1874. The first principal was Prof. Miles Ellsworth.

—Presbyterian Church of Nichols was organized in 1859. The first minister was Rev. G. M. Life. Church erected in 1865.

—Emanuel Coryell, Jonathan Platt, Col. Richard Sackett, Major John Smythe, John Russell, Daniel Shoemaker, Isaac Sharp, Pelatiah Pierce, Ebenezer Ellis, were pioneer settlers in Nichols, and soldiers of the war of the revolution.

—The River Valley Methodist Church was organized as a class, as early as 1815. Erected a church in 1873. Minister in charge, Rev. John Griffin. The first meetings prior to the erection of the church were held in the log house of Joseph Utter.

—Asbury Methodist Episcopal Church was organized in 1817, with four members; Elijah Shoemaker, Phebe Shoemaker, Daniel Shoemaker, and Maria Shoemaker. First minister Rev. John Griffin. Prior to this, services had been held by itinerant minister.s

—Gamaliel Barstow was born July 20, 1784. Settled in Nichols in 1812, member of assembly five terms, state senator, judge, justice of sessions, member of congress, state treasurer, and filled other important trusts. He died March 30, 1865, aged 81 years. He was one of the most distinguished men of Tioga county.

—The first white child born in the town was Daniel Pierce, in 1787.

—A disastrous flood occured in the Susquehanna at Nichols, March 17, 1865.

—Nichols was named in honor of the original patentee of the township.

—Nichols Methodist Episcopal Church organized as a class, in the year 1829.

—The Free Meeting House was erected upon lands donated by Nehemiah Platt, in 1830, by Hezekiah Dunham, contractor. The trustees were Emanuel Coryell, Nehemiah Platt, Gamaliel H. Barstow, Peter Joslin, Jonathan Hunt, Ezra Canfield, John Castle, Edwin Ripley, Wright Dunham, John Pettis, Sylvester Knapp, Cyrus Field, Daniel Ferguson, Justus Brown, James Thurston. In order to assist in the construction of the church, slips or pews were sold, but with the understanding that they should be free, ranging in price from $20 to $100. Nehemiah Platt, Emanuel Coryell, William Platt, and Jonathan Platt each took a slip giving the $100, for the same. The church was free to all denominations.

Owego Township.

Owego was organized by an act of the legislature of New York, Feb. 16, 1791,. See 3, G. 343, also 2, K. &R. 54, session 29, chapter 29, 4, W. 339, 2, R. L. 106, also session 45, chapter 75, laws of 1822, page 26. It is situated in the south eastern portion of Tioga county. The east branch of the Susquehanna enters the township from the east, dividing it into nearly two equal parts.

—It is bounded on the north by the town of Newark Valley, on the east by Broome county, on the south by the Pennsylvania state line, and on the west by the towns of Nichols, Tioga and Candor. It was within this township that some of the very earliest settlements were made in southern New York, by white men and bona fide settlers, as early as 1785. One hundred years ago.

The first record of the officers of the township now to be found are those of the year 1800, in which it appears that David Pixley, acted as chairman, when on the third day of April, 1800, the officers elected were John Brown, supervisor; Lemuel Brown, town clerk; Asa Bement, Asa Camp, Henry Stewart, assessors; Jesse Gleason collector; Lemuel Brown, Vine Kingsley, overseers of the poor; Stephen Mack, Stephen Ball, Henry Stewart, constables; Stephen Ball, Vine Kingsley, fence viewers: Vine Kingsley, pound master.

The name Owego is of Indian origin, and was variously spelled, Owegy, then Owago, Ah-waga. The meaning of the word is "Where the valley widens."

Early settlers:—Amos Draper, John McQuigg, James McMaster, William McMaster, William Taylor, Robert McMaster, John Nealy, William Wood, Caleb Nichols, Simeon Nichols, Hicks Horton, Richard Searles, Ashahel Pritchard, Samuel Stewart, Benjamin Brown, Jeremiah Brown, Abijah Foster, Eleazer Talcott, Abraham Hoagland, Aaron Truman, Elijah Walter Isaac Whittemore, Michael Lainhart, Hiram Buck, John T. Pettibone, Gideon Brownell, Abram Cole, Alvin Hollister, Jacob Becker, James

Phillips, Joseph Dodge, Alva Griffin, Lewis Oakley, William M. Richardson Levi Green, Benjamin Green, Moses Ingersoll, Judson Spencer, Jonathan Truesdell, Aaron Steele, Abraham Williams, Adam Gould, Ezra Talmage, James Archibald, Caleb Lamb, Smith Payne, Daniel Payne, Henry Wait, Stephen Warid, David Briggs, Isaiah Mathews, James Newman, Joshua White, Thomas Pettis, William White, Theodore White Wilson White, Henry Blow, Francis Blow, James Blow, Timothy Robertson, A. P. Robertson, Nathan Bostwick, Olney Aldrich, Levi Thurston, Searl Pearl, Laurin Pearl, Nicholas Groesbeck, Leonard L. Barton, Silas Moore, Nathaniel Catlin, William French, James Clark, Nathaniel Goodspeed, Eli Gilson, Clark Hull, G. W. Southwick, James Hill, John Bills, Abel Bills, Asa Camp, Benjamin Tracey, Anson B. Glover, Isaac Harris, Simeon Brown, Amariah Barney, Henry Billings, Chauncey Billings, Joseph S. Dean, Vincent Gland Josiah Meah, David Foster, John Goodenow, Joseph Griswold, Job Pearshall, Levi Morton, Francis Lamont, C. T. Bell, Deacon Armstrong, William Foster, Charles Webster, David Fleming, Reuben Hatch, Amzi Steadman, Walter Herrick, Thomas Parks, Mason Webster, Moses Grimes, Casey Cortwright, Ezekiel Mead, Daniel Ferguson, Ahirah Anderson, Moses Darling, B. D. Montayne, Jacob Heinstrough, Joseph Heinstrough, Cyrenus McNiel, Joseph Mersereau, John Camp, Joseph Gaskell, Elijah Walter, William A Ely, William Pumpelly, Lemuel Brown, Luke Bates, Titus Chapman, Joel S. Page, Joshua Whiting, Mason Waddells, Joshua Ferris, John Murphy, David Thurston, George Matson, Gurdon Hewett, Stephen Strong, Nathan Camp, Frederic Camp, Herman Pumpelly, John Burt, Joseph Ely, John Kelly, Phillip Goodman, Stephen B. Leonard, Walter Herrick, Thomas Stockey, David Fleming, Freelove Forsythe, David Darling, Richard Searles, Brier Truesdell.

—Amos Draper settled in 1785.

—Elgin Talcott died Jan. 27, aged 81 years.

—Dorothea Talcott, died April 14, 1838, aged 85 years

—Dr. Jedediah Fay died April 22, 1848, aged 62 years.

—The first tannery was erected in 1795, by Lemuel Brown.

—Olive Curtis born in 1770, and died in 1859, aged 89 years.

—Mrs. Abigail Huntington died June 18, 1815, aged 43 years.

—Gen. Oliver Huntington, died Nov. 13, 1823, aged 51 years.

—Stephen B. Leonard (editor) died May 8, 1876, aged 83 years.

—Elizabeth, wife of Elgin Talcott, died Jan. 15, 1848, aged 60 years.

—Tioga County Temperance Society organized in Owego, May 12, 1854.

—The Washingtonian Temperance Society was organized in Owego, in 1842

—Selecta Draper, born June 19, 1788, was the first white child born in the town.

—John McQuigg, James McMaster, were the original patentees of the land where the village of Owego now is located.

—March 22, 1822, Owego was fixed by an act of the legislature as a half shire, and a court house directed to be built. It remained a half shire until the formation of Chemung county, in 1836, and the county seat of Tioga county ever since.

—Owego has a fine free library.
—First alarm bell purchased in 1867.
—Owego Brass Band organized in 1857.
—The first school teacher was John Kelley.
—Caleb Nichols built the first saw mill in 1797.
—Fire Police of Owego organized Feb. 20, 1869.
—Capt. Luke Bates built the first tavern, in 1795.
—The Erie Railroad was opened in 1849 to Owego.
—Owego Fire Department chartered April 17, 1862.
—The first school house was erected in Owego, in 1817.
—Ahwaga Lodge F. A. M., No. 587, organized in 1864.
—Owego Lodge No. 204, I. O. O. F., instituted Feb. 6, 1846.
—Tioga Lodge, No. 335, I. O. O. F., instituted Oct. 28, 1872.
—Destructive fire in Owego Aug. 5, 1841, and April 27, 1845.
—Ancient Order of United Workmen, was organized May 23, 1877.
—Jehiel Dean, built the first framed house in the village of Owego.
—Owego Lodge, No. 54, Knights of Honor, instituted Dec. 30, 1874.
—The first fire steamer was purchased and brought to Owego, in 1866.
—The whole business portion of Owego was destroyed by fire in 1849.
—Owego Academy established in 1828. Prof. Joseph Ely, the first principal.
—William A. Ely, a pioneer and distinguished business man died Nov. 27, 1873, aged 84.
—Amos Draper erected the first house in Owego, in 1785, and sowed the first crop of wheat, in 1787.
—June 1841, the sum of $300 was voted to construct two reservoirs for holding water for fire purposes.
—Mail route established through Owego in 1799. Post office established in 1801. David Jones the first post master.
—The steamboat "Lyman Truman," built in 1875, and launched into the Susquehanna at Owego in the Spring of 1876.
—Lyman Truman was president of the First National Bank of Owego. Senator in 1857, and a prominent business man.
—The Philosophian Literary Society having for its object the improvement of the colored people was formed in 1876.
—Friendship Lodge, No. 153, F. A. M.. re-organized in 1849. E. S. Madden, W. M; E. S. Sweet, S. W; S. B. Leonard, J. W.
—Friendship Lodge F. A. M., No. 140, formed in 1804. Mason Wattles, master; Joshua Ferris, senior warden; John Murphy, junior warden.
—Hon. John M. Parker was a member of congress, justice of the supreme court, and a very distinguished jurist. He died in the year 1873, aged 68 years.
—Owego has a lodge of R. A. M., and a council of Royal, and Select Masters, and an Eastern Star lodge of Masons, beside a lodge *Phila de Afrique*, styled the Evening Star Lodge.
—Owego was incorporated as a village, April 4, 1827. President, James Pumpelly; trustees, Eleazer Dana, Harmon Pumpelly, William A. Ely, James Pumpelly, Jonathan Platt; clerk, Ezra S. Sweet.

—Owego Driving Park association organized in March 1871, by Dr. T. S. Armstrong, W. H. Corey, A. D. Thompson, G. M. Righter, R. C. McNeal, George Kipp.

—March 20, 1804, the county clerk's office, by an act of the legislature was directed to be located within three miles of Owego, upon the north side of the Susquehanna.

—Bridge across the Susquehanna at Owego erected in 1828. James Pumpelly, president of the company. Bridge erected and completed Nov. 4, 1868. Cost $54,550.

—The first parade of the Owego Fire Companies, took place Oct. 10,1842. Delegations of fire companies were present from Ithaca and Binghamton. An address was delivered by S. S. Sweet, Esq.

—Thomas I. Chatfield represented Tioga county in the assembly in 1852. Member of the state senate in 1872-3, delegate to the national republican convention in 1868, and has held numerous local offices.

—Hon. Stephen Strong, was district attorney of Tioga county for many years. County judge, and member of congress, and was one of the most able and distinguished members of the Tioga county bar, he died in 1866, aged 75 years.

—Hon. Thomas C. Platt was a county clerk, member of congress, and a United States senator, in 1881; has been president of several railroad and express companies, and one of the most distinguished men in the county of Tioga. He is the descendant of one of the first pioneer settlers of the county.

—Owego Gas Light Company organized March 20, 1856. Capital $40,-000, with W. F. Warner, president; stockholders and directors, W. F. Warner, Wm. H. Bell, Prentice E. Ransom, A. P. Storrs, Orin S. Truman, S. S. Truman, F. E. Platt, John Danforth, L. N. Chamberlain, F. I. Chatfield, works constructed on contract by Mr. William Bucknell, of Philadelphia. Gas first let into mains Oct. 15, 1856.

—No gentleman in southern New York has contributed more to the historical literature of the southern tier, or more dilligent research of historical data, than Judge Charles P. Avery. He was the life of the Southern Tier Pioneer Association which was organized in 1852, comprising pioneers and sons of pioneers in the counties of Steuben, Chemung, Tompkins, Tioga, Chenango and Broome, in New York, and Susquehanna and Bradford, in Pennsylvania. He was also deeply versed in Indian lore, and the customs, habits and settlements of those aborigines, and as a local historian could not be excelled. He was twice elected judge of Tioga county, and was a distinguished member of the bar.

Richford Township.

The town of Arlington was formed by an act of the legislature April 18, 1831, and by an act of the legislature, April 9, 1832, it was changed to the name of Richford. It is situated in the extreme northeastern portion of Tioga county. It is bounded on the north by Cortland and Tompkins, and on the east by Broome, on the south by Berkshire, and on the west by the Tompkins county line. It was taken from the northern portion of Berkshire.

At the election for town officers held April 9, 1832, at the house of Simeon M. Crandall, the officers elected were; William Dunham, supervisor; John C. Steadman, town clerk; William Belden, George P. Simmons, Jesse Moore, assessors; Laurin F. Curtis, Hubbard F. Wells, and Heman Daniels, commissioners of highways; Jacob Burgett, Elijah Powell, Tower Whiting, commissioners of schools; Simeon Griffin, Israel Wells, Edward W. Suydam inspectors of schools; Nathaniel Johnson, William G. Raymond, overseers of the poor; Obediah L. Livermore, collector; Hiram Tyler, John Talmage, constables: Seth B. Torrey, sealers of weights and measures; Platt T. Grow, Erie Osborn, David Garretson, justices of the peace.

Early settlers:—Eben Harris, Beriah Wells, Nathaniel Johnson, Samuel Smith, Samuel Gleazen, William Belden, Paul Stevens, Jeremiah Campbell, Caleb Gleason, Jesse Gleason, Ezekiel Rich, William Dunham, Elijah Dewey, Samuel Collins, Dr. Hezekiah Seaman, Stephen Wells, Deodatus Rice, Thomas P. Brown, William G. Raymond, Nathaniel Johnson, Joseph Bayette, Rev. Seth Bush, O. L. Livermore, L. R. Griffin, Laurin F. Curtis, Simeon Griffin, Chauncey L. Rice, Gad Worthington, John C. Steadman, Erie Osborn, Dr. Elijah Powell, Hubbard Wells, Caleb Arnot, Amzi Norton.

—The first church erected was in 1822.

—The first school house was built in 1820.

—The first school meeting was held in 1813.

—Ezekiel Rich was the first tanner, in 1820.

—The first settler was Eben Harris, in 1809.

—William Dunham was the first post master.

—Beriah Wells built the first tavern, in 1811.

—Hubbard Wells built the first brick dwelling.

—Caleb Arnold built the first saw mill, in 1817.

—William Belden taught the first school, in 1816.

—Catskill turnpike built through the town in 1816.

—East creek was one of the old Indian trails or paths.

—Dr. Hezekiah Seaman was the first physician, in 1825.

—Rev. Stephen Wells was the first Methodist minister, in 1811.

—Mrs. Evan Harris was the first who died in the town, in 1811.

—The Valley Lodge No. 463, I. O. G. T., instituted Dec. 11, 1867.

—The first blacksmith shop was built in 1823. Amzi Norton, blacksmith.

—The Free Will Baptist Church was organized in 1863, by Samuel Wilsey.

—A Christian Church was organized in 1851. Rev. William Grimes was the first minister.

—An Episcopal Church was organized in 1835, Rev. Carter Bailey, first Episcopal minister.

—Elijah Dewey was married to Lucy Johnson July 3, 1817, the first marriage in the town.

—The Southern Central railroad runs through the town, and has a station at the village of Richford.

—Chauncey Rich, son of Edward Rich, was early engaged in lumbering, and as a merchant.

—Joseph Bayette, a Frenchman, made cigars in the eastern portion of the town, many years ago.

—Edward Rich, an early settler, kept a hotel and run a line of stages from Cortland to Owego.

Spencer Township.

Spencer was formed by an act of the legislature, Feb. 28, 1806, taken from Owego. Boundaries changed in 1811, and 1824. It is situated in the northwest portion of Tioga county, and is bounded on the north by Tompkins county, on the east by Candor, on the south by Barton and Tioga, and on the west by Van Etten, in Chemung county. The principal village in the township is Spencer, which for several years was the half shire of Tioga county, a court house, jail, and county clerk's office, having been erected there. The Utica, Ithaca, & Elmira, the Geneva, Ithaca, & Sayre, railroads pass through the township, and have stations at Spencer. Spencer was named in honor of Judge Amos Spencer, a distinguished jurist.

The first town election was held April 1, 1806, at the Inn of Jacobus Schenicks, and the officers elected were, Joel Smith, supervisor; Joshua Ferris, town clerk; Edward Hobart, Daniel H. Bacon, Levi Slater, assessors; Moses Read, Benjamin Jennings, Joseph Barker, commissioners of highways; Lewis Beers, Samuel Westbrook, overseers of the poor; Isaiah Chambers, collector; John Shoemaker, Nathan Beers, William Cunan, John Murphy, Isaiah Chambers, constables; John F. Bacon, John McQuigg, John Malks, Jacob Swartwood, pound masters; John I. Speed, John English, Joseph L. Horton, Jacob Harrington, Alexander Ennis, Lewis Beardsley, fence viewers.

Early settlers:—Benjamin Drake, Joseph Barker, Edmond Hobart, Rodney Hobart, Phineas Spaulding, John B. Underwood, John Hall, John McQuigg, Daniel McQuigg, Judge Joshua Ferris, William Hugg, Isaac Hugg, Dr. Holmes, Stephen Bidlack, Judge Henry Miller, Andrew Purdy, Thomas Mosher, Caleb Valentine, Leonard Jones, John Jones, Richard Ferris, David Ferris, George Watson, Truman Colwell, Joshua Colwell, Abram Colwell, Benjamin Colwell, Gen. George Fisher, Thomas Fisher, Solomon Mead, John Mead, Joseph Cole, Alvin Barton, Cyrus Woodford, Thomas Andrews, Hartman Lotze, Joel Smith, Daniel H. Bacon, Levi Slater, Moses Read, Benjamin Jennings, Carmi Benton, John A. Nichols, Peter Lott, Abraham Garey, Thomas Andrews, Samuel Doolittle, Urban Palmer, Stephen Dodd, Geo. K. Hall.

—Dr. Holmes was the first physician.

—Joseph Hollister was the first lawyer.

—Samuel Doolittle opened the first store.

—Benjamin Drake erected the first grist mill in Spencer.

—Edmond Hobart raised the first crop of wheat in the town.

—Deborah Drake was the first white child born in the town.

—Benjamin Drake and Joseph Barker, were the first settlers, in 1794. Benjamin Drake settled on the present site of the village of Spencer.

—North Spencer is a post town, and Cowell's Corners is a hamlet.

—Spencer Village was the county seat, of Tioga county, from 1812 to 1821.

—John B Underwood and Polly Spaulding, were the first couple married in Spencer.

—Henry Miller, an early settler, was a judge of the court of common pleas of Tioga county.

—The Union Church at North Spencer, was organized with 30 members, in 1870. Cost $1,600.

—The old grave yard was opened for interments in 1800. The new cemetery was opened in 1864.

—Judge Joshua Ferris, an early settler, was a soldier of the revolutionary war. He was a surveyor.

—Joseph Barker was the first school-master. He came from Wyoming, Pa. in 1794. He was justice of the peace for 28 years.

—Andrew Purdy kept the first hotel in Spencer. He was a gentleman of fine address, and genial manners, and wielded a great influence in public affairs.

—Spencer Grange, No. 315, was organized march 24, 1875, with twenty-eight members. Officers; John Hallock, M,; L. W. Hull, secretary; W. H. Fisher, reporter.

—The First Baptist Church was erected in 1830, located east of the village of Spencer. In 1853, a church was erected, costing $4,000. It has a large membership.

—The First Methodist Episcopal Church was organized in 1809. Members, Peter Lott and wife, Jeremiah Andrews, Esther Dean, Abraham Garey, Hester Ann Purdy.

—Stephen Bidlack, an early settler, was the son of Captain James Bidlack, who was killed at Wyoming, Pa. His wife was Lois Ransom, daughter of Captain Samuel Ransom, who was also killed at Wyoming.

—Spencer village is an important station upon the Utica, Ithaca, & Elmira railroad, and the Geneva, Ithaca, & Sayre railroad. It is a busy, wealthy, and thriving village of about 1,000 inhabitants,

—The First Congregational Church was organized in 1815, with seven members, Daniel Hugg, Achsah Hugg, Urban Palmer, Lucy Palmer, Stephen Dodd, Mary Dodd, Clarissa Lake. Rev. Seth Williston, a missionary from Connecticut, the first minister.

—Live Oak Lodge, No. 547, Knights of Honor, was organized March 28, 1877. Officers, J. Nicholas, past Dictator; Charles E. Butts, dictator; M. B. Ferris, financial reporter; I. S. Stancliff, treasurer; S. Seely, chaplain; L. Larue, guide; M. P. Howell, assistant dictator; D. L Snook, vice dictator.

—Spencer Lodge, F. A. M., No. 290, was instituted June 7, 1853, by Reuben H. Walworth, W. M. grand master. Officers, George W. Hathaway W. M.; George K. Hall. S. W.; Elihue Butts, J. W.; John Vose, treasurer; Elijah Daimon, secretary; Benjamin Sniffin, chaplain; James Van Etten, S. D.; Samuel Bliven, tiler.

—The First Baptist Church was organized in 1799, by Phineas Spalding and Feb. 11, 1810, Elder David Jaynes preached to fifteen members, Phineas

Spalding, Susannah Spalding, John Cowell or Colwell, Deborah Cowell, Thomas Andrews, Jemima Andrews, Joseph Barker, Phebe Barker, Mehitable Hubbard, William Hugg, Lydia Hugg, Polly Underwood, Benjamin Cowell, Benjamin Casterline, Ruth Casterline.

—Spencer Chapter No. 49, order of Eastern Star, was instituted June 6, 1877. Officers, Mrs. M. Seeley, W. matron; Miss Frances Seeley, assistant matron; Jonathan Nicholas, patron; Nellie Spalding, conductress; A. Seeley, treasurer; W. B. Georgia, secretary; Helen Lawrence, assistant conductress; F. Spalding, warden; V. Lawrence, sentinel; Mrs. I. Howell, Mrs. E. M. Hutchins, Mrs. C. J. Fisher, Mrs. W. Skillings, Mrs. W. B. Georgia, points.

Tioga Township.

Tioga township was first organized by an act of the legislature, March 14, 1800, taken from Union. Boundaries changed Feb. 1806, 1808, 1813, and finally, at session No. 47, chapter 100, laws of New York, 1824, it was left as it now is. It is now bounded on the north by the towns of Candor, and Spencer, on the east by Owego, on the south by the east branch of the Susquehanna river, and on the west by the town of Barton. Along the Susquehanna river the soil is alluvial, with gravelly soil upon the uplands to the north. Tioga Center and Smithboro are villages in the town.

Early settlers:—Isaac D. Fowler, Jacob Ford, Peter W. Yates, Josiah Richardson, Benjamin Cole, John Ransom, James Burnette, Robert R. Burnette, Amos Draper, *Jonas Williams, Jesse Miller, Samuel Ransom, Andrew Alden, Prince Alden, Ezra Smith, Isaac Boardman, John Gee, James Scoonover, Nathaniel Goodspeed, Francis Gregg, James Brooks, Cornelius Brooks, Josiah Cleveland, Dr. Samuel Tinkham, David Pixley, Joel Farham, Jeremiah White, William Taylor, Noah Goodrich, Eliakim Goodrich, Nathaniel Catlin, John Hill, David Mersereau, Cornelius Taylor, John Smith, Caleb Leach, Lodowick Light, William Ransom.

—John Hill was the first carpenter.

—The first blacksmith was John Denio.

—Lodowick Light built the first tannery.

—The first school house was built in 1796.

—The first store was opened by John Light.

—The first tavern was kept by Samuel Ransom.

—The first church was erected in Tioga, in 1812.

—Rev. David Jayne was the first preacher, in 1794.

—Col. David Pixley built the first grist mill, in 1791.

—Ebenezer Mecklen drove the first mail coach through the town.

—The first recorded death was that of David Pixley, June 6, 1799.

—The first log house was built by Major William Ransom, in 1788.

—The First Baptist Church was organized in 1796, by Rev. David Jayne.

—The first post office was established in the town, in 1812. Isaac Boardman the first post master.

---

*By a division of the townships, the names of some of the early settlers frequently occur in several places, although they did not change their residence.

—An Indian burying ground was on Pipe creek.

—Halsey Valley is a post town, and quite a lively business center.

—Major William Ransom and Rachel Brooks, were the first couple married in 1792.

—James Brooks, Levi Light, Stephen Pepper, Deacon Ross, were soldiers of the war of 1812.

—Smithboro is situated upon the north bank of the Susquehenna river, and contains about six hundred inhabitants.

—Caleb Leach, an old pioneer of Tioga, made the first auger in the United States. It is now in the museum at Plymouth, Mass.

—Samuel Ransom, Cornelius Brooks, Nathaniel Catlin, Jonathan Catlin, Col. David Pixley, John Hill, John Gee, Josiah Cleveland, were revolutionary soldiers.

—Major William Ransom brought an apple tree from Wyoming and set it out, and it was parent of a number of the early orchards in Tioga, and along the river in Tioga county.

—Methodist Episcopal Church at Smithboro was organized Nov. 19, 1832, John Light, Andrew Bonham, Benjamin Brooks, trustees. The church was erected by carpenters, C. C. Yontz, William Crotchley.

—The Protestant Episcopal Church at Smithboro, was organized in 1866, with R. J. Fesch, first minister; John C. Gray, Burr L. Pearshall, wardens; Gilbert Pearshall, G. C. Chase, John C. Pearshall, T. C. Coryell, W. C. Randall, O. A. Barstow, vestrymen; church erected in 1874.

—Josiah Cleveland, a pioneer in Tioga, and a revolutionary soldier, was in the battle at Bunker's Hill. In 1843, when the monument at Bunker's Hill was completed, he was present at the ceremonies upon that occassion, and died at the foot of the hill, where sixty-eight years before he had fought for the establishment of the Independence of the thirteen colonies.

SCHUYLER COUNTY, NEW YORK.

By an act of the legislature of the state of New York, passed April 17, 1854, the county of Schuyler was formed, taken from the counties of Chemung, Steuben and Tompkins. It is bounded on the north by the counties of Yates and Seneca, on the east by the counties of Tompkins and Chemung on the south by the county of Chemung, on the west by the county of Steuben. Its county seat is Watkins, a beautiful village at the head of Seneca Lake. The county lies in the valley of Catharine creek, and east and west of the valley, and east and west of Seneca Lake, and embraces a fine fruit growing and agricultural district.

The local history of Schuyler county extends back to the revolutionary war and beyond. General Sullivan in 1779, in his expedition against the six nations, came down the valley of Catharine creek, and on the east side of the Seneca Lake, destroying the orchards and cornfields of the Indians, which he then found, located upon lands now within the limits of Schuyler county. The lands around the beautiful Seneca Lake were the choice hunting grounds of the red man, and the waters of the lake their favorite fishing resorts, and where they had for centuries established their rude huts, planted their corn, and gathered the fruits of their orchards.

One of their aged Queens, Catharine Montour, had her home in a village near the present village of Havana. Sullivan's men found her at her Indian village, "Catharinestown," where she had been left in a helpless condition by the Indians who fled before the invading army of Sullivan. They treated her kindly, and provided for her wants. It was in her honor that the town of Catharine, and the creek was named, and the township of Montour given.

The fame of Catharinestown was heralded far and wide, and the fruitful orchards and productive lands upon the borders of Seneca Lake were described by Sullivan's soldiers, to attentive and listening ears among the heroes of the continental army, which as soon as peace had been declared, and the lands open for occupation, came thronging into the lands of the Senecas. Syndicates existed in those days, and large tracts were secured by capitalists and notably among these in the present limits of Schuyler county were Royal Flint, Jonathan Lawrence, Robert C. Livingston, John Lamb, Melanethon Smith, James Watson, and John W. Watkins, and known as the "Watkins and Flint purchase,' see history of Watkins.

The formation of no county in the state was attended with more bad feeling and litigation than Schuyler. The germs, which resulted in its formation in 1854, were planted in 1836, when the county of Chemung was formed, and the county seat located at Elmira. The citizens of Catharine, Montour, Dix, Catlin, Veteran and Cayuta, wanted the county seat located at Horse Heads. It was nearer the geographical center of the new county of Chemung, and the citizens of the towns named irrespective of political parties claimed that they did not have an opportunity of being heard before the committee of the legislature, before whom the formation of the county of Chemung, and the location of the county seat was refered, and Elmira selected. From that time until the formation of the county of Schuyler was accomplished, the project of a new county was secretly, and quite often publicly and openly avowed by citizens of Veteran, Catharine, Dix and Cayuta. and enlisted sympathizers in Reading and Tyrone, in Steuben county, and Hector in Tompkins county. After being disappointed in the selection of the county seat, the citizens of Catlin, Veteran, Dix, Catharine, Cayuta and Erin, with the nominal consent of the town of Big Flats, compelled the selection of Horse Heads, as the central point for holding county conventions and general parades of the militia, and organized rifle companies of the county. In the matter of the distribution of public offices in the county for years the location of the candidate had as much to do with his election, as his capacity, ability and fitness, resulting in each locality, putting forth its most available candidate. The interrogatory for years, when a candidate was proposed for any county office was "Is he a sympathizer or a friend of Elmira, Southport and Chemung, or does he favor Dix, Catharine. Cayuta, and Veteran." These things prevailed in the Democratic conventions, and in the whig conventions, and like Banquo's ghost, "it would not down." The writer of this sketch, distinctly recollects how it was discussed in the election of Col. Jacob Westlake, for member of assembly, in 1837, and the selection of Hon. Hiram White, of Cayuta, in 1838, the selection of Judge Joseph L. Darling, of Catharine, in 1846, and Judge John W. Wisner, of Elmira, and Judge James Dunn, of the same place, how it entered into the nomination of Samuel Minier, for sheriff of Big Flats, in 1840 or 41, and his selection of William Skellinger, of Havana, as his deputy and also in the election of Mr. Skellinger, for sheriff in 1846. There was an under current quietly at work for many years, encouraged by such gentlemen of the northern portion of Chemung county as Major Erastus Crandall, Elijah Sexton, and Jabez Bradley, of Veteran, Charles Cook, Elijah Hinman, Guy Hinman, William Skellinger, Doctor Watkins, Alva Nash, Judge Simeon L. Rood, Hiram W. Jackson, George B. Guinnip, Green Bennet, and others of Dix and Catharine, irrespective of party, which was certain to culminate in an open rupture and division.

The citizens of the southern portion of the county were aware of these dissatisfactions, and such men as the late Hon. John G. McDowell, George W. Buck of Chemung township, Solomon L. Smith, Philo Jones, and others of Southport, William R. Judson, John W. Wisner, Lyman Covell, Judge Hiram Gray, Thomas Maxwell, William Maxwell, John Arnot, Capt. Samuel Partridge, and citizens generally of Elmira, were trying to avert the impending crisis, and reconcile the differences, and jealousies. The question would come up in an indirect form every year at the annual meeting of the supervisors, in the selection of the equalizing committee, to fix the taxable rate of the lands in the various towns of the county. It was the southern portion arrayed against the northern portion of the county, and the northern portion of the county arrayed against the southern portion, and the result was inevitable, and when Schuyler county was formed, no one was surprised however much they were opposed, or in favor of it. It is the sincere belief of the writer that had Horse Heads been named as the county seat of Chemung, in 1836, Schuyler county would not have been formed, and Chemung would have retained her original territory intact. The battle of Schuyler did not end in the strife for the passage of a legislative act authorizing its formation, but a long and bitter controversy grew out of the location of its county seat. All is peace now, and may she enter upon a course of uninterruted prosperity.

The first county officers were, Judge, Simeor L. Rood; county clerk, Algernon E. Newcomb; sheriff, John S. Swartwood; treasurer, Charles J. Broas; district attorney, Lewis F. Riggs; school commssioner, William C. Gulick; surrogate, Simeon L. Rood; member of assembly, Henry Fish of Mecklenburg.

The commissioners to locate the county buildings were Delos De Wolf, of Oswego county; Edward Dodd, of Washington county; Vivins W. Smith, of Onondaga county. They fixed the location at Havana. A court house was erected, and afterwards sold. A court house, jail and other buildings were erected at Watkins; and a series of litigations commenced which our space will not permit to enter into detail. Suffice it, that the county seat was finally located at Watkins.

The Chemung Canal was completed in 1833.

The Elmira & Jefferson railroad was completed in 1849. Now under the control of the Northern Central R. R.

The Syracuse, Geneva & Corning railroad was completed in the year 1877.

Its first board of supervisors consisted of Leroy Wood, of Cayuta; Phineas Catlin, of Catharine; W. E. Boothe, of Dix, Henry Fish, of Hector; Edwin C. Andrews, of Reading; George Clark, of Tyrone; A. S. Newcomb, of Orange; H. M. Hilliman, clerk.

The first term of circuit court was held at Havana, Aug. 19, 1859, Ransom Balcam, justice; Minor T. Broderick, J. B. Wilkins, justices of sessions.

MEMBERS OF ASSEMBLY.—Henry Fish, 1858; Isaac D. Mekeel, 1859; Edwin H. Downs, 1860; Abram V. Mekeel, 1861; Alvin C. Hause, 1862; Samuel Lawrence, 1863; Lorenzo Webber, 1864 5; Samuel M. Barker, 1866-7; George Clark, 1868-9; William C. Coon, 1870-1; Harmon L. Gregory, 1872; Jeremiah McGuire, 1873; Harmon L. Gregory, 1874; William H. Fish, 1875; William Gulick, 1876-7; Abram V. Mekeel, 1878-9; Lewis Beach, 1880-1; Minor T. Jones, 1882; Adrian Tuttle, 1883; J. Franklin Barnes, 1884; Fremont Cole, 1885.

SHERIFFS.—John J. Swartout, 1854; Elvin K. Mandeville, January 26, 1856; Moses F. Weaver, November, 1856; Robert Lockwood, 1859;

Peter C. Hager, 1862; Chester M. Hager, 1865; Charles W. Claugherty, 1868: John S. Swartwood, 1871; John Wood, 1874; Herman, L. Easterbrook, appointed Dec. 19, 1876; Henry B. Catlin, 1877; George E. Hurd, 1880; John M. Wakeman, appointed April 1, 1882; James W. Lyon, 1882, the present incumbent.

COUNTY JUDGES.—Simeon L. Rood, 1854; George C. Shearer, 1862; Benjamin W. Woodward, 1866; George C. Freer, 1870; Oliver P. Hurd, 1876; Martin J. Sunderlin, 1882, present incumbent. The County Judge is the Surrogate.

COUNTY CLERKS.—Algernon S. Newcomb, 1854; John Hollett, 1857; Devalson G. Weaver, 1860; Edward Kendall, 1866; Myron H. Weaver, 1875; Arthur C. Woodward, 1878; Arthur C. Woodward, 1882, present incumbent.

DISTRICT ATTORNEYS.—Lewis F. Riggs, 1854; Marcus Lyon, appointed March 12, 1855; Daniel Jamison, 1855; Henry C. VanDuser, 1858; John W. Brown, 1861; Samuel C. Keeler, 1864; Oliver P. Hurd, 1867; William L. Norton, 1870; Charles H. Fletcher, 1873; Charles W. Davis, 1876; W. LeRoy Norton, 1879; Washington Robertson, 1882, present incumbent.

COUNTY TREASURERS.—Charles J. Broas, 1854; Cyrus Roberts, 1857; Adrian Tuttle, 1860; Jacob Fitzgerald, 1863; James Cormack, 1866; Levi Shepard, 1869; Abram S. Stothoff, January 10, 1873; William H. Watt, November, 1873; Jesse Lyon, 1879, present incumbent.

SCHOOL COMMISSIONERS since organization of the county in 1854: William Gulick, Cyrus Roberts, Daniel Beach, Charles G. Winfield, Lauren G. Thomas, James H. Pope, Duncan C. Mann, Charles T. Andrews, Lauren G. Thomas, Augustus C. Huff. Term three years.

The first grand jury of Schuyler county was composed of Orange Hubbell, Charles G. Tuthill, Charles Babbitt, J. Brown, B. Carpenter, William Vaughn, Stephen Thayer, William Slawson, D. W. Goodrich, W. Buck, N. Fish, Samuel Vaughn, A. Stoll, W. A. Hurd, E. I. Agard, Fred L. Lane, L. Mix, W. Hubbell, M. Colegrove, G. C. Brown, E. W. Prentiss, Samuel Ross, jr. John J. VanAllen, District Attorney.

Schuyler County Medical Society was organized Dec. 29, 1857. Members: Thomas Shannon, J. W. Thompson, G. D. Bailey, Nelson Winton, E. B. Wagner, N. Niverson, S. B. Nichols; first president, Doctor Nelson Winton; J. W. Thompson, vice president; Thomas Shannon, secretary; S. B. H. Nichols, treasurer; Nelson Niverson, G. D. Bailey, E. B. Wager, censors.

Schuyler County Homeopathic Medical Society was formed July 9, 1872. Officers: William Gulick, president; Alexander V. Stobbs, vice president; A. P. Hollett, secretary and treasurer. G. A. Tracey, E. W. Lewis, C. B. Knight, censors.

Schuyler County Agricultural Society was organized March 14, 1855, John Woodward, president; Cyrus Sebring, Hiram White, Cornelius Harring, Eli C. Frost, Charles Mathews, vice presidents; Orlando Hurd, secretary; Thomas Evans, treasurer; Henry Fish, Morderica Carbon, Jacob Hendricks, John Roberts. Isaac P. Seymour, Robert Hughey, Solomon Williams, John Ennis, George G. Freer, Executive Committee.

Schuyler County Bible Society organized in the month of February, 1856.

The *Chemung Democrat* was issued in 1840, at Havana.

The *Independent Freeman* was issued June 15, 1850, by William B. Slawson & Co.

The *Watkins Republican* was issued June, 1854, by J. K. Averill.

The *Schuyler County Press* was issued in 1858, by S. M. Taylor.

The *Son of Temperance* issued in 1860, by A. C. Lumbard.

The *Schuyler County Democrat*, issued 1865, Watkins, S. C. Clizbee editor.

The *Watkins Independent* was established in 1866, by S. C. Clizbee.

The *Schuyler County Times* was issued in 1873, by Thomas & Gates.

The *Havana Journal* was issued Sept., 1849, by Waldo M. Potter.

The *Havana Enterprise* was issued in May, 1872, by W. H. Page.

The *Corona Boracallis* was issued in the year 1851.

The Schuyler County Teachers' Association was organized in the year 1859. The first officers were: D. H. Stoll, president; Henry C. Howard, vice president; Mary E. Duryea, treasurer; Sarah Dakin, secretary; Daniel Beach, county commissioner of common schools.

Post offices in Schuyler county.—Alpine, Altay, Beaver Dam, Bennettsburg, Burdette, Catharine, Cayuta, Cayutaville, Havana, Hector, Lawrence, Logan, Mecklenburg, Moreland, North Hector, North Reading, Odessa, Orange, Perry City, Pine Creek, Pine Grove, Reading, Reading Center, Reynoldsville, Searsburg, Smith Valley, Sugar Hill, Townsend, Tyrone, Watkins, Weston.

Catharine Township.

The town of Catharine was organized at the twenty-first session of the Legislature of the State of New York, March 9th, 1798 - taken from Newtown. (See also Session 46, Laws of 1822). It is bounded on the north by the town of Hector, on the east by Newfield in Tompkins county, on the south by Cayuta and Veteran, and west by Montour. It is situated on a plateau about three hundred and fifty feet above the Waters of Cayuga Lake, and is a fine agricultural township. Cayuta Lake, a clear body of water, is within the township. It covers an area of nearly four hundred acres. Catharine, Alpine and Odessa are villages in the town. Catharine stands upon the site of a village for many years known as "Johnson's Settlement." At the first election for town officers, held May 15, 1798, the officers elected were: Phineas Catlin, supervisor; Joshua Ferris, town clerk; David Culver, Selah Saterlee, James Bowers, assessors: John W. Watkins, Phineas Catlin, overseers of the poor; George Mills, jr., collector; David Culver, Isaac Terwilliger, Selah Saterlee, overseers of highways; John W. Watkins, James Broderick, Phineas Catlin, school commissioners; James Broderick, commissioner of highways; Abram Coryell, David Culver, jr., George Mills, jr., constables.

Early settlers: John Mitchell, Josiah Hinman, Elijah S. Hinman, David E. Beardsley, Ebenezer Mallory, Samuel Winton, Solomon Boothe, Elijah Boothe, Isaac Boothe, John Coe, Ichabod Meeker, Simeon Lovell, Isaac Lyon, John Stiles, Lemuel Shelton, William H. Prince, James Osterhout, Zachary A. Lewis, Eli Beardsley, Eaton Agard, Barnabas Miller, Phineas Catlin, J. W. Nevins, Isaac Paulding, Isaac Buckalew, James Smith, Gerard Smith, Sylvanus A. Beeman, Michæl Connor, Samuel Lawrence, Joseph Lawrence, Titus F. Mix. Samuel Mix, David Olmstead, sr., Elijah Sturdevant, John Chapman, Henry Chapman, Francis Sackett, Abel Mead, Abijah Wakeman, Isaac Ganung, George Shelton, John Foster, Robert Johnson, Aaron E. Mallory, William P. Mallory, Caleb Robinson, Robert Lockesby, John H. Rumsey, Walter Lyon, Lewis Beardsley, James Broderick, George Mills, sr., John W. Watkins, Phineas Catlin, David Culver, James Bowers, Isaac Terwilliger, Joseph Lyon, Abel Peet, David Olmstead, jr., Coleman Olmstead, Richard Wilcox, David Sturdevant, Jonathan Sturdevant, Joshua Ferris.

—John Mitchell was the first *bona fide* settler.

—Odessa was named by John Foster, in the year 1827.

—Elijah Boothe opened the first store, in the year 1800.

—Isaac Swartwood built the first saw mill, in the year 1799.

—Abel Peet died in the year 1800, the first death in the town.

—The first marriage was that of Samuel Winton and Alice Hinman.

—The first grist mill was erected in the year 1801, by David Beardsley.

—Charles Mitchell was born in the year 1801—the first white child born in the town.

—Joseph Lyon taught the first school in the present town of Catharine, in the year 1802.

—The First Baptist Church of Alpine was organized July 11, 1874, by Rev. J. Hendricks.

—The town of Catharine derives its name from Queen Catharine Montour, an Indian half-breed.

—The First M. E. Church of Odessa was organized in the year 1870. Church erected in 1877

—The first religious society was organized by the Methodist Episcopal Church, in the year 1805.

—St. John's Episcopal Church of Catharine was formed in the year 1809. Church erected in the year 1811.

—Methodist Episcopal Church of Alpine was formed March 19, 1874—Rev. G. S. Watson first minister in charge. Church erected 1874; cost, $5,000.

—M. E. Society of Catharine was organized in the year 1805. Church erected in 1834. Trustees: Samuel Agard, Simeon Lovell, Sewell Pike, Jesse Lyon, Levi Mallet.

—The First Free Will Baptist Church of Odessa was formed July 2, 1841, at the house of John Foster. Church erected in 1856. Rev. Francis A. Wildman was the first minister.

—Catharine Library Association formed April 1, 1817. Its first trustees were: Elijah S. Hinman, Samuel Agard, William H. Prince, George Hibbard, Uriah Parsons, Chester W. Lord, Enoch Merchant.

—Highland Grange, No. 22, organized Nov. 4, 1873: Jesse Lyon, Master; George N. Wager, secretary; George Winter, treasurer; Sarah E. Hall, Flora; Mrs. Ellen Hitchcock, Ceres; Cynthia Cushing, Pomona.

—The First Wesleyan Church of Odessa was organized in the year 1856. Rev. P. S. Slosson minister in charge. First trustees; Daniel Adams, John A. Reed, Lorenzo Brown, John Rumsey. Church erected 1856; cost $2,500.

—The first post office at Johnson Settlement was established in the year 1816. Chester W. Lord was the first postmaster.

—Alpine Grange, No. 229, was organized August 24, 1874: James Fitzgerald, master; A. S. Wood, overseer; J. B. Farr, secretary; S. C. Bolger, treasurer; Mrs. Mary VanLew, Flora; Rhoda Cure, Pomona; Mrs. S. C. Bolger, Ceres.

Cayuta Township.

By an act of the legislature of the state of New York, at its 47th session, March 30, 1824, Cayuta township was formed, taken from Spencer, Tioga county. Its boundaries were changed in 1854, when it became a portion of Schuyler county. It is one of the smallest townships in area, in Schuyler county. It is situated in the highland in the extreme southeastern portion of the county. It is bounded on the north by the town of Catharine, in Schuyler county, and Newfield in Tompkins county, on the east by Newfield, in Tompkins, and Van Etten in Chemung; on the south by Van Etten, and Erin in Chemung county, and on the west by Veteran, in Chemung county, and Catharine in Schuyler county.

At the first election held after the formation of Schuyler county, held May 9, 1854, the officers elected were Leroy Wood, supervisor; William Brown, town clerk; John White, justice of the peace: Salmon F. Chase, superintendent of schools; Emanuel Ennis, assessor; Peter Ennis, Commissioner of highways; Jacob Linderman, Edward Lyon, overseers of the poor; John A. Banfield, collector; John A. Banfield, Abram Lockerby, John E. Torry, Jacob Van Kurin, William B. White, constables; Samuel Roberts, Walter Archibald, inspectors of election; Alanson J. Cleveland, scaler of weights and measures.

Early settlers:—Capt. Gabriel Ogden, David Jaynes, Harmon White, Hiram White, Jonathan Thomas, Joseph Thomas, Benjamin Chambers, Jeremiah Taylor, John Ennis, Emanuel Ennis, Saunder Ennis, Benjamin Ennis, Robert Lockerby, Moses Brown, Langstaff Compton, Edward Reynolds, Henry Smith, Ebenezer Edwards, Robert Lockerby, Jesse D. White.

—John Ennis erected the first grist mill, in 1817.

—Robert Lockerby taught the first school, in 1805.

—Joseph Thomas died in 1802, the first death in the town.

—Jesse White built a saw mill, in 1816, the first in the town.

—Rosetta Thomas was born in 1804, the first birth in the township.

—The first religious services were held by Rev. Mr. Jaynes, in 1802.

—Post office established in 1815. Jesse B. White, was the first postmaster.

—The first Baptist Church in the present limits of Cayuta, was organized in 1877.

—Ebenezer Edwards was married in 1802, to Sarah Odgen, the first marriage in the town.

—A Free Church, open to all evangelical denominations, was erected in 1859. Cost $1,500. First trustees, Leroy Wood, Samuel Brown, Salmon F. Chase.

—Cayuta Rural Cemetery Association was incorporated Oct. 12, 1874. Trustees, Charles R. Swartwood, John S. McDuffee, Ira B. Jaynes, John G. Reynolds, Henry G. Smith, Samuel S. Brown, John Boyer.

Dix Township.

The town of Dix was organized April 17, 1835, chap. 98, page 82, laws of New York, taken from the town of Catlin. As now constituted, Dix is bounded on the north by the town of Reading, on the east by the valley of Watkins, and the town of Montour, on the south by the town of Catlin, and on the west by the town of Orange. It is situated on the west of the valley of Catharine, upon the rolling lands and plateaus, overlooking the Seneca Lake, and some of the finest landscape views in the state can be obtained from points in this town. Its soil is very productive. The Syracuse, Geneva & Corning railroad passes through the township in a north east, and south west direction, having stations at Beaver Dam, and at Watkins Glen, originally in the town, but now in the corporation of Watkins.

The Northern Central railroad runs along its eastern boundary, having a station at Havana, and at Watkins, thus accommodating the citizens of Dix with ample railroad facilities. It was named in honor of Hon. John A. Dix, subsequently Governor of the state. There are several hamlets and villages in the town, among them Beaver Dam, Moreland, Townsend, and the incorporated village of Watkins.

Early settlers:—John Diven, William Baskin, Jacob Mills, Jacob Mills, Jr., Mathias Miller, Thomas L Nichols, Ebenezer Buck, Obediah Phinney, Joseph Hitchcock, Christian Crout, William Lane, George Frost, John P. Cornell, George W. Bronson, Amos Royce, Judge John Crawford, Claudius Townshend, Underhill Frost, John Platt, Brewster Platt, Col. Green Bennett, Charles Bennett, Thomas Eddy, Elisha Bronson, Simeon L. Rood, Bela Sanford, Ira Sanford, Rev. John Gray, Daniel Tracy, William H. Smith, David Pike, H. R. Lybolt, J. B. Coates, Daniel Hughey, Nelson Lybolt, James Wedgewood, Joseph Cole, Elijah Phelps, Edward Lee, Archibald Tilford, Ebenezer Perry, Joshua Pierce, John Crout, Abram P. Crout, Gardner Krum, Jonas Blower, Dodo Benson, Eleazer Cole, I. Bramhall, Consider E. Evans, Thomas Eddy, Nathan Miller, John W. Chapman, Daniel D. Giles, Daniel H. Bolt, Daniel Kent, Ira Dodge, John C. Thayer, John V. Rose, Lewis Miller, W. S. Beers, Rev. Edward Hotchkiss, Harlem Cole, Almon Beecher, William Hardenberg.

—W. S. Beers built the Beaver Dams tannery, in 1837.

—Green Bennett built a saw mill on Bower's Creek, in 1828.

—Samuel Hubbell built a grist mill in VanZandt's Hollow, in 1828.

—John Griffith was the first death at Townshend setttlement, in 1832.

—The first store at Beaver Dams was opened by Abram P. Crout, in the year 1829.

—David H. Bolt, kept the first tavern at Townshend settlement, in the year 1823.

—Post office established in 1830, at Beaver Dams, David Davison was the first post master.

—Post office established at Moreland in 1836, Judge John Crawford the first post master.

—Moreland and Beaver Dams are stations on the Syracuse, Geneva & Corning railroad.

—Beaver Dams derives its name from two beaver dams in the creek at that place.

—First Baptist Church of Townsend, was organized in the year 1833. Church erected in 1849.

—Col. Green Bennett was superintendent of the Chemung Canal, and for many years was prominent in the affairs of Chemung county.

—The Baptist Church of Moreland was organized in 1830, Rev. Thomas S. Sheardown, was the first preacher. Church erected in 1843. Cost $3,000.

—Methodist Episcopal Church of Beaver Dams, organized in 1832 as a class. The first minister in charge was Rev. A. C. Orcull. Church erected in 1858

—Moreland Cemetery Association was incorporated Sept. 26, 1872. Trustees, Henry Gray, Jonathan Sturdevant, John Deum. Benjamin Clark, secretary.

—The First Presbyterian Church of Moreland, was organized Nov. 4, 1834. The first trustees were John C. Thayer, Lewis Miller, John V. Rose, church erected in 1834.

—Phineas Catlin was appointed one of the commissioners in 1797, to lay out a road from Catskill Landing, on the Hudson river to Catharine's Town. His associates were Mathew Carpenter and John Hendy.

—The First Universalist Society of Dix was organized Feb. 26, 1848. Rev. Ethan Carpenter was the first minister. Trustees were George McAlpine, Benjamin Priest, Henry Johnson. Moderator, Joseph Cole; clerk, W. S. Beers; church erected ih 1853. Cost $2,000.

Hector Township.

Hector was organized as a part of Cayuga county, at Session No. 25, March 30, 1802—taken from Ovid—embraced in Tompkins county by act of the Legislature, April 7, 1817, and in Schuyler county in the year 1854. It is situated on the eastern shore of Seneca Lake and approaches within six miles of the western shore of Cayuga Lake. The surface gradually ascends from the shores of Seneca Lake until it reaches an altitude of about six hun dred feet, and then descends toward Cayuga Lake. It is the largest town in Schuyler county. It was within its limits that the Indians of the Six Nations had corn fields and orchards which were destroyed by General Sullivan, hitherto referred to in his campaign in 1779. The history of the township affords material for a very large volume. It is bounded on the north by Seneca county, on the east by the towns of Ulysses and Enfield in Tompkins county, on the south by Catharine and Montour in Schuyler county, and west by Seneca Lake. It is rich in agricultural and the orchard products.

Early settlers: William Wickham, John Livingston, Stephen Pratt, Reuben Smith, Henry Smith, Jabez Smith, Daniel Everts, Grover Smith, Samuel Hanley, Richard Ely, Elisha Trobridge, Caleb Trobridge, Nathaniel Pritchard, Herman Trobridge, Amasa Mathews, Daniel Mathews, Sylvanus Mathews, Stephen Mathews, Capt, Jonathan Owen, William Bodle, Henry Sayler, Daniel Larrison, Capt. Joseph Hager, Joseph Gillespie, Joseph McIntyre, William McIntyre, John Mears, George Howell, Robert Durland,

William Spalding, Cornelius Humphrey, William Carman, Charles Carman, Morris Carman, Richard Carman, Joshua Makeel, Jesse Makeel, James Stillwell, Isaac Stillwell, Richard Sutfin, Robert Curry, Benjamin Gilmore, James Gilmore, Garrett Clawson, Benjamin Coddington, John M. Coddington, General William Himrod, Joel Reynolds, Timothy Schofield, Augustus Ely, John Kinan, Thomas Kinan, Daniel P. Budd, Joseph Potter, Sullivan D. Hubbell, John Proper, Peter Woodward, William Martin, Thomas Sears, David Sears, Christopher Smith, John Smith, Joseph Jewell, Zera Carter, Abiel Gardiner, Ebenezer Jewell, Elias Jewell, Jonathan Slocum, William McCann, Robert Armstrong, A. Dee, Dea German, Jacob Hager, Jabez Smith, Brickley Monell, Wilcox Buckbee, Mowbry Owen, Zalmon Barber, Abner Tremain, John Mears, James Bowley, Ashbel Tremain, William Jaycox, Robert Swartout, Reuben Wood, Samuel Seeley, George Wood, Thomas Coon, Thomas Searles, Henry Jeffreys, James Thompson, John Mackey, Daniel Thompson, John K. Mathews, William Barber, Phineas Bennett Martin Keep, Jacob Banker, M. J. Jackquish, Dr. Henry Fish, Thomas Edgerly, Samuel Seaton, Dr. Edmund Brown, Daniel Jackson, Uzel Barker.

—The first town tax collected was $300.

—Richard Ely was the first tanner in the town.

—Wm. Wickham kept the first hotel in the town.

—John Livingston taught the first school in the town.

—Hector was named by the land commissioners in 1790.

—A violent tornado occurred at Hector in the year 1876.

—Burdette Grange No. 263, was organized in Nov., 1874.

—Samuel A. Seeley erected a woolen mill in the year 1801.

—Hector Ely was the first white child born, January 21, 1796.

—The first store was opened at Hector Falls by John B. Seeley.

—The first death in the town was William Wickham, Nov. 2, 1800.

—In the year 1816 the frost destroyed nearly all the crops in Hector.

—The first church organization was the Presbyterian, Sept. 10, 1809.

—Reuben Smith built the first saw mill in the town, in the year 1795.

—William Wickham settled on the Sullivan road, cut through in 1779.

—Mecklenburg Union Cemetery Association incorporated March, 1853.

—Mrs. William Wickham built the first framed house, in the year 1802.

—Wm. Wickham was drowned at the head of Seneca Lake, Nov. 2, 1800.

—Stephen Pratt and Elizabeth Livingston were the first couple married in Hector.

—The first religious services were held at McIntyre Settlement, in the year 1805.

—The first Presbyterian church was erected at Peach Orchard in the year 1818.

—The first permanent settler in Hector was William Wickham in the year 1791.

—Hector post office established in the year 1803. Grover Smith was the first postmaster.

—The first town meeting in Hector was held at the house of Grover Smith, in the year 1802.

—Dr. Henry Fish was the first member of assembly for Schuyler county.

—Burdette post office was established March 6, 1819, Joseph Carson, post master.

—Mecklenberg post office established June 2, 1826, John Sayler post master.

—Mecklenberg Lodge, No. 609, Sons of Temperance, organized August 18, 1877.

—The bell in the church spire at Burdette was cast in Spain in the year 1788.

—M. E. Church Class formed at McIntyre Settlement in 1804. Church erected in 1822.

—Samuel Hanley was a Captain in the revolutionary war. He was an early settler in Hector.

—M. E. Class formed in 1824 at Mecklenburg, Uzel Baker, leader. Church erected in 1840.

—Perry City post office Hector township, was established July 31, 1815, Thomas Edgerly post master.

—Hector has been in Montgomery, Herkimer, Onondaga, Cayuga, Seneca, Tompkins and Schuyler counties.

—The Logan Methodist Church organized as a class in 1815. Chauncey Smith leader. Church erected in 1832.

—Burdette was originally known as Hamburg, then Tadpole, and finally christened Burdette by Richard Woodward.

—Christian Church organized at Searsburg in the year 1817. Rev. Mr. Chase the first minister. Church erected in 1839.

—Baptist Church, Peach Orchard, constituted April 11, 1820. Rev. O. C. Comstock the first minister. Church erected in 1833.

—The Baptist Church of Bennetsburg was organized in the year 1809. James Reynolds was its first minister. Church erected in 1829.

—The Baptist Church of Burdette was organized in the year 1836. Rev. James Reynolds was the first minister. Church erected in 1836.

—M. E. Church was organized at Steamburg in the year 1856. First minister in charge, Rev. William Potter. Church erected in 1857.

—The Baptist Church of Mecklenburg was organized July 5, 1825, at the house of Jeremiah Ayers. First minister, Rev. John Sturdevant. Church erected in 1835.

—Mecklenberg, Reynoldsville, Bennettsburg, Burdette, Peach Orchard, North Hector, Logan, Steamburg, Perry City, Cayutaville, are villages and hamlets in Hector.

—M. E. Church, North Hector. Class organized in 1852, by Rev. John Robinson. Elias Byram first class leader. Church organized in 1857 and church edifice erected.

—Seneca post office in Hector township established July 1, 1814, D. Burroughs, postmaster. Discontinued Oct. 30, 1830, and again established in 1846, with Hiram Milliman post master.

—North Hector Baptist Church organized Nov. 28, 1821, at the house of John Goltry, and was incorporated Nov. 1830. The first minister was Rev. J. P. Woodworth. Church erected in 1831.

--The Peach Orchard church was raised without the use of ardent spirits. Believed to be the first edifice of any kind raised in the country adjacent without that article to stimulate the people engaged in erecting them.

—The Presbyterian Church of Mecklenburg was organized by the Rev. Henry Ford, June 10, 1833. Elders: James Bodle, John W. Mathews, James Woodford, Sullivan D. Hubbell, Wakeman Lyon. Church erected in 1842.

—Samuel Hanley, Richard Ely, Nathaniel Pritchard, Amasa Mathews, Captain Jonathan Owen, Henry Sayler, Joseph Gillespie, Cornelius Humphreys, Benjamin Coddington, Peter Woodward, were pioneer settlers and soldiers in the revolutionary war.

—Methodist E. Church, Burdette, was organized as a class in 1833, Wm. Himrod, leader. Church organized Feb. 16, 1839. Church erected in 1845. Trustees: Elijah Baker, George V. Minard, Harlow Hubbell, Benjamin Benson, William T. Allen, William Himrod, John Dickinson.

—The Presbyterian Church of Burdette was organized Feb. 14, 1826. Nathan Smith, Robert McCrary, George Owen, elders. Church was erected in 1827, Rev. Jabez Chadwick the first minister. Building committee in 1827 was David Kimble, Dr. Edmund Brown, Daniel Jackson.

—The Episcopal Church organized at Peach Orchard in the year 1827. The members consisted principally of the Woodward family, who were English and erected a church. They were the ancestors of Judge Woodward, of Schuyler county, and Dr. William Woodward, of Chemung county.

—Society of Friends was organized in 1813. First members were: Eber Crandall, Charles Carman, Mary Carman, Caleb Carman, Anna Carman, Thomas Frost, Mary Frost, Jesse McKeel, Amy McKeel, Joshua McKeel, Hester McKeel, William Carman, Phebe Carman, Philadelphia Ammock. Church erected in 1826.

—The Presbyterian Church at Peach Orchard was constituted Sept. 15, 1809, by Revs. Charles Mosher and William Clark. Original members were: Anna Seaton, Thomas Morton, Judah Brewer, Samuel Seaton, Anna Gillespie, John Messler, Chloe Scovill. Elders: William Himrod, Jabez Havens, Thomas Morton, Samuel Seaton. Deacons: Samuel Seaton, Jabez Havens. Rev. William Clark, first minister. Church erected in 1818.

—The first temperance society organized in Hector; its preliminary meeting was held in a bar room, March 18, 1828. April 9, 1828, it was fully organized at the Ely school house: William Smith, president; S. H. L. Warner, secretary. First members: William Smith, S. H. L. Warner, Ephraim Birge, Richard Smith, Caleb Smith, Chauncey W. Smith, Joseph Jewell, Henry German, A. M. Comstock, Augustus Ely, John Lambert, Charles Everetts.

Montour Township and Havana Village.

Montour was organized by an act of the legislature, of the state of New York, March 3, 1860, taken from the western portion of the town of Catharine. It is bounded on the north by Hector, on the east by Catharine, on the south by Veteran, and on the west by Dix, and is one of the smallest townships in area in the county of Schuyler. The principal village within its limits is Havana, which was incorporated in 1836.

At the first election held for the village of Havana June 7, 1836, William L. Noble, John G. Henry, Edwin H. Downs, Hiram W. Jackson, William Skellinger, were elected trustees; Hiram W. Jackson, president; Sylvester Hazen, clerk; Peter Tracy, treasurer; Alexander Clauherty, constable and collector; Josiah C. Robinson, David Lee, Sidney S. Decker, assessors.

At the first election held for the town of Montour, May 1, 1860, Charles Cook was elected supervisor; William H. Skellinger, town clerk; John I. Lawrence, Charles J. Broas, Amos Hoyt, Minor T. Broderick, justices of the peace; Adam J. Campbell, Asa Fox, Samuel W. Sacket, assessors; Russell W. Leavenworth, Caleb Hill, commissioners of highways; William McDonald, overseer of the poor; Hiram W. Jackson, Joseph B. Wilkins, Alpheus Keyser, inspectors of election; Robert F. Hedges, collector; Chester C. Sheffield, Henry W. Severn, Robert F. Hedges, Nathaniel C. Williams, constables.

Early settlers:—Phineas Catlin, Anthony Broderick, Joseph Frost, Asa Coe, William Lyon, Samuel Bennett, David Lee, Israel Lee, Samuel Nichols, William Ayers, Henry Ayers, Ebenezer B. Crofut, Thomas L. Fanton, Minor L. Sherwood, Joseph Brown, Nathaniel Thompson, John C. Larew, Albert Brown, George C. Wickham, Solomon Williams, Jacob Hendricks, James P. Shearer, Samuel W. Sackett, J. Laban, A. M. Freeman, Jonathan M. Couch, Charles Cook, Silas Walcott, George Mills, James Wilson, John Richardson, William McClure, Phineas Bowers, John King, Henry Stevens, David Ayers, Thomas Nichols Jr., Dr. George W. Hinman, George Kimball, Joshua Morse, Ebenezer Risley, Darius Ballou, Abram Massiker, Roswell Wakely, Daniel Tracy, John F. Phelps, William T. Jackson, Samuel G. Crawford, John W. Jobbett, F. D. Goodwin, Flaviel Gaylord, John G. Henry, Hiram W. Jackson, Adam G. Campbell, Minor T. Broderick, Elijah Hinman, Alva Nash, Nathan Hall, Peter Quick.

—The first sloop was launched in 1796.

—Charles Cook settled in Havana in 1829

—George Mills was the first merchant, in 1805.

—George Mills kept the first tavern in Havana.

—Cook Academy was established April 12, 1854.

—William T. Jackson built a woolen mill, in 1836.

—The first steamboat was the Seneca Chief, in 1828, July 4.

—George Kimball was the first blacksmith in Havana, in 1801.

—Silas Walcott was the first permanent white settler at Havana.

—William Skellinger built a foundry and machine shop, in 1834.

—Bowers and Kimball built the first grist mill in Havana, in 1802.

—Havana Stoneware manufactory established by Charles Cook, in 1844.

—William Skellinger was deputy sheriff of Chemung county, from 1840 to 1843, and sheriff of Chemung county from 1846 to 1849.

—Havana received its name in 1829. It had previously been known as Catharine's town and Mill's Landing.

—Post office first established at Catharine's town, in October, 1802. George Mills first post master.

—Bank of Havana was incorporated Nov. 10, 1851, Charles Cook, president; C. C. Clark, cashier.

—*She-qua-gah* was the Indian name for the Havana Falls, and signified roaring waters.

—Louis Phillippe afterwards King of France, was a guest at the old hotel kept by George Mills in 1797.

—Patrons of Temperance of Havana, organized January 12, 1878. A. S. Durkee, W. S.; R. T. Dearborn, W. P.; Susan Stotenburg, secretary; G. Thompson, treasurer.

—Havana Division No. 55, Sons of Temperance, organized Sept. 1, 1873. Rev. I. Hendricks, W. P.; R. Burchfield, W. A.; P. Hendricks, R. S.; R. Ershine, F. S.; A. S. Durkee, T.

—Montour township derives its name from the Indian half breed Queen, Catharine Montour, who resided at Havana, or within the limits of the township in 1779, and previously.

—Montour Post, No. 22, G. A. R., was instituted Sept 14, 1871. Hull Fanton, commander; E. Miller, S. V.; H. L. Couch, J. B.; A. P. Hallatt, adjt.; Frank Vanduzer, quarter-master.

—Myrtle Lodge No. 731, F. A. M., was instituted March 3, 1860. John E. Mulford, W. M.; A. H. Decker, S. W.; Alpheus Keyser, J. W.; Bela P. Beebe, Treas.; William H. Skellinger, Sec.; M. G. Lewis, S. D.; Daniel L. Couch, J. D.

—The M. E. Church of Havana, was formed as a class, in 1820, organized as a society in 1829, and incorporated in 1835. Church erected in 1832. First trustees were Elijah H. Goodwin, Silas E. Ayres, Elijah White, William Skellinger, Jacob Walker.

—Montour Grange, No. 356, P. of H., was organized Sept. 6, 1875. Master, Joel A. Bailey; Overseer, James P. Shearer; secretary, I. H. Smith; treasurer, George Corwin; Ceres, Mrs I. H. Smith; Pomona, Mrs. Isaac Peck; Flora, Nettie Shearer.

—Havana Literary Library Association was organized in 1872. Elma A. Gillespie, Lucy A. Tracy, Elbert P. Cook, trustees; Miss Mary Hinman, secretary; Willis H. Tracy, treasurer; Mrs. G. W. Carpenter, librarian; Miss Frank J. Hinman, assistant librarian.

—St. Paul's Episcopal church organized April 10, 1856. First rector Rev. Peter S. Ruth; William Skellinger, Adam G. Campbell, wardens; Seth L. King, Edwin H. Downs, Calvin VanDusen, Charles Cook, George T. Hinman, Orvile Harris, Robert P. Beebe, Archibald Campbell, vestrymen. Church erected in the year 1853. Cost $12,000, was the gift of Hon. Charles Cook.

—First Presbyterian Church of Havana, was organized in 1829. The first members were, Flaviel Gaylord, Garrett Compton, William P. Lee, Charles G. Judd, Cyrus Hickox, Lewis B. Butler, Jonathan P. Couch, Stephen P. Butler, Stephen Gabbitt, Abigail Gaylord, Elizabeth Lee, Hannah Denton, Elizabeth Cummings, Alice Hibbard, Harriet Dresser, Lucy Butler, William T. Jackson, John Compton, Eliza Cleveland, Mary Compton, Margaret Cornell. First minister, Rev. James Boyle. First elders, Flaviel Gaylord, Charles G. Judd. Trustees, John D. Downs, Calvin Cooley, David Lee, William P. Lee, Myron Collins, William T. Jackson, John P. Cornell. Church erected in 1832.

—The Northern Central Railroad runs through the town of Montour, from north to south, and has a station at Havana.

—The First Baptist Church of Havana was organized April 10, 1869, by Rev. H. E. Ford. The first officers were, L. C. Crandall, Jacob Yaple, E. W. Cook, deacons; G. W. Hall, E. T. Merritt, Henry Whitford, F. A. Ganung, E. W. Cook, Minor T. Broderick, trustees. Church erected in 1873. The gift of E. W. Cook.

—Montour Cemetery Association organized August 13, 1860. Peter Tracy, president; George W. Jackson, vice president; Dr. George T. Hinman, secretary; John F. Phelps, treasurer; John F. Phelps, George W. Jackson, Adam G. Campbell, George T. Hinman, Peter Tracy, Caleb Hill, Minor T. Broderick, trustees.

—Havana Lodge No. 56, I. O. O. F., was established Feb. 4, 1846. Freeman D. Goodwin, Noble Grand; Green Bennett, Vice Grand; G. D. Bailey, secretary; David Evans, treasurer; Charter members, Green Bennett, J. D. Bailey, George Quinn, Daniel Evans, Freeman D. Goodwin, Alva Nash, Alonzo Gaylord.

—*Than-and-an aga* Encampment No. 38, I. O. O. F., instituted in 1847. First officers George T. Hinman, C. P.; Calvin Spalding, H. P.; G. D. Bailey, S. W.; Caleb Hill, J. W.; H. L. Couch, scribe. Charter members D. L. Couch, Caleb Hill, G. D. Bailey, D. W. Whippy, George T. Hinman, Calvin Van Dusen, Calvin Spalding, H. L. Couch, C. E. Noble.

MONTOUR! HAVANA! SCHUYLER!

These name are very suggestive Montour is of French and Indian origin. Havana of Spanish, and Schuyler of the Dutch Patroons, who first established themselves upon the waters of the Hudson. The name of Montour recalls the early settlement of Canada and the occupation of that country, and a large portion of New York, western Pennsylvania, and the northwest and the south by the French people, and the intermingling of the French and Indian races, the cruel wars waged against the English settlers and their descendants within the present limits of the United States, until the time when French occupation and domination in the territory referred to surrended to the English, and the coalition of the "mother country" or England with these red men to subjugate her own offspring, the American Colonists. Havana recalls the conquest of Mexico by the Spanish, and the islands adjacent, and the wresting of the Andes, and Amazon countries from the aborigines. Schuyler and Montour brings us down to a later, and more local history of our struggles with the English and their allies, the Six Nations, and the cruel deeds perpetrated at Cherry Valley, and in the valley of the Wyoming, and the tributaries of the Susquehanna, and the terrible and just retribution which overwhelmed the Indians in the valley of the Chemung, and in this the very home and garden of the Six Nations. Montour, Havana, and Schuyler county, and the country adjacent is truly historic ground. That one locality should by accident or design assume names so very suggestive of the struggles that have taken place upon the western hemisphere is indeed very remarkable.

It is also very suggestive of the trials, litigations and difficulties that have attended the history of Havana, Montour, and Schuyler county, in contending for their civil rights amid so many rivalries. Montour, Havana, and Schuyler, have survived and grown rich and prosperous as a township, village and county, and to-day with her schools and colleges, her fertile fields, her railroads, and steamboats, the influence of her press, her cascades and glens, her health resorts, and her busy and intelligent population, she maintains a high position among her sister townships, villages and counties in the state.

Orange Township.

The town of Jersey was organized by an act of the legislature of New York, February 12, 1813, as a town in Steuben county—taken from Wayne—and by an act of the legislature passed April 20, 1836, the eastern portion of Jersey township was formed into a town under the name of Orange. A portion of Hornby was annexed April 11, 1842, and part of Bradford township annexed April 17, 1854. It became a town of Schuyler county at its formation in the year 1854. It is bounded on the north by Tyrone and Reading, on the east by Catlin in Chemung county, and Dix and Reading in Schuyler county, on the south by Steuben county, and west by Steuben county. Its principal stream is Mead's creek, which flows south and west and discharges its waters into the Conhocton river. It is situated in the highlands in the south western portion of the county. The election for town officers as the town of Orange was held May 17, 1836, at the house of Alonzo Gaylord. The officers elected were: Alonzo Gaylord, supervisor; Stephen Northrop, town clerk; John Allen, Ira Nash, justices of the peace; Chancey Hewett, Andrew Webber, assessors; Joel Hathaway, overseer of the poor; Matthias Crotchley, commissioner of highways; Myron A. Smith, commissioner of schools; Thomas S. Nichols, Archibald Scoby, inspectors of schools; Benjamin Priest, collector; Abraham Allen, Benjamin Priest, Joseph F. Babbitt, Cornelius Harrington, constables.

Early settlers: Henry Sweitzer, Peter Sweitzer, Jacob Sweitzer, William Sweitzer, Henry Sweitzer, jr., John Sweitzer, Francis Yager, Samuel Skomp, Abram Bosombarach, Frederic Bartles, Isaac Dewitt, Abram Dewitt, Asa Nash, Thomas Hurd, Chapman Miller, Jedediah Miller, Daniel Curtis, Andrew Fort, William Wilkins, Ebenezer Buck, Obediah Phinney, Thomas L. Nichols, William Webb, Dr. Silas B. Hebard, Abram L. Lybolt, Henry Triphagan, Phineas Young, Brigham Young (the Mormon preacher), Jacob Fenner, Henry Miller, Jacob Miller, Joshua Chamberlain, John Dyer, Thomas Dyer, Walter Hurd, Sylvenus Arnold, Darias Hewett, William Conlogue, Miles Hotchkiss, Demas Hotchkiss, Solomon Northrup, Andrew Fort, Daniel Curtis, David Kimball, Henry Gardiner, Jared Stephens, William Dewitt.

—Thomas Hurd kept the first tavern in 1817.

—Walter Hurd opened the first store in the year 1823.

—The first settler was Henry Sweitzer in the year 1802.

—Daniel McDougal taught the first school in the year 1818.

—William Conlogue built the first saw mill and grist mill in the town in the year 1818.

—The first marriage was Abram Bosombarach and Anna Sweitzer.

—Joshua Chamberlain built the first framed house in the year 1819.

—Henry Sweitzer built the first house in the town, in the year 1802.

—Dr. Silas B. Hebard was the first resident physician, in the year 1818.

—Mead's Creek post office was established in the year 1822. David Kimball was the first post master.

—William Dewitt was the original owner of the land where the village of Monterey is now located.

—Henry Sweitzer, William Sweitzer, John Sweitzer, John Dyer, were soldiers in the war of 1812.

—Monterey was originally known as "Gaylord." The name Monterey was given it in the year 1848.

—A number of the settlers were from Orange County, New York, and hence the adoption of the name of Orange.

—The Presbyterians organized the first religious society in the year 1824. Rev. Joseph Crawford was the first minister.

—Brigham Young preached as a Reformed Methodist in the town of Orange—afterwards espoused the Mormon religion.

—Monterey is a village in the town of Orange, containing about four hundred and fifty inhabitants, situated upon Mead's creek.

—Orange Lodge, No. 621, F. & A. M., was organized Sept, 5, 1866: Z. F. Wilder, W. M.; A. J. Van Gorden, S. W.; D. W. Bennett, J. W.; Curtis Maltby, Treas.; W. J. Hummiston, Sec.; Thomas J. Crouch, S. D.; Leroy Gaylord, J. D.; Ephraim Barkley, S. M. C.; John Rowley, J. M. C.; Charles Sedam, tyler.

—The First Methodist Episcopal Church of Orange was organized in the year 1827, by Rev. Peregrine Hallett; First members were: Levi Miller, William Conlogue, Solomon Northrup, Demas Hotchkiss, Jedediah Miller, Miles Hotchkiss, Andrew Fort, Daniel Miller, John Miller. Church erected in the year 1830.

—The Baptist Church of Orange was organized July 15, 1837, by Deacon B. J. Overhiser. In the year 1840 it was made an Independent Church. The members were: B. J. Overhiser, E. Tompkins, S. Dewitt, D. Galtry, P. Andrews, S. Doane, M. Chamberlain, H. Bryant, S. Bancroft, M. Morse, A. Overhiser, L. Burgess, L. Bryant.

—Orange Grange, No. 229, was organized Nov. 26, 1874; First officers: William C. Gray, master; Curtis Maltby, overseer; William H. Bartlett, lecturer; George Chrisjohn, steward; C. Chamberlain, assistant steward; Andrew Ellison, chaplain; D. R. Miller, treasurer; J. C. Merrill, secretary; William Warden, gate keeper; Mrs. C. Maltby, Ceres; Mrs. D. Miller, Pomona; Mrs W. Warden, Flora; Mrs. C. Chamberlain, lady assistant steward.

—Monterey Lodge, No. 1,010, Knights of Honor, instituted April 5, 1878: J. W. Baker, dictator; Lorenzo Alden, vice dictator; G. W. Hummiston, assistant dictator; F. S. Baker, reporter; J. J. Overhiser, treasurer; Alonzo Tucker, financial reporter; A. S. McIntyre, chaplain; W. A. Thomas, guide; J. C. Vine, guardian; Charles Mathews, sentinel; George Kals, past dictator, were the first officers.

—Henry Skomp was the first white child born in the town.

—Presbyterian Church of Mead's Creek was organized January 3, 1824, by Rev. Joseph Crawford. First ruling elders were: Samuel Adams, Henry Gardiner, Jared Stephens. First members: Henry Gardiner, Kate Gardiner, Mrs. Mary Ann Miller, Lyman Johnson, Dorcas Johnson, Mary Chamberlain, Mary Ann Hurd, Sarah Kimball, Darius Hewett, Lydia Hewett, Jared Stephens, Hannah Stephens, Clarissa Hewett, Nancy Kimball, Rebecca Curtis, Daniel Curtis, Sabra Ware, Lucy Goodrich. Church erected in 1834.

Reading Township.

The town of Reading was formed by an act of the legislature, Feb. 17, 1806, as a town in Steuben county, taken from Fredericktown. See also session 47, chap. 171, laws of 1824, and laws of 1854. It is bounded on the north by the county of Yates, on the east by Seneca Lake, on the south by Dix and Orange, on the west by Orange and Tyrone. The town of Reading is beautifully located on the west shore of Seneca Lake, and is rich in the orchard and agricultural products. The Northern Central railroad, and the Syracuse, Geneva & Corning railroad pass through the township.

Early settlers:—John Dow, David Culver, Alexander Hinton, William Roberts, Joseph Roberts, James Roberts, John Roberts, Valentine Hitchcock, Richard Phillips, Elisha Benedict, John French, Samuel Gustin, Elida Parker, Alfred Rich, Anson Rich, James Calvert, Alpheus Calvert, George Calvert, John Calvert, Andrew McDowell, Caleb Fulkerson, Richard Laning, Daniel Shannon, Anson Sutton, Nathaniel Sutton, John Sutton, John Davis, Alpheus Davis, Asaph Corbett, Jason Peck, Erastus Peck, Tenant Peck, Benoni Peck, Lewis Lafevre, Thomas Torrance, John Diven, John Diven Jr., Francis Diven, George Diven, William Diven, John Hurlburt, John Hurley, James Drake, Jonathan Tremain, James Hayes, Alpheus Schofield, Abner Piper, Ichabod Andrews, Amherst Andrews, Daniel C. Norris, Samuel Norris, Samuel Sellen, Wesley Sellen, Zebina Sellen, Major Sellen, John Sellen, William Sellen, Samuel Ross, James Ross, Alexander Ross, William Ross, Samuel Ross Jr., Alonzo Simons Hiram Chapman, Ira Parker, Abner Hurd, Ephraim Ainsley, James Drake, John Carpenter, Chester Corbett.

—The first town meeting was held in 1806.

—Elida Parker built the first saw mill in 1805.

—David Culver opened the first tavern in 1801.

—David Culver Jr., opened the first store in 1806.

—The Methodist erected the first church, in 1818.

—David Culver built the first framed house in 1807.

—The only highway in Reading, in 1807, was the Lake road.

—Judge John Dow harvested the first crop in Reading, in 1798.

—The first birth was Miner Culver, son of David Culver, in 1801.

—Lucy Dow, daughter of Judge Dow, taught the first school, in 1807.

—The post office in Reading was established in 1816. Hiram Chapman first post master.

—Elisha Culver and Susan Diven were married in 1805. The first marriage in the town.

—Reading Center is a station on the Syracuse, Geneva & Corning R. R.

—The Syracuse, Geneva & Corning railroad was constructed through Reading, in 1877.

—The first religious society organized was the Baptist, under the ministration of Rev. Roswell Goff, in 1809.

—John Roberts was the first blacksmith. His anvil was placed on a maple stump, and all out doors was his shop.

—The Jefferson and Canandaigua railroad was constructed through Reading, in 1852. It is now controlled by the Northern Central railroad.

—John Dow was the first settler in Reading, in 1798. He was justice of the peace, supervisor, judge and member of the legislature, and died in 1853. He was from Voluntown, Windham county, Connecticut, and was one of the old vanguards of democracy.

—Reading Grange, No. 50, organized January 15, 1874. J. W. Warner, master; Thomas Ellis, overseer; A. W. Sutton, lecturer; M. W. Sutton, steward; H. D. Skiff, assistant steward; James O'Daniels, chaplain; G. S. Hilliman, treasurer; Isaac Conklin, secretary; Eugene Smith, gate keeper; Mrs. Frank Diven, Ceres; Mrs. Mary Hilliman, Pomona; Mrs. Jane Ellis, Flora, Mrs. Adaline Skiff, lady assistant steward.

—The Baptist Church of Reading was organized January 12, 1833, by Rev. Thomas S. Sheardown, assisted by representatives from Trumansburg Plainville, Tyrone, Hector, Barrington, Elmira, and Southport; Rev. A. Abbott, presided. The first members were John Carpenter, James Hawkins, Ann Weaver, Deborah Hawkins, M. Granby, Margaret Hurley, Benjamin Drake, Russell Skiff, John Hurley, Catharine Drake, Sarah Skiff, Elizabeth Skiff. Church erected in 1835.

—The Second Baptist Church of Reading was organized March 4, 1808, by Rev. Roswell Goff. Its first members were Rhoda Peck, Jerusha Culver, Thankful Davis, James Drake, John Hurlburt, Hannah Hurlburt, John French, Rebecca French, Lewis Lafevre, Nancy Lafevre, John Hurley, Margaret Hurley, John Sutton, Elizabeth Sutton, Elisha Benedict, Thankful Benedict, Ephraim Ainsley, Jessie Whitkin, Sarah Roberts, Susannah Culver, Reliance Wait, Mary Benedict, Anna Hitchcock, Anna Miner, Zelina Ward, Alpheus Calvert, Polly Benedict. Meetings were held in private dwellings and groves, organization dissolved in 1833.

Tyrone Township.

At the forty-fifth annual session of the legislature of New York, April 16, 1822, the town of Tyrone was formed as a township in the county of Steuben—taken from Wayne township. By the act of the legislature in 1845 it became a town in the county of Schuyler. It is situated in the north west corner of the county of Schuyler, and is bounded on the north by the county of Yates, on the east by Yates and the town of Reading, on the south by Orange, on the west by Steuben county. There are two small lakes in the town, known as Lake Lamoka and Lake Wanetta, otherwise Mud Lake or Little Lake. The streams are the big and little Tobyhanna. The surface is broken and uneven but well adapted to grazing. The first election for town officers was held Feb. 4, 1823, at the house of Joseph Hause; Enoch De-

Camp, president of the board of election, and John Arnold, clerk. The officers elected were; William Kernan, supervisor; John Arnold, town clerk; John Sebring, Abram Fleet, overseers of the poor; Benjamin Doughty, Peter Disbrow, Jesse Whitcomb, assessors; Stiles Beach, Michael Jordan, Daniel Childs, jr., commissioners of highways; Abel Kendall, William Kernan, Joseph Jessup, commissioners of common schools; Runyon Compton, collector; Runyon Compton, B. C. Kelley, Constables; Joel Fero, Enoch DeCamp, Sylvanus Arnold, inspectors of common schools; Thomas Humphrey, pound master; John Sebring, Morris F. Hause, Enoch DeCamp, fence viewers: Runyon Compton, George Marrow, Robert Lang, Abel Kendall, Richard J. Beebe, Edward Jessup, Aaron Swartout, William Hause, Levi Price, Watson Prentiss, Ebenezer Russell, Benjamin Smith, James D. Davis, Hugh Jamison, Peter S. Lewis, James Van Duser, B. C. Kelley, Asa Hedge, Enoch DeCamp, William Kernan, Jonathan Compton, William Andrews, Solomon Smith, Abraham Hoover, Joel Mead, George McGowan, Asa Fero, John Smith, Abijah Vining, Solomon Gee, path masters; John Arnold, Benjamin Sackett, Jesse Whitcomb, Henry S. Williams, justices of the peace by appointment.

Early settlers: Joshua Wixson, Elisha Wixson, Thaddeus Bennett, Justus Bennett, Gersham Bennett., Abram Bennett, Albert Stothoff, Abram Fleet, Daniel Foster, Benjamin Harding, Gamaliel Townshend, Zebulon Dean, Harlem Sears, Solomon Wixson, Ephraim Thomas, Sanford O'Conner, Bernard Hedman, Charles McDermostreau, William Kernan, John Teeple, Geo. Teeple, Capt. Sohn Sebring, Daniel Jessup, Joseph Jessup, Edward Jessup, Nicholas Jessup, Hugh Jamison, Henry S Williams, James Clark, Levi Price, James Price, Seth Clark, Benjamin Clark, Joseph Sunderland, Daniel M. Sunderland, John Young, Joseph Young, Phineas Young, Brigham Young, Lorenzo Young, Abel Kendall, Silas Kendall, Lyman S. Kendall, Abel Kendal jr., Stiles Beach, Captain Coon, John Silsbee, Henry Swartout, Benjamin Sackett, William Jordan, Jesse Jordan, Dr. Rogers, Michael Jordan, Obediah Beach, Peter Hanmer, John Arnold, Daniel Arnold, Isaac Arnold, Lyon Gardiner, Robert Lang, Moses Little, Isaac Little, Benjamin Little, James Van Duser, Josiah Gregory, Isaac Van Duser, Phineas Fullerton, Norman Walcott, Jonathan Davis, William Dewitt, Zebulon Dean, John White, Ira Dean, John Jessup.

—John Teeple was the first surveyor in town.

—Hugh Jamison taught the first school in Tyrone.

—John Arnold was the first post master at Tyrone.

—Squire Teeple kept the first hotel in the year 1805.

—Altay was originally known as "Kendall Hollow."

—William Bennett was the first death in the township.

—Daniel Foster was the first blacksmith in the year 1803.

—John Arnold built the first framed house in the year 1816.

—Dr. Charles Waldo was the first physician in the year 1815.

- Elisha and Joshua Wixson were the first settlers in Tyrone.

—Harlem Sears was the first miller in the town in the year 1802.

—The Baptists organized the first religious society in the year 1813.

—Rev. Thomas Brown was the first resident preacher in the year 1820.

—The Bennetts cleared and opened the first farm in the year 1800.

—Joseph Sunderland established the first tannery in the year 1802.

—Wayne village is partly in Tyrone and partly in Wayne township.

—The Pultney estate erected the first grist and saw mill in the year 1802.

—Tyrone village, Altay, Wayne, Pine Grove, are post offices in the town.

—Brigham Young's father, John Young, was a soldier of the revolutionary war.

—Simeon Fleet was born Feb. 1, 1804, the first white child born in the town.

—L. B. Gibson built the first steamboat which plied on Lake Lamoka, Sept. 1, 1878.

—The first stage passed through Tyrone in the year 1821, owned by John Magee of Bath.

—Tyrone township furnished one hundred and twenty soldiers to the Union army in the late rebellion.

—Benjamin Harding and Lucinda Townshend were married in the year 1805, the first marriage in the town.

—Dennis O'Conner opened the first store in the year 1810, and was post master. The office was known as Roscommon.

—The town of Tyrone was named by Gen. William Kernan, an old settler and pioneer, father of United States Senator Francis Kernan.

—Thomas O'Conner, an early resident of Tyrone, was the father of Hon. Charles O'Conner, the distinguished lawyer of New York city.

—Lamoka Lodge, No. 463, F. A. M., was chartered Weston Lodge, June 21, 1859. Its first officers were: William Gulick, W. M.; Horace Dean, S. W.; A. J. Van Gordon, J. W.

—Tyrone Knights of Honor was organized August 12, 1878: David W. Bennett, dictator; James M. Conklin, vice dictator; Charles T. Willis, assistant dictator; Freeman W. Little, F. R.; Benjamin Lawrence, R.; Emerson R. Bissell, P. D.

—The methodist Episcopal Church of Pine Grove was formed as a class in the year 1829. Church erected in the year 1848. First members: Jabez Hanmer, Ellen Hanmer, J. G. Gray, James Smith, Angeline Smith; Ardilla Bost, Harry Gray, Patience Wilber, Austin Wilber.

—The M. E. Church, Tyrone village, organized Oct. 11, 1828, by elder Nathan Dodson. William White was the first class leader. First members: William White, Emily White, Ira A. White, Fidelia White, Stiles Beach, Lydia Beach, Enos Mead, Joseph Carter, Isaac Van Liew, Charles Weller, Stephen H. Arnold. Church erected in 1842.

—Tyrone Baptist Church was organized at the house of David Hite, Nov. 22, 1815, Elnathan Finch, moderator; J. C. Osgood, clerk. First members: Phineas Fullerton Norman Walcott, Jonathan Davis, William Dewitt, Hope Carpenter, Daniel Jessup, Jonas Davis, George Davis, Mehitable Davis, Mary Gilbert, Phebe Carpenter. Elder Phineas Fullerton was the first minister. Church erected in 1830.

—The Baptist Church of Wayne village was organized March, 1819, in Frederick Townshend's barn: Elder Peter Powers, moderator; Elder Samuel Bigelow, clerk. Elder Daniel Sherwood was the first minister. First members: Ephraim Wright, Elizabeth Chase, Lydia Sunderlin Eli Northrop, Joseph Sunderlin and wife, Frederick Townshend and wife, Elizabeth Disbrow. Church erected in the year 1830.

—The Presbyterian Church of Tyrone was organized Feb. 21, 1832, by the Presbytery of Bath. First members: Henry S. Williams, Henry Booram, Lewis Ferris, Runyon Compton, M. W. Comstock, Joel Fero, Cyrus Sebring, Samuel Turner, J. A. McCoy, John Hughey, John Stokes, Daniel Hughey, Robert Sprowl, James Hughey, James Allison, Andrew Herpending. The church erected in 1853.

—The Altay Baptist Church was organized at the house of Thomas Rozell, Dec. 11, 1824. Rev. B. C. Brown was the first minister. First members: Abel Kendall, Thomas G. Corey, William Robinson, Thomas Caswell jr., Beriah C. Brown, Ebenezer Brown, Daniel Brown, Cyrus Maynard, Abel Kendall jr., Josiah Jackson, Silas Kendall, Elizabeth Davidson, Myram Caswell, Mary Owen, Mary Kendall, Mary Corey, Miriam Robinson, Elanor Caswell, Paulina Brown, Orilla Brown, Parmelia Brown, Mary Maynard, Elizabeth Jackson, Elizabeth Kendall, Mary Force, Sophia Force, Eva Kendall, Clarissa Hughey. Church erected in the year 1842.

Watkins Village.

Watkins, the county seat of Schuyler county, situated at the head of Seneca Lake and named in honor of Doctor Samuel Watkins, a prominent land owner, and an early resident, and distinguished citizen is one of the most pleasant and delightful villages in the state. The elegant private residences, the public buildings, its hotels, and the romantic scenery of its glen, and the inviting waters of the lake, make it a great resort for the invalid and those who desire rest and recreation. The views obtained from it and the surrounding hillsides cannot be excelled. Its settlement and history dates back to revolutionary days, and Indian legends are connected with its occupation by the warriors of the Six Nations.

It was known in former times as Salubria, and Jefferson, but was finally incorporated under the name and title of Watkins, April 8, 1852. From the most authentic source (the records having been destroyed,) it is believed that the following named gentlemen composed the first official board of the village. William E. White, Winthrop E. Booth, George C. Quinn, Orlando Hurd, Benoni Peck. Trustees; William H. Williams, treasurer; Enoch Armitage, clerk.

—The first hotel was erected in 1801.

—David Cutler was the first settler in 1788.

—Watkins Gas Light Company organized in 1869.

—St. Mary's Temperance Cadets organized in Jan. 173-.

—The first store was opened in 1815, by Allen & Vedder.

—The Watkins Exchange Bank established July 17, 1876.

—The first church in Watkins was completed May 10. 1833. Presbyterian.

—Duncan S. Magee died May 6, 1869, in the thirty-eighth year of his age.

—The first boat upon Seneca Lake was built by General Charles Williamson, agent for the Putney estate, and plied between the present site of Watkins and Geneva, in 1796.

—Watkins Union School established by an act of the legislature, April 3, 1863.

—The Catholics have fine grounds laid out into a Cemetery near Glenwood.

—The Elmira & Jefferson railroad was opened from Elmira to Watkins, Dec. 3, 1849.

—Fire Department was organized at Watkins in 1853. First foreman James Haywood.

—Hon. John Magee erected a Presbyterian Church in Watkins, in 1867-8 at a cost of $50,000.

—Dr. Samuel Watkins died in 1851, aged about 80 years. He was born on Long Island in 1771.

—St. Mary's Catholic Church erected in 1865, Rev. Father Dennis English priest in charge, cost $23,000.

—Catholic Temperance Society organized in 1876. Thomas H. Barrett, president; John Moran, vice president.

—Hon John Magee removed from Bath to Watkins in 1864, and died April 5, 1868, in the seventy-fourth year of his age.

—The first name of the post office established at Watkins, was known as "Catlin" Nov. 27, 1823, John Diven post master.

—Dr. Samuel Watkins became a resident in 1828, laid out the village, erected the Jefferson House in 1834, and also erected dwellings and stores.

—Post office changed name from Catlin to Salubria, November 2, 1829, and to Watkins Sept. 20, 1852, and July 1, 1874, established as a money order office.

—Canadesaga Lodge, No. 196, I. O. O. F., was organized August 20. 1868, C. Broderick, N. G.; Henry D. Staring, V. G.; J. D. Booth, secretary; H. J. Baldwin, treasurer.

—Seneca Council Royal and Select masters, organized April 20, 1870. Dispensation granted to M. L. Egbert, W. E. Woodward, C. E. Robbins, John H. Ellis, George Norman, George Bradley, Adna Barker, S. W. Cass.

—Ladies Library organized Jan. 1, 1870. First officers, Mrs Lousia H. Dent, president; Mrs. Daniel Beech, Mrs. T. B Sellen, Mrs. Dewitt Freer, Mrs. Mary Roe, vice presidents. Miss Helen Kingsbury, recording secretary.

—First National Bank of Watkins was organized in March, 1864. Capital $50,000; George G. Freer, president; Incorporators, George G. Freer, John Knight, Martin S. Phinney, John B. Hinman, E. L. Sawyer. It was subsequently reorganized as "The Schuyler County Bank."

—St James Episcopal church organized Sept. 14, 1830. Vestrymen, William B. Ireland, Winthrop E. Booth, Alanson G. Everts, Asa A. Norton Charles Tillinghast, Samuel J. Beebe, Ebenezer Harvey, John Mitchell. Church erected in 1831. Trinity Church, New York, donated $300 towards its erection. Rev. Dr. Mason, president of Geneva College, held the first service in the month of August, 1831. New Church erected in 1864, and dedicated August 18, 1866, by Bishop Coxe. Cost of Church $8,000, Rev. Duncan C. Mann, rector.

—Watkins Chapter, No. 182, R. A. M., organized under dispensation June 20, 1864; Isaac S. Marshall, H. P.; David P. Day, K.; Daniel Beech, scribe. Companions, O. W. Lackey, Israel Jocobson, J. J. VanGorder, Daniel Disbrow, David C. Row, Abram Beals, John McIntyre, W. A. Bronson, Lemuel Hudson.

—Presbyterian Church organized Sept. 10, 1818. First members, William Baskin, Catharine Baskin, Elijah Bacon, Ruth Bacon, John Diven, Eleanor Diven, Charles T. Brown, Bradley Thompson, Miss Olive Bacon, Miss Sarah Thompson, Miss Sarah VanZant, Mrs. Anna Norton, Mrs. Polly Smith, Mrs Patty Phinney, Mrs. Jane Baskin, Mrs. Elizabeth Diven.

—The First Baptist Church of Jefferson was organized by Rev. Thomas S. Sheardown, Oct. 2, 1846. First members, John Mosier, Albert Wilson, William Kinner, William Pratt, T. L. McWhorter, R. Russ, Mary Kinney, Caroline Mosier, Sarah Pratt, Emeline Mosier, Lucinda Cass, Charlotte Mosier, Helen Edgertown, Fanny Winfield, Sarah Wilson. Church erected in 1851

—Glenwood Cemetery established March 15, 1865, the donation of Hon. John Magee, and Hon. George Freer, to the trustees of the village of Watkins. It is a beautiful spot upon the hillside overlooking the village of Watkins, and the waters of Seneca Lake. Dr. Samuel Watkins, Hon. John Magee and wife, John Magee Jr., Duncan S. Magee, Hebe Ellsworth Magee, Hon. George G. Freer, and many others are interred in this cemetery.

—Jefferson Lodge, No. 332, F. A. M., was instituted under dispensation Dec. 19, 1853, Lemuel Hudson, W. M.; Abel B. Ferrell, S. W.; Ebenezer Thayer, J. W.; Members George B. Gunnip, Oscar Holden, Benoni Peck, Judson Heath, Alonzo Simmons. Lodge worked under dispensation until August 9, 1854, when the following officers were installed by Brothers James S. French, and Squire Newton, of Union Lodge of Elmira; Lemuel Hudson, W. M.; Judson Hewett, S. W.; Ebenezer Thayer, J. W.; Lot B. Davis, S. D.; William Thompson, J. D.; George B. Guinnip, treasurer; Oscar Holden, secretary; Lemuel H. Thompson, tiler.

TOMPKINS COUNTY, NEW YORK.

Tompkins county was formed by an act of the legislature, April 17, 1817—taken from Cayuga and Seneca. Its lineage extends back to Onondaga, Herkimer, Montgomery, Tryon and Albany counties. It was named in honor of Governor Daniel D. Tompkins. The county of Tompkins when formed contained the towns of Hector, Ulysses, and Covert taken from Seneca county, and the town of Dryden and a part of the towns of Locke and Genoa from Cayuga county. On the 22d of March, 1822, it received accessions to its territory, of Danby, Caroline and Cayuta, from Tioga county, Cayuta afterwards being divided and a portion named Newfield was retained in Tompkins. In the year 1853 a portion of Newfield was attached to Chemung county, and in april, 1854, the town of Hector, which was situated in the north west portion of the county along the banks of Seneca Lake, and containing some of the finest agricultural lands in the county, was detached to aid in the formation of the county of Schuyler. Tompkins, as originally formed, had within its limits quite a portion of Cayuga Lake, and extended westward to the Seneca Lake. For further particulars in relation to formation of townships see township histories in this work. Tompkins county is bounded on the north by Cayuga and Seneca counties, on the east by Cortland and Tioga, on the south by Tioga, Schuyler and Chemung, and on the west by Chemung and Schuyler, and its county seat is Ithaca. Its first county officials were: Oliver Comstock appointed first judge, April 10, 1817; D. W. Bruyn, appointed surrogate, March 11, 1817; Herman Camp, appointed sheriff, April 11, 1819; Herman Bloom, appointed sheriff, June 26, 1817; David Woodcock, appointed district attorney, April 15, 1817. The justices of the peace appointed in 1817 were: W. Wigton, Eliakim Avery, A. D. W. Bruyn, Henry Bloom, Charles Bingham, Nathaniel F. Mack, John Sutton, Simeon F. Strong, Joseph Goodwin, John Bowman, J. Bennett, Samuel Love, John Ellis, William Martin, Peter Rappleyea, Chester Coborn, Thos. White, Richard Smith, H. D. Barto, Caleb Smith, Peter Whitmore, J. Weaver, Stephen Woodworth, Lewis Tooker, John Bowker, Charles Kelley, C. Brown, 2d, James Colegrove, Abijah Miller. The first term of general sessions was held commencing May 28th 1817, in Ithaca, in the town of Ulysses. Present, John Sutton, senior judge; Thomas White, Richard Smith, John Ellis, judges and justices of the peace; Charles Bingham, Parley Whetmore, John Bowman, William Wigton, associate justices. The first petit jury was summoned to appear at the September term in the year 1817, and consisted of Samuel Knapp, Marvin Buck, John Collins, Oliver

Miller, Abner N. Harland, Horace Cooper, John Sniffen, Aaron P. Matthews, John Waldson, Caleb Davis, Augustus Ely, Peter Van Vliet. The first court of common pleas was held commencing on the 4th Tuesday of May, 1817, Senior Judge John Sutton presiding. At this term a grand jury was summoned to appear, by John Ludlow, coroner. The first board of supervisors of Tompkins county met in the year 1817. They were: John Sutton, of Ulysses; Parley Whetmore, of Dryden; Samuel Crittenden, of Division; Richard Townley, of Lansing; Levi Wheeler, of Covert, and Richard Smith, of Hector.

MEMBERS OF ASSEMBLY.—Samuel Crittenden, John Sutton, 1818; Samuel Crittenden, John Sutton, 1819; Herman Camp, Joshua Phillips, 1820; Samuel Crittenden, Peter Hager, 1821; Samuel Crittenden, Peter Hager 2d, 1822; Jacob Conrad, Peter Hager 2d, 1823; Peter Hager 2d, Nicoll Halsey, 1824; Josiah North, Jared Patchin, 1825; Nathan Benson, David Woodcock, 1826; Nathan Benson, Benjamin Jennings, John Sayler, 1827; Amasa Dana, Samuel H. Dean, Josiah Hedden, 1828; Amasa Dana, Samuel H. Dean, Jonathan B. Gosman, 1829; Elijah Atwater, Jonathan B. Gosman, Ebenezer Mack, 1830; John Ellis, Jehiel Ludlow, John Sayler, 1831; John Ellis, Horace Mack, John J. Speed jr., 1832; Thomas Bishop, Daniel B. Swartwood, Ira Tillotson, 1833; George B. Guinnip, Charles Humphrey, Thomas B. Sears, 1834; Charles Humphrey, Parvis A. Williams, Caleb Woodbury, 1835; William R. Fitch, George B. Guinnip, Charles Humphrey, 1836; Lewis Halsey, Benjamin Jennings, 1837; Elbert Curtis, Robert Swartwood, 1838; David Bower, Jesse McKinney, 1839; W. H. L. Bogert, Robert Swartout, 1840; Levi Hubbell, Alpha H. Shaw, 1841; Charles Humphrey, Bernardus Swartout, 1842; Sylvester Larned, George T. Spink, 1843; Peter Lownsberry, Charles M. Turner, 1844; Sherman Miller, Lyman Strawbridge, 1845; James W. Montgomery, Henry S. Walbridge, 1846; Samuel Lawrence, Henry W. Sage, 1847; John Jessup, Alpheus West, 1848; Darius Hall, Chas. J. Roundsville, 1849; Henry Brewer, Elias W. Cady, 1850; Alexander Graham, Benjamin G. Ferris, 1851; Alvan Hunt, Stephen B. Cushing, 1852; David Crocker jr., Ebenezer S. Marsh, 1853; Benj. Joy, Eli Beers, 1854; Frederic S. Dumont, Justus P. Pennoyer, 1855; Wm. C. Coon, Rob't S. Hyde, 1856; Alex. Bower, Elias W. Cady, 1857; Edward S. Esty, 1858; Wm. Woodbury, 1859; Jeremiah W. Dwight, 1860–61; Ezra Cornell, 1862–63; Henry B. Lord, 1864–65; Lyman Congdon, 1866; John H. Selkreg, 1867–71; Anson W. Nettles, 1872–73; William L. Bostwick, 1874; George W. Schuyler, 1875; Samuel D. Halliday, 1876; Silas R. Wicker, 1877; Samuel D. Halliday, 1878; Charles M. Titus, 1879–80; Truman Boardman, 1881; John E. Beers, 1882; John E. Cady, 1883–84; Hibbard Clark, 1885.

SHERIFFS.—Herman Camp, 1817; Henry Bloom, 1817; Nicoll Halsey, 1819; Nicholas Townley, 1821; Ebenezer Vickery, 1825; Thomas Robertson, 1828; Peter Hager 2d, 1831; Minus McGowen, 1834; Jehiel Lucknow, 1837; Edward L. Porter, 1839; Ephraim Labar, 1842; John P. Andrews, 1845; Charles C. Howell, 1848; Lewis H. Van Kirk, 1851; Richard J. Ives, 1854; Smith Robertson, 1857; Homer Jennings, 1860; Edward Hungerford, 1863; Eron C. VanKirk, 1866; Horace L. Root, 1869; E. C. VanKirk, 1872;

Barnard M. Hagin, 1875; William J. Smith, 1878; J. K. Follett, 1881; J. Warren Tibbitts, 1884, present incumbent.

Constitutional Convention of 1821 assembled August 28 and adjourned November 10. Delegates from Tompkins county were Richard Smith and Richard Townley.

Constitutional Convention of 1846; delegates from Tompkins, Thomas Sears, John Young.

The first clerk of Tompkins county was Archer Green, appointed April 11, 1817.

The first congressman from Tompkins county, after its formation, was Hon. Oliver C. Comstock, of Trumansburg.

Stephen B. Cushing was elected attorney general of the state, in 1855.

George W. Schuyler was elected state treasurer in 1863, and appointed superintendent of the banking department in 1866.

By a resolution of the board of supervisors of the county of Tompkins, adopted Nov. 23, 1827, the sum of $4,000 was voted to be raised for the purpose of erecting a county poor house. A committee was appointed, consisting of Samuel Sharp, of Dryden; John Guthrie, of Gates; Sullivan D. Hubbell, of Hector; Elbert Curtis, of Danby; Nicoll Halsey, of Ulysses; Gilbert J. Ogden, of Enfield; John White, of Newfield; Nicholas Townley, of Lansing; Ira Tillotson, of Ithaca; Charles Mulks of Caroline, to select the site and superintend the construction of the buildings. The poor house was erected about four miles from Ithaca.

The Tompkins county court house and jail were first erected in the year 1818. A new court house was erected in the year 1855.

The county of Tompkins consists of nine townships, Caroline, Danby, Dryden, Groton, Enfield, Ithaca, Lansing, Newfield and Ulysses, and a large number of villages and hamlets. The largest incorporated village is Ithaca, situated at the head of Cayuga Lake, covering the valley of the inlet, and extending east and west upon the hillsides. Some of the finest farming lands in the state are found in Tompkins county on the eastern and western shores of Cayuga Lake, and upon the hillsides and plateaus. One of the earliest chartered railroads in the state had its initial point at Ithaca and its termini at Owego. Its public men have been distinguished for their learning, ability and enterprise, filling honorable positions from justice of the peace to governor of the state. Its schools, academies and colleges rank high in the scale of intelligence and efficiency, and its internal improvements in the shape of railroads and telegraphs, although not quite as extensive as some counties, still afford ample facilities for cheap and rapid transportation

Post Offices.—Asbury, Brookton, Caroline, Caroline Centre, Caroline Depot, Danby, Dryden, East Lansing, East Newfield, Enfield Centre, Etna, Freeville, Groton, Groton City, Ithaca, Jacksonville, Lake Ridge, Lansingville, Ludlowville, McLean, Midway, Newfield, North Lansing, Peruville, Pony Hollow, Slaterville, South Danby, South Lansing, Stratton, Taughannock Falls, Trumansburg, Trumbull Corners, Varna, Waterburgh, West Danby, West Dryden, West Groton, Willow Creek.

Hon. David Woodcock, a member of the Tompkins county bar, and a distinguished public man, died at Ithaca in 1835.

Andrew D. W. Bruyn, a distinguished lawyer, died at Washington, while discharging his duties as a member of congress, in 1838.

Amasa Dana, who had represented the county of Tompkins, in the state legislature several terms, and in congress several terms, a distinguished member of the Tompkins county bar, died at Ithaca, December 24, 1867, aged 76 years.

Hon. Charles Humphrey, an old member of the Tompkins county bar, died at Albany, while attending a session of the Supreme Court, July 18, 1850.

Hon. Stephen B. Cushing, a distinguished member of the Tompkins county bar, and Attorney General of the state in 1856, died suddenly in New York City, in 1865.

Tompkins County Agricultural Society organized March 1, 1820. President, William T. Southworth; vice presidents, Alexander Bowers, George Robertson, Peter Himrod, William Morrison, Job Allen; corresponding secretary. Platt Ketchan; recording secretary, Jacob G. Dyckman; treasurer, Luther Gere; auditor, William R. Collins. Committees; Ulysses—James Truesdell, Joseph Goodman, Richard Smith; Hector—Eranthus Everetts, Jason Atwater, Richard Manning; Dryden—Hooker Ballard, James Weaver, Peleg Ellis; Lansing—Edward Walker, John Bowker, Daniel Bush; Groton—Nathan Benson, Admantha Blodgett, Daniel Bradley. Farm Committee; Hector—William Martin, Gilbert Stevenson, Thomas Sears; Ulysses—Samuel Rolfe, John King, John McClellan; Groton—Josiah Willowby, Benjamin Thomas, Isaac Allen; Lansing—John Nettles, James McKinney, Simeon Strong: Dryden—Jesse Stout, Daniel Brown, Amos Lewis. Publication Committee; O. C. Comstock, Thomas Johnson, David Woodcock, Gilbert Seaman, Archer Green. Subscription Committee; Ulysses—Ebenezer Mack, John McClellan; Hector—Peter Hager, Robert Swartout; Dryden—William Wigton, Hooker Ballard; Lansing—John Ludlow, Nicholas Townley; Groton—John Allen, Augustus Crarey.

Tompkins County Medical Society was organized in 1818. Members, Daniel Johnson, George W. Phillips, John W. Phillips, Charles Emmons, Jason Atwater, Israel Young, Augustus Crarey, D. L. Mead, P. A. Williams, Dyer Foote, Alexander M. Comstock, A. J. Miller, C. C. Comstock, A. C. Haight.

A public road was built from Oxford in Chenango county, to Ithaca, during the years 1791-2-3, the contractor was Joseph Chaplin.

In 1804, the Susquehanna and Bath Turnpike was incorporated. It passed through the present towns of Caroline, Dryden, Ithaca and Enfield.

The Owego and Ithaca Turnpike was incorporated in 1807. Road completed in 1811.

The Geneva and Ithaca Turnpike was completed in 1811.

The Cayuga Steamboat Company was organized Dec. 15, 1819. President David Woodcock; Directors, Oliver Phelps, James Pumpelly, Joseph Benjaman, Lewis Tooker; treasurer, Charles W. Conner; secretary, Charles Humphrey; Agent for construction of a boat, Oliver Phelps. The steamer "Enterprise" was launched May 4, 1820, amid great rejoicing. The engine was made in Jersey City. This was the first steamboat on Cayuga Lake, her engine was 24 horse power, the boat was capable of carrying 120 tons. This boat connected with a line of stages from the east, and a line at the foot of the lake for Buffalo.

The "Telemachus" was launched in 1828, the "Dewitt Clinton" in 1829, the "Simeon Dewitt" in 1836, besides a whole fleet subsequently.

The Ithaca & Owego railroad company was incorporated January 28, 1828, and completed in 1834. Its first officers were, President, Francis A. Bloodgood; Treasurer, Richard V. Dewitt; Secretary, Ebenezer Mack; Directors, S. Dewitt Bloodgood, Andrew D. W. Bruyn, Cornelius P. Hermans, Myndert Van Schaick, James Pumpelly, Alvah Beebe. After having a varied history, January 1, 1855, it was leased to the Deleware, Lackawana & Western R. R.

April 9, 1832, a charter was granted to the Ithaca & Geneva railroad. Capital $800,000.

April 16, 1834, the Ithaca & Port Renwick R. R. was chartered.

In Sept. 1820, the Ithaca Canal Co., was organized. Nothing however was accomplished.

The Ithaca & Athens railroad was chartered in 1867. Capital $2,000,000. The road was opened 1871.

The Geneva & Ithaca Railroad Company was organized in 1871. Capital $1,250,000. It was opened in 1873. It is now under the control of the Lehigh Valley Railroad Co.

The Cayuga Lake R. R., was incorporated in 1869. Captial $1,000,000. Opened in 1874. This is also under the management of the Lehigh Valley Railroad Co.

The Ithaca & Cortland Railroad Company organized in 1869. Capital $500,000. Opened in 1871. Finally consolidated under the name of the Utica, Ithaca & Elmira R. R., and recently changed to the Elmira, Cortland & Northern Railroad.

The Catskill & Ithaca railroad was chartered April 21, 1828. Capital $1,-500.00. No road was constructed.

The Ithaca & Auburn railroad chartered in May, 1836, no work done.

The Chemung & Ithaca railroad chartered May, 1837. Capital $200,000. Not constructed.

The Sodus Canal Company organized in 1829. This was a project to unite the waters of the Cayuga Lake with the Ontario, at or near Sodus Point. Never constructed. Charter expired by limitation.

From 1807, to 1857, many stage routes were established, radiating from Ithaca, and John Bartley's friends claim that he was the first stage driver who "tooted" his horn in the village of Ithaca.

The *Seneca Republican* was established July 4, 1815, by Jonathan Ingersoll, and in 1823, its name was changed to "*The Ithaca Journal*" and published by Ebenezer Mack. It has been a great absorber of rival papers. A daily was issued July 1, 1872.

The Ithaca Chronicle was established in 1820, by D. D. Spencer, afterwards issued as the *Ithaca Democrat*.

The Groton Balance was issued in January, 1831, by H. P. Eels & Co.

The *Coon Skinner*, a weekly democratic campaign newspaper, was issued in July, 1844.

The Weekly Ithacan was issued May, 1856, by Asahel Clapp.

The Lake Light, an anti-masonic paper was issued at Trumansburg, Oct. 10, 1827, by Phelps & Broome.

The Anti-Masonic Sentinel was published at Trumansburg, Feb. 5, 1829, by R. St. John.

Trumansburg Advertiser was issued July 4, 1832, by David Fairchild.

Trumansburg Sun was issued Dec. 2, 1840, by John Gray.

Trumansburg Herald was established March 7, 1846, by S. M. Day.

Trumansburg Weekly Independence was issued November 5, 1851, by William K. Creque.

Trumansburg News was issued in 1860, by Himrod & Osborn.

Trumansburg Sentinel issued April 5, 1866, by Oscar M. Wilson.

The Republican Chronicle was established at Ithaca, June, 1820, by Spencer & Stockton.

The Western Messenger was established in Ithaca, in 1826, by A. P. Searing.

The Jeffersonian and Tompkins Times was issued in Ithaca in 1835, by Charles Robbins.

The Tompkins Volunteer was issued in 1840, by H. C. Goodwin.

The Flag of the Union was issued at Ithaca in 1848, by J. B. Gosman.

The Western Museum and Belles-lettres Repository issued at Ithaca, in 1821, by A. P. Searing.

The Ithacan was issued Nov. 28, 1868, by Bragdon & Cunningham.

The Ithaca Daily Leader was issued November 1, 1869, by William A. Burritt.

The Dryden Herald was issued in 1871, by William Smith.

The Groton Journal was issued by H. C. Marsh, Nov. 9, 1866.

The Philanthropist, a Universalist newspaper, was issued in 1831, at Ithaca, by O. A. Bronson.

Rumsey's Companion was issued at Dryden in 1856, by E. D. Rumsey.

The Templar and Watchman was issued at Ithaca, in 1853, by Orlando Lund.

Caroline Township.

The town of Caroline was organized Feb. 22, 1811, then in Tioga county, session 34, taken from Spencer. See also Session 45, Laws of 1822, chapter 75. It is situated in the extreme southeastern portion of Tompkins county, and is bounded on the north by Dryden, on the east by Richford and Berkshire, in Tioga county, on the south by Candor in Tompkins county, and on the west by Danby Its surface is hilly and uneven. The streams of the township run southward, and empty into the Owego Creek, and westward and northward into Cayuga Lake. The name of Caroline was given it by Dr. Joseph Speed, a prominent citizen, in honor of his daughter Caroline. Caroline, Caroline Center, Slaterville, West Slaterville, Speedsville, and Brookton, (formerly Mott's Corners,) are villages in the township.

At an election held for the selection of the first town officers of the township, held at the Bush Tavern, on the second Tuesday of April, 1811,

William Rounsville was elected supervisor; Levi Slater, town clerk; Ephraim Chambers, Nathaniel Toby, Laban Jenks, assessors; John Robison, Nathaniel Toby, Moses Reed, commissioners of highways; Charles Mulks, collector; John Robison, Joseph Chambers, overseers of the poor; Richard Chambers Robert Hyde, constables; Dr. Joseph Speed, Charles Mulks, Robert Freeland, fence viewers; Robert Bush, pound master; Ephraim Chambers, and John Robison, were appointed justices of the peace, by the council of appointment at Albany. After the year 1826, the office of justiec of the peace became elective by the people, and in 1827, Dr. James Ashley, was then elected to serve one year, Milo Heath two years, Aaron Curtis three years, and Dr. Silas Hutchinson four years.

Early settlers:—Capt. David Rich, Mrs. Earlsey, with five sons, and five daughters, named Richard, William, John, Johnson, Joshua, Elanor, Sally, Betsey, Mary, Kate; Gen. John Cantine, John Cantine Jr., Charles Cantine, Moses Cantine, Joseph Chambers, Richard Bush, Hartmore Ennist, Benona Mulks, Levi Slater, John Robison, Lemuel Yates, Mathew Jansen, Benjamin Tracey, Daniel Newkirk, Rev. Garret Manderville, John Rounsevell, Joel Rich, George Vickery, Sylvester Rounsevell, John Doty, Deacon Booth, Jonathan Norwood, Robert Freeland, Henry Quick, Jacob Quick, Augustine Boyer, Robert Hyde, Dr. Joseph Speed, Henry Speed, Aaron Bull, Moses Reed, Joseph Goodrich, Andrew Van Luven, Jonah Cass, Isaac Miller, Nathaniel Gosper, Joseph Smith, Marcus Parmeton, Bartholomew Green, Alexander Stowell, Abraham Boice, Dr. James Ashley, Jonathan Snow, John Taft, Peter Lounsberry, Martin Merrill, Charles Cooper, George Blair, Lyman Cobb, Lemuel Yates, Lyman Rawson, Richard Bush, Laban Jenks, Henry Morgan, Israel Mott, John Mott, Isaac Goodale, Hugh Boyer, Calvin Clark, James Livermore, John Taft, Abel Gates, Ezekiel Jewett, John Groat, Jeremiah Kinney, Joel Rich, Israel Paine, Daniel Hedges.

—The first tavern was kept by Richard Bush, in 1801.

—The first store was opened by John J. Speed, in 1806.

—A log school house was erected in 1802, at Slaterville.

—Speedsville was named in honor of John J. Speed Sr., an early settler.

—The first tannery was built by Solomon Robinson and Daniel Hedges, in 1816.

—Slaterville is named in honor of Levi Slater, the first settler in that vicinity.

—Boiceville, or West Slaterville, was originally named after Abraham Boice, an early settler.

—Slaterville post office was established in 1823, John Robison was the first post master.

—The Caroline post office was established in 1810, Dr. Joseph Speed was the first post master.

—Gen. John Cantine erected the first grist and saw mills, at the place now known as Brookton, in 1800.

—Methodist Episcopal Church of Caroline Center, was organized by Rev George Harmon, in 1820. Church erected in 1825. Cost $1,000. New Church erected in 1866. Cost $3,000.

—The post office at Caroline Center was established in 1838, Hiram S. Jones post master.

—Methodist Episcopal Church of Speedsville, organized as a class in 1820. Church erected in 1851.

—The Reformed Dutch Church was erected in 1820, the first church edifice in the town of Caroline.

—The Universalist Society of Caroline was formed April 26, 1827. Rev. N. Doolittle, the first minister.

—First Baptist Church of Caroline was organized in 1814, Rev. Plin Sabin first minister. Church erected in 1848.

—Captain David Rich was the first settler in the town of Caroline, in 1795, he died in March, 1852, aged 92 years.

—The Caroline Literary Association was organized in January, 1818, and a circulating library was soon after founded by the society.

—Congregational Church of Mott's Corners was formed March 28, 1868. Rev. William A. Hills, first minister, church erected in 1868.

—Lyman Cobb, author of Cobb's spelling book, and a series of school readers, was an early settler of Caroline, and a prominent teacher.

—St. John's Protestant Episcopal Church was first organized at Richford. Established at Speedsville in 1842. Rev. George Watson, missionary; Hiram Bliss, Town Whiton, wardens.

—Caroline Lodge No. 681, F. A. M., was constituted in Nov. 1867. First officers, Dr. W. C. Gallagher, W. M.; Moses Munson, S. W.; Job Norwood, J. W.; R. G. Speed, sec.; R. M. Wood, treas.

—Speedsville Lodge No. 265, F. A. M., was constituted June 11, 1851. The first officers were Robert H. Hyde, W. M.; Thomas Band, S. W.; Lyman Kingman, J. W.; Leonard Legg, sec.; Robert E. Muir, treas.

—Gen. John Cantine, who settled in Caroline, in 1798, was one of the three commissioners to survey and settle the difference between New York and Massachusetts, in regard to the title of Western New York. He erected mills in 1800.

—The Dutch Reformed Church was organized in 1810, by Rev. Garret Manderville. Among it early members were Joseph Chambers, Oakley Bush, Widow Elanor Earsley, her sons William Earsley, and John Earsley, Betsey Yates, wife of Pardon Yates, and daughter of Widow Earsley. Church erected in 1820.

—The First Methodist Class was organized in 1812. First minister in charge was Rev. John Griffin. Nov. 28, 1831, it was organized as the "Garretson Society of the Methodist Episcopal Church," and subsequently assumed under a charter the name of the First Methodist Episcopal Church of Caroline. Church was dedicated in 1834, by Rev. Silas Comfort.

Danby Township.

By an act of the legislature passed February 22, 1811, the township of Danby was formed from Spencer as a township in Tioga county, and in the year 1822 it became a township in Tompkins county, and in the year 1839 a portion of Caroline was attached to it. It is bounded on the north by Ithaca and Dryden, on the east by Caroline in Tompkins county and Candor in

Tioga county, on the south by Spencer in Tioga county, and on the west by Newfield in Tompkins county. The first town election was held March 12, 1811. Stephen Beers jr. was elected supervisor; Uri Hill, town clerk; Nathan Adams, Aaron Bennett, Benjamin Jennings, assessors; John Yaple, Seymour A. Adams, Hudson Jennings, commissioners of highways; Jacob Yaple, Stephen Beers, overseers of the poor; Beardsley Clark, constable and collector; Hudson Jennings, constable; Lewis Beardsley, Hezekiah Clark, John Dumond, John Yaple, fence viewers; Hezekiah Clark, pound master.

Early settlers: John Dumond, Isaac Dumond, Jacob Yaple, John Yaple, Doctor Lewis Beers, Jabez Beers, William R. Collins, Joseph Judson, Elias Deyo, David Clark, Lewis Beardsley, Benjamin Jennings, Hezekiah Clark, John Pumpelly, Philo Hall, Benajah Tichnor, Abner Beers jr., Nathan Beers, Comfort Butler, Nathan Adams, Seymour H. Adams, David Smith, Elbert Curtis, S. Bates, Charles Wright, Samuel Swartout, Thomas Swartout, James Swartout, John Swartout, Abram Swartout, Peter Davis, William Davis, John Masterson, Spencer Elston, Jacob Wise, John Elyca, John Miller, Moses Barker, Uri Hill, Aaron Bennett, Seymour H. Adams, Hudson Jennings, Beardsley Clark, Hezekiah Clark, John Patchen, James Briggs, Isaac Briggs, Moses Banfield, Amos Hall, Leonard Hall, Silas Hall, Isaac Jennings, Joseph Rogers, Luther Foster, Erastus Pierce, James Grimes.

—The first death was Mrs. Rogers, in 1797.

—Hezekiah Clark kept the first tavern in Danby in 1809.

—The first saw mill was erected by John Dumond, in 1797.

—First Presbyterian Church was organized in Danby in 1807.

—The first store was opened by Abner Beers, in the year 1805.

—The first framed house was erected by Dr. Lewis Beers, in 1801.

—The first birth in the town was Isaac Dumond, August 12, 1795.

—Jacob Yaple built the first grist mill in Danby, in the year 1799.

—The first church edifice was erected by the Presbyterians, in 1820.

—The post office was established in Danby, 1801, Lewis Beers, post master.

—Danby Mutual Fire Insurance Company, organized Sept., 1860. Capital $60,000.

—The first school house was erected in the town in the year 1799—Joseph Beers the first teacher.

—Church of New Jerusalem, at Danby, was organized May 30, 1816. Erected a church in 1826.

—South Danby M. E. Church was organized in 1830. Erected a church in 1836. Rev. Peter Compton, first minister.

—The first dwellings were erected by Isaac Dumond, John Dumond, John Yaples, Jacob Yaples, in the year 1795.

—West Danby Baptist Church was organized in 1821. Church erected in 1840, under the pastorate of Rev. Mr. Gross.

—Dr. Lewis Beers, of Danby, was appointed the first judge of the court of common pleas of Tompkins county. He was also the first and only president of the Owego and Ithaca Turnpike Company, which position he occupied for twenty-nine years.

—The Methodist Episcopal Church, West Danby, was organized in 1869. Rev. E. G. Hall, first minister. Church erected in 1870. Cost $3,500.

—Methodist Episcopal Church of Danby was established in 1811, with five members. Incorporated in 1832 and erected a church. Rev. Morgan Freeman was the first minister in charge.

—Danby Pioneer Grange, No. 230, organized Sept. 5, 1874. Joel Banfield, master; Brazella Dorr, overseer; W. E. Chapman, secretary; L. C. Burs, treasurer; Miss Clara Roper, Ceres; Mrs. J. E. Judson Pomona; Miss Mrs. W. E. Chapman, Flora.

—Christ Protestant Episcopal Church, Danby, was organized July 12, 1826. First Rector, Rev. Lucius Carter. Wardens: Daniel Williams, Walter Bennett. Vestrymen: Aaron Bennett, David Marvin, Isaac Jennings, Timothy St. John, Hanford Bradley, Zekiel Sanford, Benjamin Banker, Lawrence VanKleeck. Church erected in 1834. Cost $3,500.

—The Soldiers' Monument Association was organized July 24, 1866. The object of the association was the erecting of a suitable monument to perpetuate the memory of the soldiers from Danby who lost their lives in the defense of the Union during the war of the rebellion. The worthy object was finally accomplished and a monument erected, upon which is inscribed the names of forty-five men who gave up their lives that the Union might be maintained. They are: 137th Regiment, Company K—Ephraim Dunham, died Nov. 18, 1862, aged 21 years; Charles F. Stoddard, Dec. 23, 1862, aged 23 years; Benjamin Clark, died July 2, 1863, aged 19 years; Alexander B. Hance, Oct. 29, 1863, aged 26 years; J. Willis Hance, died Oct. 29th, 1863, aged 20 years; Charles K. Swartout, died May 2, 1863, aged 23 years; Hudson Jennings, died Nov. 27, 1863, aged 24 years; Elijah Ryant died July 17, 1864, aged 42 years. 139th Infantry, Company I—Bradford C. Hallett, died Sept. 30, 1864, aged 23 years; Christopher Piatt jr., died Nov. 24, 1864, aged 30 years; Charles J. Voorhis, died April 2, 1865, aged 21 years; Daniel B. Carson, died April 13, 1865, aged 22 years; William Ostrander, died April 23, 1865, aged 30 years. 109th Regiment, Company A—Hebron Maybee, died Feb. 24, 1864, aged 34 years; Samuel C. Bogardus, died March 3, 1864, aged 20 years; Daniel S. Briggs, died March 16, 1864, aged 51 years; Harrison Little, died May 12, 1864, age 22 years; John G. Nichols, died May 12, 1864, aged 24 years; Daniel H. McPherson, died Aug. 2, 1864, aged 24 years; William H. Debell, died Aug. 19, 1864, aged 20 years; Reuben B. Young, died Aug. 31, 1864, aged 21 years; Abram R. Morse, died Oct. 3, 1864, aged 39 years; Percival S. Foster, died Nov. 3, 1864, aged 20 years; Julius Ostrander, died Nov. 22, 1864, aged 21 years; Marcus Crance, died Jan. 25, 1864, aged 18 years; Theodore F. Angle, died Jan. 25, 1864, aged 24 years; Robert W. Sage, died Sept. 13, 1862, aged 20 years. 21st Regiment Cavalry, Company M—Samuel A. Atwell, died April 10, 1864, aged 18 years; Hamilton M. Schuyler, died Aug. 16, 1864. Company L—Fernando Stanley, died March 24, 1864, aged 26 years. 6th Regiment Artillery, Company B—Lafayette Crance died July 17, 1864, aged 20 years; Peter Westervelt died February 24, 1865, aged 29 years. 16th Artillery, Company A—Thomas Edson died Jan. 30, 1864, aged 26 years; John Deputron, died April 25, 1864, aged 20 years. Company B—Ira Hanford, died March 20, 1865, aged 39 years; Hiram Hanford, died Sept. 23, 1864, aged 27 years; Homer C. Clough, died Dec. 24, 1862, aged 19 years; Charles Whitmarsh died, aged 30 years. 47th Regiment Infantry—Company K—Charles H. Ryant died July 17, 1884, aged 21 years. 64th Regiment Infantry, Co. K—Horace K. Dumond, died July 2, 1865, aged 23 years. 76th Regiment Infantry, Co. F—Henry H. McFall, died Dec. 13, 1862, aged 22 years 86th Regiment Infantry, Company C—George W. Wright, died Nov. 29th, 1863, aged 22 years. 109th Regiment Infantry, Company K—Ira Martin, died July 2, 1863, aged 19 years. Signal Corps—William L. Vorhis, died Nov. 30, 1863, aged 19 years. Pennsylvania Regiment—Edwin L. Beach, died April 27, 1864, aged 28 years.

Dryden Township.

Dryden was formed pursuant to an act of the legislature, as a town in Cayuga county, Feb. 22, 1803, taken from Ulysses, and by an act of the legislature of 1817, became a porti n of Tompkins county. It is bounded on the north by Groton, on the east by Cortland county, on the south by Richford in Tioga county, and Caroline and Danby in Tompkins county, on the west by Ithaca and Lansing, and is one of the largest and most populous townships in the county.

At an election held for the town of Dryden, in the county of Cayuga, now Tompkins, March 1, 1803, at the house of George Robertson, the officers elected were George Robertson, supervisor; Joel Hull, town clerk; John Ellis, Joel Hull, Peleg Ellis, assessors; Daniel Lacey, constable and collector; Phillip S. Robertson, William Garreson, poor masters; William Harned, Ezekiel Sanford, Lewis Fortner, commissioners of highways; Joseph Schofield, David Foot, Ebenezer Clauson, Amnah Peet, fence viewers; John Montayne, pound master.

Early settlers:—Amos Sweet, Ezekiel Sanford, David Foot, Ebenezer Clauson, George Robertson, Phillip S. Robertson, Jared Benjamin, Daniel White, George Knapp, Lyman Hurd, John White, Ruloff Whitney, Nathaniel Sheldon, Peleg Ellis, John Ellis, Joel Hull, James Lacey, Thomas Lewis, Benjamin Lacey, Daniel Lacey, Thomas Lacey, Richard Lacey, Peter Snyder, Christopher Snyder, George Dartt, Henry Naile, Jacob Crutts, Andrew Sherwood, Thomas Sherwood, William Sweazy, James Cooper, Edward Griswold, Abraham Griswold, Seth Wheeler, Seth Wheeler Jr., Enos Wheeler, Jesse Bartholomew, Jacob Primrose, Henry Primrose, Lewis Primrose, Jacob Rhodes, Joseph Hart, Thomas Southworth, John Southworth, Samuel Skellinger, Abram Woodcock, Timothy Owens, Elijah Dimmick, William Miller, Reuben Brown, Ithaman Whipple, Aaron Case, Abner Carpenter, James McKee, Luther Weeks John Horner, John Minnier, Benjamin Fulkerson, Abram Hoagland, Nicholas Hile, Stephen Yeoman, George Gray, Zephoniah Brown, Samuel Girvin, Robert Hollingshed, Ichabod Parmenter, Benjamin Ganung, Henry Teeter, John Cornelius, Joel George, Obediah Brown Jr., Ashael Bouton, Jonathan Luce, Richard White, John Wickham, John Waldron, Israel Brown, Ichabod Barnes, Enoch Pixley, Michael Blue, Nathaniel Luther, John Van Mater, Peter Bush, Morris Bailey, Israel Soutwick, Daniel Ogden, James McElheny,

Nathan Legg, William Callan, Caleb Carr, Peleg Carr, Job Carr, William Smith, Samuel Clark, John Conklin, James Yeoman, Obediah Brown, Lewis Fortuer, William Garreson, William Harned, Amnah Peet, Joseph Schofield, John Montayne, Derrick Sutfin, Jacob Snyder, Samuel Hemingway, Amos Lewis, Isaiah Giles, David Lewis, Benjamin Jennings, Rev. Daniel McArthur, Thomas Jamison, David J. Baker, Rice Weed, Elias W. Cady, Parley Whitmore, Paul Ewers, Capt. John Gardiner, Abram Post, Eli Card, Jacob Van Order, Anson Teeter, Joel Rumsey, Henry Herrington James McLean, Titus Foote, Friendly Williams, Welcome Williams, Jacob Lumbard, Jacob Stickles, Parley Whitmore, Rev. Jeremiah Osborn.

—Joel Hull was the first surveyor.

—Joel Hull opened the first store in 1802.

—Daniel White built the first grist mill, in 1802.

—George Robertson kept the first tavern in 1801.

—George Robertson harvested the first crops in 1798.

—Amos Sweet built the first house in Dryden, in 1797.

—Dr. Nathaniel Sheldon was the first physician in 1797.

—Nathaniel Shelden built the first framed house in 1798.

—Daniel Lacy taught the first school in the town, in 1802.

—The Baptist organized the first religious society in 1804.

—Lyman Hurd brought the first horse into Dryden, in 1800

—Ruloff Whitney built the first saw mill in the town, in 1799.

—Lyman Hurd built the first framed barn in the town, in 1801.

—Gretchen Snyder died in 1802, the first death in the township.

—H. D. Rumsey issued the first newspaper in the town, in 1856.

—John Southworth built the first brick house in the town in 1836.

—The town was named in honor of John Dryden, an English poet.

—Rev. Jeremiah Osborn of the Presbyterian Church, was the first resident preacher.

—The first births in the town were in 1802, a pair of twins to the wife of Lyman Hurd.

—The post office was established in Dryden in 1814, Abrabam Post the first post master.

—Ruloff Whitney was married to Susan Glenny, in 1800 The first marriage in the town.

—The first highway was opened through Dryden by the state, in 1795. It was called the "Bridle Road," Joseph Chaplin was the contractor.

—Phillip Robertson, George Knapp, Benjamin Lacey, Andrew Sherwood, Edward Griswold, Paul Ewers, Capt. John Gardiner, were early settlers and soldiers in the revolutionary war.

DRYDEN VILLAGE.

At the first election held in the village of Dryden for the selection of village officers, Aug. 15, 1857, D. P. Goodhue, Rochester Marsh, Isaac Ford, John B. Sweetland, William W. Tanner were elected trustees; Augustus H. Phillips, Orrin W. Wheeler, John C. Lacey, assessors, Godfrey Sharp, collector; Horace G. Fitts, treasurer; Thomas J. McElheney, clerk; Godfrey Sharp, pound master. The trustees selected, David P. Goodhue, president.

The committee appointed by Judge Wisner to hold the election consisted of Edwin Fitts, John B. Sweetland, S. D. Hamlin. It is reported that Peter Snyder in 1874, held a family re-union, at which five hundred and forty of his descendants were present.

The First Baptist Church of Dryden was organized Feb. 29, 1804. Samuel Hemingway, deacon; John Wichkam, clerk. Members, Francis Miller, Elijah Denmick, Silas Brown, Ebenezer Brown, Nathaniel Luther, Job Carr, Ziba Randall, Timothy Owens, Jonathan Dunham. Henry Dunham, Joshua Jay, Abraham Woodcock, Nathan Dunham, Joel Whipple, Samuel Skellinger, Morris Bailey, Orpha Luther, Asher Wickham, Mehitable Carr, Betsey Brown, Abigail Dimick, Mary Owens, Lucy Dunham, Kate Woodcock; Rev. Mr. Shedd the first minister.

—Dryden Village has a fire department.

—Great fever and ague epidemic in 1804.

—Dryden Lodge, No. 472, F. A. M., was organized March 20, 1859.

—Dryden Lodge, No. 390, I. O. O. F., was instituted May 15, 1875.

—Dryden furnished 333 soldiers to the Union army during the late rebellion.

—During the war of 1812, only fourteen settlers were left at home. The others had gone into the service.

—Etna Grange, No. 387, was instituted in April, 1875. A. L. Tyler, master; William Hanford, overseer; G. E. Hanford, secretary.

—Methodist Episcopal Church of Dryden Village, was organized as a class in 1816, by Rev. AlvinTorry, an initinerant. Church erected in 1832. First resident minister in charge was Rev. J. T. Peck.

—The Dryden Agricultural Society was organized in March, 1856. Officers, Elias W. Cady, president; Jeremiah Snyder, vice president; David P. Goodhue, treasurer; Otis E. Wood, secretary.

—The M. E. Church, West Dryden, was formed in 1811, as a class by Rev. George Densmore. Members of class, Shelden Andrus, and wife, Samuel Fox, and wife, David Case, and wife, Sarah Freeman.

—The First Methodist Episcopal Church of Etna, was organized April 13 1835. Church erected in 1837, trustees, Dr. Harris, James Freeman, John H. Porter, Alva Carr, Oliver Baker, Michael Vanderhoof, Richard Bryant.

—A special town meeting was held July 9, 1814, for the election of the first board of school commissioners. Joshua Phillips, John Ellis, and Peleg Ellis were chosen. The total amount disbursed that year for salaries of twelve teachers was $192.47.

—The First M. E. Church of Varna was formed Jan. 5, 1842. Church erected in 1843. Rev. W. H. Miller, first minister in charge; trustees, Hoffman Steenberg, Isaac Seaman, William Cobb, John Munson, Robert C. Hunt, George Emmons, Benjamin Davenport.

—Freeville is the railroad center of the town of Dryden. The Utica, Ithaca & Elmira, now the Elmira, Cortland & Northern, R. R., the Owego & New York, R. R., the Southern Central R. R., the Delaware, Lackawanna & Western, R. R. converge at Freeville.

—Catholic Church of McLean Village, was formed in 1841, at the house of Michael O'Byrne. Church erected in 1851. First communicants, Michael

O'Byrne, John Keenan, Patrick Corcoran, Mathew O'Byrne, James Walpole, Patrick Kane, Thomas Kane, Patrick Donnelly.

—The First Presbyterian Church at Dryden, was formed by Rev. Jabez Chadwick, Feb. 17, 1808. Members, James Wood, Stephen Myrah, Benjamin Simons, Derrick Sutfin, Abraham Griswold, Juliann Turpening, Anson F. Griswold, Isabel Simons, Rebecca Myrah, Sarah Wood, Elizabeth Tappan, Jerusha Taylor. In 1816, Rev. Jeremiah Osborn became the resident minister, church erected in 1821.

Enfield Township.

The town of Enfield was organized by an act of the Legislature at its 44th session, March 16, 1821, taken from the southern portion of Ulysses. It is bounded on the north by the town of Ulysses, on the east by Ithaca, on the south by Newfield, and on the west by Hector, Schuyler county. It is situated in the highlands between the Cayuga and Seneca Lakes.

The early settlers were John Giltner, Judah Baker, Ashel Lovell, John White, Peter Banfield, John Applegate, Gilbert Longstreet, Samuel Rolfe, Daniel Konkle, Joseph Rogers, Isaac Beach, John Beach, James Bailey, James Rumsey, Isaac Rumsey, Benjamin Ferris, Timothy F. Nobles, Squire J. Nobles, John Nobles, Amos Ogden, Gilbert J. Ogden, John Cooper, Reuben D. Lyon, Abram Longcoy, Isaac Chase, James Newman, Nathaniel Newman, Elder Ezra Chase, David Thatcher, John Townshend, Orson Bostwick, T. J. Porter, John Sheffield, Samuel Harvey, Jesse Harriman, Walter Payne, Charles Woodward, J. B. Williams, F. S. Williams, Jarvis Langdon, Oliver Rumsey. Christopher Miller, David Atwater, Jonathan Rolfe.

—Moses Lovell was the first postmaster.

—The first settler was John Giltner in 1803.

—Judah Baker set out the first orchard in 1806.

—Walter Payne was the first supervisor in 1821.

—Benjamin Ferris built the first saw mill in 1812.

—The first church organized was the Baptist in 1817.

—The first resident minister was Elder Chase in 1813.

—Isaac Rumsey built the first grist mill in the town in 1817.

—John Applegate opened the first tavern in the town in 1807.

—The Christian Church of Enfield was organized in 1821, by Rev. Ezra Chase.

—The first school house was erected in 1809. William Bundy was the first teacher.

—Jesse Osborne and Rachel Chase were married in 1809—the first marriage in the township.

—The M. E. Church of Enfield was organized January 19, 1835. Rev. Joseph Pearshall the first minister in charge,

—The Presbyterian Church of Enfield was organized February 14, 1832, Rev. William Page, of Ithaca, supplying the pulpit. In 1835 a church was erected. February 28, 1838, Rev. Warren Day was stated preacher and remained six years. Mr. Jarvis Langdon, afterwards a distinguished and prominent citizen of Elmira, was at one time a member of this church.

—The Baptist Church of Enfield was instituted in 1817. Rev. John Lewis, first preacher, erected a church in 1842.

—In 1823 a French Canadian by the name of Francis Dezaac, having some misunderstanding with some farmers of Enfield and Ulysses, went to Canada and gathered a quantity of Canada thistle blows or seed and returned and stealthily sowed them over several fallows, and along the highways of those towns and escaped from the country. But the mischief he committed sixty odd years ago has not been remedied, and has cost the farmers of Tompkins, Seneca and Cayuga thousands of dollars.

Groton Township.

The town of Division was organized at the 40th session of the legislature of the state of New York, April 7, 1817, and at the 41st session, March 31, 1818, it was changed to Groton. Taken from the town of Locke. It is situated in the north-eastern portion of Tompkins county, and is bounded on the north by Cayuga county, on the east by Cortland county, on the south by Dryden and west by Lansing.

At a town meeting held pursuant to an act of the legislature, April 15, 1817, the officers elected were Samuel Crittenden, supervisor; Admantha Blodgett, town clerk; Benjamin Williams, Nathan Benson, William Cobb, assessors; Ezra Loomis, collector; Ezra Carpenter, David Morton, overseers of the poor; Jonathan Bennett, Isaac Allen, John Benedict, commissioners of highways; Spencer Crary, Jenks Carpenter, Ezra Andrews, constables and pound masters; Ezra Carpenter, Nathan Benson, James Luther, commissioners of schools; Joshua Dean, Amantha Blodgett, Seth Blood, Sumner Brown, John Hale, Daniel Ladd, inspectors of common schools. At this town meeting a large number of path-masters, etc., were chosen, which will give the reader a fair idea of the names of the early settlers and residents of the town sixty-eight years ago. District No. 1, James Henshaw; No. 2, Ezra Andrews; No. 3, Luther Trumble; No. 4, Eber Curtis; No. 5, Alanson Campbell; No. 6, John Orr; No. 7, Seth G. Goodin; No. 8, William Crary; No. 9, Ezra Hollister; No. 10, Isaac Allen; No. 11, John Howe; No. 12, Edward Perry; No. 13, Joshua Stevens; No. 14, Thomas Jones; No. 15, James Austin; No. 16, Abner Atwood; No. 17, Henry Homer; No. 18, John Newland; No. 19, Samuel Chapman; No. 20, Daniel Ogden; No. 21, Michael Grummon; No. 22, Henry I. Brinkerhoff; No. 23, David Niven; No. 24, Daniel Bill; No. 25, Jeremiah Dimon; No. 26, Zadoc Weeks; No. 27, Asa Maine; No. 28, Richard Francis; No. 29, Ashbel West.

Early Settlers:—John Perrin, Ebenezer Williams, Ezra Carpenter, Lemuel Perrin, S. J. Carpenter, Ephraim Spalding, Michael Grummon, Ezra Loomis, Samuel Ingalls, Silas Stuart, Jonas Williams. Samuel Crittenden, Christopher Pipher, Asa Church, Henry I. Brinkerhoff, Sylvenus Larned, Dr. Wright, Thomas Johnson, Jeremiah Elston, Daniel Luther, Dr. Nathan Branch, Jonathan Bennett, Peleg Hathaway, Abiatha Hathaway, Ezra Loomis, Samuel Ingalls, Silas Stuart, Benjamin Williams, David Hicks, William Hicks, James Hicks, Abner Atwood, Capt. Daniel Niven, Lemi Bradley, Jesse Bartholomew, Aaron Benedict, John Benedict, William S. Clark, William Cobb, Daniel Maltby, Zackeus Maltby, John Shaw, Daniel

J. Shaw, Amos Cobb, Anson Hanchett, Nicholas Rowe, Rev. Benjamin Whipple, David Whipple, Jonathan Whipple. John Guthrie, Samuel Hogg, Joseph Alling. Joseph Henshaw, Henry Carter, David Morton, Morderica Morton, Andrew Leonard, Zackeus Morton, Joseph Allen, Araph Allen, Isaac Allen, Luther Trumble, Luther Trumble jr., Simon Loomis, Nathaniel Loomis, Luther Loomis, Edward Loomis, Daniel Loomis, Dr. Richard Lanning, Samuel Noyes, G. J. Ackley, Joseph S. Hart, Amasa Cobb, Daniel Marsh, John Benedict, Daniel J. Shaw, Samuel H. Starr, John Neill, Newell F. Murdock, Nicholas Barney, Amos Norton, Abram Byington, Jesse Read, Adam Bullard, William Randall, Roswell Randall.

—Samuel Love was the first tanner.

—John Perrin made the first brick in the town.

—John Perrin was the first merchant in Groton.

—John Perrin built the first house in Groton in 1797.

—Jonas Williams built the first framed house in 1807.

—Benjamin Williams was the first postmaster in 1812.

—The Baptists erected the first framed church in 1819.

—Ebenezer Williams planted the first apple tree. in 1798.

—Andrew Allen and David Allen were the first blacksmiths.

—Dr. Nathan Beach was the first resident physician in 1803.

—Jonathan Bennett was the first jutsice of the peace, in 1805

—The Congregationalists organized the first religious society in the town in 1805.

—Chauncey Trumble was the first superintendent of a Sunday school in the town.

—The first marriage in the town was Jonas Williams jr., to Miss Hathaway in 1805.

—Jonas Williams built the first saw-mill in 1810. He also built the first grist mill in 1812.

—The first school house erected in the town was in 1805. It was made with hewed logs.

—Congregational Log Church erected in 1810. It was the first church edifice in the town.

—M. E. Church of McLean Village was formed in 1829. Church erected in 1832. Cost $1,500.

—Ebenezer Williams was the first surveyor in the town. Samuel Crittenden came in soon after.

—Rev. Benjamin Whipple, David Morton, Admantha Blodgett, Simon Loomis, early settlers of Groton, were soldiers of the revolutionary war.

—Groton village was incorporated June 11, 1860, by order of the judge of Tompkins county. F. H. Robertson, Harvey D. Spencer and John G. Stevens, were directed by the court to hold the first election for village officers. In pursuance of the order an election was held July 7, 1860, at the house of Dexter Allen. Officers elected were Robert C. Reynolds, Philander H. Robertson, William Williams, William Woodbury, Daniel S. Delano, trustees; Lyman Perrigo, Horace Williams, assessors; J. Nelson Lester, collector; F. C. Reynolds, treasurer; D. V. Linderman, clerk; T. C. Joy, pound masters.

—Rev. Benjamin Whipple was the first resident minister in 1805.

—St. Mathew's Protestant Episcopal Church organized in 1817, by Rev. William A. Clark.

—Roman Catholic Church organized in 1870, by Rev. Father Gilbert, of Ithaca, erected a brick church in 1873. Cost $3,000.

—Groton Academy founded in 1832, Prof. S. W. Clark, first principle. It is now known as Groton Union Graded High School.

—Baptist meetings were held at McLean, as early as 1805, by Rev. Benjamin Whipple. Church organized Jan. 24, 1824. Elder Platt was the first resident minister. Amos Hart, Ithaman Whipple, first deacons. Church erected in 1828.

—M. E. Church of Groton Village was incorporated July 18, 1836, by Rev. L. H. Reddington and Justus P. Pennoyer. First trustees Justus P. Pennoyer, Josiah P. Ingraham, Augustus C. Marsh, Hiram Young, Daniel Tarbell, Simon Loomis, church erected in 1842.

—Groton Lodge, No 496, F. & A. M., organized in May, 1869. First officers, Dexter Allen, W. M.; Martin S. Delano, S. W.; Norman Gibbs, J. W.; Albert Osmond, secretary; Orrin Clark, treasurer; S. S. Reynolds, S. D.; J. Lester Jr., D.; Leonard Stoddard, tiler.

—Zion Protestant Episcopal Church of McLean Village incorporated Sept 23, 1833. Samuel Starr, Heber Foote, wardens; Miles Riggs, Alva Jarvis, Richard Lanning, Adolphus Jarvis, William Braybook, Philo Beers, Erastus Bradley, vestrymen. Rev. Humphrey Hollis first rector. Church erected in 1849. Cost $1,000.

—The First Baptist Church of Groton Village was organized August 27, 1806, by a committee from several churches in the adjoining section of the country. It was termed the First Baptist Church of Locke, but changed its name from Locke to Groton when the name of the township was changed in 1818. At its organization the members were Ezra Luther, Lemuel Perrin, David Morton Jr., John Lee, Andrew Leonard, Alfred Carder, Alanson Thomas, William Fisk, Oliver Luther, Benjamin Luther, Asa Luther, Nathaniel Luther, Daniel Luther, Enoch Benedict, David Whipple, Benjamin Whipple, Benjamin Thomas, Anson Hanchett, John Perkins, James Smith, James Luther, Ebenezer Thomas, Smith Covert, Jonas Williams, Jenks Carpenter, Daniel Pierce, Elijah Moore, Joel Whipple, Rebecca Luther, Sarah Whipple, Mary Luther, Amelia Perrin, Sarah Lee, Mary Benedict, Hannah Pipher, Oliver Hinman, Christiana Fisk, Hannah Luther, Nancy Luther, Beulah Luther, Asenath Thomas, Abigail Burrows, Deborah Morton, Ann Leonard, Orpha Luther, Jerusha Perkins, Mercy Hathaway, Rhoda Carpenter, Mary Williams, Jane Moore, Lydia Whipple, Prudence Carpenter, Elanor Williams, Elsie Thomas, Hannah Hathaway, Mary Kennedy, Rebecca Pierce, Phebe Pierce, Rebecca Morton, Mary Morton, Sarah Thomas, Jane Stewart, Patty Perrin, Ruth Carpenter, Jane Bevina, Lucy Vanarsdale. The first baptisms were Enoch Benedict, Benjamin Luther, Mary Benedict, Nancy Luther, Olive Luther, Alfred Carder, Asa Luther. Oct. 11, 1806, Benjamin Thomas, Asa Luther, James Smith, were chosen deacons. Elder Starr was the first minister. Church erected in 1819. The church exercised a broad influence over that section of the country.

—Groton furnished 385 soldiers and one seaman in the late rebellion.

—First Wesleyan Methodist Church of Groton was organized in 1844.

—The Elmira, Cortland & Northern railroad, and the Southern Central railroad pass through the town of Groton, each having several flag and other stations.

—First Universalist Society of Groton was organized April 21, 1832. Rev. Walter W. Bullard, was the first minister, Caleb Woodbury, Eben Mix, Abraham Phinney, Daniel Ladd, Sylvenus Larned, Hiram Byington, first trustees. Church erected in 1843. Cost $3,000.

—First Christian Church of Groton was organized in 1831, by Rev. Ira Brown. First members, Thomas Sherman, Clark Reynolds, Hannah Sherman, Israel Thompson, Solomon Loomis and wife, Abigail Brown. First deacons, Solomon Loomis, Thomas Sherman. Church erected in 1833. Cost $1,200.

—The first National Bank of Groton was charted May 1, 1865, Capital $100,000. First officers, Charles Perrigo, president; S. Hopkins, vice president; D. H. Marsh, cashier; Charles Perrigo, Lyman Perrigo, Clinton Bowker, D. H. Marsh, John Green, S. Hopkins, S. C. Reynolds, John G. Stevens, A S. Beach, C. P. Atwood, Henry Allen, John W. Halladay, Artemus Backus, directors.

—The Congregational Church of Groton Village was organized March 12, 1849. Its first trustees were Sylvenus Delano. Stephen H. Shaw, William Allen, Calvin C. Goodley, Claudius B. Jewell, Orlando Childs. Church dedicated January 29, 1851. Cost $3,000. Building committee, William Allen, J. J. Reynolds, R. C. Reynolds, Orlando Childs. First minister Rev. H. A. Sackett.

—Congregational Church of West Groton was organized in December, 1816, at the house of Ichabod Brown, by Rev. Joshua Dean. The original members were John Hall, Ichabod Brown, Dinah Whiting, John Seaton, James Travis. John Seaton was the first deacon and clerk. In 1817, Daniel Brown, Rebecca Steves, Christianna Hogg, William Tallman, Olive Brown, Anna Tallman, Mary Seaton, Mrs. Miller, Susannah Allen, William Whiting were taken as members. Rev. Isaac Eddy was the first minister. Church erected in 1833.

Ithaca Township and Village.

By an act of the legislature passed at its 44th session, March 16, 1821. Ithaca was formed, taken from Ulysses. It is bounded on the north by Ulysses and Lansing, on the east by Dryden, on the south by Danby and Newfield, and on the west by Enfield. It is situated at the head of Cayuga Lake. It has a genealogy running back through the history of the counties of Cayuga, Seneca, and Onondago. In 1794, it was a town in Onondago county.

April 3, 1821, at a town election for the town of Ithaca, in Tompkins county, held at the court house Nathan Herrick was elected supervisor; Isaac Beers, town clerk: Caleb Davis, William P. Burdick, Richard Pew, assessors; Ebenezer Vickery, collector; Eliakim Dean, Jesse Merrick, overseers of the poor; David Coddington, Joseph Pew, Moses Davenport, com.

missioners of highways; Amasa Woodruff, Ebenezer Vickery, constables; Andrew D. Bruyn, John Johnson, John Whiton, commissioners of common schools; Isaac Beers, Reuben Judd, Benjamin Pelton, inspectors of common schools; William T. Southworth, Charles Humphrey, Luther Gere, commissioners of schools and Gospel Lot; David Curtis, pound master.

Early settlers:—Jacob Yaple, (Iable,) Isaac Dumond, Peter Hinepaw, William Van Orman, Robert McDowell, Ira Stevens, Jonathan Woodruff, Abraham Smith, Joseph Smith, Nehemiah Woodruff, Charles Woodruff, Richard Loomis, Walter Wood, George Sager, Simon Sager, Bezeal Holley, Abram Lightfoot, Abram Markle, Henry Markle, Isaac Patchin, Abram Davenport, Benjamin Pelton, Richard W. Pelton, Richard Pangborn, Abram Johnson, Jeremiah Jeffrey, Joseph S. Sidney, Jonas Whiting, John Smith, Archer Green, Jabez Hanmer, Francis King, Moses Dewitt, William R. Collins, John Landon, Caleb B. Drake, David Woodcock, Joseph Burnett, Luther Gere, Ebenezer Mack, Horace Mack, Benjamin Ferris, Jeremiah S. Beebe, David Quigg, David B. Beers, William Leslie, Charles Humphrey, Roger Delano, Peter Bois or Boyce, Jacob S. Vrooman, Oliver Wisewell, Stephen Segwick, Peter Chesebrough, Hudson Gaskill, Henry Ackley, Julius Ackley, Marcus Stigney, Henry Hibbard, John McDowell, Thornton Fleming, Elias De Pew, Garret Shoemaker, Cornelius Shoemaker, Benjamin Johnson, Salmon Buell, Edward Davids, Daniel Bates, Comfort Butler, George Carpenter, William Butler, Timothy Hollister, Otis Eddy, Nathaniel Davenport, George Blythe, Jacob Shepard, Henry Stringer, James Johnson, William R. Collins, Ira Tillotson, Joseph Benjamin, Higbee Burrell, Samuel Benham, Thomas Downing, Herman Camp, Henry Bloom, Alexander Smith, Henry McCormick, John McCormick, Barney Gibbs, Levi Williams, Isaac Teeter, Edward Oliver, Rev. Doctor Baker, Walter Wood, Peter Fisher, Dr. Hartshorn.

—John Belcher was the first singing teacher.
—David Quigg was the first merchant in 1801.
—Ithaca Gas Works were established in 1853.
—Robert Maines was the first barber in Ithaca.
—Oliver Wisewell was the first lawyer in Ithaca.
—The Ithaca academy was incorporated in 1823.
—Rachel Allen was the first death in the year 1790.
—Gardner & Butler were the first tanners in Ithaca.
—Ithaca Fire Department incorporated April 1. 1871.
—The first physician who located was Doctor Frisbee.
—Peleg Chesebrough was the first tailor in Ithaca in 1799.
—Hudson Gaskill was the first blacksmith in Ithaca in 1798.
—Horace King published the early history of Ithaca in 1847.
—William Linn published a life of Thomas Jefferson in 1834.
—Abram Markle built the first framed house in the year 1800.
—Eureka Fire Company No. 4 was organized March 11, 1842.
—Torrent Bucket Company No. 5 was organized March 2, 1843.
—June 15, 1825, Ebenezer Mack established a circulating library.
—Luther Gere built the first tavern in 1805 in the town of Ithaca.
—The first minister was Rev. Garret Mandeville in the year 1805.

—A public well was dug in the year 1821.

—Ebenezer Mack published a life of Lafayette in Ithaca in 1841.

—Lyman Cobb first published his spelling book in Ithaca in 1821.

—Cataract Engine Company No. 7 was formed December 31, 1863.

—The First Unitarian society was organized in November, 1865, by Rev. William H. Fish.

—Abram Davenport, married to Mary Johnson 1798, was the first marriage in the town.

—The Presbyterian church was organized January 24, 1804, by Rev. Jedediah Chapman.

—Cornell free library was incorporated April 15, 1864. Was dedicated December 20, 1866.

—The first post-master was appointed by President Jefferson in 1804 at Ithaca, Richard W. Pelton.

—Methodist Theological and Historical Library association established in 1821. David Ayers, librarian.

—The Free Methodist church was formed November 6, 1871. Trustees, William Webley, William Sullivan, Ezekiel Osborn.

—First National Bank of Ithaca was organized in 1864. Capital $150,000. Ebenezer T. Turner, president; Alonzo B. Cornell, cashier.

—Catholic church erected in 1835 by Rev. Father Gilbride. Subsequently a new church was erected under the direction of Rev. Bernard McCool.

—The Merchants' and Farmers' Bank was organized April 18, 1838, capital $150,000, by Timothy S. Williams, Manwell R. Williams, Josiah B. Williams.

—Ithaca Water Works incorporated June 25, 1853, Henry W. Sage, Alfred Wells, Charles E. Hardy, Anson Spencer, Joseph E. Shaw, were the incorporators.

—September 24, 1831, the New Jerusalem Church library was formed; Isaac N. Beers, Jesse D. Smith, Benjamin G. Ferris, Harvey Bailey, Lewis Beers, trustees.

—The Tabernacle Baptist church was organized June 17, 1870. Trustees, Franklin Hooker, William R. Norton, Nathan McKean, John Linderberry, Bennett J. Mix.

—St. John's Episcopal church was organized April 8, 1822. Prior however there had been services held. Rev Samuel Phinney was the first rector. Church erected in 1824.

—Reformed Protestant Dutch church was organized April 2, 1830, by Rev. John H. Schemerhorn. The first services were held in the court house. Church erected in 1831.

—In 1826 the Ithaca Methodist Literary society was formed. Henry H. Moore, Benjamin S. Cook, C. J. Heath, Ithiel Potter, John Perkins, Amasa Dana, David Ayers, trustees.

—Mr. Howe was the first school teacher in Ithaca in 1804. He was the forerunner of the grand army of pedagogues who have pursued their labors in Ithaca from that day to the present.

—St. Paul's Episcopal church was organized September 30, 1874. Wardens, William D. Willson, Willard Fish; vesterymen, Charles Babcock, J. M McMurray, Robert Richardson, T. F. Crane, John Snaith.

—A branch of the Bank of Newburgh was established in Ithaca in April, 1815, Charles W. Conner, Cashier; William R. Collins, Luther Gere, Benjamin Drake, Andrew D. W. Bruyn, were directors.

—Ithaca Savings Bank was organized April 17, 1863. Did no business. Charter revived April 3, 1868. Ezra Cornell, president; William Andrus and George W. Schuyler, vice-presidents; O. B. Curran, treasurer and secretary; F. L. Finch, attorney.

—First Baptist church of Ithaca was organized in Danby in 1821, and transferred to Ithaca October 18, 1826, the first meeting being held in the court house; Rev. O. C. Comstock minister in charge. A brick church was erected in 1831 costing $7,000.

—October 2, 1818, at a public meeting it was resolved to construct a school house. John Woodcock, James Collier, were appointed a subscription committee. The result of this meeting and subsequent meetings was the incorporation of the Ithaca academy in 1823.

—The African M. E. Zion church was formed December 16, 1833, with seventeen members. Trustees, William Augustus, Francis Collins, James W. Lewis, William Newcomer, John Wilkins, David Hector, Thomas Jackson, James Collins, John Shaw. The first minister was Rev. Henry Johnson.

—Bank of Ithaca was chartered in 1829, capital $200,000, Luther Gere, Ansel St. John, Cashiers; Andrew D. W. Bruyn, Daniel Bates, James Nichols, Benjamin Drake, Jeremiah S. Beebe, Henry Ackley, Calvin Burr, William Randall, Stephen Tuttle, Jonathan Platt, David Hanmer, Ebenezer Mack, Directors.

—Tompkins County Bank was chartered in 1836, capital $250,000, Herman Camp, President; Seth H. Mann, Cashier; Timothy S. Williams, Jeremiah S. Beebe, Horace Mack, William R. Collins, Robert Halsey, Edmond G. Pelton, Julius Ackley, Chauncey L. Grant, Moses Stevens, Edward C. Read, Charles Davis, Augustus C. Marsh, Directors.

—Hook and Ladder Company No. 3, was organized January 31, 1831, members—Benjamin Drake, Erasmus Ballard, David Woodcock, Hart Lee, George P. Frost, Peter DeReimer, Orestus S. Huntington, William Hoyt, John Chatterton, Jonathan Shepard, Ira Tillotson, Daniel T. Tillotson, John Hollister, William Cooper, Asaph Colborn, Isaac B. Gere.

The act of incorporation was passed April 2, 1821, which among other things defined the boundaries, and gave directions how the property should be assessed and taxed for the purpose of erecting suitable town buildings, the purchase of fire engines, etc., etc.

—November 22, 1820. Joseph Benjamin, David Woodcock, Edward Edwards, Benjamin Drake, Isaac Beers, Henry Ackley, Ben Johnson, Jesse Merritt, Charles Humphrey, Daniel Bates, Ebenezer Mack, Ira Tillotson, Benjamin Pelton, Luther Gere, Jeremiah S. Beebe, gave notice that they should apply to the Legislature for the passage of an act incorporating the village of Ithaca.

—The establishment of Cornell university grew out of an act of congress passed July 2, 1862, appropriating public lands for educational purposes. Hon. Ezra Cornell donated to the institution at first $500,000 and subsequently made otherdonations. Hon. Henry W. Sage and others also made large endowments, and the state made an endowment of land scrip representing 990,000 acres of U. S. government lands, which were principally located in the state of Wisconsin by the trustees, thus making it one of the most richly endowed and wealthy institutions of learning in the United States.

—The Methodists first met for worship at the house of John McDowell in June, 1794, by William Colbert, an itinerant missionary. The first revival in the church occurred in 1794 under the ministration of Rev. John Brodhead, when Mrs. John McDowell, Peter Van Orman and wife, George Sager and his mother, William Pangburn, Richard Pangburn, Elias DePew, Abram Smith, Mary Smith, Catharine Hinepaw, William Jackson, Rachel Jackson, Dr. Simmons, Garret Shoemaker and wife, Cornelius Shoemaker and wife, became members. A church was erected in 1820. Cost $5,000.

—July 24, 1824, a meeting was held by the citizens in relation to the erection of a public market house, August 6, 1824, the trustees resolved to erect a market house twenty by forty, Lucius Wells and Nathan Herrick were appointed a committee to superintend its construction. August 25, the building was completed and eight stalls were rented for one year—No. 1, Jacob Wood, $16.75 ; No. 2, Job Beckwith, $19.00 : No. 3, E. Champlain, $13.81 ; No. 4, J. Lewis, $14.25 ; No. 6, David Curtis, $14.25; No. 7, E. Champlain, $13 75 ; No. 8, Samuel Hill, $12.25 ; a total of $104.06. Every day except Sunday was a market day.

—June 6, 1823, the Trustees purchased of Samuel Mesrereau, of New York, a fire engine for $300. The names of the first fire company were : Otis Eddy, Charles Humphrey, John Johnson, Julius Ackley, Henry Hibbard, Samuel L. Sheldon, Robert J. Renwick, Joshua H. Lee, Nathan Cook, Henry K. Stockton, John Tillotson, Ebenezer Thayer, Samuel Reynolds, Ira Patterson, Lucius Wells, Horace Mack, Newton Gunn, Jonas Holman, Edward L. Porter, Edward Davidson, Amasa Woodruff, Samuel Buchanan, Ephraim Porter, James Chapman, Joseph Esty, Willard W. Taber, George P. Frost, Frederic Deming, Charles Hinckley, Henry S. Walbridge, Henry H. More, Daniel Pratt, Joseph Burritt, Stephen B. Munn Jr., Henry W. Hinckley, Gifford Tracey, Jacob Wood, Andrew J. Miller.

—May 12, 1828, a second company was formed under the title of Rescue No 2. The new company was given the old engine and the old company took the new engine. Those constituting Rescue No. 2 were : Sylvester Munger, J. Newton Perkins, Sylvester Hunt, George Hollister, Adolphus Colborn, John R. Kelley, John M. Cantine, Benjamin G. Ferris, Hunt Pomeroy, William B. Kelley, Elias Colborn, Uri Y. Hazzard, Ithiel Potter, Elbert Kane Daniel Young, Ira Bower, Isaiah Hunt, R. A. Clark, Anson Spencer, Urbana Dunning, James Wynans, E. H. Thomas, Charles Cooley, David Elliott, George McCormick, David Ayers, Jacob Yaples, John Colston, Stephen Turtlelot, James W. Sowles.

—The first Board of Village Officers were: Daniel Bates, President; William R. Collins, Andrew D. W. Bruyn, Julius Ackley, George Blythe, Trustees ; Nathan Herrick, Henry Ackley, Assessors ; Charles W. Connor, Miles Seymour, Jesse Grant, Fire Wardens ; Charles W. Conner, Treasurer ; Augustus P. Searing, Clerk ; Thomas Downing, Collector ; David Curtis, Pound Master. This was the initial step taken in organizing the village government of Ithaca, which from time to time as exigences or necessity required, extended the limits of its boundaries, and increased its powers until the spectacle is now presented of an incorporated village with schools, academies, and colleges of learning—with elegant public and private buildings and a population of about fifteen thousand inhabitants enjoying under a village charter all the conveniences of a city with scarcely any of its burdens.

Lansing Township.

Lansing was organized at the fortieth session of the legislature of New York, April 7, 1817—taken from Genoa in Cayuga county.

It is bounded on the north by Cayuga county, on the east by Groton and Dryden, on the south by Ithaca, and on the west by Cayuga lake. It is beautifully located on the eastern shore of Cayuga lake and is one of the finest towns in Tompkins county.

The first township election was held April 15, 1817, at the house of Samuel Howe.

Early setttlers;—Silas Ludlow, Henry Ludlow, Thomas Ludlow, Samuel Baker, Ebenezer Haskins, Benajah Strong, Salmon Strong, Joel Bacon, Daniel Bacon, John Bowker, Joseph Bowker, Noah Bowker, Andrew Myers, Moses DePew, Nicholas DePew, Ephraim Blue, Richard Townley, Joel Himrod, Abraham Minier, George Rhodes, Frederic Storms, Henry Bloom, Abram Bloom, Peter Conrad, Tillman Bower, Hontetter Bower, Samuel Bower, Adam Bower, George Bower, John Holden, John Beardsley, Robert Alexander, Weston Allen, Micajah Starr, Deacon Joseph Gillett, Solomon Kellogg, Jonah Tooker, Henry Teeter, John Mead, John Garrison, Major Stevens, William Gibbs, Samuel Gibbs, Daniel White, Albert White, William Goodwin, Jacob Shoemaker, John Osmun, Abram Van Wagner Samuel R. Brown, Reuben Brown, George LaBar, Daniel Norton, Joseph Gibbs, Samuel Davis, Cornelius Harring, John Kimple, Col. John Harper, Sidney Drake, Nathaniel Hamilton, David More, Jonathan Colborn, Thomas Hamilton, John S. Holden, John Royal, Daniel DeCamp, John Learn, Jacob Conrad, Reuben Colton, Thomas Dougherty, Samuel Brown, Joseph Wyckoff, Aaron Hadden, Joseph Nettles, John Brown, Joseph Miller, Joseph North, Joseph Ives, Abram Miller, Dr. Hutchinson, Benjamin Grover, John Kelley, Calvin Burr, James A. Burr, Oliver Phelps, Arad Joy, Jacob Morrell, Mark Hagar, Benjamin Joy, Benjamin Buck, Casper Fenner, Silas K. Newton, David Crocker, Rev. John Bacom, John Guthrie, Peter Hinepaw.

—Samuel Baker was the first blacksmith in 1794.

—Lansingville was formerly known as Teetertown.

—Thomas Dougherty built the first tannery in 1800.

—Oliver Phelps built the first steamer on Cayuga lake.

—Samuel Baker sent the first boat load of wheat to market.

—The first stock of goods was sold by John Guthrie in 1794.

—Henry and Thomas Ludlow built the first grist mill in 1795.

—John Beardsley built the first framed house in the year 1796.

—Mrs. Catharine Bloom died in 1798. The first death in the town.

—John Beardsley's house had glass windows in 1796. The first in the town.

—The first tavern was built by Thomas Ludlow in 1793. It was built of logs.

—The first post office was established in 1808. Abijah Miller the first postmaster.

—The first church society was organized in 1794 and a log church erected in 1799.

—The first marriage in the town was Henry Bloom and Catharine Goodwin in 1794.

—Methodist church at Ludlowville was organized in 1817. Church erected in 1825. Rev. Hiram Gee preacher in charge.

—The First Presbyterian church of Lansingville was organized in 1804. Rev. Jabez Chadwick the first minister. Church erected in 1805.

—The Baptist church of North Lansing was organized March 7, 1849. The first minister was Rev. William H. Delano. Church erected in 1852.

—Lansing Temperance society was formed in 1828. Thomas Ludlow, president; Nicholas Townley, secretary. It celebrated its semi-centennial in 1878.

—Captain Benajah Strong, Ephraim Bloom, John Beardsley, John Mead, Daniel Norton, John S. Holden, Jacob Morrell, were early settlers and soldiers in the war of the revolution.

—The Baptist church of East Lansing was organized March 27, 1804. Rev. Mr. Tuttle was the first minister. The first members were: William Stebbins, Phebe Buck, John Bowker, Reuben Colton and wife. Church erected in 1822.

—The German Lutheran church was founded in 1803. Rev. John Hontz was the first minister. The members of this church were scattered over a very large territory extending into Cayuga county. Rev. Deidrich Villiers preached at the place twenty-five years.

—The Presbyterian church of Ludlowville was organized September 9, 1817. Rev. William Adams the first minister. The first trustees were: Gideon Morehouse, Ebenezer Brown, Joshua Jennings, John Bowman, Thomas Ludlow, Julius Ackley, Abijah Miller, Oliver Phelps, Edward Walker. Church erected in 1825.

—The First Baptist church of Lake Ridge was organized October 31, 1796. Rev. Micajah Starr the first minister. Benajah Strong the first deacon. Joel Baker clerk. The first members were: William Avery, Micajah Starr, Abigail Woodruff, Anna Starr, Jerusha Bacon, Benajah Strong, Pierpont Bacon, Joel Bacon, Thankful Bacon, Sarah Bacon, Luther Barney, Lydia Gillett, Charles Townley, Abigail Strong. Church erected in 1840.

—The first quarterly meeting of the M. E. church was held in Lansing in 1797. At that time a class was organized with Reuben Brown leader. First members: Abram Minier and wife, Reuben Brown and wife, William Gibbs and wife, Robert Leidle and wife, James Egbert and wife, Walter Brown and wife, Samuel Baker and wife. A log church was erected in 1797. The framed church in 1802. It was the first framed church in the Genesee conference. In 1833 erected a brick church.

Newfield Township.

Cayuta was organized at the 34th session of the legislature of New York, Feb. 22, 1811, as a town in Tioga county, taken from Spencer. At session 45, name changed to Newfield, by act of March 29, 1822. Newfield is situated in the southwestern portion of Tompkins county, and is bounded on the north by Enfield and Ithaca, on the east by Danby, on the south by Van Etten in Chemung county, and Cayuta in Schuyler county, on the west by Cayuta and Catharine in Schuyler county. The principal village of the township is Newfield, a station on the Geneva, Ithaca & Sayre R. R. In 1875, a large portion of the business places was destroyed by fire. But substantial brick buildings have taken their place, and Newfield is an active and busy place.

Early settlers:—James Thomas, Joseph Chambers, John White, David Linderman, Richard Sebring, Barnabas Gibbs, John C. Gibbs, Phillip La Bar, Jonathan Compton, James Todd, Abraham Brown, Isaac L. Smith, Charles Gillett. Ebenezer Patchen, James Murray, Stephen Green, Jeremiah Green, James Douglass, Daniel Strong, Eliakim Dean, William Dudley, William Stratton, Samuel K. Rogers, Herman Parker, James Trumble, Jacob A. Trumble, James Douglass, J. V. Clark, Joseph Stubbs, Lewis Hughes, Daniel Strang, Harvey Linderman.

—The first school house was erected in 1805.

—Benjamin Sebring was the first post master.

—George Dudley opened the first store in 1815.

—Eliakim Dean erected the first grist mill in 1811.

—Samuel K. Rogers erected a carding machine in 1815.

—The first church was erected by the Presbyterians, in 1832.

—The Geneva, Ithaca & Sayre R. R., runs through the township.

—Benjamin Sebring kept the first hotel. He was from Pennsylvania.

—The first saw mill was built by Eliakim Dean, in 1809, at Newfield village.

—The First Christian Church of Newfield was organized May 20, 1854. First minister Rev. Ezra Chase. Church erected in 1858.

—The First Baptist Church of Newfield was organized in 1820, by Rev. Mr. Oviatt; Elijah B. Georgia, Nathan Stewart, first deacons. Church erected in 1842. Cost $3,000.

—First Presbyterian Church of Newfield was organized in 1819, by Rev. William Leavensworth. Church erected in 1832. First trustees, Daniel Crowell, Miller Wood, Hobert Estabrook, Charles McCorn, Simeon T. Bush. First clerk, James Todd.

—Newfield Grange No. 242, was organized Sept. 1874. Stephen Davenport, master; L. T. Carpenter, overseer; E. A. Curtis, secretary; George W. Protts, treasurer; Miss E. Shaffer, Flora; Mrs. Mary A. Douglass, Pomona; Mrs. G. C. Everhart, Ceres.

—The First M. E. Church of Newfield was organized in 1834. Rev. Moses Adams the first resident minister in charge. Church erected in 1835. Trustees, Daniel B. Swartwood, Benjamin H. Clark, Samuel Sebring, Israel Mead, Abram Dudley, H. M. Ferguson, Charles M. Turner, David Murray.

Ulysses Township.

Ulysses was organized by an act of the Legislature April 1801, see also session 26, and session 44, laws of 1821. It is bounded on the north by the county of Seneca, on the east by Cayuga Lake, on the south by Enfield and west by Hector in Schuyler county. The Taughanock Creek flows from the west, crossing the township in the northern portion, and discharging its waters into Cayuga Lake. It was originally a large township, it is now one of the most productive townships in the county, and nicely located.

The first town election was held April 7, 1795, at the house of Peter Hinepaw. Andrew English was elected supervisor; Abram Markle, town clerk; Andrew English, Isaac Patchin, William Norman, assessors; Joseph Weston constable and collector; Peter Hinepaw, Phillip Tremain, James Smith, commissioners of highways; Nathaniel Davenport, Robert McDowell, overseers of the poor; Peter Dumond, Richard Goodwin, Henry Davenport, overseers of highways; John Yaple, William Norman, fence viewers; Richard McDowell, pound master. At the time that the above named election was held the towns of Enfield and Ithaca were included.

Early settlers:—Jacob Yaple, (Iable) Isaac Dumond, Peter Hinepaw, Samuel Weyburn, Abner Tremain, Phillip Tremain, Benjamin Tremain, John McLallen, Stephen Richards, Levi Valentine, Jeremiah Ayres, Jesse Harriman, Richard Goodwin, Benjamin Goodwin, Daniel Norton, James F. Curry, James Centre, David Atwater, Thomas Cooper, Benjamin Lanning, Robert McLallen, Jacob Chambers, Doxy Lane, Job Rogers, Dr. Peter Rose, Robert Henshaw, Jonathan Owens, Albert Crandall, Jeptha Lee, Wilson Stout, Nathaniel Mack, John Mack, Alexander Bower, Richard Ayers, Herman Camp, Allen Pease, Dr. O. C. Comstock, Frederic Burlew, Abraham Updyke, Isaac Updyke, Jacob Updyke, John Creque, Lyman Strobridge, Henry D. Bartow, Samuel Vance, David C. Williams, Nicol Halsey, Henry Taylor, Michael Snell, Benjamin Hinckley, John Havens, Bethniel Bond, Samuel Cheseman, John Trembly, Jacob Putnam, Daniel Holmes, Joshua Hinckley, Merritt King, Richard Henshaw, Thomas Martin, David Smith, Jonas Whiting, Archer Green, Robert Ruhey, Michael C. Snell, Amasa Andrews, Michael Kirkendall, Abram Johnson, Charles Bingham, Arthur S. Johnson, John Rudy.

—John McLallen built the first tavern.

—John Pettis was the first blacksmith.

—The first settler was Samuel Weyburn.

—The first post office was established in 1811.

—The first lawyer was H. D. Bartow, in 1814.

—The first church was erected of logs in 1811.

—Dr. O. C. Comstock was the first post master.

—David Atwater built the first saw mill in 1796.

—The first physician was Dr. Peter Rose in 1797.

—The first Sunday school was established in 1823.

—Abner Tremain erected the first grist mill in 1794.

—The first birth was Calvin Tremain, Sept. 13, 1794.

—The first store was opened by Robert Henshaw, in 1802.

—Jesse Harriman built the first framed house in 1800.

—*Taughannock* means Falls in the Woods.

—The Taughannock Falls are 215 feet high.

—Society of Friends was established in 1864.

—Trumansburg Village was incorporated in 1872.

—The Trumansburg Academy was erected in 1855.

—The Indian name for Cayuga Lake was *Guenguch.*

—The first marriage was John McLallen, Dec. 12, 1799.

—The first church organization was the Presbyterian, in 1803.

—Taughannock No. 132, I. O. O. F., instituted Dec. 23, 1844.

—The first brick dwelling was erected by James McLallen, in 1826.

—Harmony Lodge No. 306, Knights of Honor instituted Oct. 3, 1877.

—The Geneva & Ithaca Turnpike was completed through Ulysses, in 1811.

—The first one who preached in the town was Rev. Valentine Cook, in 1794.

—St. James Catholic Temperance and Benevolent Society organized Feb. 28, 1874.

—St. Jame's Catholic church erected in 1856. Rev. Father Gilbert the first priest.

—Lyman Strobridge, Henry Taylor, Col. Henry Camp, were soldiers of the war of 1812.

—The first school house was erected in 1805. The first teacher was Stephen Woodruff.

—Willow Creek, Taughannock and Trumansburg are stations on the Geneva, Ithaca & Sayre R. R.

—The bar room of John McLallen was used as a place of holding religious services for several years.

—Samuel Vance died March 19, 1877, aged 106 years, he was born in New Brunswick, New Jersey.

—The Baptist church was organized Aug. 26, 1819, by Rev. O. C. Comstock. Church erected in 1824.

—M. E. church of Trumansburg organized Jan. 4, 1831, by Rev. William M. Jones. Church erected in 1831.

—The First M. E. church class was formed in 1803, with Richard Goodwin leader Church erected in 1825.

—M. E church at Jacksonville was made a separate charge in 1842. Rev. S. W. Alden the first minister in charge.

—Ulysses, while a portion of Onondaga county, for the year 1796, received £5, 8s, 6d, 3 farthings, as a portion of school moneys.

—Abner Tremain, Richard Goodwin, Benjamin Lanning, Jeptha Lee, were early settlers and had served as soldiers in the revolutionary war.

The first school meeting was held in the town June 21, 1796. The first school commissioners were Robert McDowell, Daniel Turrell, Jeremiah Jeffrey.

—The First Presbyterian church of Trumansburg was organized Jan. 10, 1803, at the house of David Atwater, by Rev. Jedediah Chapman. Rev. Garret Manderville was the first regular minister. Trustees, James Crawford, Elias Smith, Isaiah Crawford.

—The Union and Horticultural Society was organized Aug. 1, 1858. Hon. Truman Boardman was its first president; Lewis Porter, vice president; Joseph H. Biggs, secretary; F. S. Dumont, treasurer; J. D. M. Smith, clerk.

—Protestant Episcopal church organized Jan. 25, 1871, by Rev. T. S. Randolph. Officers: Henry D. Bartow, William Willis, wardens; James R. Willis, William B. Dumond, Edmond Pearshall, Warren Halsey, Jared S. Halsey, John D. Woodward, Clark Daggett, Benjamin Dunning, vestrymen; David Dumond, treasurer; Stephen Clough, secretary. Church erected in 1877.

—The first Masonic Lodge was instituted June 5, 1818, and known as Fdelity Lodge. The first officers installed June 24, 1818 were Henry Taylor, W. M.; Edward Ely, S. W.; Zachariah P. Smead, J. W.; Horace Osborn, treasurer; Elijah H. Goodwin, secretary. The first initiation was John Creque. During the Anti-Masonic excitement this lodge maintained its standing with the Grand Lodge. Many unlawful acts were committed by the Anti-Masons. The names of the twelve members who remained true to their masonic views were, Nicoll Halsey, John Creque, Lyman Strobridge, Nathaniel Ayers, Henry Taylor, Milo Van Dusen, Uriel Turner, James McLallen, Isaac W. Hart, David K. McLallen, Philemon H. Thompson, Elias J. Ayers. Henry Taylor the first W. M. of the lodge was born Sept. 3, 1873, the day that the treaty of peace was signed between United States and Great Britain.

ERRATA.

PAGE 163 In the first line of the fifth paragraph reads "Conhocton" instead of "Cowanesque."

PAGE 152. In the fourth paragraph from the bottom of the page, insert the word "Crandall" after Major Erastus.

PAGE 176. Near the top of page "The first load of coal from Blossburg" should be "1840" instead of "1859."